TWO-WAY MIRROR

*The Life of Elizabeth
Barrett Browning*

TWO-WAY MIRROR

The Life of Elizabeth Barrett Browning

FIONA SAMPSON

W. W. NORTON & COMPANY
Independent Publishers Since 1923

For information about permission to reproduce selections from this book, write to
Permissions, W. W. Norton & Company, Inc., 500 Fifth Avenue, New York, NY 10110

For information about special discounts for bulk purchases, please contact
W. W. Norton Special Sales at specialsales@wwnorton.com or 800-233-4830

Manufacturing by Lake Book Manufacturing

Library of Congress Cataloging-in-Publication Data

Names: Sampson, Fiona, author.
Title: Two-way mirror : the life of Elizabeth Barrett Browning / Fiona Sampson.
Description: First American edition. | New York, NY : W. W. Norton & Company, 2021. |
    Includes bibliographical references and index.
Identifiers: LCCN 2021004103 | ISBN 9781324002956 (hardcover) | ISBN 9781324002963 (epub)
Subjects: LCSH: Browning, Elizabeth Barrett, 1806–1861. | Poets, English—19th century—
    Biography.
Classification: LCC PR4193 .S26 2021 | DDC 821/.8 [B]—dc23
LC record available at https://lccn.loc.gov/2021004103

W. W. Norton & Company, Inc., 500 Fifth Avenue, New York, N.Y. 10110
www.wwnorton.com

W. W. Norton & Company Ltd., 15 Carlisle Street, London W1D 3BS

1 2 3 4 5 6 7 8 9 0

For Peter
'… last, an amethyst.'

Contents

A note on names ix

Acknowledgements xi

List of illustrations xiii

Frontispiece From within 1

Book 1 How (not) to belong 13
    Opening Frame 35

Book 2 How to be ill 38
    Second Frame 46

Book 3 How not to love 48
    Third Frame 72

Book 4 How to manage change 74
    Fourth Frame 97

Book 5 How to lose your way 99
    Tain 124

Book 6 How to be dutiful 126
    Sixth Frame 149

Book 7 How to desire 151
    Seventh Frame 183

Book 8 How to be autonomous 185
    Eighth Frame 220

Book 9 How to lose a body   222
    Closing Frame   258

Notes   261
Index   305

A note on names

Elizabeth Barrett Browning's family called her Ba throughout her life; Robert Browning took up the habit. But for all its affection, this diminutive is redolent of the way she's been diminished, both personally and poetically, in popular accounts. The poet signed herself EBB, and this shorthand is a godsend to researchers. But initials aren't a name, just a slightly dehumanising, paralegal formula. So I've chosen the reasonable onlooker's position and call my protagonist Elizabeth from Book 2, where she comes of age. Other family members are called by the names her own usage settled on: 'Papa', 'Treppy', 'Uncle Sam', 'Stormie'; but not 'Addles' for Henrietta.

In refusing the premise of slavery, I won't accept that people *are* 'slaves' or can *be* 'property'. Where people in this story are enslaved, that's how I refer to them; I use quote marks to indicate contemporary usage of 'buying' and 'owning' without accepting the terms.

Acknowledgements

I am extremely grateful to Jill Bialosky at W. W. Norton, Cecily Gayford at Profile and Markus Hoffmann at Regal Hoffmann Associates for this commission. My gratitude also goes to the Society of Authors for a Writer's Award, and to Archipelago Publishing House, Dajana Djedović and the Museum of Language and Letters at Tršić for a residency, which enabled me to work on this book. I'd like to thank my agent Sarah Chalfant for her insightful guidance and the extraordinary fillip of her support; Susanne Hillen for her consummate copy-edit; and above all and always, my husband and first reader, Peter Salmon, for putting up with the nineteenth-century women who have taken residence with us.

I've benefited hugely from the generosity of the Provost and Fellows of Eton College, who have granted permission for quotation from the unpublished Browning letters as well as image reproduction rights. I would like to thank Michael Meredith, Browning scholar and College Librarian Emeritus, for his ready intellectual hospitality.

This book wouldn't have been a realistic possibility without the mighty, exemplary and pioneering work of Philip Kelley, Browning scholar and advocate, including the monumental and still-growing corpus of *The Brownings' Correspondence*, some of it co-edited with Ronald Hudson, Edward Hagan and Scott Lewis, published by Wedgestone Press. Now largely digitalised and freely available online, the *Correspondence* is the indispensable Browning resource, and my references follow its cataloguing system throughout: www.browningscorrespondence.com. Since 1979, the National Endowment for the Humanities, an independent United States federal agency, has supported the Brownings' Correspondence Project with twenty-one grants totalling $3.612 million: for this visionary support everyone with any interest in the Brownings and their work must be profoundly grateful.

From the outset, Philip Kelley has been a truly generous correspondent, and I'm most grateful to him for welcoming me into the community of EBB obsessives. More, he has with extraordinary generosity read this book in manuscript, correcting errors and supplying illuminating details and connections from his wealth of knowledge: an act of exceptional support from a world-leading expert to a colleague he's never met. Such errors as remain are all my own.

Illustrations

A shoulder of Hope End parkland. (Author's photograph.)

Hope End House in the early nineteenth century. (Reproduced by kind permission of the Master and Fellows of Balliol College.)

Cinnamon Hill Great House, Jamaica. (By permission of Glen Carty.)

Ba aged around eight with family pet Havannah. (Reproduced by permission of the Provost and Fellows of Eton College.)

Ba aged twelve, with brothers Bro and Sam. (Reproduced by permission of the Provost and Fellows of Eton College.)

Elizabeth aged fifteen. (Reproduced by permission of the Provost and Fellows of Eton College.)

Elizabeth with Flush at Wimpole Street in the mid-1840s. (Reproduced by permission of the Provost and Fellows of Eton College.)

Outside view of Casa Guidi today. (Author's photograph.)

The interior of Casa Guidi. (Author's photograph.)

Elizabeth and Robert in 1853; matching portraits by Thomas Buchanan Read. (Armstrong Browning Library, Baylor University, Waco, Texas.)

Outside view of the Brownings' apartment building in Via de Bocca di Leone, Rome. (Author's photograph.)

Studio photograph of Elizabeth in Le Havre, 17 September 1858. (Armstrong Browning Library, Baylor University, Waco, Texas.)

An engraving from the Le Havre sitting annotated by Dante Gabriel
    Rossetti. (Armstrong Browning Library, Baylor University, Waco,
    Texas.)
Detail of the same image as used by Rossetti for his portrait.
    (Armstrong Browning Library, Baylor University, Waco, Texas.)
A bronze cast from 1853 of Elizabeth and Robert's clasped hands.
    (Armstrong Browning Library, Baylor University, Waco, Texas.)
Portrait in oils of Elizabeth aged fifty-three. (© National Portrait
    Gallery, London.)
Elizabeth and eleven-year-old Pen in Rome, June 1860. (Armstrong
    Browning Library, Baylor University, Waco, Texas.)
Drawing of Elizabeth in Rome, February 1861. (Armstrong Browning
    Library, Baylor University, Waco, Texas.)
Elizabeth a month before her death, photographed on 27 May 1861.
    (Armstrong Browning Library, Baylor University, Waco, Texas.)
Robert and Pen photographed in Venice on 14 November 1889.
    (© National Portrait Gallery, London.)

Frontispiece:
From within

understand
That life develops from within.

In my favourite portrait of Elizabeth Barrett Browning she simultaneously turns away and looks back over her shoulder at us. Of course in
one sense every historical figure does this: glancing over their shoulder
towards the future where we're watching them, even while they face away
from us into their own time. But Barrett Browning makes the gesture
particularly provocative. Her wide, sensual mouth dips and rises in a curly
bracket. Sceptical, even teasing, her gaze has a directness that seems startlingly modern.

Which is an irony, since it's an image that has been constructed by
thoroughly old-fashioned means. The frontispiece for the fourth British
edition of her bestselling verse novel *Aurora Leigh* is an engraving after an
ambrotype taken specifically for this purpose. On the afternoon in September 1858 when a shutter falls on the poet's half smile, in a stuffy studio
on Le Havre harbour-front, photography is understood to be neither
artistic, nor detailed, enough for portraiture. It will be another half-dozen
years before Julia Margaret Cameron starts to produce her famous, markedly Pre-Raphaelite images of friends and family. And so the portrait

that eventually results from this sitting won't be created by the photographer, but by a founder member of the Pre-Raphaelite Brotherhood itself.

Dante Gabriel Rossetti is a friend of 'EBB', as his celebrated subject likes to style herself, and of her husband and fellow poet Robert Browning. He's a poet himself, and from its outset a decade ago the Brotherhood has placed literature, philosophy and the book arts – illustration, fine printing, binding – at the heart of its work. This commitment is combined with a personal acquaintance that surely makes Rossetti the safest of hands for the urgent refashioning of Barrett Browning's public image.

But his are not to be the only hands her image passes through. First it's engraved by a less stellar craftsman, Thomas Oldham Barlow. The artist edits the result:

> The hair brought a little more down more over the forehead, and the parting line not left quite so raw. More tone on the forehead and indeed all over the face. The mouth is considerably in need of correction [...] by adding a line of shadow all along the top of the upper lip, thus lessening the curve upward at the corners.

Notes and sketches sprawl over Rossetti's offprint from the engraver's block. It would be easy to jump to the conclusion that this creator of sultry images of his own lovers – dreamy Lizzie Siddal, heavy-lidded Jane Morris – would like to 'correct' the poet's appearance. But far from disparaging her, Rossetti wants his engraver to be more faithful to the 'photograph portrait' they're both working from, for example by removing 'a sort of smile not in the photograph & not characteristic of the original'.

He's had plenty of chances to study this 'original' at the Brownings' home, 'an evening resort where I never feel unhappy'. In the two years since the hugely successful appearance of *Aurora Leigh*, Elizabeth's pioneering, nine-book *Bildungsroman* which is the first to tell the story of a woman becoming a writer, Rossetti has admired her work and become eager to paint her. Initial impressions – 'as unattractive a person as can well be imagined. She looks quite worn out with illness, & speaks in the tone of an invalid' – have turned to admiring protectiveness. Now he replaces the photographer's stock studio furniture with a symbolic writing desk, and instructs Barlow to 'darken' their subject's hair and enlarge her signature dark eyes in order to make her look a little younger and less 'worn out with illness'. After all, this portrait's whole purpose is to 'extinguish' what her husband calls 'certain horrible libels on humanity published as portraits of her in America': portrayals all too similar to Rossetti's own first impressions.

Earlier, shipping the photograph to *Aurora Leigh*'s American publishers, Robert has assured them just a shade too urgently that, 'What you receive, is the sun's simple truth without a hair's breadth of retouching.' Well. Up from Italy to spend summer 1858 with Elizabeth's English family, the Brownings have picked out Le Havre as a halfway meeting point. On the very last day of what turn out to be two unsatisfactory, tiring months at the Normandy port, Robert finds a 'clever man' to conduct a photographic session with his camera-shy wife. But the result seems to justify her resistances. Jean Victor Macaire-Warnod and his brother Louis Cyrus Macaire, who share the waterside studio, are renowned technical pioneers. Yet the photographic image that will briefly see commercial distribution in North America, and be so proudly donated to the Authors' Club of New York by *littérateur* Richard Henry Stoddard, is an oddly unclear and generic image. The poet's publishers, C. S. Francis & Co, do not use it themselves.

Look closer though and, for all Robert's insistence that there isn't 'a hair's breadth of retouching', the picture turns out to have been clumsily overpainted. In fact within two sentences his letter contradicts itself, framing Macaire-Warnod as 'the Artist' who's worked up detail that got lost in making this copy. Yet with its brushstroke hair, torso straight as a ruler, and expressionless face, this naïve rendering is hardly the work of a professional. Who apart from Robert – who is a keen amateur artist – could have a motive for intervention so strong that it overrules plain sight and common sense like this?

We can't be absolutely sure we've caught him red-handed. The great American photographer Mathew Brady seems to have been authorised to sell prints of the image Francis & Co received, for $3 a pop, though it's hard to believe that he would have retouched so clumsily. But what we do know is that, luckily, Robert has kept back an untouched original. It's this version that Barlow and Rossetti use, and we can see a detail of it in copies taken by British photographers Elliott and Fry. In it, the unexpurgated Elizabeth Barrett Browning has a dark shadow of tiredness or pain under her left eye, and the greying of her hair is difficult to assess, but she's every bit as characterful as Rossetti's recreation. This real-life woman has dark eyes and arched, dark eyebrows. Her nose is long; so is her upper lip, with its sexy overbite. Her face is asymmetric. Cover the right side and the left seems soulful and focused; cover the left and the right appears amused.

In the twenty-first century we recognise instantly the Brownings' anxiety about this key publicity shot, and their need to control the image of the international celebrity that fifty-two-year-old Elizabeth Barrett Browning has become. As readers we like to feel, with Elizabeth's fictional alter ego Aurora Leigh, that 'This special book [...] stands above my knowledge, draws me up.' Yet we also expect a glossy, artfully posed author photo; it's almost as if we need an ideal appearance to embody the mind we idealise as we read. In our own post-postmodern times, the Romantic cult of the visible and what it can express seems gobbled up by its own children, the visually framed identities that 'are' our social media selves. Elizabeth's struggle with her portrait reminds us that this process is nothing new.

The irony is that, despite being so anxiously aware of the ramifications of image-making, she's destined to become a notorious object lesson in how distorted ideas about famous individuals get established. The Brownings would have been astonished and mortified to see myths about their private life obscure first her work, and eventually even her identity. Let's remind ourselves that Elizabeth Barrett Browning is a pivotal figure, changing the direction of English-language poetry and influencing both her contemporaries and subsequent generations of poets and readers. In her lifetime, acknowledged as Britain's greatest ever woman poet, she receives international critical acclaim and attracts a huge readership. Yet within seventy years of her death, popular culture will have reduced this figure – who when she died was mourned as a public, political heroine in revolutionary Italy – to a swooning poetess in whose little, couch-bound life only a tyrannical father and an ardent poet-lover contribute drama.

The damage will be done above all by Rudolf Besier, author of *The Barretts of Wimpole Street*, a man of whom it's probably safe to say that he makes no particular study of how women emerge as writers: though he seems happy to incorporate gossip to gee up this drama. In the 1980s Lady Anne Holland-Martin will recall to the Browning scholar Philip Kelley how, at the after-party for its premiere at the Malvern Festival Theatre, 'It was felt [Besier's] play needed a dramatic impact. During the conversation, those who had lived in the community for generations recalled in vivid terms the handed-down memories about Edward Moulton-Barrett ... the rest is history.' Three film versions follow Besier's 1931 Broadway hit: a Norma Shearer and Charles Laughton vehicle (1934), 1957's remake with Jennifer Jones and John Gielgud, and the 1982 TV movie with Jane Lapotaire and Joss Ackland. There are also no fewer than seven further remakes for television of Besier's domestic melodrama.

By the 1970s – when Saul Bellow, Philip Roth and John Updike crowd the book charts – the roaring boys of North American literary criticism will go a stage further, maligning Elizabeth Barrett Browning as relevant to the history of literature only through marriage or, worse, as hindering that real writer, her husband. In 1973's *Oxford Anthology of English Literature*, handsome paired volumes designed as an authoritative student resource, Lionel Trilling and Harold Bloom pronounce:

> Miss Barrett became an invalid (for still mysterious reasons) from 1838 to 1846 when [...] she eloped with the best poet of the age. Her long poem *Aurora Leigh* (1856) was much admired, even by Ruskin, but is very bad. Quite bad too are the famous *Sonnets from the Portuguese* [...] Though the Brownings' married life was reasonably happy, Mrs Browning's enthusiasms [...] gave her husband much grief.

But perhaps the tendentiousness of this is unsurprising. The *Anthology's* editors print just one minor poem by Elizabeth Barrett Browning; but then the only other writing by women to feature in its more than four and a half thousand pages comprises one minor poem each by Edith Sitwell and Stevie Smith, two by Emily Brontë, and passages from Dorothy Wordsworth's private journals: in total, fewer than two dozen pages, or around 0.5 per cent of their 'canon'. Literary revisionism on this scale is strenuous stuff. Excluding all of the Brontë novels, Jane Austen, Mary Shelley, George Eliot and Virginia Woolf can be neither innocent nor accidental; and it illustrates vividly how literary canons are not born, but made.

Within the continual process of reputation-making and remaking that is literary history, Elizabeth Barrett Browning remains a bellwether for the rising and sinking stock of women writers. It's probably no coincidence that the melodramatic exploitation of her life story comes to an end in the 1980s as women's writing becomes more widely read, rediscovered, taught. Half a century earlier, when *The Barretts of Wimpole Street* was already a cultural phenomenon, Virginia Woolf (who went to see Besier's play) summed up the poet's then standing:

> Passionate lovers, in curls and side-whiskers, oppressed, defiant, eloping—in this guise thousands of people must know and love the Brownings who have never read a line of their poetry. […] But fate has not been kind to Mrs. Browning as a writer. Nobody reads her, nobody discusses her, nobody troubles to put her in her place.

Yet Woolf was herself complicit. Her comments date from the year she published *Flush: A Biography*, her own version of the famous costume drama – written from the point of view of Elizabeth's pet spaniel.

Today, we can't ignore how central the construction of identity is to Elizabeth Barrett Browning's story; and how this holds as true for her life itself as for the myth-making that surrounds it. Hers is a story about how a writer *becomes* – and that's what this book tries to mirror. Elizabeth dramatises the two-way creation of every writing self, from without and from within. That the life of the body both enables and limits the life of the mind is the paradox of the thinking self. John Keats's early death, or the seventeen-year-old poet-suicide in Henry Wallis's 'The Death of Chatterton', are moving because they remind us that a dead poet falls silent. But life imposes its own limits on the writer. For every Lord Byron or Malcolm Lowry, seizing the day in ways that their work celebrates, there is a John Clare or a Primo Levi trying to write experience away.

Writers' bodies create resistances, forcing interplay between self and world. Elizabeth Barrett Browning turned twelve in 1818, the year that Frankenstein's creature first found out how deeply the wearer of a body can be changed by what happens to it. And perhaps it's no accident that he is the creation of another woman writer. There are so many reasons why women may find that their bodies define their lives to a greater extent than do men's that it's surely no surprise if they chose to write about embodiment.

It used to be a feminist truism that René Descartes had it wrong, and there is no separation between mind and body. Yet bodies *do* disguise, shield, and isolate minds. A woman being whistled at by scaffolders may be mulling her dystopian novel, the mother in the labour suite may have done pioneering work on biodiversity, that figure wearing the Marigolds may be a leading human rights lawyer. More: to spend any time with someone whose body is failing is to understand that recognising the unimpaired selfhood 'within' it is both human and humane. So are we ghosts in a curvaceous machine, to borrow from the twentieth-century British language philosopher Gilbert Ryle's formulation? Or do we inhabit the body in ways that are inseparable from how we think and feel? Or, again, do many Western philosophy courses start with the thought experiment that goes, *How do you know you're not a brain being stimulated in a vat?* because, in a way, that's what we dream of? A virtual life, in which we experience ourselves as pure will, without the resistances of the concrete world?

Today, the screen world seems to offer us this ideal existence. And if we turn back two centuries, we find Elizabeth Barrett Browning, too, used the written word in 'virtual' ways to take part in the wider world while remaining bodily at home on her daybed. For she does see herself as a ghost in a machine; her strong-willed thinking self as set within an often frustrating body. It isn't only that illness and contemporary ideas of femininity exclude her from much that she longs to do and be. Living in the shadow of mortality from young womanhood onward, she wants urgently to continue to exist after bodily death, and for her loved ones to continue to exist too; as both Nonconformist Christianity and the spiritualism she explores assure her they will. This separation of mind – whether as 'soul' or 'ghost' – from body is unfashionable in the twenty-first-century West, but to dismiss it is to fail to understand how Elizabeth and her contemporaries experience embodiment. In the event, the thinking self who speaks in Elizabeth Barrett Browning's work *has* triumphantly outlived her bodily existence. But how telling it is that the fictionalised character of 'Elizabeth' that's replaced her in the popular imagination – someone passive and poorly, bullied and rescued, barely even a poet – is almost entirely bodily, scarcely a mind at all.

Yet there's another turn in the story. This often triumphant life is also the mirror and beneficiary of its brutal times. Jamaican and Madeiran ancestry make Elizabeth question her own ethnicity. A sensibility that will change the course of literary history is built on a shifting, uncertain self-image. But if we think that the shadowy self she imagines in the mirror is truly black, or that she's haunted by the figure of another self denied the leisure and literacy that have made her a poet, we should think again. Elizabeth Barrett Browning is the daughter and granddaughter of slavers: it's their prodigious sugar fortunes that have allowed her extraordinary talents to develop. Even her elopement is financed by this money, despite the fact that by the time she runs away both she and her husband are abolitionists.

The self jars against circumstance. When Elizabeth emerges from this mercantile and firmly unliterary background as a child prodigy, and declares not only that she will be a poet, but that she already is one, it should be a reach too far. In 1806, the year of her birth, women can neither vote nor, in England at least, own property once married. Even the wealthiest receive relatively little formal education and are barred from all but the oldest 'profession'. On marriage, they pass from their father's control to their husband's without becoming citizens in their own right. So it's not surprising that, at the start of the nineteenth century, women writers tend to emerge in the company of literary men who have brought them along too; whether by accident or design. The exceptional talents of Maria Edgeworth (1768–1849), Mary Shelley (1797–1851) and the Brontë sisters (born between 1816 and 1820) were all first recognised by educated, intellectual fathers.

Elizabeth's father, though no *littérateur*, also encourages his young daughter; perhaps she owes her remarkable confidence to him. 'Literature was the star which in prospect illuminated my future days [;] it was the spur which prompted me .. the aim .. the very soul of my being', she asserts at fourteen. Born nine years after Mary Shelley and ten before Charlotte Brontë, she starts writing as a child of six, by her own reckoning, and doesn't stop until five weeks before she dies. Her first surviving poem, 'On the Cruelty of Forcement to Man', is written in the Herefordshire country house of her childhood; her last, 'The North and the South', almost four decades later in Rome in May 1861, the month before her death.

The eponymous narrator of *Aurora Leigh*, the masterpiece Elizabeth publishes at fifty, is transfixed by a similar passion:

> I may love my art.
> You'll grant that even a woman may love art,
> Seeing that to waste true love on anything
> Is womanly, past question.

The rhetoric sounds like an own goal. In fact it's strategic. Lacking both social agency and an education in the classical arts of logic and rhetoric that father, brothers, husband have received, a woman born at the start of the nineteenth century is unlikely to win arguments by *reasoning* about who or what she is. She must learn instead to be stubborn; irrational. To claim that she too is a poet, she must arm herself with her own weakness, which is to say her enthusiasm:

> I lived, those days,
> And wrote because I lived—unlicensed else;
> My heart beat in my brain.

My heart beat in my brain: it sounds like fury or madness. But the pulse is metrical, not manic. Elizabeth's success will be indubitable, the kind poets dream of and rarely achieve. *Aurora Leigh*, with which she crowns that success, will be an instant bestseller, its first edition selling out within a fortnight, and it will go on to be one of the best-read literary works of the second half of the nineteenth century. This verse *Künstlerroman* – the story specifically of a maker's development, or *Bildungsroman* – will influence generations of poets and writers. Among the many women for whom it is immediately formative are George Eliot, Charlotte Mew, the writing duo who make up 'Michael Field', and Emily Dickinson – who hangs the Rossetti portrait of Elizabeth in her room. But its success isn't limited by gender. Leading male writers, among them Rudyard Kipling, John Ruskin, Algernon Swinburne and Oscar Wilde, will celebrate the work for decades to come.

Aurora Leigh is a work of fiction, not memoir. Its nine books map only indirectly onto the nine 'books' of its author's own life. If it is any kind of

'How to' *vade mecum*, it's less a guide to practical professional steps than to thinking of oneself *as* a woman writer. Elizabeth's own life story works in similar ways, that is, not so much guide as inspiration. But in portraying the development of a woman poet, *Aurora Leigh* does give us clues as to how its author herself managed to emerge.

On her twentieth birthday the verse novel's protagonist, orphaned Aurora, refuses a marriage both loving and advantageous in order to dedicate herself to writing. Just before she does so, she crowns herself with a poet's wreath:

> What, therefore, if I crown myself to-day
> In sport, not pride, to learn the feel of it.

Not pride, but *to learn the feel of it*: there's a crucial distinction. If she delayed until she, or the world, felt confident that she deserved poetic laurels, how long would Aurora, or Elizabeth, wait?

In fact, laurel wreaths will crown Barrett Browning's coffin: what use are they to her by then? But practising, *learning the feel* of the 'the tender pricking' of literary laurels, of how to 'tie … rhymes', is a way of *doing* without having to look at what you're daring to do. Modest and incremental, it's like the domestic arts Aurora Leigh already knows. This is how the young woman slips past the gatekeepers of the feminine self and starts to write.

> Then I sate and teased
> The patient needle till it split the thread,
> Which oozed off from it in meandering lace
> From hour to hour.

I like that oozing thread, which just doesn't want to lie down. As it slips out of the needle, between the fingers that try to knot it tight, it's a little metaphor for creative disobedience.

Practice makes perfect, as many a sampler instructed the girl who was embroidering it. But Elizabeth hasn't always been patient. At thirteen, in the Preface to her first printed work, *The Battle of Marathon*, she's all innocent insouciance:

> Happily it is not now, as it was in the days of POPE […]. Now, even

the female may drive her Pegasus through the realms of Parnassus, without being saluted with the most equivocal of all appellations, a learned lady; without being celebrated by her friends as a SAPPHO, or traduced by her enemies as a pedant; without being abused in the Review, or criticised in society.

Unfortunately, the reception of her adult work will show that this isn't always true. And two centuries later, we need to catch on if we find ourselves thinking, 'Happily it is not now, as it was in the days of ELIZABETH BARRETT BROWNING.' For while Elizabeth is very much a creature of her own times, she also fits our own: as a woman working on the problem of how to be herself. And despite the years of practice to come, this early teenager has her eye on the prize. Already she 'never can be satisfied with [...] the comparative respect / Which means the absolute scorn'. What matters to her isn't producing tolerable verse but being a true poet, judged by the highest standards. *Her heart beats in her brain.*

Still, the question remains hanging: what if women *can't* produce real art?

Among our female authors we make room
For this fair writer, and congratulate
The country that produces in these times
Such women, competent to ... spell.

In this biting parody of a kind of reviewing she has actually experienced, the poet comes close to revealing herself. But Elizabeth Barrett Browning is not 'Aurora Leigh'. Real life differs from fiction, partly because the verse novel's author has 'money and a room of her own', in the famous phrase Virginia Woolf will coin seventy years from now, in *A Room of One's Own*.

Yet critical reception *is* a kind of mirror, even a distorting one, in which writers check their progress however much they intend not to. Reading is another. Everyone needs a companion in their sentimental education. And for a writer developing in provincial isolation, books take the place of a peer group. As a young woman, Elizabeth has plenty of accounts of the writer's struggle to keep her company. Influential, form-expanding Romantic biographies and memoirs like Jean-Jacques

Rousseau's *Confessions* (1782) and William Godwin's *Memoirs of the Author of a Vindication of the Rights of Woman* (1798) have long been in print. In the year she turns eighteen, '*Lives of the Poets*, Boswell's *Life of Johnson*, Southey's *Life of Nelson*, Lockhart's *Life of Burns*, Moore's *Life of Sheridan*, Moore's *Life of Byron*, Wolfe's *Remains*', can be read even in remote Yorkshire vicarages – as we learn when Charlotte Brontë recommends them to a friend. They are certainly available to a wealthy family like the Barretts.

Of course, these are all books by men. What would the sentimental education of a woman look like? It is Elizabeth herself who will, eventually, provide an answer. *Aurora Leigh* is fiction, not biography. But literary biography is always a *Bildungsroman*, the story of how a thinking, feeling self emerges. And in this, intimate respect, the story Elizabeth Barrett Browning tells in *Aurora Leigh* is also the one her life story tells us, for:

> poets [...] understand
> That life develops from within.

Book One:
How (not) to belong

And ankle-deep in English grass I leaped
And clapped my hands, and called all very fair.

Sun beats down on a shoulder of parkland, parched grass crackles underfoot, blowflies and mosquitoes hover among odours of meadowsweet and wild hop. The steep hillside is covered with drying hay that catches the ankles, but at the crest you feel on top of the world. Turn north and almost at your feet is a steep cut running east towards the Malvern Hills. Turn south and a dramatic natural amphitheatre commands the Hereford plain. Two strikingly different worlds fit together here along a single geological seam. In one direction stylish villas, a sign of Malvern's emerging fashionability, dot the wooded slopes of Colwall. In the other, a rural hinterland reaches south and west to the border of Wales.

What are the very first things we remember? Bursts of light and colour perhaps, with the luminous quality of glass. Moments that remain as images, if not complete stories. For a four-year-old called Ba, this is her first summer in the dazzlingly fertile Herefordshire countryside; her previous homes, in County Durham and then near London, can already be little more than trace impressions. Here everything is hyperreal. Footpaths disappear into thickets; nettles taller than a man spill across fields.

Even the hot, stormy weather is exceptional. Later this summer a 'very remarkable water-spout', with 'two branches bent nearly, or perfectly, at right angles to each other' will be observed off the Kent coast at Ramsgate; one of the largest tornadoes ever recorded in Britain will flatten a trail at Fernhill Heath, just the other side of the Malverns.

It's even headier down in the closed-off valleys known locally as Hopes. Ba's family have recently settled in one of these 'ripples of land', where the outside world disappears. But from Oyster Hill, this high point of their estate, 'Commanding the romantic scenery of the Malvern and the adjoining hills, with views [...] highly interesting and of great extent', everything in the vicinity can be surveyed – just as it is designed to be. In 1810 British wealth still broadly correlates with landowning. If anything, landed gentry have tightened hold on their estates in recent decades, as the paralegal process of enclosure abolishes the common land on which tenants used to support themselves. The old subsistence farming strips are being replaced by money made visible as ornamental parks and newly managed fields 'tied up fast with hedges, nosegay-like': the Agricultural Revolution has transformed land, for those who own it, from a reliable but rather unexciting asset into a fashionable, and briskly profitable, gentleman's hobby.

Unlanded money finds itself in something of a hurry to join the action, and Ba's father is no exception. His wealth is prodigious, but it's been generated by international trade and is held largely offshore. The precisely calibrated English class system will be only too happy to point this out to him as an inferiority. What's more, he was born abroad, in Jamaica. So this Herefordshire estate called Hope End is the first British property he's owned. It came on the market last autumn and, tucked away in the heartlands of rural Britain, seems to us now a surprising choice for a merchant with an eye on the rest of the world. But after some prevarication – and hard bargaining – Ba's father has bought nearly 500 acres, with a Big House, farm buildings and cottages, 'to make yourself, Brother & Sister & dear Mamma happy', as he tells her. It sounds like a fairy tale, and in a way it is; though as in any fairy tale not everything's quite as it appears. The debt of happiness 'dear Puss' must repay her father will eventually come to seem outsized, even grotesque.

But today's four-year-old is too young to understand emotional blackmail – and too busy being excited about a forthcoming trip to the seaside. 'My dear Grandmama, I love you very much', she writes in mid-July. 'We are going to the sea on Monday week, we are all very sorry you are gone away, you had better come with us to the sea, we all send you kisses.' Impetuous and loving, this note is about as far from a duty letter as any small child could get. Its delighted recipient responds:

> This Morning post brought me a Letter very prettily written indeed for a little Girl of four Years old, so pleas'd am I, that I cou'd not let the day pass without writing a few lines, to thank my Beloved Child […] I am so proud of my Letter that it shall be put in a very careful place, till my Darling pet grows up.

And Papa's mother continues: 'Ask Bro when I am to have a Letter from him, I hope he is a good Boy, & attends to his Book—He will never be a Man till he does—.'

Which is striving, ambitious stuff, since Ba's little brother is only three; but also a form of affection. This is a self-made family, its style noticeably modern, and nicknames are intimate currency. Three-year-old Edward, who as eldest son confusingly bears what is also his father's and indeed his great-grandfather's name, will be 'Bro' for the rest of his life. 'Ba' was christened Elizabeth after Grandmama, whose own nickname is 'Bessey'. The children's baby sister Henrietta is 'Addles', and the nine siblings yet to be born will include 'Stormie' (Charles, who was born in a storm) and 'Daisy', real name Alfred (perhaps from 'Oops a daisy'?). In their parents' generation, Papa's sister Sarah, dead at twelve, remains forever 'Pinkie', while on their mother's side unmarried Aunt Arabella is 'Bummy'.

It's all mortar for the life being built at Hope End. We get a first glimpse of Ba's new home in a letter her father sends her:

> This Morng we again went to Hope-End and compleated our tour of it, besides looking thro' the center of the Estate and examining the Cottages; We shall go tomorrow to inspect the Timber &c—The more I see of the Property the more I like it […] There is no fruit whatever this year in the Garden, but should we be fortunate enough to be here next year no doubt we shall have abundance.

Since at this point his little daughter is just three, of course he's really addressing Mamma, who'll be reading the letter aloud. Behind the rather sweet, fatherly gesture we catch sight of something else; something evasive, even controlling. Papa is not actually consulting his wife over this life-changing move.

In fact, the splendidly if repetitively named Edward Barrett Moulton-Barrett knows perfectly well that – after almost a year first in west London and then with her mother-in-law in Surrey – his wife would prefer to go back 'to the dear North', where she grew up and where the couple first settled. Ba's Mamma was born Mary Graham-Clarke in Newcastle upon Tyne in 1781, and raised, partly in the city centre and partly a couple of miles away at stately Kenton Lodge in Gosforth, the eldest child of a wealthy industrialist: John Graham-Clarke's town house at 14 Pilgrim Street, and his many mercantile concerns including breweries, sugar refineries and a small fleet of ocean-going ships, have become city landmarks. He may share the civic pride that created the elegant Grainger Town terraces and mighty warehouses of eighteenth-century Newcastle, but his money is newer still. He has other local businesses too, including a flax mill, a colliery and a glassworks, but his international trade is built on the daily luxuries, beer and sugar, that entrepreneurs like him are now establishing at the heart of British life.

However, on the July afternoon when Ba surveys her new home, Graham-Clarke is already seventy-three. Closer to his homesick daughter's centre of emotional gravity are her six surviving siblings and her mother Arabella, a lively woman with artistic leanings who is two decades her husband's junior. Besides, Graham-Clarke has little leisure for playing the family man; his hands are full becoming an industrialist. Yet he's not entirely self-made. Part of his wealth comes from his wife's dowry and inheritance, and in his twenties he made an equally advantageous first marriage. Only recently arrived in the city, he married a wealthy widow called Elizabeth Rutter, at a stroke acquiring her late husband's highly successful brewing business and effectively 'marrying-in' to her in-laws, highly respected in Newcastle for decades. And perhaps the key legacy is one he received a quarter century ago when, at the age of fifty, plain John Graham found himself able, by dint of taking the double-barrel

'Clarke', to inherit from an uncle who wanted his name to continue with his money.

Easy money: dirty money. Beyond the peaceful Herefordshire 'Hills, vales, woods, netted in a silver mist / Farms, granges, doubled up among the hills; / and cattle grazing in the watered vales', that seques-ter Ba and her parents, on the other side of the Atlantic, lies another very different set of estates. At his death eight years from now, John Graham-Clarke will have interests in at least thirteen Jamaican sugar plantations, where he holds enslaved more than six hundred men and women with their children. And these ugly figures are just a snapshot. Ba's maternal grandfather doesn't simply 'own' and exploit these people, he 'buys' them from slavers too. By 1810 steam-driven sugar mills have been introduced in the Caribbean, but cane remains labour intensive. It takes around 350 man-hours and over thirty bullock-pair hours to plant a single hectare, and 990 man-hours to harvest one tonne. People are worked to death on the Jamaican plantations and, in the dark arithmetic of slavers, must be replaced. It's true that by the time Ba arrives at Hope End Britain has passed the Abolition of the Slave Trade Act (1807), but in practice the slave trade won't be stamped out in the Caribbean until 1811.

Nothing mitigates her grandfather's culpability. A strategic, hard-headed ex-militiaman from East Yorkshire, Graham-Clarke was neither young nor unworldly by the time he acquired his Jamaican estates. His single visit to that island, in the early 1790s, consolidated relationships with other planter families, but produced no gesture of remission or compassion for his enslaved labour. For nineteenth-century commercial ambition is shameless. Enormous wealth is already being generated for British industrialists, even those who own no slaves and pillage no colo-nies, by indentured and child labour in factories, mills and mines. Unlike plantation slavery, this on-shore exploitation offers no fig leaf of invis-ibility to those who profit from it: conditions in local factories and mills like the ones Graham-Clarke owns are starkly visible. Yet they persist. Seamen, including his own crews, routinely brave danger, floggings and near starvation, even though the Tyne dockside, where they tie up, runs right by the city centre. In 1810 this is still small enough for rich and poor to live within sight, sound and smell of each other. Even the vertical slums around Black Gate are less than half a mile from Graham-Clarke's Pilgrim Street home. It's in this brutally desensitising era that businesses like his are beginning to flex global muscle.

Since his alliance-building visit to the Caribbean, Ba's dynamic grandfather has become a key English contact for many Jamaican plantation owners. Among them are the Barretts of Cinnamon Hill. Graham-Clarke became important to this family in 1792, when pater-familias Edward Barrett saw his daughter Elizabeth's offspring, Sarah, Edward and Samuel, off to England for their education. The grandchildren had become his responsibility when their father, Charles Moulton, left them. Elizabeth soon followed her children to London. But there – though her boys were under the legal guardianship of James Scarlett, the brilliant Jamaican-born lawyer and family friend who would become Lord Abinger – she was in effect a woman alone, since she was accompanied only by her best friend, Mary Trepsack. A family dependent whose father was an impoverished planter and mother a slave, 'Treppy' will remain a central, much-loved Barrett figure right through the lives of Elizabeth Moulton's grandchildren – as her loving nickname indicates. But she's a woman of mixed heritage and relatively poorly off, and in the world of men she has even less power than her friend.

By contrast, Graham-Clarke was well-placed to become de facto mentor to the wealthy Barrett boys. Edward, the elder son and so primary heir, fell into the habit of staying at Pilgrim Street. Perhaps he was already falling for the family's eldest girl, Mary. Although four years her junior, before he even came of age he'd decided to marry her. His youth meant that the marriage needed family approval, but this presented no problem, for Barrett wealth represented a dynastic opportunity for Graham-Clarke. Indeed in some lights, Mary appears a bit like a honeytrap set for the young, fatherless heir.

Whatever the case, Edward Barrett Moulton-Barrett soon proved himself no pushover. Realising his new father-in-law had stopped paying for sugar received from the Barrett plantations, in November 1807 he instructed Philip Scarlett, his attorney and the brother of his actual legal guardian, to refuse Graham-Clarke further shipments: 'He has not for the last two years settled our account [...] it is an unpleasant business and has given me great uneasiness but it is a duty I owe to myself [...] I do not wish this to be known.' A peculiarly intimate trust, in a man who must have been a kind of father figure to the youth, had been broken; and with it, perhaps, some vital faith in human nature. Just three months later, the twenty-two-year-old gave his County Durham landlord notice and moved his new family to the other end of England.

I do not wish this to be known. It is possible that this delicacy means Mary has no idea why her husband moved abruptly south. But she seems to have been raised biddable. As she grows up, Ba will find her mother's apparent submissiveness infuriating, and even in maturity she'll give no sign of understanding that it might have been strategic; recalling only something that sounds like passive aggression – 'A sweet, gentle nature, which the thunder a little turned from its sweetness—as when it turns milk—One of those women who never can resist,—but, in submitting & bowing on themselves, make a mark, a plait, within, .. a sign of suffering' – and certain that no such feminine 'sweetness' forms part of her own character. How ironic that by the time she writes this she'll be making similar displays of tractability herself.

But perhaps our mothers are the people we understand least. Mary Moulton-Barrett is in fact a strong woman, physically able to bear twelve children and determined against the tide of the times to ensure the intellectual development of her eldest daughter – and indeed all her brood. Yet maybe it *is* a tendency to yield that causes her to appear sanguine about slavery, gossiping that 'I rejoice to hear that Mrs T. has had a letter from James, giving an excellent account of himself, of the crops, & of his happiness in [the plantation at] Mont Serrat.'

Is this a domestic survival technique, in an era when women face economic, and so physical, destruction if they cease to comply with their menfolk? And what if it is – can there be a sliding scale of complicity? In 1810, more than 10 per cent of wealthy Britons are profiting from slavery: money that will never return to the enslaved people who created it, but remains in the British economy into the twenty-first century. Over two centuries on, the murky waters of the Atlantic slave trade lap at all our feet, whether as deficit or profit. Even four-year-old Ba is implicated, on that sunny hilltop where we could imagine her by now sitting down. She just doesn't know it yet.

But she does absorb the lesson of the surrounding inequality. Half a century from now, she'll indict the false promise of rural beauty created by exploitation:

> And cottage-gardens smelling everywhere,
> Confused with smell of orchards. 'See,' I said,
> [...]
> 'Who says there's nothing for the poor and vile
> Save poverty and wickedness? Behold!'
> [...]
> But we indeed who call things good and fair,
> The evil is upon us while we speak.

In July 1810 the view from Hope End is indeed 'good and fair' with orchards and hop yards that will later earn a local MP the sobriquet Member for Cider. Arable yields are high. Red-flanked, white-faced Hereford cattle dot the countryside like toys. But these model landscapes tell a kind of lie. Despite a good climate and rich, loamy soil, this is a poor county. Herefordshire's farm labourers are the majority population, and most earn less than they need to survive. Like other forms of wealth, agricultural profits flow up, not down, the social scale. Besides, the region's remote. The shallow, seasonal River Wye, hardly even a glint from the Hope End viewpoint, can't compete with the industrial arteries constructed during the recent 'canal mania'. Turnpike roads are excellent for the new Post Routes but too expensive for agricultural transport, and so old drovers' tracks still crisscross the county, their green lanes crowding with up to four hundred beasts at a time.

But mostly it's not drover's cries but the tap-tapping of building works that float up to Ba's summer vantage point. In the valley below her, an ostentatious new mansion is under construction. Work started almost as soon as the family arrived last autumn. Already, she and her lucky siblings have the run of:

> a lawn in front, with a fine sheet of water stored with fish, fed by springs, cascade etc. [...] extensive gravelled walks, through a

shrubbery ornamented with magnificent timber trees, thriving ever-
greens, shrubs and flower borders; [...] a productive walled garden,
clothed with choice fruit trees [...] grapery &c. [...] and upwards of
four hundred and seventy acres of excellent grass and meadow, arable,
woodland, hop ground and plantation.

By her own account she becomes a tomboy, who:

could run rapidly & leap high,—and [...] had very strong wrists. [...]
She cd. climb too pretty well up trees—[...] And she liked fishing,
though she did not often catch anything. And best of all, though she
cared for bows & arrows, & squirts & popguns—best of all, did she
like riding ... galloping till the trees raced past her & the cloud were
shot over her head.

So rambunctious is she that by the time she turns eleven Grandmama
worries about her modesty:

I have sent you six slips to wear under your frocks, you are now too
big to go without them [...] Now My darling Child you must allow
me to say I think you are too BIG to attempt fighting with BRO [...]
I have seen him very rude & boisterous with you & Harry He is now
a big Boy fit only to associate with Boys NOT GIRLS.

But this outdoor life is conspicuously healthier, particularly for the
girls, than the conventional alternative; besides, Hope End is far enough
from even the nearest cities, Hereford and Gloucester, to escape the dangerous infections bred by overcrowding or dirty water. So the death of one
of the children is met with appalled dismay. When four-year-old Mary
dies suddenly in March 1814, ten days after Ba's eighth birthday, the family
are stunned. Papa even lets them all make a rare, extended trip north to
recover. They visit his brother, Ba's Uncle Sam, in Yorkshire for a month,
and go on to his parents-in-law in Newcastle for another three. After this
period of shocked mourning the subject is closed and the family continue
to thrive. But it's the first cold draught from outside the hothouse.

Ba is eleven when that hothouse, Hope End mansion, is completed.
Family portraits from this time show a tumbling flock of children, all
sporting identical, gender-neutral page-boy haircuts, and dressed alike
in shift frocks with empire waistlines. The effect is of the freedom and

benign mischief of putti; there's even a poodle playmate called Havannah. Only Ba already has her characteristically rounded cheeks and chin, her pout, and somewhat darker hair.

By the time she's twelve, the expression captured by the well-known portraitist William Artaud has become meltingly sweet. It's a good look with which to disarm critics of female precocity. Though he's accustomed to spending time with distinguished and highly able members of the establishment, Artaud certainly falls for it. He tells a friend that Ba:

> possess[es] an extraordinary genius. She has a command of language and ideas that is quite marvellous and her versyfication is sufficiently varied and harmonious. She absorbs the learned languages as freely and as rapidly as chalk does water [...]. She has all the engenuous simplicity and airy volatility of spirits of the most sprightly of her age and sex. [...] She is idolized by her parents and yet such is the excellence of her disposition that I think she is not in the least danger of being spoilt.

Perhaps the girl on the edge of puberty wears her precocity lightly because she's used to it. With her mother's guidance, since she was eight she has been reading big-scale texts full of ethical argument: Alexander Pope's translation of the *Iliad*, Shakespeare's *Othello* and *The Tempest*, passages from John Milton's *Paradise Lost*. She was also eight when she received a 'ten shilling note' to reward 'some lines on virtue' written for her father. His delighted response addressed her as 'Poet-Laureat of Hope-End'; she took this compliment seriously, as only a little girl who adores her Papa can, and resolved that she would be a proper Laureate, producing odes for every domestic occasion.

Unlike most eight-year-olds though, Ba kept her resolution. She wrote a second poem to her father just three days later. The next month saw verses for her mother's birthday and for Henrietta ('But now you have a horrid cold, / And in a ugly night cap you are rolled'), and a sonnet celebrating the 'recovery of little Arabella, from a dangerous illness':

> When Death's pale hand o'er Baby spread,
> The pillow raised her little head,
> Her face was white, her pulse beat low,

From every eye sad tears did flow.

If this seems a little morbid, that's perhaps not surprising. Papa's accolade came just five weeks after little Mary's death, and these first family poems are written through the ensuing period of mourning at Hope End and during the family's trip north.

However seriously Ba takes her own poems, occasional verse is in fact another of the family's 'things'. Her grandmother Graham-Clarke writes accomplished poetry, and over the years Ba's siblings and Mamma will try their hand at it too. Like the family nicknames, these rhymes play with language as something shared, a kind of insider speak, and the domestic magic of using words to build a shared understanding is something Ba will never quite shake off. Years from now, a distinctively Victorian alignment with the people at home will remain close to the heart of her adult work.

Meanwhile, when she gets to fourteen Ba looks back at how this eight-year-old self:

> first found real delight in poetry [...] too young to feel the loveliness of simple beauty, I required something dazzling to strike my mind— The brilliant imagery the fine metaphors and the flowing numbers [...]
>
> At nine I felt much pleasure from effusions of my imagination in the adorned drapery of versification [...] At this age works of imagination only afforded me gratification [...]
>
> At ten my poetry was entirely formed by the style of written authors and I read that I might write.

These memories come from 'Glimpses into My Own Life and Literary Character', one of three notebook self-portraits Ba composes in a burst of adolescent self-consciousness between the ages of twelve and fifteen. Perhaps naïvely, she cites John Locke's foundational 1689 work of philosophical empiricism, *An Essay Concerning Human Understanding*, to argue that she's not being vain: self-examination can 'bring us great advantage in directing our thoughts in the search of other things'. Precocious or not, her self-scrutiny is typical for a teenaged girl in veering towards the excessively self-critical. 'My Character and Bro's Compared' is peppered with judgements like 'ardent', 'enthusiastic', 'impatient' and 'not content till I excel', which a disinterested observer might recognise as signs of an unusual intelligence struggling with being forced to go at trotting pace.

Still, this fourteen-year-old is guided more by emotional intuition than rational proposition – 'I feel uncontroulable contempt for any little-ness of mind, or meanness of soul [...] & prejudice I detest' – professes a 'patriotism enthusiastic & sincere', and claims to 'understand little of Theology', although at twelve she passed through a phase of 'enthusiastic visions', since regretted. She's also capable of touchingly straightforward adolescent angst: 'In society I am pretty much the same as other people only much more awkward much more wild & much more mad!!'

But behind all this there's a nagging sense of talent being wasted: of a mind consuming itself. Idyllic though life at Hope End is, far from being stretched Ba is being held back a year by sharing lessons with Bro, her younger brother who, 'tho by no means difficient has no chance in competition with her', as William Artaud puts it. Youthful intelligence must find its own way, and it does so chiefly through reading. 'At eleven I wished to be considered an authoress. Novels were thrown aside. Poetry and Essays were my studies & I felt the most ardent desire to understand the learned languages.'

Ba starts Latin, her first 'learned language', in 1816, having begun French a few months earlier. The following summer she takes up Greek – with the Classics tutor who was officially brought in for Bro – finding, 'I like this language a lot, because [...] I will be able to read Plato, and all the great authors of Greece.' And not just read: within a couple of years she'll be composing her first Greek ode. For now, though, it's with still childish tactlessness that she admonishes her Uncle Sam, 'I'm astonished that you don't want to travel to Greece, where can one take more instruc-tion, or more pleasure, than from the broken monuments which are the tombs of the greatest people in the universe?' But after all, she is only eleven. And what's more, she's writing in French – under the tutelage of a Madame Gordin, who comes in twice a day and sets correspondence as homework.

It would be difficult to make such an arrangement in rural Here-fordshire, but the family are spending summer 1817 at newly fashionable

Ramsgate. Much to Ba's irritation this Kent seaside resort has also produced a dancing master: 'I don't like dancing at all.' Her mind is on Higher Things. She's already composing French and Latin verse,

> sitting in 'my house under the sideboard,' in the dining room, concocting one of the soliloquies beginning:
> 'Qui suis je? autrefois un general Romain:
> Maintenant esclave de Carthage je souffre en vain'

as she'll recall decades from now in a vignette of her ten-year-old self, still playing house under the furniture of the adult world at the same time as she plunges determinedly out of her depth.

This is touching, funny – and priggish. Talent is Ba's privilege and her Achilles heel. At fourteen, when Bro goes away to school, she becomes doubly anguished by the loss of her closest companion and her own exclusion from education. Perhaps triply so, as sexless tomboy freedom is exchanged for the young woman's body that will handicap so many of her pleasures:

> Through the whole course of my childhood, I had a steady indignation against Nature who made me a woman, & a determinate resolution to dress up in men's clothes as soon as ever I was free of the nursery, & go into the world 'to seek my fortune'.

'Poor Beth,' she'll write later, slipping discreetly into third person:

> had one great misfortune. She was born a woman. Now she despised nearly all the women in the world [...]—She could not abide their littlenesses called delicacies, their pretty headaches, & soft mincing voices, their nerves and affectations. [...] One word Beth hated in her soul ... & the word was 'feminine'.

Ba is articulating here the frustration of generations of women who hate, not their bodies and their own selves, but the constrictions of gender roles. There are pleasures and there are pinch points, and we should be careful about reducing such resistances to aspects of 'femineity' to the single-pointed essentialism of gender dysphoria: that 'real' women couldn't possibly feel like this is the claim made by centuries of misogynists.

Ba is growing up in an era when even the daughters of the wealthy must rely on paternal goodwill – and culture – to patch together an education beyond the feminine accomplishments she's bored by: 'I hate needlework & drawing because I never feel occupied whilst I work or draw—'. Her father keeps a country gentleman's library: a cosmopolitan affair, as British education at the start of the nineteenth century is, well stocked with the classics, key Enlightenment belles-lettres, and some of the Romantics. With her mother's guidance, by her early teens she has read the American revolutionary thinker Thomas Paine, Locke's fellow British empiricist David Hume, the great French secularist Voltaire, a translation from the German of Johann Wolfgang von Goethe's *The Sorrows of Young Werther*, arguably the most influential *Bildungsroman* in European history, and that Genevan-born Romantic with a more political take on the nature of the self, Jean-Jacques Rousseau. She's such 'A great admirer at thirteen' of Mary Wollstonecraft's *A Vindication of the Rights of Woman* that two years later her mother is worrying 'Mrs Wolstonecrafts system' will turn her into 'an old maid' with '*singleness of will &c.*'

Yet it's Mamma herself who gave Ba permission to read Wollstonecraft at this formative age. The surrendered wife imagined by future biographers is nothing like this real-life woman, viewed by her contemporaries as 'Mary and her little coterie of independent females'. Ambitious for her children's development, it's she who keeps them at their lessons when Papa is away on business, and who commissions and collects much of Ba's juvenile creativity, including a fragmentary 'Essay on Woman', written at sixteen in response to Alexander Pope's 'Essay on Man':

> Are vases only prised because they break?
> Then why must woman to be loved be weak?

But it's not just 'femineity' that's engaging Ba's emerging political awareness. Turn back once more to 1817, and we find the eleven-year-old drafting a furious letter to Lord Somers, owner of nearby Eastnor Castle, who to neighbourhood chagrin is about to be made Lord Lieutenant of Herefordshire, and will shortly gain an Earldom. He's among House of Lords supporters of the government's suspension of habeas corpus – the right to be tried in one's own presence, and therefore fairly – on the grounds that there are too many political subversives around. Moreover, his pamphlet *A Defence of the Constitution of Great Britain*, published this same year, argues that the right to vote should be curtailed; parliament doesn't need to sit every year. Ba's fiery letter denouncing his attacks on 'liberty' can't have done neighbourly relations much good, if it was ever actually sent, but she doesn't seem to notice the paradox inherent in arguing for legal and democratic rights as the daughter and granddaughter of slave 'owners'. She's not alone in this. Her slaver father and Uncle Sam are both at the same time politically progressive Whigs.

Is youthful idealism in particular always separated by a few degrees from daily life? Ever since her very first poem, 'On the Cruelty of Forcement to Man', protested press-ganging, liberty has been a recurring theme for Ba. The high point of her early seriousness is *The Battle of Marathon*, a 1,500-line retelling, in the heroic couplets she's coming to favour, of a key moment in the Greco-Persian wars. Her Preface frames this story not as adventure but as a moral parable about 'one little city rising undaunted, and daring her innumerable enemies, in defence of her freedom'; and it's surely better to hold such ethical ideals than not. How then do we judge a young person who develops a social conscience before she knows all the facts, or has the economic and social agency to act?

It's unclear how well-informed Ba is about the sources of her family's wealth as she enters her teens. But *The Battle of Marathon* has cost her too much effort and emotion to be a game. Started in the summer she was eleven, it takes her over two years to complete. Her father, the dedicatee, has it printed in a private edition of fifty copies for her fourteenth birthday. Though this is vanity publishing, it is her first book, and some of its strongest passages show a precociously adult, assured ear, as when Ba brings Athena to Athens to give false council:

> Doubt clouds the Goddess' breast—she calls her car,
> And lightly sweeps the liquid fields of air.
> When sable night midst silent nature springs,
> And o'er Athena shakes her drowsy wings,
> The Paphian Goddess from Olympus flies,
> And leaves the starry senate of the skies.

Still, even the most austerely intellectual young girl enjoys high days

and holidays. The plays Ba puts on with her siblings are undeniably literary achievements – that first French tragedy is succeeded by *Socrates, of
the Laurel of Athens* when she's eleven, and *The Tragedy of Laodice* when
she's thirteen – but organising the straggle of little siblings to perform
must be chaotic fun too. There are trips to join Grandmama and Treppy at
the smart new spa town of Cheltenham, just twenty-five miles away. And
when Ba was nine, she managed to invite herself along on her parents'
expedition to France simply by dint of jumping into the carriage with
them.

Yet this turned out to be the most intellectually formative of treats.
Travelling by way of Calais, Boulogne, Abbeville and Amiens, the family
followed a trail of ecclesiastical architecture to Paris, where they spent
three weeks at the Hôtel de Rivoli 'with French windows opening upon
the Thuillerie Gardens, & Palace'. Ba and her mother frequented the
nearby Louvre, 'the most magnificent thing in the world I am sure', and
the Jardin des Plantes. They were joined by Uncle Sam, and went with
him to the Théâtre Français and the Opéra Comique before returning to
England via Rouen, where they viewed another cathedral and the spot
where Joan of Arc was burned at the stake. It was the start of Ba's lifelong fascination with Europe, and fuelled her desire to learn languages. It
also differed markedly from the longueurs of life back home:

> Hope End in spite of the romantic prospects which environ it in
> spite of the beauty of beholding Nature wrapt in her bridal robe
> which we have at present IS dull and IS lonely [;] the sun rolls over
> our heads—no Papa is here to greet us.

This is a fascinating glimpse of how important her father's charisma
is to the creation of this happy home. For every idyll is part fantasy, and
Hope End in particular is being built with blood money. For, to an even
greater extent than Graham-Clarke's, Barrett wealth comes from sugar
plantations. Ba's father was born Edward Barrett Moulton at Cinnamon
Hill in St James, Jamaica, in May 1785, and spent his first seven years in
the elegant eighteenth-century Great House overlooking Montego Bay.
It's a beautiful spot, among aromatic cinnamon trees, that by the 1970s
will be seductive enough for country and western star Johnny Cash to

move in. The estate that surrounded young Edward, though, was one of several sugar plantations owned by his maternal grandfather Edward Barrett and worked by enslaved people.

Edward's mother was a Barrett, his father a Moulton, and when he was thirteen and living in England, he and his brother added a second 'Barrett' to their names in order to inherit from their maternal grandfather, who by then had neither surviving sons nor other legitimate grandchildren. As it had with the Clarke estate, money wanted to follow the family name. Once again, this required a complex process involving a Royal Warrant. That John Graham-Clarke was on hand to guide the youths through this suggests that he might even have proposed the idea. (Was he already planning a dynastic marriage?) When, later that same year, the teenaged Edward's grandfather died, he left some 84,000 acres of sugar plantation where around 2,000 people were enslaved: a substantial legacy indeed.

The Barretts seem to believe themselves to be of mixed heritage. Hercie Barrett, Ba's four times great-grandfather, arrived in Jamaica in 1655, an officer in the army that captured it from Spain. As a reward, in 1663 King Charles II granted him land: a colonist, then, but not yet a slave owner. Subsequent generations, however, changed this, and the intervening century and a half has been plenty long enough for the kinds of consensual and non-consensual relationships across ethnic divides, both acknowledged and otherwise, that produce mixed-heritage populations in long-colonised societies. When she's nearly forty, Ba will write to her lover that she herself has 'the blood of a slave':

> I would give ten towns in Norfolk (if I had them) to own some purer lineage than that of the blood of the slave!—Cursed are we from generation to generation!—I seem to hear the 'Commination service'.

This letter has been much quoted, including by commentators who believe that it displays not anxiety about heritage but right-minded abolitionist guilt. But the (racist) phrasing is clear. 'Some purer *lineage* than that of the blood' addresses ethnicity, not the blood on the family's hands; and that Commination Service, already almost obsolete in Elizabeth's lifetime, tries to ward off divine punishment not so much for any particular sin as for the 'original sin' of being born.

Internalised racism is a baroque falsehood. Shame is a complex, unreasonable emotion, and shame and anxiety about something understood as one's very identity is both profoundly unreasonable – no one can help how they're born – and particularly complex because it concerns what is inescapable. From a twenty-first-century perspective, though, Barrett mixed heritage would be brilliant news. How exciting if the cultural game changer that Elizabeth Barrett Browning will become proves to have broken open not only the male canon but the canon of white writing too.

Which is why it's important to be careful with the actual recorded facts. Disappointingly, Ba's closest relatives whose mixed heritage is certain aren't people she's actually descended from but are lateral kin: second cousins who are the children of Grandmama's profligate brother George Goodin Barrett. Three years after Papa and his siblings arrived in Britain, this second, illegitimate set of Edward Barrett's grandchildren made the same Atlantic crossing. Their mother Elissa Peters was of mixed heritage. She had been enslaved until the death of her late 'owner', to whom she was 'given' by his father. When George Goodin died she was freed, and sent with her six children by him to John Graham-Clarke, to be settled in Newcastle under the terms of their father's will, that they 'not fix their abode in Jamaica but do settle and reside in such countries where those distinctions respecting colour are not maintained'. This optimistic construction of race relations in early nineteenth-century Tyneside all too conveniently tidies the children away from their late father's property.

The roots of Barrett privilege are in shallow soil. The family are paradoxically placed as beneficiaries of the very racism that causes them such anxiety. The customary behaviour of the Jamaican plantocracy does indeed make mixed heritage somewhere in the branching tree of their ancestors a reasonable hunch, but hunches aren't history. Nevertheless, if race is at least partly a social construct – not a set of essentialist, eugenical capacities – shouldn't we count it a kind of victory for nineteenth-century black writing that a woman who with relatively good reason *believes herself* to be of mixed heritage achieves literary superstardom before 1850? For Elizabeth is certainly not doing what later generations will call 'blacking up' in that posthumously much-quoted, but in fact very private, letter to her lover: on the contrary, she's confessing a secret.

If Ba has already encountered difficulty in imagining herself into the role of woman poet, imagining herself as black woman poet must be, for her time and class, almost unthinkable. The only precursor the forty-year-old who'll write this letter might have heard of is Phillis Wheatley, the African-born poet who was raised as a slave in Boston, Massachusetts and created a sensation in 1773, when she moved to London and published a poetry collection, *Poems on Various Subjects Religious and Moral*, under the patronage of the Countess of Huntingdon. She is in a way Elizabeth Barrett Browning's alter ego, the kind of outlier, impossibly-best-case chance Elizabeth might have had if she'd been born enslaved. Later admired for her classicism, in her own time much of Wheatley's celebrity was based precisely on the perceived *anomaly* of her gifts: 'These poems display no astonishing works of genius, but when we consider them as the productions of a young, untutored African, who wrote them after six months careful study of the English language, we cannot but express our admiration.'

The exception is often viewed as an imposter, and the Barrett family disease is imposter syndrome. Ba's father was only briefly exposed to the hurly-burly of school. Sent to Harrow at twelve, he left abruptly within a year. In the family version that will be passed down by Robert Browning, he was humiliatingly bullied by an older pupil for whom he was supposed to fag (that is, act as servant). Such bullying is endemic, indeed structural, to famous boys' schools of the time; condoned as a way to 'knock the corners off' spoiled youngsters, teach discipline, and help them internalise the potency of hierarchy.

Papa certainly has faith in hierarchy. A decade on from Ba's idyllic first Herefordshire summer, he sends his own eldest two sons to Charterhouse even though he himself did not cope at school. But with what, exactly? Was he, for example, flogged – like a 'slave', as he may have experienced it? He's said to be dark complexioned, like Ba. Was there racism in the abuse? Or, more complex, might his family have *feared* an element of racism? In the family version the older boy who 'punished' the teenager, allegedly for burning his toast, was expelled: how hard did Harrow try to soothe a pushy colonial family?

Whatever happened, both brothers were withdrawn from school and, although Edward Barrett Moulton-Barrett went up to Trinity Hall Cambridge at sixteen, his corners clearly never were knocked off. By the time he got to university, he may also have had a stiffening sense of his fatherless family as dysfunctional. Unlike his brother Sam, Papa will never return to Jamaica, the place where their own father scandalously separated from or possibly even deserted them and their mother. For Ba's paternal grandfather Charles Moulton left the family soon after his third son had been conceived. Worse, his brother Robert Moulton later defrauded Papa, the eldest of the three, of up to £30,000, asserting that Charles had given him power of attorney and laying claim to manage Edward's estates while he was still a minor.

Despite all this, Charles has maintained some contact. By the time Ba turns seven he is living in England. Land tax records for 1812–13 show him residing at Epsom, Surrey, in a house belonging to the Barretts. But Ba never meets this missing grandparent. The begging letter he sends her father at this period elicits a brusque rebuttal. Still, his trickster figure resurfaces periodically. In *The History of Parliament*, where he earns a mention when his second son, Uncle Sam, serves as MP for Richmond, Yorkshire, he has become a 'merchant, of Hammersmith, Mdx. and New York'. In fact he seems to hail from the island of Madeira, nearly 700 kilometres off the coast of Morocco, whose population at the time of his birth comprised primarily the descendants of early Portuguese settlers, and slaves from Guinea, Algeria and the Canary Islands.

How aware of this is Ba? Many years in the future she'll fall in love with a man whose terms of endearment for this brown-eyed, dark-haired woman include 'the little Portuguese', a pet name eventually to be immortalised in the title of her *Sonnets from the Portuguese*. But her feelings about this part of her family history are mixed. From childhood, Elizabeth Barrett Moulton-Barrett signs herself 'EBB', omitting the initial *M* because, 'I fell into the habit [...] of forgetting that I was a *Moulton*, altogether.' She'll publish her breakthrough book, *Poems (1844)*, as 'Elizabeth Barrett Barrett'.

If Ba's internalised racism whispers that her ancestry constitutes a 'taint', there's just the faintest hint of another 'taint' too; one she may not even be aware of. Perhaps it's not surprising that, with the not-disinterested John Graham-Clarke increasingly replacing other mentors, Edward Barrett Moulton-Barrett rushed into early marriage. But there's an additional whiff of haste about this wedding, which took place on 14 May 1805, a fortnight shy of his twentieth birthday, and was announced only retrospectively. When Ba was born as early as decently possible just forty-two weeks later, on 6 March 1806, her father was still a couple of months short of his own legal majority. Her first brother, Bro, followed her with remarkable speed the following June, and such reproductive assiduity reminds us just how young a father Edward is.

But there is another possibility. Mary and Edward married – in style, despite the haste – at the newly consecrated, fashionable St Nicholas's Church, Gosforth. Given this, and the local standing of Mary's family, it's somewhat surprising that, when baby Ba arrives, she's christened privately at just three days old, on 9 March 1806. No evidence survives to suggest that she's particularly frail. Noticeably, this firstborn isn't celebrated with a holiday on the family's plantations, though first son Bro will be. And when he's christened, on 10 February 1808, the two-year-old Ba is rechristened in public alongside him.

It's almost as if she's been smuggled into the world. Her private christening is conducted by a good friend who just happens to be visiting the new parents that week. William Lewis Rham, a Cambridge friend of Edward's, is on his way to becoming a leading agriculturalist; he's also the rector of a parish far out of sight and mind in Wiltshire. He's doubtless delighted to inspect the agricultural potential of the estate his friend has recently rented, Coxhoe Hall in County Durham. But it must be odd and embarrassing for the young, unmarried priest to coincide with, if not an actual birth, then the lying-in that followed it. On the other hand, with his relatively little experience of infants, Rham would be the perfect choice for officiant if one had anything questionable to cover up: such as, say, a baby who appears less a newborn than three or four months old. Which raises the question: could the consistently precocious Ba in fact have been born a little earlier than her recorded birth date, so perilously soon after her parents' hasty marriage, and so close, at less than sixteen months, to Bro's arrival?

Whatever the case, for all his wealth, by July 1810 Ba's twenty-five-year-old Papa has plenty of reasons to feel insecure. A broken home, immigration, anxieties about ethnicity and class, compromised wealth, early marriage and possibly accidental fatherhood, manipulation by an absent father, his father's brother *and* his father-in-law: with so little to rely on, the psyche needs compensatory structures. Small wonder he's throwing so much money and energy into creating his ideal home.

Hope End house, finished the year he turns thirty-two, is a young man's indulgence. The Barrett circle are more interested in extracting merchandise and money from Jamaica than in the kind of magpie cultural orientalism that Queen Victoria's imperial reign will soon popularise, yet this great statement is built in the very newest, orientalist style. With its minarets, ogee drop-shaped windows and second-floor roundels, it has more than a little in common with the fashionable Picturesque, that newest cultural trend for strikingly ornamented, even whimsical forms of planting and building, for which Herefordshire friends and neighbours will turn out to be the intellectual powerhouse. Edward Barrett Moulton-Barrett doesn't employ an architect, simply turning to landscape architect J. C. Loudon, who is redesigning the grounds, for occasional advice. The result is a fabulously expensive piece of outsider art.

The house being built in 1810 below Ba's parkland viewpoint looks like the folly it is – yet it has a disconcerting, Gaudi-like sense of fluidity. The building pushes and pulls old Palladian proportions to create a flowing modernist structure that's a whole century ahead of its time. But, as it amplifies the original gesture of relegating the old, Georgian mansion that so resembled Cinnamon Hill to a stable block, some deeply personal, Freudian logic seems to be trumping economic and aesthetic sense.

Perhaps unsurprisingly, in 1873 a subsequent owner will pull everything down and start again. But for the space of Ba's childhood the house that Papa built represents everything that's prodigious, expansive and progressive – and everything defensive and compromised – about the Barretts. Risk-taking, pioneering, fundamentally domestic and not a little vulgar, Hope End may be a monument to invention as survival strategy – and the precursor to the adult Ba's own *sui generis* creativity.

[*Opening Frame*]

That great twentieth-century Italian, the novelist Italo Calvino, says that:

> Both in art and in literature, the function of the frame is fundamental. It is the frame that marks the boundary between the picture and what is outside. It allows the picture to exist, isolating it from the rest; but at the same time, it recalls – and somehow stands for – everything that remains out of the picture.

Calvino is a hugely sensual, visual writer, an artist of the coloured world. So perhaps it's not surprising that he pictures storytelling this way. But this is much more than a nice literary metaphor; it's an idea about how stories work. As Calvino points out, a frame isolates, identifies, and so shows up what it contains. It especially highlights what's hard to see. In his own most famous novel, 1979's *If On a Winter's Night a Traveller*, a framing structure challenges us to think about both what's true, and how we can know that it is.

Calvino's frame is his book's 'outer' narrative about 'you' the reader. This kind of literary device is nothing new, though most introduce characters who then narrate the work's 'inner' stories. The world's oldest literary text, *Gilgamesh*, a survivor from the second millennium BCE, starts by imagining the discovery of (in turn more) ancient tablets recording the story it goes on to tell. In the middle

ages, the Scheherazade stories collected in the Islamic
Golden Age as *One Thousand and One Nights*, and
Giovanni Boccaccio's fourteenth-century *The Decameron*,
offer us parables about storytelling as survival. Scheherazade
needs to enchant her husband the Sultan so that he
won't execute her; the ten young people who narrate the
Decameron are self-isolating from plague.

We know from her 1842 essay, 'The Book of the Poets',
how highly Elizabeth Barrett Browning values Geoffrey
Chaucer's framed compendium of *The Canterbury Tales*:
'And he sent us a train of pilgrims, each with a distinct
individuality apart from the pilgrimage, all the way from
Southwark and the Tabard Inn, to Canterbury and Beckett's
shrine: and their laughter never comes to an end, and their
talk goes on with the stars.' Two of the English canon's most
famous frame novels, Mary Shelley's three-ply *Frankenstein*
– in which Walton the Arctic explorer frames Frankenstein's
own storytelling, which frames his creature's – and Emily
Brontë's *Wuthering Heights*, narrated by the housekeeper,
are written by women who are Elizabeth's contemporaries;
of those published in the century before her birth, Laurence
Sterne's *Tristram Shandy* could be described as all frame.

So it's not surprising that when she comes to write
the full-length fiction that is also her *ars poetica*, she plays
with interlocking frames. In *Aurora Leigh* her eponymous
protagonist's own story periodically frames others. Letters
tell their own stories; so, at greater length and in person,
do the heroine's beloved cousin Romney, her nemesis Lady
Waldemar, and her protégée Marion. And positioned at the
heart of this verse novel is a story we don't get to read: the
entirely fictional, semi-autobiographical poetic masterpiece
with which Aurora justifies her life choices and proves her
identity as a poet. This imaginary book, the volume we can
never open, is in a sense Aurora Leigh's *Aurora Leigh*. But

because we don't get to read it, it exists as pure symbol, representing poetry itself: everything the writer of the real book within which it appears believes about her own life's purpose and has spent it doing. Which is how Elizabeth contrives to frame her own self – her own life, love, beliefs and art – within the story of Aurora Leigh.

Elizabeth's life usually comes to us as a story ready-framed by cliché: the love story, the history of nervous invalidism, or the Victorian family melodrama. That's especially ironic because her actual life was as a woman who revolutionised poetry, and she inspired generations of other readers and writers, particularly women. It's also just plain wrong. Elizabeth is not a character. She has none of the plasticity of fiction. She was a real person – which means that writing about her has certain obligations and limits. Of course, rather like those other arts where faithfulness is taken for granted – translation, documentary – biography grapples with its own interpretive nature. But struggling with something is not the same as cheating.

Aurora Leigh frames this book. I've even borrowed its nine-book structure and the frontispiece of early editions. This isn't to claim that the verse novel is 'really' an autobiography, a memoir, or even a *roman-à-clef*: it's not. The course of its heroine's life does not follow its author's. But the work is Elizabeth's great account of a literary development that in one absolutely central way does resemble her own: it's the story of someone who becomes herself through becoming a poet. This is the story I believe Elizabeth would have wanted to have told about herself; the frame she deserves.

Book Two:
How to be ill

I did not write, nor read, nor even think,
But sate absorbed amid the quickening glooms [...]
Dissolving slowly, slowly, until lost.

Summer once again; but now it's 1821 and Ba is fifteen. The sash window throws a double lozenge of pale West Country light onto a wall; it scarcely seems to move as hours pass. In a panel of sky, gulls wheel and tumble above the River Severn. There's little for the eye to catch on and less to do: though the bedroom's spacious enough and comfortable, it lacks personal clutter. 'I am as happy as possible and have delightful fun', Ba claims bravely in a letter to her sister Henrietta. But this is simply not true.

She's confined to the newly built, no-frills Gloucester Spa Hotel. Just over the road stands a utilitarian, single-storey Pump Room where iodine-rich spring water is dispensed. It's all a world away from nearby Cheltenham, the holiday town famous for its palatial neoclassical Pump Rooms, public gardens and private spas. But Ba is in Gloucester for her health, not a holiday, and the spa is medically endorsed by a local celebrity. Driven, influential and polymathic, Dr John Baron is also physician at Gloucester General Infirmary, has a large private practice, is publishing research into TB, and is advocating the vaccinations introduced by his friend, the pioneering Edward Jenner – and when Gloucester County Lunatic Asylum opens a couple of years from now, he'll serve as a consultant there, too.

In a portrait painted just a year ago, Baron sports a cravat and silk waistcoat, turns up his velvet collar lapels and generally looks like what he is: a man unused to being crossed. But Ba, the indulged first child of a highly privileged family, and what's more a teenager, is strong-willed too. She and Henrietta call Baron 'Dr BARREN' (which may be how the Scot pronounces his own name), and she grumbles that 'he seems to have a penchant for the *pillow*'.

She grumbles equally about getting up:

> I was out in my chair the day before yesterday but was certainly the worse for it. Yesterday the bath was tried but no sooner had the hot water touched my back than I was in agony. I could not remain in, an instant.

But a little inconsistency is par for the teenage course. Besides, by the summer of 1821 she's been ill for some months, and her diagnosis continues to elude the doctors. This is enormously frightening at a time when almost anything, from a common cold to an infected splinter, could be fatal. Ba's next surviving letters are dictated to her brother as if she hadn't the strength to write herself.

One reason she's here is that both a London doctor, Dr George Ricketts Nuttall of Dean Street, Soho, and Dr William Cother from Worcester – a second opinion the family has called in – are at a loss as to the nature of her 'interesting case'. Cother's diagnostic letter, based on the patient's own account, is the most detailed version we have of the symptoms of this adolescent illness which will determine the course of her life. According to this, it starts with periodic headaches. After seven weeks, pain moves to:

> the right side, that is about the center of the angle formed by the greatest projection of the ribs, the umbilicus, and the anterior superior spinous process of the os ilium. The pain commences here is carried to the corresponding region of the back, up the side to the point of the right shoulder, and down the arm [...] the paroxysms

[are] accompanied by convulsive twitches of the muscles, in which the diaphragm is particularly concerned.

The narrative diagnosis invites the reader to join in the detective work of medicine. Reading these letters two centuries later, it's striking how much dialogue there is between the patient, the doctors, and their client her father. At the end of May, when Ba is still at home, Dr Nuttall – well-known as a lecturer, author of medical books and Physician to the Westminster General Dispensary – holds to his opinion that she's suffering from indigestion. He writes from London with a series of intimate questions about flatulence and bowel movements: 'You have too much good sense, my dear Elizabeth, not to be candid with me, on a point, of so much moment to yourself [...] In matters of this kind, false delicacy might, & have, often, led to the most ruinous consequences.' Patient confidentiality, or the march of time, mean that, perhaps happily, we have no record of Ba's reply as to whether she's been passing, in the doctor's colourful words, 'clay-coloured, or greenish, or blackish, or frothy, or mucous, or yeasty motions', or suffered 'much distension from wind, & does it escape?'

Instead, we watch as Nuttall, Cother and others gradually eliminate the most likely causes of her symptoms. 'Your active turn of mind, & *inactive state* of body, together with your age &c incline you, as well as other young bodies under similar circumstances, to dyspeptic complaints', Nuttall suggests. But his warning seems arbitrary. The high-spirited Ba is no indoor geek, even though she's made the transition from childish bodily freedom to the inhibitions of adolescence: gentility expects a girl her age to muffle her body elaborately and adopt a sedentary lifestyle – just as her newly arriving menstrual cycle may make her feel, especially at first, that her body is busy with its own secret affairs.

Still, Nuttall won't be the last clinician to warn writing women about imaginary dangers posed by an 'active turn of mind'. Does his patient object? We can't be sure, but it's just three weeks after this pronouncement, on 24 June, that Cother is called in to give his opinion – which is that something serious *is* amiss: 'Probably referable to derangement in some highly important organ [...] At the same time that I confess, the positive proofs are wanting of the existance of diseased spine, I must say that this is the best inference, I could draw.'

From her room in Gloucester, Ba protests the frightening diagnosis that 'the spine' could be 'the seat' of her illness even while insisting that she's sicker than Mamma realises. Small wonder if she sends mixed messages as she waits nervously to see what Dr Baron will find when he comes, soon after her arrival, 'to examine my back accurately and with particular care in order either to remove or satisfy his own doubts'. Unfortunately for her the upshot is that he agrees with Cother, and recommends confinement in a spinal sling. Ba is to spend the coming months 'a young lady on her back'.

It's bad news. But all the same, 'I do not wish to return home my dearest Mamma till I am well and perhaps the wish may be natural considering that illness casts a shade of apathetic gloom.' And it could be worse. She won't actually be subject to fierce mechanical traction; her spine will be held motionless in position, perhaps lightly stretched by gravity. Ba and her doctors have left no description of this sling, but those in use at this time are harnesses, often with front and back plates for the torso and a collar that fits under the chin. Since the seventeenth century, doctors have also been using Francis Glisson's hanging sling, which suspends the vertebral column from a collar round the patient's neck; Ba is lying down, and hers may be attached to the bedhead. The apparatus, with its pulleys and cord, looks a bit like the imaginary home-made machines of Heath Robinson, or Wallace and Gromit. For the patient herself, though not particularly painful, it is restricting. Ba can't move her head, which makes reading difficult and writing impossible.

By the time 1821 turns into 1822, her bravado has worn off. She writes to Aunt Bummy with understandable self-pity:

> I have often entertained hopes that you and dear Grandmama might be inclined to enliven my confinement but alas! how often have I been disappointed! I fear many months must yet pass ere I change my position and tho' I endeavour to be as patient as I can yet dearest Bum the prospect is melancholy. Oh! how I *do* wish you were here but it would be too much I fear to ask!

Company is the only way out of the imprisoning, imprisoned body in the apparatus. Ba arrived in Gloucester accompanied by her favourite uncle, Sam, and she will always remember how he 'was [...] to *me* Uncle

brother friend & nurse when I lay in the long weary sickness at Gloucester. I can never forget *that* —& the gratitude and the love were as one.'
Papa's unmarried brother is standing in for the man himself, who will visit
just once, around New Year. By autumn 1821, the patient has 'my learned
companion Master Bro by the side of my classical couch hurling a look of
contempt at Doctor Baron and of defiance at little Tommy Cooke.' Aged
just fourteen, Bro as eldest son is taking his turn as Papa's deputy. But
he's also Ba's favourite brother, and this temporary renewal of childhood
complicity must feel like some kind of remission.

The siblings have two months together, recreating their old intimacy,
before late October brings a visit from Mamma – who has brought along
the family's third son, six-year-old Stormie – heralding Bro's return to
school. Luckily, the renewed separation causes no relapse; Ba's mother
finds her 'considerably better'. And when no family are in attendance
there's always 'Little Tommy Cooke', who 'is quite divine and excels at
my toilet with as much grace as ever'. This diminutive says a lot: for all Dr
Baron's social climbing, in 1821 gentry regard doctors as little more than
expert servants. Whether he's a medical student, as seems likely, or just
a male treatment assistant, Cooke assumes primary nursing responsibilities. Coming from a large family, Ba is probably used to a lack of privacy,
but intimate care by a young man implies to the twenty-first-century
observer that some boundary is being crossed. Yet in 1821 it's not unusual.
Hospital nursing is regarded as such dirty work that the women who take
it up are, in Florence Nightingale's words, 'too old, too weak, too drunken,
too dirty, too stupid or too bad to do anything else'.

There's yet one more medic involved. Back in spring 1821, before
Nuttall and Cother were called in, family doctor Mr John Carden examined Ba. In early autumn he reappears at the Spa Hotel to prescribe
'setons' or puncture threads, which, like the cupping (applying a hot cup
to the skin to raise blisters) she has already endured, are supposed to facil-
itate the discharge of undesirable matter. Carden is sure that an external
cause, whether poison or an infection, is the root of Ba's illness, because
when he was first called in she, Henrietta and Arabella were all suffering
from the same symptoms. He prescribed all three a bark draught (a kind
of tonic given for scurvy and as an astringent) and as a follow-up added

valerian, which in the twenty-first century will still be a herbal remedy for
diseases of the nervous system. This apparently cured Arabella, but both
elder girls went on (coincidentally?) to develop measles; at which point
Ba's recovery halted.

Contemporary sources suggest that the bark Carden prescribed may
have been elm, which is only very mildly toxic. Much more harmful is
the opium Ba has been prescribed, presumably also by him. As Cother
remarks with acerbity in June, 'I understand she has taken a variety of
powerful medicines without any permanent benefit. Opium at one time
relieved the spasms but it has ceased to have that effect.' He's right. It's
a powerful drug for a young body to tolerate. Small wonder that by the
time he examines her:

> The mind has ceased in a great degree to engage in those investiga-
> tions and pursuits which formerly constituted it's greatest delight,
> and there appears to be a degree of listlessness perceptible to those
> around her.

Even in tiny quantities opiates are famously addictive; and they consti-
pate. No surprise that someone who's also confined to bed has lost her
appetite. The fifteen-year-old, 'has only a relish for highly seasoned food.
She has shrunk so much as to have produced in the minds of her friends
great anxiety.'

It also sounds very much as though she's depressed. In the strange
limbo of the room at Gloucester, her life is to all intents and purposes
suspended: rather like her spine in its harness. Despite Mamma's 'daily
dispatches', this time emptied of everything and everyone she loves must
drag. In the monotony it would be easy for symptoms to enlarge to the
point of hypochondria. But is Ba a hypochondriac? This first illness is the
start of the mythologising of Elizabeth Barrett Browning. Future pop
psychology will decide that she is the very type of a Victorian invalid:
suffering from psychosomatic or even hysterical symptoms in protest at
her restrictive family life, or faking illness in order to free herself from
the conventional roles played by young women of her time, or anorexic,
or definitively suffering from one or another specific complaint. Imaginative diagnoses of her deepest psyche crowd around her bedside, as if

biographers and dramatists weren't voyeurs but counted along with her doctors and family.

We don't. But we do have the benefit of hindsight. We know that Ba will recover from this crisis – if not completely – and live another forty, highly productive years. We also know that she'll suffer continued ill health. What we can't be certain about is whether she's being irrevocably damaged by the treatment she's receiving now. Months confined to bed on a regime of opium would be enough to stop the healthiest teenager being able to take more than a few steps at a time, and the sling's ortho-paedic interference can only exacerbate this weakness. So it's not surpris-ing that, by the time Ba gives up hope of a complete cure and returns to Hope End in May 1822, she's scarcely able to walk.

But there's more to it than this. Ba has contracted *something*. Viewed from the twenty-first century, her symptoms suggest nothing so much as viral infection followed by post-viral syndrome. Today, debate tries to bring her symptoms, formulated in nineteenth-century terms, into the brightly lit modern consulting room. In 1989, D. A. B. Young started a discussion in the *British Medical Journal* by arguing that Ba had initially fallen ill with what was 'certainly an encephalomyelitis of one kind or another'. He sug-gests that this could have been measles encephalitis, or that the 'measles' she and Henrietta caught was actually misdiagnosed poliomyelitis. Polio would certainly explain her later difficulties with exertion and even breath-ing, which Young startlingly, and fascinatingly, associates with possible deformity of the spine caused by polio-related scoliosis. The excruciating spasms Ba suffers aren't dissimilar to those experienced by anyone with a major spinal prolapse. The slow onset of 'paralytic scoliosis with thoracic involvement' – up to two years after infection – would also explain why doctors examining Ba specifically for spinal disease in the weeks imme-diately after she became ill could find nothing wrong. Young also follows the trail of Pen Browning's loyal belief that his mother suffered a spinal injury associated with riding, or preparing to ride, her pony. This would be a palatably romantic version of continuing spinal problems. More recently, looking in another direction, Anne Buchanan and Ellen Buchanan Weiss have noticed the similarity between the triggers Ba reports and those for the rare muscle-weakening disorder, hypokalemic periodic paralysis.

Equally possible is that the agonising spasms that Ba experiences at the peak of her illness are tardive dystonia, caused by specific substances acting on the dopamine receptors in her brain. Her full body spasms that centre on a particular point, and difficulties with walking that includes 'sciatic' cramping, are a close match. In twenty-first-century Britain, tardive dystonia occurs as a side effect of drugs prescribed for psychosis. But dopamine receptor inhibition is also a side effect of magnolia, a remedy widely prescribed in nineteenth-century England for a range of illnesses, and just as likely as elm to have been the main ingredient in Carden's bark decoction. (Wouldn't it be in keeping with Ba's passionate impatience to overdose in order to try to speed up a cure?)

Each of these competing theories is plausible. The trouble with posthumous speculation is that clinical diagnosis relies on a kind of habeas corpus – actual examination to contemporary clinical standards – and Ba simply isn't here for even the most distinguished clinician to examine. To understand her ill health, the best we can do is not to conjecture, but to understand it in the way she and those around her did: *as* the symptoms she experienced. To know what Ba's life was *like*, we have to know what it was like for her to suffer *as* she did, without the 'voice-over' of a posteriori knowledge. We have to try to step out of our comfortable positions as onlookers in order to feel as Ba herself does. Framed by apparatus in her Gloucester bedroom, all she knows is that:

> The suffering is agony, and the paroxysms continue from a quarter of an hour to an hour and upwards [...] The attack seems gradually to approach its acme, and then suddenly ceases—during its progress the mind is for the most part conscious of surrounding objects but towards its close, there is generally some, and occasionally, very considerable confusion produced by it.

[*Second Frame*]

Is a biography a kind of portrait? This book started by
looking at Elizabeth in Dante Gabriel Rossetti's 1858
engraving. Picture biography like this – picture portraiture as
something actually 'painted on the wall' – and you're almost
certainly imagining a face.

But why should faces matter so much? The twentieth-
century philosopher Emmanuel Levinas says they are
where we encounter each other. Faced with someone else,
we realise that we must take them into account in our
understanding of the world, that 'My freedom does not
have the last word; I am not alone.' What flows from this
recognition, in other words, is everything that makes us
human: love and morality, society and intimacy. The human
face is the 'source from which all meaning appears'.

Levinas was born in Kaunas in what's now Lithuania
in 1906 and, like his compatriot the poet Czesław Miłosz
(who was born just 40 miles north and five years later),
lived through most of the twentieth century; he died on
Christmas Day 1995. Miłosz wrote that, 'My generation was
lost. Cities too. And nations.' But Levinas was Jewish, and
so the century he lived through was darker still, although
he survived the Second World War by being interned as a
French prisoner of war.

In the 1920s he had studied at the University of Freiburg.
His professors there were two great innovators of our
understanding that you must include the human *having* the

experience inside your philosophical frame, otherwise you're noodling in ideal space: father of phenomenology Edmund Husserl, and Martin Heidegger, that dreamer of human Being. Both philosophers may at this point have appeared close to the heart of the culture and traditions Elizabeth Barrett Browning had believed in so deeply. Yet Heidegger's ideas were soon to fail the test: he became an active Nazi collaborator, and was complicit in the professional destruction of his Jewish mentor, Husserl.

So there's a profundity to Levinas's ideas about personhood. 'To begin with the face as a source from which all meaning appears, the face in its absolute nudity', he says in 1961 in *Totality and Infinity*, 'is to affirm that being is enacted in the relationship between men' (that's to say, people). Our human duty is to sustain that other face: to keep alive the other self who is recognised and created in this encounter – and in so doing to become human ourselves.

For without selfhood no set of features has any especial meaning. They could just be shapes 'painted on the wall'. The phrase comes from Robert Browning's poem, 'My Last Duchess'. In that famous fable of coercive control, a jealous Duke has his wife murdered and replaced by her portrait – which, unlike the living woman, is absolutely compliant. The face in the frame, Browning's poem reminds us, is no longer a self and cannot meet our gaze.

Book Three:
How not to love

What
He doubts is, whether we can do the thing
With decent grace we've not yet done at all.

In 1822, turning sixteen brings no particular privileges. British women don't come of age in any civic sense: it will be nearly a hundred years before any get the vote. For the well-off, girlhood merges into maturity in a procession of pretty, high-waisted dresses, with no stronger demarcation than the putting up of long hair. Meanwhile, the technical age of consent is still, shockingly, twelve.

So Elizabeth's birthday this March has no special significance. All the same, it's no fun spending it at the Gloucester Spa Hotel. The usual anniversary poems arrive by post but are no replacement for a proper family party. Henrietta inadvertently rubs salt in the wound: 'We had famous toasts after dinner […] the first that […] this time next year [you] may be here enjoying both health and happiness [,] the second for your nurses.' To make the patient feel still more left out, another baby brother, Septimus, has just been born.

Perhaps unsurprisingly, two months later she's home. But it's a difficult transition, because she hasn't yet been cured. The carriage journey across half of Gloucestershire is painful and jolting for a body grown accustomed to nothing but a spinal sling; when she arrives, her family are shocked to see that she can only walk a few steps. Immediately, as she's helped to the room that will be her world in the coming months, she replaces little Arabella as the invalid sibling.

Yet there are compensations to this removal from the quotidian hurly-burly. Elizabeth takes after Papa in flourishing with seclusion. She loves 'silence & quietness & a sight of the green trees & fields out of the window'. She also shares her father's single-pointed determination; and now, in her own sanctum, she's free to read and write to her heart's content. The apprentice writer finds herself, at sixteen, released from boring 'accomplishments' and domestic, daughterly duties. Even formal study is no longer compulsory. Instead, shawled and wearing an invalid's lacy mob cap, she reclines among cushions like royalty at a levée. The role of invalid is semi-public, part of the world if set apart, and Elizabeth's room is a public as well as a private space, one designed equally for night and day, sleeping and waking.

When Henrietta sketches Hope End, we see how snugly the house fits among wide lawns, where the brothers play cricket between the trees as shadows lengthen first one way, then the other. Elizabeth is confined to an upper floor, but the mansion sits down low in its valley, and from her window she can see the elaborate, Picturesque-style lake and shrubbery below her, and, further away, the estate orchards, hop yards and woods. She even glimpses the bare tops of the Malvern Hills. But what dominate her view are trees:

First, the lime,
[…] past the lime, the lawn,
Which, after sweeping broadly round the house,
Went trickling through the shrubberies in a stream
Of tender turf, and wore and lost itself
Among the acacias, over which you saw
The irregular line of elms by the deep lane
Which […] dammed the overflow
Of arbutus and laurel. […] Behind the elms,
And through their tops, you saw the folded hills
[…] the woodlands.

This is a Hope End of the mind, transformed by memory three decades from now into the childhood home of *Aurora Leigh*'s eponymous heroine. In 1822, the halls and stairwells of the actual house below Elizabeth echo with the continuing chaos of childhood. The schoolroom where she and Bro 'conversed, read, studied—together [...] fagged at the grammar, wept over the torn dictionary—triumphed over classical difficulties', has been handed on to younger siblings. Alfred and Septimus are still infants in the nursery, but Henrietta, Arabella, Charles, George and Henry are all now aged between four and thirteen, 'my gardeners and *scufflers*', as their mother calls them:

> George & Stormy are cleaning the walks, A. *scuffling* up Henttas walk to the Cottage & Henry helping Emma to spread out the Nursery tea on the grass—a busy but very quiet school day we have had—[Arabella] gave us a gay cottage breakfast on her birth day, under Minnys directing taste [...] Seppy is sneezing with a little cold—[...] & is as sentimentally melancholy [...] as the strawberries will permit.

However, Elizabeth's invalid status has shifted a double burden of daughterly responsibility onto thirteen-year-old Henrietta, effectively forcing her, since Bro and Sam are away at school, into the role of eldest child at home. Entering adolescence just as her big sister returns from Gloucester, Henrietta is in many ways what Elizabeth might have been: an artistic child growing up into a conventional young woman. She writes verse and, like her mother, also sketches; the family appreciate her poems and pictures. But they don't view her as *gifted*, and for her – as for Arabella – there's to be no dispensation from daughterly duties.

Perhaps this is partly an accident of birth order. Firstborn children fascinate their parents, initiating what later siblings more or less repeat; as a third child and second daughter, 'Addles' is unenviably 'also-ran'. On the other hand, talent undeniably exists – and she lacks it, for all the upbringing she shares with Elizabeth. This spring she writes her mother a birthday ode so bad it's almost good:

> Oh say what love I bear
> To whom? except my mère

For whom this day I offer up my prayer
And may it very soon be granted
For virtue in her is indeed strongly planted.

Does Henrietta herself know how terrible this verse is? And does she recognise how much Elizabeth's continuing closeness to Bro keeps her at a distance? The two eldest siblings are still a pair. Writing from school, Bro nags his sister about exercise:

So my dear Miss Bazy you need not fret yourself into the Lumbago, nor keep your '*well leg*' in bed a bit the more for it nor need it prevent the other from following it a bit the more tardily.

He launches into the geeky discussions of classical metre he knows she loves:

M is also cut off as 'Sepulchrum horrificum' i.e. sepulchr' horrificum, if a vowel precedes two consonants it is long and you may not have a word of more than three syllables at the end of a line.

More surprisingly, he sometimes has to push her to write back. 'I have no idea of writing every other day to you as I hitherto have done without having some return [...] Dab it but your a cool hand by Jove!!' he announces from Grandmama's in Marylebone, where the boys spend school breaks that are too short to make the long trip home to Herefordshire. But he writes again the next day anyway, because the support works both ways. Sam, naughtier as well as younger, is proving more of a responsibility than a confidant. In this era, when fathers don't want to be troubled with details of their sons' lives, and mothers don't understand educational experiences they've never had, a sister who can follow at least part of what Bro is doing – even though she refuses to acknowledge the discomfort and violence of school – is a huge emotional support.

In turn he understands how important it is that she keep working:

But those hundred lines [...] when I came away you had A HUNDRED LINES to complete the poem, and though you have most certainly, got on most surprisingly, you are still in the same place, with a HUNDRED LINES before you.

He doesn't need to worry. 'Miss Bazy' is taking months over her new poem precisely because she's working hard on it. Not for her 'effusions' scribbled down in haste: she'll never be that kind of Romantic, even though this is the era of the Romantic second generation, and George Gordon Lord Byron and Percy Bysshe Shelley are poetry's rising stars. She admires these figures not as peers but across the gulf that lies between writers and readers, although she's only fourteen years Shelley's junior. But her own tastes also hark back to what came before literary Romanticism, immersing her in the ancient Greek and Latin canon and guiding her towards poets, like Alexander Pope, who have already brought classical metres into English prosody.

Elizabeth wants to be an accomplished classicist as well as a poet, and she reconciles these twin ambitions through the belief that classical Greek scansion is the ideal form for English verse. The influence of this bifocalism will be enduring. For slowly, in the teenager's bedroom with its country views, the famous future poet is being formed. Classical poetry feels authoritative and timeless to her. Both Pope's straight-talking clarity and the plain speech of translation, which the classical tradition *is* in English, will find their way into her mature work. And, within this same tradition, extended narrative form passes from Homer, Virgil, Ovid and even Julius Caesar on its way to eighteenth-century pastiche in Pope's *The Dunciad* and *The Rape of the Lock*, on through Byron's *Don Juan*, which is being written and published even as Elizabeth sits here, and will eventually make space for the verse novel that is to be arguably her own most influential work.

All the same, in the high room at Hope End, she does also read Shelley, who drowned so shockingly this summer. His *Adonais*, on the death of John Keats, appeared last July while she was seriously ill in Gloucester, and must trigger intimate feelings of identification. It's not surprising she describes it as an 'exquisition':

> Within the twilight chamber spreads apace
> The shadow of white Death, and at the door
> Invisible Corruption waits.

For all her steely insistence on technique, she has a literary crush on

Byron, too. Before she fell ill, she believed she would be 'Very much in love when she was fifteen,—[…] Her lover was to be a poet in any case— and [she] was inclined to believe that he wd. be Ld. Byron.'

Only Bro seems to understand the deep division in her character that this marks. The intrinsically disobedient creativity of that wild girl, his boisterous sister Ba, hasn't disappeared within the self-disciplined intellectual, the apparently obedient daughter, of their late teens. Elizabeth is *both* strong-willed and obedient, hot and cold, Dionysian and Apollonian. For her nineteenth birthday her favourite brother gives her 'a very beautiful *silver remember* medal of Lord Byron'. 'I was at a loss to discover which it most resembled Ld Byron, or myself', he tells her, and while siblings may joke around, it's a piece of striking self-identification by the blond, seventeen-year-old youth with the smouldering, infamous – and dead – peer; one which suggests an unspoken, intense intimacy.

And it *is* unusual for a teenaged boy to have his sister as best friend. But in these first years back at Hope End, Elizabeth, working through layers of loss – of health, independence, a chance at education – seems oblivious that Bro adores her, as she does of the possibility he jokingly suggests that 'your friend Tommy' Cooke, the Gloucester medic, has feelings for her. Poets are much safer targets for a crush than flesh-and-blood young men. Confined to the pages of books, Byron and Shelley can fill her imagination as pure visionaries, activists and role models. One of her first publishing successes, when she's eighteen, is the appearance of her 'Stanzas on the Death of Lord Byron' in *The Globe and Traveller*:

> He *was*, and *is* not! Graecia's trembling shore,
> Sighing through all her palmy groves, shall tell
> That Harold's pilgrimage at last is o'er—

It's a virtuoso technical homage written in Spenserian stanzas, the exact form of Byron's famous *Bildungsroman, Childe Harold's Pilgrimage* – though, at only four stanzas to the original's 555 pages, very much shorter. Such detail probably escapes her proud family. Elizabeth is visiting Cheltenham with Grandmama and Treppy when the poem appears, so Mamma reports:

> Taking the paper, with a becoming carelessness of air, I asked [Papa]

what he thought of those lines, he said, 'They are very beautiful indeed the only I have seen at all worthy the subject.' I cannot help thinking, replied I, that we know something of the Author. 'They cannot be Ba's' said he, taking the paper from me to read them again, [']tho' certainly when I first read them, they reminded me greatly of her style—had you any idea they are hers?['] 'I have a *conviction* of it,' said the conceited Mother, pouring out the tea with an air that threatened to overflow the tea tray.

As she grows stronger, Elizabeth will enjoy such stays away. A year after her return from Gloucester, the family decamped to the Normandy resort of Boulogne for seven months. Only eight years after the end of the Napoleonic Wars, Boulogne was already a popular bathing resort, though its prosperity still depended on herring. Eighteen months later in July 1825, and back across the Channel, Elizabeth and Henrietta go to live with Grandmama for almost a year in newly fashionable Hastings. These eighteen months at the seaside take Elizabeth away from her concentrated life at Hope End, but stamp her imagination. She's at the lovely, responsive age when anything can change the way in which the self forms, and the 'glorious sea! from side to side / Swinging the grandeur of his foamy strength' will appear almost too frequently in the poems she goes on to write in her twenties.

But these are in the future. It's while she's at Hastings that Elizabeth's second volume appears, three weeks after her twentieth birthday. *An Essay on Mind*, its philosophical title poem running to 1,462 lines and accompanied by fourteen 'Miscellaneous Poems', is published by a reputable London firm, James Duncan, on 25 March 1826, and underwritten by Treppy. This kind of arrangement isn't unusual, and when the edition runs to a second impression the sponsor presumably gets her money back. Still, it's fairly hard won: Uncle Sam first submitted the manuscript (to a much more fashionable publisher) a year ago. Duncan's list, though, includes the Dispensationalist periodical *The Jewish Expositor and Friend of Israel*, and the Barretts are in sympathy with Dispensationalist theologians, who justify an interest in Judaica by viewing biblical history as a series of *dispensations*: first the Jewish, then the Christian religions, and next the Second Coming. The family particularly admire a Dispensationalist lay preacher called Edward Irving; indeed Elizabeth praises him in her title poem, in a passage that stands as her adolescent *ars poetica*:

> And while Philosophy, in spirit, free,
> Reasons, believes, yet cannot plainly *see*,
> Poetic Rapture, to her dazzled sight,
> Pourtrays the shadows of the things of light;
> [...]
> Thus Reason oft the aid of fancy seeks,
> And strikes Pierian chords—when Irving speaks!

As she leaves her teens, in other words, Elizabeth already believes that poetry earns its keep by aiding serious thought; intuiting or imagining what logic cannot. This is conscientious as it is; but her Preface goes further still, spelling out the argument for 'Ethical Poetry' that her late great poems will still be making decades in the future. Although 'it has been asserted that poetry is not a proper vehicle for abstract ideas', she argues now, 'Poetry is the enthusiasm of the understanding.' And she makes her case from political poetry, predictably concentrating on the classical canon and especially on Homer who, in Edward Gibbon's words, is 'the law-giver, the theologian, the historian, and the philosopher of the ancients'.

Crammed as *An Essay*'s actual title poem is with perhaps not completely digested classical allusions, this is a young poet flexing intellectual and creative muscle. She's searching out her own means and ends, as she turns her gaze inward and takes 'Mind' as her topic. In developing the idea of the poet as a thinking self, she's discarding childish daydreams of a poetic life of chivalric action, in which she would 'Arm herself in complete steel [...] & ride on a steed, along the banks of the Danube, every where by her enchanted songs [...] attracting to her side many warriors & [...] destroy the Turkish empire, & deliver "Greece the glorious."'

Perhaps her changed circumstances have forced this shift in perception. But the result is that she's arriving at something like the famous Enlightenment idea that the self is found in and defined by thought, René Descartes's 'I think, therefore I exist'. *Cogito, ergo sum*. This line of thought allows her to sidestep the dismaying fact that it's increasingly difficult for women writers to publish *as* women. *An Essay* had to be submitted *for* Elizabeth, and is published anonymously: society, it seems, takes one look at the embodied self, and decides its limits. A woman may only do *this*, an invalid just *that*. But, veiled by the page, a former tomboy can be a poet, and a young woman an intellectual. In this, Elizabeth's experience is no outlier: Mary Shelley's *Frankenstein* appeared anonymously eight years ago, the Brontë sisters' necessarily pseudonymous *annus mirabilis*, 1847, is still twenty years in the future.

Elizabeth's *Essay* forces the traditional big questions about literature and thought through the unfamiliar paradigm of the woman writer. For though she may be anonymous to the reader, *she* knows she's a woman writing: how does this make her feel? It's turning out to be complicated – just like growing up. The cliché is that child prodigies find the passage to adulthood hard to navigate. When Elizabeth fell ill just as she was leaving childhood, her condition was disabling and sometimes frightening, but in a way it solved a number of problems. A fourteen-year-old can just about convince herself that she's still a child: she hasn't finished growing and she can still genuinely enjoy some childish things. But at fifteen this becomes a pretence. As the eldest Barrett offspring, it falls to Elizabeth to sustain the idyll of family childhood for as long as possible. Where once being old for her age pleased her father, now immaturity is required. And this isn't just about sexual innocence. It applies to autonomy and agency too. The fierce trajectory of intellectual precocity is being abruptly braked by a freeze on emotional development that's so sharp it threatens to split the teenaged self apart.

Before her illness, Elizabeth's notes to her father had already become painfully kittenish. 'My ever ever dearest Puppy', she wrote at fifteen, going on five:

> My heart whispers that you will not refuse, that you will not turn from me in anger! My dearest, dearest Puppy grant my request! […] Imagine yourself my age once more, how your heart would beat with joy at the prospect of an excursion to the metropolis! Have I tormented you? If I have, oh! forgive me.

It's with such miming of childish unselfconsciousness, of course, that self-consciousness arrives. And as Elizabeth starts to act 'in character', she becomes more conventionally feminine. Her new physical frailty helps this along, making her appear quietened, passive. Housebound as she is, she becomes a sort of *genius loci*. It would be easy to mistake her, as Papa does, for Coventry Patmore's 'The Angel in the House', 'all mildness and young trust, / And ever with her chaste and noble air'.

Self-suppression and sexual denial will pass down the line of siblings as each comes of age, and slowly become the family norm. The frustration of Elizabeth's intellectual life, on the other hand, is felt by her alone. But it's no less damaging. Autodidacticism is ultimately limiting; Elizabeth badly needs a mentor. Yet her age and gender mean that the only way she can meet any such figure will be through her family.

Uncle Sam is the obvious candidate. For years, she's crammed letters to him with puns, and notes on her precocious reading. As a kind of father substitute, or supplement, he's a safe audience for her peacock displays. An altogether less suitable possibility is Daniel McSwiney, the siblings' former tutor, who dashes off an unmistakably flirtatious postscript to one of Bro's letters, calling her 'Miss Sauce-box'. This well-educated, good-looking thirty-year-old – a dandy, as even the Barrett boys notice – comes from old Irish Catholic farming gentry; and he has form with the ladies. Youthful party-going has recently been succeeded by stormy courtship of one 'Miss Edwards'. As a fellow foreigner, McSwiney may feel it's not inconceivable that he could marry up into Barrett money; indeed, he'll go on to wed the daughter of his next employer. For Elizabeth, though, he's romantically invisible. Not only does he like a drink; much worse, he's a mediocre poet. So she carries on squeezing quotes and allusions into letters to Uncle Sam. We get the sense of a hectic, almost desperate, desire to hold on to the brilliance that has defined her. After all, child-hood talent is easily recognised: it's just a matter of being developmentally ahead of the game. But adult brilliance is defined by content – what to *do* with those unusual gifts? – and is altogether more in the eye of the beholder.

The publication of *An Essay on Mind* helps resolve all this. It's a palpable achievement, and in just a few months it sets off three correspondences that lift Elizabeth out of intellectual loneliness, transform her daily reality, and have a lasting effect on her life. The most affectionate, and ultimately longest lasting, of these exchanges is with a distant cousin. John Kenyon shares a great-grandfather with Papa, with whom he was at

Cambridge, having followed the same route from Jamaica to England for his education. When his interest in Elizabeth begins, Kenyon is a hugely sociable forty-two-year-old of independent means. The best-known portrait, a lithograph after John Collingham Moore, shows him at seventy with quizzical, warm eyes, the high-coloured cheeks that suggest a life dedicated to sociability, and the girth of an epicure.

A sometime poet and a generous patron of writers, it's only natural that when he visits Hope End in July 1826, he scrounges a copy of Elizabeth's newly published *Essay*. We can guess the light-heartedness with which he does so from the apology he writes after reading the book, when he suddenly realises that this is serious work:

> Fame, I hope if you should persevere seeking her, will not turn out to you what you have so poetically described her, and what in truth she has turned out to so many—
> —But you have plenty of time before you.

It's the start of a lifelong, and life-changing, relationship. Over decades, Kenyon will introduce Elizabeth to the key confidant of her thirties, Mary Russell Mitford, who in turn gives her the adored spaniel Flush. He will encourage his mentee and Robert Browning to meet. Eventually, he will even give the Browning couple and their son financial support.

But for all its future importance, this isn't the first friendship that Elizabeth's *Essay* produces. Since June she's been corresponding with another family friend, Sir Uvedale Price, who also lives in Herefordshire. His home at Foxley near Yazor is close to the craggy Welsh hills and less than three miles from the meandering River Wye. This is a terrain far removed from the smooth valleys of southern England, so amenable to neoclassical order and elegant, 'Capability' Brown landscapes; and Sir Uvedale has helped develop the strikingly anticlassical aesthetic of the Picturesque, which is now shaping national and international fashion. He published the work for which he's best known, *An Essay on the Picturesque, As Compared With The Sublime And The Beautiful; And, On The Use Of Studying Pictures, For The Purpose Of Improving Real Landscape*, in 1794.

The lengthy subtitle says it all. Price argued that the Romantic categories of the Sublime and the Beautiful, until then fashionable ways to think about both natural and man-made landscapes, should be supplemented by a third: the Picturesque, or in other words what works well in a picture. In eighteenth-century France, the principle had developed that gardening was a painterly creation 'designed by the man of genius, and adored by the man of feeling'. This idea was borrowed for British audiences by artist, travel writer and Anglican clergyman William Gilpin, an associate of Price's, who first cited it in 1782 in his *Observations on the River Wye and Several Parts of South Wales, etc. Relative Chiefly to Picturesque Beauty; Made in the Summer of the Year 1770*. Hugely successful, and followed by further volumes, this illustrated tourist guide created the Wye Tour, that first model of mass tourism, quickly popular even among the wealthy as the Napoleonic Wars made traditional Grand Tours problematic.

Sir Uvedale lives upriver from all the excitement, yet by the time his relationship with Elizabeth springs to life, those thirty-odd miles of river trip between Ross on Wye and Chepstow, featuring gorges, overhanging woods, old towns, ruined castles and the ruins of Tintern Abbey, are the epitome of Picturesque fashion. More exciting for Elizabeth, though, is that Sir Uvedale is friends with William Wordsworth, whose own Wye Tour resulted in his famous 'Lines Written a Few Miles above Tintern Abbey, on Revisiting the Banks of the Wye during a Tour, July 13, 1798'. Elizabeth will admire and advocate Wordsworth throughout her life, and this poem, with its mixture of applied philosophy and picturesque description, seems clearly to have influenced her. Wordsworth writes:

> Once again I see
> These hedge-rows, hardly hedge-rows, little lines
> Of sportive wood run wild: these pastoral farms,
> Green to the very door; and wreaths of smoke
> Sent up, in silence, from among the trees!

Half a century later *Aurora Leigh* echoes:

> Behind the elms
> And through their tops, you saw the folded hills
> Striped up and down with hedges, (burly oaks
> Projecting from the line to show themselves)
> Through which my cousin Romney's chimneys smoked

As still as when a silent mouth in frost
Breathes.

Price is an Oxford-educated socialite who has married into the Irish aristocracy. Wealthy and sophisticated, he counts as friends both prominent Whig politician and sometime Foreign Secretary Charles James Fox, and Sir George Beaumont, who has helped found the National Gallery. So he has no need to tolerate fools or to pander to lady hobbyists; and he recognises that Elizabeth is neither. Their correspondence is intensely serious and focuses on ancient Greek verse-forms, which both believe are the appropriate discipline for English verse. For all his resistance to neoclassical landscape, Price has received an excellent classical education, and he devotes pages to close reading of Elizabeth's use of metre. She responds in kind, displaying the width and depth of her knowledge: her first letter alone recruits Abraham Cowley, Thomas Gray, Sir John Denham, Edmund Spenser, John Milton and Alexander Pope. The tone of intellectually engaged argumentation is one a young man of her age and class might share with his college tutor, something Price recognises and commends: 'This very amicable controversy, may, I think, be of use to us both; for you are well furnished with arms, & dextrous in the use of them.'

But Price is seventy-nine when this correspondence starts. When he dies just over three years later, in September 1829, Elizabeth is – luckily perhaps – still too young to understand quite how rare such formative friendships are. She grieves for Sir Uvedale of course, and composes an exequy; but she isn't devastated. She isn't even fully convinced by his legacy, which after all surrounds her. Papa's house at Hope End is a gigantic Picturesque folly. But Elizabeth is not at all convinced that she doesn't prefer the 'Sublime' and 'Beautiful', comparing, 'Herefordshire all hill & wood—undulating & broken ground!' with 'Worcestershire throwing out a grand unbroken extent [...] to the horizon! One, prospect attracting the eye, by picturesqueness: the other the mind—by sublimity.'

Perhaps that's partly because this 'sublime' vicinity has produced the third, and most intense, of her new friendships. Hugh Stuart Boyd, a forty-five-year-old *soi-disant* scholar living off the proceeds from his County Antrim estates, has settled in nearby Malvern. With his wife Anne and daughter Annie, five years Elizabeth's junior, he lives first at Ruby Cottage, Malvern Wells, and then, from May 1828, at Woodland Lodge, Great Malvern. Boyd is so impressed by Elizabeth's *Essay on Mind* that in February 1827 he writes to her out of the blue and without being introduced. It's a not insignificant gesture that verges on social transgression.

The letter itself is lost, but we know something of what it contains from Elizabeth's reply. Evidently, he's enclosed some verses in Greek addressed to her, but also expressed interest in her 'improvement'. Combining flattery with criticism is, did she but know it, the classic move an older man makes on a younger woman. It works so well because young women are so often in the grip of self-criticism; learning the delicate paradox of excelling at being secondary. And Elizabeth, on the cusp of twenty-one, responds. Like many women her age, she's been practising self-flagellation, behind the stalking horse of self-improvement, for years. Besides, she's already primed by her father to attach herself to authority, and to believe that criticism is a sign of male affection. Indeed Boyd's letter arrives just when she's feeling demolished by her father's dismissal of a new poem, 'The Development of Genius': she simply assumes that his verdict is both authoritative and disinterested. She seizes on Boyd's approach and fires off in response one of her epistolary pyrotechnics, full of allusions and accompanied by some Greek verses of her own.

She also starts a one-step-forward, two-steps-back dance that we'll come to recognise:

> I regret that the distance between Hope End & Malvern, & my own incapacity to walk or ride far, should present anything like an obstacle to my availing myself immediately of Mr Boyd's very kind offer of pointing out to me personally his objections to my Essay.

For Elizabeth may be intellectually accomplished but rural seclusion – not to mention a deeper retreat, into the privacy of her own room – has turned the confident, boisterous child into a shy young woman who hates going out and about. She especially hates paying visits, which in these days of slow travel often require an overnight stay. It's not a solitary vice. Social shyness is a sanctioned family trait. Henrietta records a day in February 1827 on which:

Mama was on the lawn superintending the dusting of the curtains, luckily she escaped before [a cold-calling family] saw her. Luncheon was ordered, I was sent for & there they sat never attempting to go till it was becoming quite dark [...] Pray fancy Mama & me by ourselves obliged to entertain these four people.

Elizabeth even found visiting Sir Uvedale Price challenging. Though her trip to Yazor in October 1826 went well – he entrusted her with the proofs of his *An Essay on the Modern Pronunciation of the Greek and Latin Languages* – their intimacy remains founded on the extraordinary mutuality of their literary confidence. So her reluctance to turn what quickly becomes an in-depth epistolary relationship with Hugh Stuart Boyd into something in real time is not surprising. Eight months in, convention will remain an alibi for shyness: 'As a *female*, & a *young* female, I could not pay such a *first visit* as the one you proposed to me, without overstepping the established observances of society.' Whether or not this is her father's view, as she claims, in the event she manages to hold off meeting Boyd for over a year – until one day in March 1828 her carriage passes him on the road.

She doesn't stop. She's on a rushed errand to prevent friends from setting out to visit her mother, who is ill with the rheumatoid arthritis that within months will kill her. But, in a sign of things to come, Boyd is so petulantly affronted by this that he threatens to leave Malvern. It's an odd reaction, one that should sound warning bells to any parent. In practice, perhaps because Mamma is so unwell, it does the opposite. The public nature of the encounter, combined with Boyd's expression of social displeasure, bounces Elizabeth *and Papa* into arranging for her to visit him without delay. Just four days later, Bro drives Elizabeth, Henrietta and Arabella over the hills to Boyd's home in Malvern Wells. Unfortunately, misjudging the steep descent from the Wyche pass, the siblings don't set the drag chain (a kind of brake). The downhill momentum of the heavy carriage makes the pony panic, gallop, and overturn them. The result is a second awkward encounter with the Boyds in the road. This time Elizabeth introduces herself, only to be 'awed [...] by Mr Boyd's silence—At last he said "I cannot help thinking that *I* was the cause—I was the cause."'

Odder still, one might think. As are the 'uncopiable compliments' which follow in his next letter. Yet still no one intervenes. At this key moment in Elizabeth's otherwise exceptionally sheltered young life she is left as utterly exposed as if she were already an orphan. John Kenyon's affection is familial, protective and proud. Sir Uvedale's respect for the young woman is exceptional given her age and gender; but it's the generosity of a man near the end of a long, successful life, for whom the phenomenally able daughter of old friends is pure bonus. He's the intellectual mentor Elizabeth has lacked, and wants nothing in return but the odd burst of brainy sparring.

Hugh Stuart Boyd is a very different. A restless soul who carts his womenfolk from place to place, he has never worked. The official tragedy of his life is that fifteen years ago he began to lose his sight and has become completely blind. Despite being now unable to read or write, he sees himself as both a scholar of Greek, and a poet. Plucky indeed – even Miltonian – which is certainly how those around him view it. But the degrees of separation that blindness can create have not so much opened up imaginative mental space as reinforced a native dogmatism. Boyd is locked in an obsession with a particular method of Greek scansion that – luckily or perhaps unluckily for Elizabeth – happens to be the same one Sir Uvedale advocates. Yet the unintentionally comic dead hand of his verse makes clear how very little he understands about *poetry*. In a verse about walkers killed by lightning, for example:

Awhile they sailed on pleasure's golden tide—
A storm arose; the lightning came: they died—
If upon them Heaven's dart unsparing flew,
Think that the next dread shaft may light on you.

Elizabeth, usually so quick to joke about bad verse, is courteous in response, praising Boyd's 'smoothness of versification'. But there's no getting around it. This is a lesser talent. Boyd is no Sir Uvedale. Yet, far from developing a reciprocity, he expects to criticise Elizabeth – and to receive only praise from her. Perhaps he finds reciprocity difficult in general. Or he doesn't like joining in: even though he seems to have enjoyed studying under a personal tutor, he left Oxford without a degree.

Elizabeth has been raised in sympathy with independent-mindedness; but her father's solitariness differs from this. Unlike Papa, Boyd has never tried to put down roots; he hasn't created a home of his own, and his only child was born six years into what is perhaps not a terribly successful marriage.

In February 1827, when Boyd writes his first fishing letter to Elizabeth, Anne Lowry Boyd has less than ten years left to live. Her husband, by contrast, still has plenty of twinkle; Elizabeth describes him as 'rather young looking than otherwise'. He is 'moderately tall, and slightly formed. His features are good [...] His voice is very harmonious and gentle and low.' It soon transpires that her new friend needs an amanuensis to help with his correspondence and to read aloud in both English and ancient Greek, and he seems to find that young women fulfil this role particularly well. As Aunt Bummy will comment tartly, 'Really *all* the young ladies in the neighbourhood seem to me to be in the habit of going to see that poor man.'

To be fair to Boyd, he's no Humbert Humbert. The many young women he invites into his home are not *chronologically* children. Yet, as he must be aware, socially imposed innocence has kept them naïve and vulnerable to manipulation. And, while they may initially be drawn in by a feminine sense of 'doing good works', the bitchiness with which they compete for Boyd's favour makes it clear where the power lies. 'Eliza told me that Miss Steers walks out with Mr Boyd whenever she can. So [...] he is not afraid of disgracing *her* by his "slovenly appearance"!!', Elizabeth bursts out petulantly, before recording with shock – and envy? – that Boyd has advised Eliza to read Henry Fielding's risqué, picaresque novel *Tom Jones*.

Although she sounds like a teenager, Elizabeth is by now in her early twenties, and not without admirers of her own. In 1829 she receives a Valentine ode under the pseudonym of Italian dramatist Alfieri, which hints heavily that its author knew her as a child:

> Immortal B—t! [...]
> Tis thine to call 'the days of childhood' back,
> And, with thy sounds of magic minstrelsy,
> Recal the memory of past times to me.

[...]
Years have rolled on—oh, there are memories
Of blasted hopes—and mine is one of these.

The period 1829–30 also sees her involved in an extensive correspondence with classicist and lexicographer Edmund Henry Barker. Yet she remains a desperately inexperienced young woman, and by 1831 her emotions and desires have been kettled inside family life for years. She's twenty-five: an age at which her own mother was the married mistress of Coxhoe Hall, and had given birth to Elizabeth herself. In this fugue state of inauthenticity and repression, greatly exacerbated by raw but unspoken bereavement when Mamma dies unexpectedly in late 1828, it's no surprise that the young woman should fall in love by way of 'exalted' literary passions that helpfully conceal her own feelings. After all, if she asks herself why 'Mr Boyd' matters to her so much, she has only to reach for her own Preface to the *Battle of Marathon*: 'Poetry is the parent of liberty, and of all the fine arts.' The Achilles heel of young poets, their idealistic passion for writing, creates ready fodder for the literary casting couch.

The relationship is manipulative from the outset. Elizabeth's very first entry in a diary she keeps for eleven months from June 1831 records, 'I suspect that [Mr Boyd's] regard for me is dependant on his literary estimation of me, & not great enough, for me to afford the loss of any part of it.' Love capriciously withheld, or simply not requited, can be addictive, forcing the lover to understand that what affection *is* bestowed by the beloved is conditional, and to scrutinise their own behaviour for ways to 'earn' more. Nothing else makes sense of the incompatible 'truths' that the beloved claims to return their love, yet doesn't show it. When this is sustained for years by the alibi that consummation is impossible because the beloved is married – and, as so often the case with older men and younger women, Boyd is – the unspoken contract becomes increasingly abject, creating an association between love and suffering.

'Why shd. I wish so much to be with a person, who certainly does not wish *so much* to be with me. Why shd. I take pleasure in lacerating myself, & kissing the rod?' By now Elizabeth's every encounter with Boyd is barbed with anxious comparisons. In November, 'He does not like Miss Bordman as much as he used to do. He says that he does not like her *much*', but in December he names Harriet Mushet, a 'rival Queen'. At this game's perverse arrival point, pleasure vanishes even for the instigator, as tearfulness replaces wide-eyed eagerness and, in the cliché, 'She's just no fun anymore'. But, missing infusions of admiration, even the manipulator may come to believe in his own affection. 'He put his hat before his face, & talked […] "of course he felt gratified and obliged by the sentiments I expressed." "*Gratified & obliged!*"—Well!'

There is simply no excuse for this. Fanning the flames is no way to handle a crush:

> Mr Boyd attacked me & made Miss Steers attack me on the subject of science standing higher in the scale of intellect than poetry. […] And when she was gone, Mr Boyd said—'I hope you did not think that I wished Miss Steers to stay for my own sake. I was quite disinterested about it—'.

But at twenty-five Elizabeth is caught in a perpetual adolescence of obedience: she doesn't yet recognise the flawed human three-dimensionality of older men. 'How I ought to love him!—*ought*!—how I *do*!—' she frets, about her father. And she obeys Boyd too, as he puts her through her paces, even though by now she realises her feelings for him are adulterous:

> How could I write a diary without throwing upon paper […] the thoughts of my heart as well as of my head?—& then how could I bear to look on *them* after they were written? Adam made fig leaves necessary for the mind, as well as for the body.

This diary entry is one of the first times she mentions a separation between the 'thoughts of my heart' and 'the thoughts of my head'. What she does next – of course – is to share the insight with Boyd.

Three weeks later, 'On opening my drawer I saw the ms of *Thoughts versus Words*, & a *Thought struck* me that I wd. address & send it to Mr Boyd.' The piece is full of confident humour and her years of study:

> Philosophical Thought [is] a personnage of retired habits and eccentric disposition […] a silly report was once spread about his children the Ideas having had the use of their eyesight from the moment of their entrance into the world. […] Poetical Thought […]

is still a great dresser, & flirts away most vigorously with the Words. [...] Philosophical Thought & Poetical Thought used to be good friends—but [...] from the beginning there have been temporary coldnesses between them,—and they had one serious quarrel about Plato.

The philosophical in-jokes are executed with such lightness of touch that it would be easy to miss how watertight these allusions are: Plato banned poetry from his ideal *Republic*, characterising it as both emotive and imitative; in the same work he produced his famous image of the cave, in which we sit seeing only the shadows of things, not the things themselves. And miss them Boyd does. Four days later he sends back a message, via his wife, saying he 'likes the talent, and nothing else, of my "Thoughts".'

The trouble with a 'mentor' whose mind is second rate, and who has complicated motives to prevent you thriving, is that their failures constitute such poor advice: Elizabeth's essay will appear in the prestigious pages of *The Athenaeum*. But not for another five years. Meanwhile, its author falls into a depression:

I feel *bitterly*— as I have felt—for some time at least. [...] Well! It is better far better that I should go away; better in everyway, & perhaps for everybody. Better for *me*, I dare say.

Which reminds us just how adolescent Elizabeth's preoccupation with Boyd is in tone. Still, it's keeping real worries at bay. A dispute over Papa's inheritance is placing the family under gathering financial pressure: the rumour is that they may even have to leave Hope End. Such a dramatic change is still for now unthinkable. Yet it would at least free Elizabeth from her impasse. For these first struggles to release herself from Boyd's emotional double bind are doomed to fail: she's fighting against herself.

In fact it is Boyd who will leave the district first, three months before the Barretts' departure, in May 1832. Yet within seven months he has brought his family to live near Elizabeth once again, and it will take her a further year and a half, until May 1834, finally to shed him. Meanwhile, the traction these two lost souls have on each other and on the people around them is astonishing. 'Empty minded, & without real *sensibility*—which extends to the tastes as well as the feelings—frivolous and flippant. What a woman to be Mr Boyd's wife!' Elizabeth tells herself in July 1831, at a time when she's inappropriately pressuring Boyd not to move somewhere more lively for his wife's and daughter's sake. Little love or sisterhood is lost between the future feminist role model and the powerless females of the Boyd household. 'How very very very unkindly [Annie] has behaved to me! I cannot bear to think of it [...] What is my sin? Having *been* anxious, & *appeared* anxious for Mr. Boyd to remain near me.' Well: indeed. Annie is Boyd's *daughter*, after all. Worse, she's one of the competitors Boyd is happy to play off against Elizabeth: 'Some talking of [Annie's] coldness to me—attributed by Mr Boyd, to jealousy [of a friend]—No love—no jealousy! Some talking of Annie abstractedly [...]—& my opinion of her manners.'

Something of what Annie Boyd feels about this paternal betrayal will be revealed after her mother's death, when she picks a Catholic to marry. Boyd is virulently and publicly anti-Catholic, and author of the fundamentalist Protestant *The Fathers not Papists*. In these circles, though, his prejudice is one of the more normal aspects of his behaviour. The Barretts are anti-Catholic too. If anything, they've shifted from the Established Church in the 'opposite' direction, towards Nonconformism. On Sunday mornings they attend the Anglican parish church, and on Sunday evenings the Nonconformist chapel at the park 'Gate', 'Driving to church— driving back again—driving to chapel—driving back again—& prayers three times at home besides!' as Elizabeth records.

They're very much in step with their times. Since its split from the Anglican Church at the end of the eighteenth century, Methodism has been developing rapidly not only in Britain but in North America and in British colonies including Jamaica, where it has become associated with the abolitionist movement. Nonconformism will continue to grow at a tremendous rate throughout Elizabeth's lifetime. Membership of the Church of England remains an essential social passport – it's a condition for matriculation at the universities of Oxford and Cambridge, for example – but Methodism's attractions for someone like Elizabeth include the movement's very active engagement with 'the Word' through Bible study, inspiring sermons – to 'make me *glow*' as Elizabeth puts it – and its flourishing hymn-writing. Papa regularly rides ten miles or more through the orchard country of north-west Gloucestershire to Bible meetings in Newent or Redmarley D'Abitot. His eldest daughter reads 'every day, seven chapters of Scripture', although sometimes she finds 'my heart & mind are not affected by this exercise as they should be'. All the same, years from now Nonconformism will be one of the things that she and her future husband have in common.

Despite this deepening religious radicalism, convention shapes Barrett family life. After all, Edward Barrett Moulton-Barrett was elected High Sheriff of Herefordshire in 1814. So now Aunt Bummy asks Elizabeth not to discuss the family's gathering financial troubles with Mr Boyd. For behind the scenes Papa has been dealing with financial (and consequently social) near-catastrophe. As Elizabeth will discover, only money's intrinsically conservative tendency to stick with the status quo has so far saved him from having humiliatingly to uproot the family from Hope End.

And this threat of a move isn't the only trauma playing itself out beyond the narrow focus of her attention. One of the main reasons her life at twenty-six is over-determined by two middle-aged men – her father, and Boyd, the man who has masqueraded as a mentor for the last five years – is that she lacks a mother's advice, attention and love. In particular, Mamma might have helped correct the intruder's destructive embroilment with her eldest child. But she has been gone for four years. The Elizabeth that Boyd has been toying with has been prey to chaotic wishful thinking and the acting out of an enormous grief.

When Mary Moulton-Barrett died in autumn 1828, she had been unwell for months. But her death still came as a profound shock to the family. She'd never fully recovered from the birth of her twelfth child, Octavius, in 1824, and when her own mother died in November 1827 she was overwhelmed by grief. In the following months, every-one put her worsening symptoms down to mourning. Finally, in May 1828, Dr Carden was sent for. He diagnosed rheumatoid arthritis, but was encouraging; later, he supported a decision to send the patient to Cheltenham. So on 30 September Mamma set out with Bummy and Henrietta for the spa town. Next day she was well enough to send home a reassuring note because 'my beloved Ba's tearful eyes as I parted with her yesterday have hung somewhat heavily on my heart'. The trio were staying 'not in the Square, therefore not quite so gay as our fancy pictured', she reported, but in charming and comfortable premises at 14 Montpellier Terrace.

Her death a week later, on 7 October, was so unexpected that even her husband wasn't at her bedside. He received the news in London the next morning – and was overwhelmed. The jumbled letter of prayer and incoherent grief he dashed off to Elizabeth in the moments before setting out for Cheltenham reveals a raw and genuine loss. For Edward Barrett Moulton-Barrett, Mary's death foreclosed what had after all been a genuine love match, and marked the end of any sense that things always turn out right.

As for Elizabeth: so long reliant on words, she now found them useless. She couldn't cry either. 'I dare say God will touch my heart & make me cry soon, & then I shall be even better than I am now—better able to read & to think', she wrote to Henrietta in Cheltenham, a couple of days after the news broke. But she revealed in the same letter that she was already resuming her bookish habits. At first glance this seems healthy: routine structures days suddenly emptied of meaning; and thinking prevents feeling. But it's also the reaction of someone trying desperately to hold on to what she knows about herself in the face of almost overwhelming pressure to fall apart. Everyone around her felt that Elizabeth, the sibling closest to their parents, and whom they perceived as the frailest among them, was in deep trouble. Bro was especially alarmed when her inability to express her feelings continued – and continued.

As Bummy, Henrietta and Papa picked up the pieces in Montpellier Terrace, Elizabeth simply shut down. 'She read [...] every letter from Cheltenham [...] without its producing the slightest effect upon her.' Partly, she may have been repeating the coping mechanism learnt at eight when her sister Mary had died. Though it seems to have been already in place even then:

> I remember [in] infancy being told by a servant [...] "that I was cold and unfeeling and that every one thought so whatever they might say"—I heard this declaration with great pretended calmness—tho my head perfectly seemed to swim [...] No! I could not preserve

buoyant spirits when the bitterness of death was at my heart! I was young very young then to govern myself—but I […] gloried in that self command, but […] when I was left alone […] with my pillow […] tears gushed wildly forth!

And now, aged twenty-two, that pattern had been confirmed. Though she's going to experience much loss in the years to come, grief will nearly always silence her.

So the twenty-six-year-old who faces the possibility of having to leave Hope End has already suffered two close family bereavements, and willed herself back from grave illness. But by a similar effort of will Elizabeth is also gradually turning herself into a major poet. For her, words represent not death but life.

[*Third Frame*]

If stories can be portraits, we also read portraits as stories. That's true even of the famous dead. In the much-copied lost mural by Hans Holbein the Younger, King Henry VIII's barrel chest and square jaw suggest to me nothing so much as a hard-drinking bully. Despite the famous smile, Mahatma Gandhi's gaze remains as steely as his spectacle frames in photographs Henri Cartier-Bresson took on the last day of his life, while I understand his body language as a public statement about the attributes of nonviolent leadership.

I mean that I read off from these portraits *directly*, as if from life. For, more than work in any other genre, portraits seem to disavow that they have been made. They ask us to be naïve literalists, to *believe* them; it's as if they want to exempt themselves from the rules of the art game. Usually we view work made in different genres – oil, miniature, fresco *With Kneeling Patron*, press photo, lightning sketch – in different ways: whether pouring raptly over vitrines or standing awestruck among the draughts in a thirteenth-century cloister. But portraits tend to cluster under the name of the sitter instead: despite the fact that their real subject isn't perhaps a *person* so much as an *encounter* between two people, the artist and her subject.

Of course, that encounter is no longer 'live' within the image. The portrait itself has broken up the reciprocity of the meeting between artist and sitter, portraitist and subject:

leaving the subject's face, but not the artist's, visible; and
the artist's experience, but not the subject's, in view. Only
in a self-portrait do both sides of this encounter still seem
present. Perhaps that's because the self experienced and the
self experiencing are both there together in the face we see.
Rembrandt van Rijn's self-portraits, for example. The way
they bring us into the presence of a compassionate, searching
and earthy self – one who appears 'dug out of humanity', as
Elizabeth puts it.

Book Four:
How to manage change

In upright consciousness of place and time.

Do we become different people in different places? Opinionated as ever, Elizabeth sums up Sidmouth within four days of her arrival:

> The town is small & not superfluously clean; but of course the respectable houses are not a part of the town. Our's is one which the Grand Duchess Helena had,—not at all *grand*, but extremely comfortable, & cheerful, with [...] pleasant green hills & trees behind. [...] You may suppose what a southern climate this is, when I tell you that myrtles & verbena three or four feet high, & hydrangeas are in flower in the gardens.

It's August 1832, and the calamity everyone's been dreading has finally occurred. Papa has been forced to sell Hope End, and the family to leave their idyll there for good. Once it's done, though, the move will feel almost inevitable. And perhaps there's a kind of relief after months of anxiety. As it turns out, Elizabeth's time in the Devon town will be one of the most 'comfortable, and cheerful' of her life, as she learns to adapt and change – and to enjoy doing so.

Over the last year at Hope End, her father has scoped out possible new addresses at Eastbourne, Brighton, and the Isle of Wight: all south-coast resorts rather than the fashionable centres that are closer to home, like Cheltenham or Bath. Perhaps he can't face meeting people he knows in his new, reduced circumstances. He has certainly been increasingly reclusive since the sale became a reality: it 'has made Papa shrink from society of any kind, lately. He would not even attend the religious societies in Ledbury, which he was […] so interested in supporting.' In 1808–09 it had taken him a year to find the Herefordshire property that has defined him, and he did so alone, leaving his wife to await his decision. Now, as he again searches alone, it's the turn of his adult children to wait powerlessly for their lives to be redefined.

At last, bounced into action by the completed mansion sale, he takes Rafarel House, part of a smart regency terrace at the western end of Sidmouth seafront. 'The drawing room's four windows all look to the sea', which is 'about a hundred & fifty yards' away; right next door is Fort Field, where local gentlemen play cricket. Perhaps this is what helps decide him: after all, he has eight sons living at home, three of whom are by now young adults with time hanging heavy on their hands. Besides, cricket is something he and his boys do together. Learnt in childhood – maybe even in his earliest years in Jamaica – it's one of few remaining constants in his vertiginously changing life. Indeed, on the family's 'very last evening' at Hope End, they go out into the grounds for a game.

It's painful to picture that final match among the valley's lengthening shadows. Henrietta made a sketch from the schoolroom window which shows woods massed on the hillside, behind a game in progress on the grass, and a church spire pricking the skyline like an eye-catcher. But this final game is also an improvised ceremony of farewell. The late August evening must feel like the end of summer in every way; when dusk falls shortly after seven there isn't even a moon to light the lawns.

Edward Barrett Moulton-Barrett has become a reflective, even a brooding man, secretive and deeply religious, certainly capable of seeing this as the end of his own life's 'summer'. He's forty-seven: no great age – and plenty young enough to play cricket – but old enough to experience a midlife crisis as everything seems to crumble around him. In the last three years he has lost the two women he depended on most in the world, the death of his wife followed a couple of years later by that of his mother, who had for so long been effectively his only parent. On top of this, his fortune has dwindled. Papa is still a very wealthy man. But he's been forced to sell the magnum opus which, like all builders of mansions, he must have imagined passing down through future generations. Perhaps it had even helped him picture, with an echo of the old Barrett imposter syndrome, eventual ennoblement and entry into the heart of the British Establishment. He loves Hope End so much that, when he dies, he'll turn out never to have relinquished the estate woodlands. In short, he sees himself as 'a broken down man'. To rebuild elsewhere – starting in the skimpy seaside terrace that he's rented for just one month – would require tremendous willpower; never his strong point. And while it's hard for us to feel sympathy for someone who continues to profit from slavery, for the man himself a strongly religious sense of obligation ratchets up the stress of feeling responsible for supporting a large number of family and servants.

The family leave Hope End in two parties. Papa, Bro and seventh son Septimus, or Sette, stay on till the house has been completely packed up. For the main group, a palindromic departure date of 23/8/1832 has been set: perhaps a superstitious choice? Setting out, they pass through the streets of Ledbury and on through familiar countryside. 'I cannot dwell upon the pain of that first hour of our journey—but [...b]efore the first day's journey was at an end, we felt inexpressibly relieved—relieved from the restlessness & anxiety which have so long oppressed us', Elizabeth admits to Julia Martin, a friend who lives at Old Colwall, the next estate to Hope End.

Grief, yes; but is there humiliation too? Julia, an Anglican vicar's daughter from the Irish Midlands, married into local gentry when Elizabeth was a susceptible thirteen. Along with Daniel McSwiney and Hugh Stuart Boyd, she's among the noticeable number of Irish acquaintances in Elizabeth's tiny social circle; one of those subtle indicators of the Barretts' level on the complex barometer of the English class system. But it's only now that real friendship develops between the women, touched into life by Julia's kindness in writing straight away to Elizabeth in Sidmouth. While they were actually neighbours, the awkward age gap of fourteen years combined with Elizabeth's intellectual snobbery to make the younger woman prefer the company of Mrs Martin's glamorously well-travelled husband James. Throughout her early twenties Elizabeth has displayed an embarrassing tendency to admire and befriend men rather than women. Over the last five years, Mr Boyd has fulfilled her need for a confidant, often in the nastiest ways, but she's beginning to feel the need for female friendships; and they are an art she must learn. At home too, though Bro and Sam are now back from school, the siblings' activities are increasingly segregated by gender, and her sisters Henrietta and Arabella have become her closest companions.

All the same, in the first weeks after Boyd's departure her letters to him are wildly inappropriate. Things she may formerly have said face to face in private now spill onto pages that will be read aloud to him; most probably by his wife or daughter, about whom she writes with presumptuous cattiness, 'I never could apprehend that a person with such breadth of chest & with so little tendency to becoming thin, was of a consumptive habit.' These rather shaming, often transparently manipulative missives are spaced out by the relatively slow responses they receive: Elizabeth evidently hasn't understood that Boyd's first letter after he left Worcestershire, 'looking back with pleasure to our past intercourse' and apologising for occasions on which he may have 'spoken to me crossly or peevishly', is a 'Dear Joanna', trying to draw a line under the addictive tangle of their relationship. In leaving Colwall for the environs of Bath, he was in every sense moving on. Now it's Elizabeth's turn to try, however clumsily, to wind him back in, though even she apprehends dimly that there are limits, and peppers her letters with apologies.

Admittedly, the newsy letters Elizabeth sends Julia Martin also tend to start with apologies for tardiness, suggesting that they are ever so slightly dutiful. She also writes to Maria Commeline, an unmarried young lady whom, typically, she got to know through her classicist father, the Revd James Commeline: 'Very amusing sensible sharp-minded people, – and as they don't spare their pricks in making remarks on their neighbours, they are considered not altogether as good-natured as they might be.' A third Herefordshire correspondent is Lady Margaret Cocks who, though she's the same age as Julia Martin, is unmarried and lives with her father,

Elizabeth's old nemesis Lord Somers, at Eastnor Castle: letters to her are busy with literary fireworks and family chatter.

She's learning discretion, however. In mid-December she tells Julia Martin, 'Mr Boyd arrived here three days ago, & is going to settle himself close to us. [...] You may suppose how astonished I was to hear of their arrival: not having an idea of its probability.' Which is disingenuous since she's been pushing for precisely this for over a month. Indeed Boyd has broken a lease and must pay double rents as a result. Small wonder if, the following May, it's with a touch of complacency that Elizabeth tells Lady Margaret how she and Boyd 'read & talk together as in old days'.

By which time everyone seemed to be settling in to Devon life. The family have stayed on at Rafarel House. Those seaside holidays with Grandmama have taught Elizabeth to enjoy the ocean, 'sublimest object in nature', and in this aftermath of Romanticism, society accultures young women to handle emotion by projecting it onto the natural world. This isn't just the literary device that, later in the century, John Ruskin will label the Pathetic Fallacy, but social convention in an increasingly unconfessional age.

As Sidmouth's tides enter Elizabeth's imagination, she'll poeticise human experience as 'a footstep on the sand / The morning after springtide'. But the endlessly watchable seaside, ozone-scented and creating its own special light, is also a playground that entices her away from her books and out for donkey rides and fishing trips:

> I don't know when I have been so long well as I have been lately [...]
> in spite of our fishing and boating and getting wet three times a day.
> There is good trout-fishing at the Otter, & the noble river Sid [...]
> My love of water concentrates itself in the boat.

However, despite its perfect location facing right onto the water, the house is turning out to be too small for the numerous Barretts crowded into it. As Arabella tells Annie Boyd, 'We are all squeezed in little rooms, two in a bed': something Elizabeth's *amour propre* has prevented her from revealing. Besides, this slice of what's known as Fortfield Terrace stands in an exposed position, and it's draughty. Should they stay or should they go? After a year of trying to make the house work, in September 1833 they move 200 yards inland, a sideways shift that's the culmination of a typical period of prevarication by Papa. After all now that, as Elizabeth will put it, the family have 'no ties to draw us or to bind us elsewhere', Sidmouth will do as well as anywhere.

To Lady Margaret Cocks she gives their new home a rather romantic spin:

> a pretty villa or rather cottage, with thatch and a viranda and a garden, and the viranda's due proportion of ivy & rose trees—about a quarter of a mile from the sea. The view of the sea is rather too indistinct to please me [...] but I am consoled by hearing it roaring, & by a genuine Devonshire lane with 'hedgerow elms,' bounding our garden.

Contemporary prints show that Belle Vue is very much more a villa than a cottage. Unlike Fortfield Terrace, it overlooks 'the little town & the church steeple'. But the family remain cut off from Sidmouth proper. 'We hear that the place is extremely full, & gay; but this is of course only an *on dit* to us.' The appointment of a drawing master, 'Mr Williams', is very welcome, but hardly compensates for continued exclusion from a social whirl which is almost within earshot. The girls feel it particularly: opportunities to meet young men and make lives of their own are narrowing. As they move into this newest home, Elizabeth is already twenty-seven, Henrietta twenty-four, and Arabella has just turned twenty.

A year into their stay at Belle Vue, Sidmouth remains, 'Very full: but our cottage stands away from everybody almost—and so do we.' Yet while his daughters' domestic lives are increasingly restricted, Papa has begun sending his sons out into the world, dispatching the third and fourth boys, Stormie and George, to study at the University of Glasgow: which unlike Oxbridge is open to Nonconformists. George will graduate in 1835 as he turns nineteen and be called to the Bar in the Inner Temple in 1838: he clearly shares some of Elizabeth's precocious braininess. But Stormie, though older by eighteen months, simply listens in on lectures because of a severe speech impediment, which is now starting to shape his future. His destiny is a life of family service looking after the Barretts' Caribbean estates.

For now though, it is Bro who, as eldest son, is dispatched to Jamaica.

Charged with an heir's responsibilities he may be, but the way his father lands him with the role is characteristically disempowering. 'Papa took him to London about a fortnight ago on *supply* business,' EBB tells Lady Margaret Cocks in November 1833, '—and we thought of seeing them both again in a few days. But it was otherwise willed by God,—and dearest Bro sailed from Gravesend two days ago.' Possibly this was a paternal strategy to avoid tearful scenes – or even to prevent himself from being dissuaded by them; Papa may be aware of his own weakness in decision-making. Choosing this time of year for the Atlantic crossing certainly seems like a poor decision. But Bro makes it safely to Jamaica: where he finds there's plenty to do.

Rumours of emancipation are in the air, but the island's Assembly has been resisting British governmental pressure even to ameliorate the conditions enslaved people endure there. Only three Assembly members voted in support of a recent proposal to end flogging of enslaved women – a trio led by Uncle Sam, who's been back at Cinnamon Hill since 1827. The years he served as MP for Richmond, Yorkshire empowered Sam to write in 1831 to his Whig colleague Lord Howick, Under Secretary for War and the Colonies and the prime minister's son, about the island's brutal conditions. But nothing changed. Less than three months after he'd sent the letter, a general strike held by 'slaves' on Christmas Day erupted into riots involving up to a fifth of the island's enslaved population, which at the time totalled around 300,000. The so-called Baptist War lasted just eleven days and was brutally suppressed: around five hundred enslaved people were killed, more than half of them by quasi-judicial execution including for trivial offences. The Assembly estimated – arguably, overestimated – the damage to (largely, its members' own) property at £1,154,589: the rioters had mostly lacked weapons, but many plantation trash houses, where the trash leaves and stems of the sugar cane are stored and dried to serve as fuel for the sugar refineries, had been set alight.

That Cinnamon Hill was one of the few estates to escape damage is no coincidence. Since arriving on the island, Uncle Sam and his wife Mary Clementina have been recognised as more moderate than their crueller neighbours. When Mary Clementina died in June 1831 she was apparently much mourned, not only back in England, but 'by all her negroes'. The couple had brought with them the Barrett family interest in Nonconformism; from England, Elizabeth's father decreed that the Baptist William Knibb should be allowed to minister to the people enslaved on his own Oxford and Cambridge estates. In 1830, when their lives had proved so chaotic that Knibb stopped the work, Papa intervened once more to enable him to continue.

Such plantocracy support is key to any amelioration of the conditions it has itself created. In the 1830s, Baptist, Methodist, Moravian and Wesleyan ministers are Jamaica's chief advocates of enslaved people's rights. If not quite preaching liberation theology, they are ministering to enslaved, free black, and mixed-heritage congregants. Enslaved people can and do become elders in these churches, to the horror of many planters. Indeed the Baptist War got its name from the leadership of Samuel Sharpe, an enslaved Baptist deacon, as well as from the spiritual and practical support that the uprising received from Nonconformist ministers. During the eighteen months between the insurrection and Sharpe's execution by hanging in May 1832, Nonconformist ministers were repeatedly accused by the Assembly and at the Courts Martial (in which landowners dispensed often summary justice for their losses) of inciting rebellion, and spreading false rumours that slavery had been abolished.

Around this very time Uncle Sam started to give the people enslaved on the Cinnamon Hill and Cornwall estates every Saturday off. Unsurprisingly, he was soon being fingered by the colonial establishment. His rescue of a minister whose chapel had been burnt down by planters prompted the custos, or warden, of Trelawny to complain, 'I *highly disapprove* of the conduct of Mr Moulton-Barrett; it has been stated to me, that *he was seen riding out of town with a Mr. Box, who I had ordered to be taken into custody as one of the incendiary preachers.*' Nevertheless Uncle Sam persisted and when, in early 1832, Knibb was arrested and his chapel razed, joined two ministers in writing an open letter of support care of the local custos – who was his own first cousin, Richard Barrett. More: after Sam himself had been appointed custos of St Ann in June 1832 by a newbroom governor, he supported an application by a Wesleyan, John Greenwood, for licence to preach, citing the Toleration Act. The courtroom in which he was hearing the application descended into mob violence; the governor sent in troops to support Sam and to maintain order.

So when Bro lands in Jamaica in December 1833 the island is, though no longer formally under martial law, in a restless state; and the Barrett name is deeply implicated in these upheavals. The following September, Elizabeth writes that her brother is still:

> an exile in Jamaica [...] there is no use in dreaming it—he *cannot* be happy there—among the *white* savages. I would rather see him in England, employed in the very humblest of honest employments.

That telling phrase, '*white* savages', represents a step in her slow coming to terms with the realities of slavery. Her conscience won't reach its public high point until 1848, when she's married to an abolitionist and living a new life at a distance from her family and its shibboleths, amid the democratic revolutionaries of Risorgimento Italy. To get to that stage, this daughter and granddaughter of slave owners will have had to move a long way from the position she holds back in May 1833, when she writes of Parliament's proposal to abolish slavery:

> The West Indians are irreparably ruined if the bill passes. Papa says that in the case of its passing, nobody in his senses would think of even attempting the culture of sugar [...] I am almost more sorry for poor Lord Grey who is going to ruin us, than for our poor selves who are going to be ruined.

On 28 August 1833, however, the Slavery Abolition Act does become law, its progress hastened by public disgust at revelations about the Baptist War.

Slavery won't be abolished in America until the 1860s, but in Britain popular opinion has been mobilising for a while. The Anti-Slavery Society was founded by William Wilberforce, Thomas Clarkson and others in 1823, when Elizabeth was seventeen. 1831, the Barretts' last full year at Hope End, saw the publication of the first British slave narrative. Mary Prince, brought to London as a domestic, had run away after ten years, found shelter with the Moravian Church, and started working for Thomas Pringle, Secretary of the Anti-Slavery Society. He transcribed and published her *The History of Mary Prince, a West Indian*

Slave, Related by Herself, an excoriating testimony that sold out three editions in a year:

> How can slaves be happy when they have the halter round their neck and the whip upon their back? and are disgraced and thought no more of than beasts?—and are separated from their mothers, and husbands, and children, and sisters, just as cattle are sold and separated? [...]—women that have had children exposed in the open field to shame! There is no modesty or decency shown by the owner to his slaves [...]. Since I have been here I have often wondered how English people can go out into the West Indies and act in such a beastly manner. But when they go to the West Indies, they forget God and all feeling of shame [...]. They tie up slaves like hogs—moor them up like cattle, and they lick them.

Despite such raw home truths, the 1833 Act still doesn't liberate people already enslaved. No one will actually be freed until 1838, after a five-year transition designed to ease the financial shock to the planters. The British government also announces a fund of £20 million – to compensate slavers, not the people they've exploited. Even when 1838 does arrive, the indentured 'apprenticeships' to which enslaved people are moved – low-paid work on inescapable contracts – don't constitute genuine freedom.

September 1833 sees Elizabeth grumbling at the same time as virtue signalling:

> Of course you know that the late bill has ruined the West Indians. That is settled. The consternation here is very great. Nevertheless I am glad, and always shall be, that the negroes are—virtually—free!

That 'nevertheless' sums up the dilemma of being born a Barrett. By now twenty-seven, Elizabeth is adult and intelligent enough to recognise that her own interests are opposed to those of the people her family enslaved. Whigs and progressives, the Barretts would be natural abolitionists – but for their own plantations. Uncle Sam's impossible solution to this paradox replaces it with another one. Trying to be a kind slave 'owner' is a contradiction in terms, since slavery is in its very nature a crime. As Elizabeth herself will put it a dozen years from now, when she has finally become a true abolitionist, 'a philanthropist & liberal who advocates the slave-trade, can scarcely be *thorough* [...]. Call it a philanthropic *veneering.*' The government's misdirected reparations compound the moral problem, ensuring that Barrett family money remains dirty; and there's a practical problem too. The alternative to complicity is to walk away into extreme poverty. None of the Barretts display this level of self-sacrificing integrity. But then in nineteenth-century Britain – as in twenty-first – nobody does.

It's autumn 1835 when Bro finally arrives home from Jamaica; in 1836 second brother Sam travels out to replace him. By now the men of the family are grappling not with the ethical fault line that runs through their fortunes, but with huge, continuing financial fallout from a more intimate threat. Before Papa had even attained his majority, the property he inherited from his grandfather Edward Barrett was being contested by a cousin, 'Handsome Sam' Barrett, who claimed a historic misattribution of holdings. This case rumbled on, finally seeming to have been settled in 1824 by order of the Council of George IV. But when Handsome Sam died in Cheltenham that very month, his younger brother Richard, a trained lawyer, took over the estate as executor and trustee and dug up paperwork allowing a fresh attack, on similar grounds, upon Papa's inheritance.

This is the same Richard who as custos tried in 1832 to have Uncle Sam arrested. (He is known to the family back in England as 'RB': initials that will acquire quite other significance in years to come.) The case won't be resolved until 'RB' dies in 1839. As one of Elizabeth's friends will summarise it, at Hope End Edward Barrett Moulton-Barrett was 'a man of £15,000 a year' until, out of the blue,

> A cousin came to him & showed him a will dated 60 years before under which he claimed £75,000. Mr Barrett, who had never heard of the claim showed the will to a lawyer who advised him to dispute it.—He did so; & after the cause had been driven from court to court it has been given against him with enormous costs & interest, so that his place in Herefordshire is sold.

By the family's third year in Sidmouth these costs, both financial and emotional, are accumulating exponentially. Papa, who has become profoundly depressed, disappears frequently 'to do his London business'. On one such trip in October 1834, he falls seriously ill with 'water on the lungs'

– in other words, pneumonia. He makes a good recovery, but it's a scare. 'Without him, we should indeed be orphans & desolate', frets Elizabeth.

Papa's nurse in London is his late mother's best friend and companion, Mary Trepsack – now living alone in Marylebone on the £2,000 Grandmama left her. Treppy's mixed heritage means that she is 'black' by her own definition, though she doesn't describe herself this way – reserving the term for others. Much loved – 'She has nursed .. tossed up .. held on her knee—Papa when he was an infant' – she personifies the family's ambivalences about race. Treppy's mother was enslaved, and though her white planter father, William Trepsack, gave the child his name and probably manumitted her at birth, she has achieved the decent comfort of her present life only paradoxically, through the lottery of bereavement. The death of her mother – who was herself of mixed heritage, in other words similarly the child of a white man – meant that Treppy escaped sharing her fate, and being raised enslaved. Next, when her father died she was rescued from his failing household to became a ward of Papa's reprobate, domestically chaotic Uncle Samuel. It was only finally on *his* death when she was thirteen that Treppy arrived at Cinnamon Hill. With so much instability in her childhood it's not surprising that she's adaptable and compliant, complicit with the system that enslaved her mother: in 1835–36 she's awarded £220/15/10d compensation for eleven slaves she herself 'owns' at the Cottage and Cinnamon Hill estates.

Trepsac is a French family name, intriguingly associated in the eighteenth-century Caribbean most strongly with the leader of the Dominican Order on Martinique: race and religion are as entangled for Treppy as for the Barrett family 'proper'. While Nonconformism offers a form of moderate radicalism that particularly suits the Barretts' ambiguous social position, in the 1830s social upheaval and religious revival are tangling on all sides. In Dublin, biblical literalists calling themselves Plymouth Brethren are rejecting the Anglicanism of the Anglo-Irish Ascendency; at the 'other' end of Revivalism the Anglo-Catholic Oxford Movement is founded by John Keble and John Henry Newman in 1833. Radical spirituality supplies drama to the drab lives of the labouring poor even as it denies their aspirations. This is a moment when Britain seems poised to follow its continental neighbours, and former colonies in North

America, into violent social revolution. But Nonconformist Revivalism preaches individual self-determination rather than political reformation. (It objects to slavery as a check on individual rights, not as a social failure.) So its social effect is stabilising rather than radicalising; it puts a brake on the political consciousness of the working people for whom it's the only access to ideas, education and collective participation.

In Sidmouth Elizabeth, too, is finding that Nonconformism offers her both a new community and ideas to explore. Marsh Congregational Chapel, where she worships, was built in 1810 and boasts an active congregation. Its minister, the Revd George Hunter, a charismatic preacher and driven leader, excels at eliciting bequests for the thriving Sunday school. He's also the perfect object for a crush, since his wife is absent, 'removed [...] by a stroke worse than death .. madness! & there is no hope of a restoration', and he has a little daughter, Mary, who turns ten in 1836. Sure enough, he soon turns up in Elizabeth's letters. Evidently, the fashionable congregation may donate to appeals but don't pay a generous salary: his 'circumstances are miserably straitened, & the only apparent opening lies [in] pupils', as she notes later, while soliciting teaching work for him. With plenty of experience of schooling younger siblings herself, she now secures permission to tutor little Mary Hunter, who goes on to become a lifelong family favourite. Papa even gives the sisters permission to accompany Hunter when he preaches out of town.

Once again Elizabeth has set up, right under her father's nose, a scenario in which she serves as helper to a married man who inspires her intellectually. But nothing indicates that the Revd Hunter is manipulative like Mr Boyd. Indeed, for all his charismatic intensity, surviving correspondence suggests a man more vulnerable than in control. Nervy and needy, like his wife he too will end his days in an asylum. And so Elizabeth's friendship with him doesn't turn into obsession but remains a conduit through which her interests and emotions can become more public and dispersed. In fact, we could say that hers is a case in which the Revd Hunter's ministry pays off. As doctrinal debates displace classical poetics in appealing to her intellectual side, the Sidmouth poems are markedly more spiritual than those that precede and follow them. A new, devotional tone appears in her correspondence.

This same tone brings her closer again to her father. Each is now seeking solace and meaning in a life whose main project seems to have been cut short. Resignation feels like the meanest of virtues, a piece-by-piece renunciation of any number of hopes. But it can also be a gesture, a way to bundle up everything that's risky, unspeakable or uncertain into one big statement of abdication. In Sidmouth in 1833–34 Papa is preparing for a future as a man of reduced significance, and Elizabeth for a spinster life of indifferent health.

She also has her first taste of failure. In May 1833 her translation of Aeschylus's *Prometheus Unbound*, together with some of her own poems, is issued by a proper, unsubsidised publisher, A. J. Valpy, in his Classical Library. It's an exciting milestone, and the submission is Papa's idea. One reason Valpy accepted the manuscript may have been a small but significant poetic triumph that Elizabeth had recently achieved. In January 1832 *The Times* rushed her poem on cholera into print a mere four days after receiving it. But when, the following month, she made the Aeschylus translation, it was her turn to rush, hurrying to complete the work within a fortnight in order to impress Boyd – a misjudgement all the more understandable in those emotionally chaotic last months at Hope End. Now the book is out, and the few reviews it receives are far from positive. Worst of all is *The Athenaeum*'s single-sentence notice: 'Take warning by the author before us.'

Perhaps this is a necessary failure. It certainly helps reset the direction of Elizabeth's work. She's twenty-eight; the time for classical studies, however advanced, is clearly over. If she doesn't step up now as a poet in her own right she never will. It can only help that within the year that inveterate classicist Mr Boyd will at last have left for London. Even so, such resets take time. Outside the window beyond her writing desk, the seasons pass. 'Sidmouth is a nest among elms; and the lulling of the sea & the shadow of the hills make it a peaceful one.' Elizabeth finally emerges from a period almost of dormition in September 1835, with the publication in *The New Monthly Magazine* of 'Stanzas Addressed to Miss Landon, and Suggested by her "Stanzas on the Death of Mrs Hemans"'. It's the first in a flurry of magazine publications over the next couple of years: not only poems but 'A Thought on Thoughts', the virtuoso prose essay that so failed to impress Boyd.

It is also the first public outing of a theme that Elizabeth will make her own two decades from now in *Aurora Leigh*: the figure of the woman poet. 'Stanzas' is a praise-song for Landon, to frame the one that Landon wrote for the poet and writer Felicia Hemans, doubling up the homage as if to go twice as far as any other poetic tribute: that 'exquisition' *Adonais*, Percy Bysshe Shelley's ode for John Keats, for example. And as in her ode for Byron, there's a secret brilliance to her technique. The repeated 'dying fall' she rhymes with is no accident. She uses the *strong*-weak stress pattern that, when it appears like this at the ends of lines, is called 'feminine'. A hobbled, 'feminine' rhythm for an ode to female role models:

> Thou bay-crowned living One that o'er the bay-crowned Dead are
> bowing,
> And o'er the shadeless moveless brow the vital shadow throwing,
> And o'er the sighless songless lips the wail and music wedding.

Meanwhile home life is changing. Early in 1835 Belle Vue is sold over the family's heads, and the usual parental prevarication – Elizabeth calls it 'a state of most metaphysical doubtfulness' – leads them back to Rafarel House for six months. In December 1835 they finally move to London. The three-year stay at the Devonshire seaside has been happier than any of them could have imagined when they left Hope End. But it's been an interlude. Now is the time to consolidate their new life: no longer landed gentry perhaps, but still wealthy international merchants. The men of the family must be in the capital. George graduates this year and has to study for the Bar. When they're not taking turns in Jamaica, the three eldest sons – Bro, Sam and Stormie – all need to be in London with Papa to manage the family sugar business. The younger boys will be closer to educational possibilities in the city. And the daughters, of course, are seen as having entirely portable lives. In any case, for them this move is not unattractive. Sidmouth, with its 'quadrilling and cricketing', may have been kept at arm's length by Papa, but it's given them a sniff of society. London seems rich with the possibility of more.

For Elizabeth, three months short of her thirtieth birthday, the city represents literary success. This is true in more ways than she perhaps realises. Witnessing her slow emotional and literary development can be frustrating. We have to remember that each step in this all but self-taught progress is actually a giant stride. *Gradus ad Parnassum.* Now, pushed and pulled by the contradictory expectations of intellect and femininity, as she stands on the brink of her thirties she needs countervailing influences from beyond restrictive family life more than ever. In crowded London, where all sorts of lives go on cheek by jowl, the truth that Papa's is not the only way of doing things will be unignorable.

Still, domestic uncertainty doesn't end straight away. Her father starts by leasing a house in Marylebone for four months, to test the family's 'capacities for living the natural term of man's life in this smoky*gen* and foggy*gen*'. Cautious in every way, he has picked the district he and the family know best: where his mother lived with Treppy for nearly four decades, where Papa and Uncle Sam, later Bro and young Sam, joined them on school breaks, and where Uncle Sam returned to stay whenever Parliament was sitting during his first three years as an MP.

The Barretts move to 74 Gloucester Place on 2 December 1835. It's a bad time of year to arrive in dirty, hectic London. The house Papa has taken is a four-storey mid-terrace with basement, faced in modest brown London brick and standing in a grid of prosperous but almost identical terraced dwellings that crisscross this low-lying west central area. No public gardens or planned vistas relieve the urban claustrophobia. Though the district includes some of the smartest houses in London, it's a shock for Elizabeth to exchange 'the sea shore, which I love more than ever, now that I cannot walk on it', for 'that long & high brick wall opposite' and the 'dash & din' of a city 'wrapped up like a mummy, in a yellow mist, so closely that I have had scarcely a glimpse of its countenance since we came'. Besides, the house, like Fortfield Terrace, is jerry-built. Within a year a storm will blow 'the chimney thro' the skylight, into the entrance passage. You may imagine the crashing effect of the bricks bounding from the staircase downwards breaking the stone steps in the process—in addition to the falling in of twenty four large panes of glass, frames & all!'

Still, wealth conjures up compensations. The next summer, to make up for the lack of a country view, Elizabeth's father imports from Jamaica for her 'two Barbary doves [...] in whose voices I seem to hear the waters & waving leaves [...] so beautiful & soft & calm.' More generally people-scape is replacing landscape. She's entering an era of important new friendships that will replace old habits – and old ties. Although Boyd is less than two miles away in Camden, contact quickly tails off in a series of excuses; Elizabeth has 'such a cough *again!* that I should hasten it to a wrong conclusion, by going out today', or is 'quite *dis*abled by a very bad cold which has kept me in my bedroom all today'.

But that '*again!*' sounds an alarm. After less than a month in the city Elizabeth has already developed a chronic cough. Smog *is* a serious, even life-threatening problem. Yet, despite discovering that London's pollution does indeed pose a risk, Papa fails once again to take decisive action. The family will remain at Gloucester Place for two and a half years. And when they do move, in May 1838, it will be to similar acommodation even closer to the centre of London. The costs to Elizabeth of these decisions will be, as future feminists would say, 'written on the body'.

For now though, as friends and visitors help put it on the map, Marylebone is slowly becoming home. One of the first in touch is John Kenyon. A decade after he had stumbled across his young relative's poetic talents, he is eager to welcome her into his richly gregarious, literary life. He has turned the home he shares with his brother-in-law, just a few blocks east at 39 Devonshire Place, into a kind of writers' salon built on personal friendship. Kenyon happened to settle near Nether Stowey in the early days of his marriage, and there befriended many first-generation Romantic writers through Samuel Taylor Coleridge. By the time he introduces Elizabeth to the London literary scene in 1835, his circle includes Charles and Mary Lamb, Walter Savage Landor, who often stays with him when in England, Robert Southey, whom he will accompany on a tour of France in 1838, and William Wordsworth. He's also friends with a number of American writers. Julia Ward Howe, who will later write 'The Battle Hymn of the Republic', describes him as 'a Maecenas of the period'. He also knows less famous but still established writers and intellectuals, such as the poet-dramatist and civil servant Bryan Waller Procter, theologians Augustus William Hare and Julius Charles Hare, and the lawyer, journalist and diarist Henry Crabb Robinson, through whom everyone in the circle is just a handshake away from the German Romantic poets, among them Goethe, Herder and Schiller, whom Robinson met during a youthful Grand Tour.

In short, it's precisely the distinguished writing world of which Elizabeth dreamt when she was a girl in Herefordshire, and its doors are suddenly open to her. Her instant, characteristic response is to be overwhelmed by shyness. Luckily, Kenyon persists. He's a generous man: one measure of his philanthropy is that his charitable donations are dispersed impersonally, by a board he appoints. And he has the gift of friendship. Crabb Robinson describes 'the face of a Benedictine monk and the joyous talk of a good fellow [who] delights at seeing at his hospitable table every variety of literary notabilities, and therefore he has been called "a feeder of lions".'

Elizabeth may be nervous of literary lions, but within a month of moving to London she's already writing to Thomas Noon Talfourd to thank him for leaving a copy of his privately printed tragedy, *Ion*, for her at their shared publisher Valpy's. A decade Elizabeth's senior, Talfourd is a barrister and writer who has already published a body of literary and legal journalism. His new play will premiere at Covent Garden in May to 'success complete. Ellen Tree and Macready were loudly applauded, and the author had every reason to be satisfied.' Talfourd's after-theatre party is 'largely attended by actors, lawyers, and dramatists', according to Crabb Robinson, who's there along with 'quantities of poets' including William Wordsworth, Walter Savage Landor – and the young Robert Browning, a twenty-four-year-old newcomer, who had published the monodrama *Paracelsus* to critical acclaim the previous summer and is included in the festivities with a toast.

Elizabeth won't be at the first-night party, of course; but she thanks Talfourd for *Ion* with a letter that combines effusiveness with criticism: 'Dare I observe that the most perceptible defect appears to me to arise from a redundancy in the language? May I observe besides that the power of concentrating thought in poetry, is a more essential one, than as it is generally estimated?' Dare she indeed, even though as it happens she's right? But Talfourd seems to have been more amused than offended by this precocious criticism. He keeps the letter in an album: where nearly a decade from now, and to her intense mortification, Robert Browning and Elizabeth's brother George will stumble upon it together.

But in the spring of 1836, the young Robert Browning is being just as clumsy as Elizabeth. The pair are tyros at the same moment, if not together. Two days after the *Ion* party, Robert writes to William Charles Macready, the great classical and Shakespearean tragedian who's playing the lead, offering to write him 'a Tragedy […] to be ready by the first of November next' on 'any subject […] any character of event with which you are predisposed to sympathize'. This bumptiouness pays off: a year from now, Macready will join the management of Covent Garden, becoming a powerful advocate for living writers' work; and on 1 May 1837 Browning's blank verse drama *Strafford*, with Macready in the title role, will open at the house for a successful five-night run.

For the next few years, Elizabeth Barrett and Robert Browning – a young man six years her junior, but whose profile is enhanced by this kind of going out and about – will move in parallel through London's culture-making circles. When they read each other, it's from within the same rich, elbowing world of poetic competitors; a cat's cradle of repeated crisscross encounters. This summer, Kenyon lends Elizabeth Robert's *Paracelsus* and she:

> wd wish for more harmony & rather more clearness & compression—*concentration*—besides: but I do think & feel that the pulse of poetry is full & warm & strong in it, […] a height & depth of thought—& sudden repressed gushings of tenderness which suggest to us a depth beyond.

Yet they never quite meet. Elizabeth's gender, her shyness and her tendency to suffer chest infections all mean that she doesn't actually enter most of the rooms in which her gifted peers join the senior poets of the day to toast, gossip or backstab each other.

The fact that she does manage to participate so fully despite this speaks to the quality of her writing. By now, au fait with how the literary world works, she's publishing regularly in literary magazines. These new poems, starting with her 'Stanzas Addressed to Miss Landon…' ode, are attracting critical attention. In July 1836, *The Athenaeum*'s 'Our Weekly Gossip of Literature and Art' singles out her ballad, 'The Romaunt of Margret', published that month in *The New Monthly Magazine*: 'We have not read such a ballad for many a day; and if its writer will only remember, that in poetry manner is a blemish to be got rid of, […] he (or she) may rank very high—what if we say, among the highest?'

And Kenyon continues to make introductions. In May, two days after

Talfourd's premiere, he persuades her to come to dinner at Devonshire Place to meet Walter Savage Landor and William Wordsworth. Against the tide of fashion, she still admires the latter greatly:

> You might think me affected if I told you all I felt in seeing the living face. His manners are very simple; & his conversation not at all *prominent*—if you quite understand what I mean by *that*. I do myself—for I saw at the same time—Landor, the brilliant Landor! & *felt* the difference between great genius and eminent talent.

The dinner goes so well that Elizabeth meets the 'great genius' not once but twice. The social texture of Wordsworth's life has been thinned by the recent deaths of Coleridge, Charles Lamb and James Hogg, and perhaps this is why 'he was very kind to me, & let me hear his conversation'. Did he but know it, he is also making a valuable literary ally, who in years to come will use her own literary prestige to advocate his work.

Right now, though, it's no surprise that the sixty-six-year-old is taken with this personable young woman. At thirty, Elizabeth seems unaware of her own charm in a way she was not in girlhood. But we glimpse it thanks to yet another of John Kenyon's introductions. The day before her dinner with Wordsworth, Elizabeth had met bestselling writer Mary Russell Mitford. She had found even this prospect so nerve-wracking that Kenyon suggested a visit to London Zoo. On 27 May, he and Miss Mitford called for Elizabeth at Gloucester Place; the ensuing carriage outing to Regent's Park marked the start of a firm friendship, one that will prove hugely influential for the young poet.

At last Elizabeth finds herself close up to a *woman* writer who can serve as both model and guide. But possibly she hadn't imagined her future quite like this. The talkative, bonneted forty-eight-year-old she now gets to know lives in relative poverty outside London, and is writing prose. Miss Mitford's home at Three Mile Cross near Reading has found fame in her 'Our Village' series, collected in five immensely popular volumes as *Sketches of English Character and Scenery*. No classic beauty, she nevertheless has the same round face, brown hair and large eyes that Elizabeth's own childhood portraits captured. Also like Elizabeth, she has thick dark eyebrows and eyes that slant as if in amusement. She looks not aesthetic but questioning, shrewd, emotionally intelligent. Small wonder, perhaps.

Miss Mitford is both unmarried *and* unsheltered. She has to support both herself and a spendthrift father by her writing – he's worked his way through both an enormous lottery win that came her way in childhood and his late wife's fortune. The writer she's become as a result is highly productive, tenacious and pragmatic. When she meets Elizabeth she's in London, therefore, on one of her periodic literary networking trips.

As a well-known playwright herself, Miss Mitford too was at that first night party for *Ion*, where she met and was (as Elizabeth will later discover) signally unimpressed by Robert Browning. By contrast, the next day Kenyon introduces her to this:

> sweet young woman [...] who reads Greek as I do French, and has published some translations from Æschylus, and some most striking poems. She is a delightful young creature; shy and timid and modest.

First impressions are reinforced the following evening:

> Miss Barrett has translated the most difficult of the Greek plays [...] and written most exquisite poems in almost every style. She is so sweet and gentle, and so pretty, that one looks at her as if she were some bright flower; and she says it is like a dream that she should be talking to me, whose works she knows by heart.

This is Miss Mitford boasting to her father about her own literary reputation; but the naïve gushiness she records is unmistakably Elizabeth's. And it's a pleasure to see 'Miss Barrett' as these letters picture her. They remind us that, far from the figure of future melodramatic fantasy, there's nothing eccentric, hysteric or gaunt about this petite, pretty thirty-year-old. Being sheltered has kept her mentally and physically young. She has a spring in her mental step, and a receptiveness to the world that's just opening up to her.

We can imagine Mary Russell Mitford in the brick-built Berkshire labourer's cottage that she shares with her father, looking out over the flower garden of which she's so proud and mulling Elizabeth's literary prospects, as she commissions the young poet for *Findens' Tableaux*, an annual she edits. When she writes in July to a friend, Lady Dacre, that Elizabeth, 'Will I think get rid of all that is painful in her shyness, retaining the most graceful modesty, if once brought forward in the Society

she is so fitted to adorn. She is very pretty, very gentle, very graceful, &
with a look of extreme youth which is in itself a charm,' Miss Mitford
seems at first glance merely to be treating the London literary 'village' just
like her own gossipy 'small neighbourhood […] where we know every
one, are known to every one, interested in every one, and authorised to
hope that every one feels an interest in us.' But in fact this is more than
idle chat. She's deftly connecting the young poet to that rare thing, a
literary network that can make particular space for an emerging woman
writer. For, under her former name of Barbarina Wilmot, Lady Dacre is
a playwright and poet, active in a circle that includes Anna Seward, Mary
Tighe, and the Ladies of Llangollen.

She's also nearly seventy, while Miss Mitford will turn fifty next year.
These distinguished, much published women understand just how hard it
is to achieve what Elizabeth wants: to be a leading writer who is a woman.
(Miss Mitford herself hoped to be the country's pre-eminent female
poet when she was young.) They also recognise how difficult it's been to
achieve what Elizabeth already has. Miss Mitford declares her Preface to
Prometheus Unbound 'unmatched in modern prose […] Depend upon it,'
she goes on, 'Her "Essay on Mind" […] contain[s] allusions to books, as
if known by everybody, which Henry Cary declared to me no young man
of his day at Oxford had ever looked into.'

This is another piece of strategic advocacy, this time to the fashionable preacher William Harness, incumbent of Regent Square Chapel,
Bloomsbury, a lifelong friend of Lord Byron's, and still a well-connected
littérateur. Miss Mitford certainly knows how to hustle, and there's a sense
of urgency to her advocacy. Within three months of meeting Elizabeth,
she has already realised that all is not well at 74 Gloucester Place:

> Of course the poverty is only comparative—people who live in
> Gloucester Place are probably what I should call rich—still with
> ten children coming into life the change is of course great; & the
> mother being dead, & the father utterly dispirited, my lovely young
> friend has been living in the middle of gaiety in a seclusion the
> most absolute […] & chiefly occupied in teaching her little broth-
> ers Greek.

Astutely, she makes the link between Edward Barrett Moulton-Barrett's depression and the restrictive 'seclusion' he imposes on his family as she urges Lady Dacre to make contact:

> If events lead her to write on, & she be blest with life & health I have no doubt of her being the most remarkable woman that ever lived. — Her address is 74 Gloucester Place—but I don't think she can be 'got at' without Mr Kenyon—John Kenyon Esqre 4 Harley Place—& he must be reached through Mr Harness.

Life inside number 74 *can* be restrictive, even suffocating. But at least Elizabeth is writing. The poems she's been working on since leaving Hope End will soon be collected and published as *The Seraphim*, which will appear from Saunders and Otley in June 1838. By then she'll be thirty-two, but her development is accelerating. As the manuscript coheres, a step change in her achievement is becoming apparent: the book marks the emergence of her characteristic poetic voice. It is storytelling that gives this new work shape: for all her training in abstract thought, as a writer Elizabeth has an irrepressible gift for picturing *how it was*. Unconventional, 'disobedient' rhyme and metre help naturalise these new poems – among them 'Isobel's Child', 'Romance of the Ganges', 'The Virgin Mary to Child Jesus' – into something that sounds, for all its mannerisms, as flexible as speech. Indeed, many of them are written in persona and narrated by a wide-ranging cast: a lover, a mother, a 'Merry Man', and even the Madonna.

As she sends off *The Seraphim* to her publishers, Elizabeth must realise that both her inner and her outer worlds are changing. The six years since they left Hope End have been a time of transition for all the family, and by shifting focus from classical studies to an imaginative world of her own creation she herself is both breaking the bounds of her confining life at Gloucester Place – and accepting them. If she's not able to range freely in the real world, very well: she'll do so in imagination. It's this internal trajectory that will paradoxically open up to her the outer life of literary friendship, stimulation and reputation. She is becoming a writer.

[*Fourth Frame*]

'What was he doing, the great god Pan, / Down in the
reeds by the river?' Elizabeth Barrett Browning asks, in 'A
Musical Instrument'. Her much-anthologised poem is a
parable about how art reduces and injures life. 'Half a beast
is the great god Pan, [...]/ Making a poet out of a man.'
Metaphorical Pan cuts down the reed with which he makes
his flute and so, though his music is 'piercing sweet':

> The true gods sigh for the cost and pain,—
> For the reed which grows nevermore again
>   As a reed with the reeds in the river.

The river running past my house in spate this February
morning is most definitely not metaphorical, and I'm out
taking photos of the scene. Flood water, coloured deep
orange by run-off from the fields, foams and falls between
the dark weeds. It's absorbing – until P calls from the
kitchen window that there's fresh coffee on the stove, and do
I want some? – No kidding! And what's more, because I like
the way he looks leaning out the window, I'll take a picture
of him too.

What I mean by this, of course, is to prolong the
moment. Instead the camera interrupts it, coming between
us. Once I lift it to focus I can see P's eyes, but he can no
longer see mine: I watch this almost instantly alter and
empty his expression. (I'd guess my eyes have changed too,
but no one can see them.)

Does this matter? I think it does. I suspect the absence of a returning gaze matters enormously. And it's not just that the camera's obscuring my face. I simply don't look at my partner's image on the camera screen the way I look at him. Actually, I even feel that this is the wrong preposition. I don't believe we usually look *at* each other the way we look *at* a picture or a screen image. I think we look more *to* or *with* each other. This image I've just stored in my camera, the one that seems to show my partner looking *at* (*to, with*) me? It's actually fake, a forgery. All it shows is him looking *in my direction*.

'A society has a duty to ban forgeries', the Belgian philosopher and psychoanalyst Luce Irigaray says at one point in 'The Blind Spot of an Old Dream of Symmetry'. This essay is the opening panel – the left-hand to the double-sided mirror – of her 1974 classic, *Speculum of the Other Woman*. In it, she talks about how women's writing, trying to fit itself to conventional literary models that are historically male, has to 'fake it', for all the world like a compliant wife. Starting with her childish fantasies about growing up to be a Byronic soldier-troubadour, Elizabeth engages with this problem quite consciously all her life. Irigaray goes on to say that 'Woman's special form of neurosis would be to "mimic" a work of art, to be *a bad (copy of a) work of art.*' Here too Elizabeth is in the frame. At least one cause of her slowness to arrive at poetic maturity must be the years she spends trying on various literary models, classical and theological. It's almost as if these genres were so much fancy dress – and writing were a kind of role play.

Book Five:
How to lose your way

[...] salt upon your lips.

Elizabeth is in bed again. The cough that's been troubling her since that first London autumn has settled on her chest. Never an early riser, now she's under orders to lie in till lunchtime and to avoid going out in a frost that is 'daggers for all weak chests'. No one's exactly worried about her: Dr Chambers is convinced that her lungs are 'without desease—but so *weak*, that they struggle *against* the cold air—which occasions the cough'. But, with 'one cold upon another falling upon the chest & producing cough', she hasn't left the house in four months.

There's nothing gentle or genteel about such a cough; about gasping for breath. Violent spasms: the whole body forced into an upright position, because to lie down is to suffocate in the too-heavy air. Coughing without drawing breath, coughing till you retch, eyes streaming, nothing to you but the red O of your coughing mouth. And then, just when you think there might be a moment's calm, the cough starting its obsessional, insatiable irritation over again. At night, loud in the silenced house, your self-conscious coughing keeps not only you but the person in the next bed, the next room, awake.

Coughing and wheezing, hacking and whooping: none of this is in the least romantic. And the paraphernalia that comes with it's not much better. Inhaling a gloop that prisms and swirls slowly in steaming water, Elizabeth has to keep moving her long hair out of the way. Besides, what to do with the gloop she herself coughs up, those slugs of yellow, grey, green mucus suddenly at the back of her throat and on her tongue? Lace handkerchiefs are wasted on this, the heavy lifting of the respiratory system.

Asthma meets bronchial infection in a cunning marriage. Asthma-narrowed bronchi are perfect harbours for infection and the gunk it produces: those gummed-up bronchioles in turn create the irritation that increases asthmatic inflammation. Untreated childhood asthma prevents the lungs developing fully, thus ensuring itself a future in the body. So Elizabeth coughs. Altogether she's finding it hard to keep her spirits up. Her third-floor back-bedroom window offers an austere view of parapets, 'high star-raking chimneys' and a slice of winter sky; indoors, the chick hatched by her Barbary doves has died after protracted ailing 'one cold night', and the parent birds are so 'spiritless, songless' that she's brought the pair into her own bedroom to warm them up. As she pets them, it's almost as if she's picturing herself as still the girl who fed the Hope End chickens by hand. She 'should name it as a grief […] to lose either of them', but caged birds are a poor substitute for country air and childhood freedoms.

Once again paper friendships keep Elizabeth occupied. But now instead of daydreaming about the ancient Greeks, or admiring writers from afar, she has actual literary correspondents. John Kenyon, who's been unwell himself, sends her a manuscript. *Poems: For the Most Part Occasional* includes 'Destiny', which takes lines from her own version of *Prometheus Bound* as its epigraph; she responds with a series of detailed critiques. Meanwhile, Mary Russell Mitford is thinking of applying for a raise in her civil list pension, and asks Elizabeth to mobilise a cousin-in-law's support.

Miss Mitford's tone is particularly warm. 'My dear Love,' she opens on 1 February 1838, 'I have got to think your obscurity of style, my love, merely the far-reaching and far-seeing of a spirit more elevated than ours.' If this doesn't embarrass the younger poet, it must boost her self-esteem.

Sure enough, she's soon asking Kenyon about possibilities for publishing *The Seraphim*. Within a month publication is underway, and with new-found confidence Elizabeth is able to decline Mr Boyd's offer to go through her proofs: 'My dear friend, I do hope that you may not be very angry, —but Papa thinks and indeed I think that as I have already *had* two proof sheets of forty eight pages, and the printers have gone on to the rest of the poem, it would not be very welcome to them if we were to ask then to retrace their steps.'

Dragons are being slain all round. 'Do you know that Mr Valpy is giving up business?' she gossips, with not a little *schadenfreude*. She's yet to forgive her former publisher for how he handled her *Prometheus Unbound* – perhaps it's a useful distraction from the book's critical failure – and has vowed 'to put no more mss to be changed to print, in Mr Valpy's hands'. She writes about her new collection to Miss Mitford with relaxed certainty, punningly invoking Lord Byron's famous take on sexual regret: 'So now, there is room for only "the *late* remorse of *fear*".' One reason for this changing tone may be developing social maturity, but Elizabeth also knows that these poems are good. With Papa, she believes the book's long title poem, 'rather a dramatic lyric than a lyrical drama', is the best thing she's written. And she has a strong vision for the volume as a whole. Like her previous books, it will start with the long piece, 'Then, would come the Poets' vow, & Margret, & several poems of a length almost equal to them, & some shorter ones at the end.'

As she writes these letters in her warm room, keeping one eye on the chill world outdoors, Elizabeth can take comfort from the fact that it's no longer just family who believe in her talent. She's joining a literary world. But by March 1838 even this busy life of the mind can't disguise the fact that she hasn't been out of the house for six months, and is 'incapable of any occupation which should not rather be called an imitation of idleness'. She's acutely aware how this gets in the way of writing, 'For altho' ambition is a grand angelic sin […] I have at any rate a long futurity of coughing [to] abstract me from it.'

Beyond her bedroom door, though, the household mood has been lightened in recent months by the promise of a permanent London address. Months of wrangling over the lease of this potential home at 50 Wimpole

Street have left the family on tenterhooks lest 'those lawyers [...] are going to rob us of it'. By spring 1838 the move seems increasingly certain. But then bad news arrives at Gloucester Place: 'How the waves of pleasure & mournfulness chase each other over the sand of life!' In February, the Barretts discover that Uncle Sam is dead. The shock affects Elizabeth, as all bad news does, psychosomatically: 'My strength flags a good deal, and the cough very little.' Uncle Sam, the family learn, died at Kingston on 23 December 1837 while trying to get home from Spanish Town to Cinnamon Hill. The cause of death was 'pulmonary consumption', or TB: so though the family back in London had no idea of it, he must have guessed that he was dying.

Possibly this is why, the previous August, he gifted Elizabeth his one-eighth share in the *David Lyon*, a working vessel once used as a convict ship, together with its latest annual profit. Uncle Sam is survived by no legitimate children, and his gift marks the special relationship the two had enjoyed since he, 'Was [...] Uncle brother friend & nurse when I lay in the long weary sickness at Gloucester'. When news of this generosity arrived, his 'kindness melted our dear Ba to *tears*, for she had thought from his long continued silence, that she *must* be forgotten.' In fact he was probably too ill for letter-writing. But she doesn't yet seem to realise the significance of the money itself. Invested, it will produce an annual income of around £200, equivalent to a little under three years' pay for a skilled labourer. Combined with around £4,000 inherited from Grandmama, also invested for her, it means that, unusually for a woman at this time, Elizabeth could afford to live independently.

This is not what happens next. Instead in a visceral reflex Papa summons his own Sam, the son who is his brother's namesake, home from Jamaica. At twenty-six the former naughty schoolboy has become one of the most gregarious, outgoing members of the Barrett clan and, sent to Cinnamon Hill in 1836, he has proved an asset in the management of family affairs. He is also a young man with an appetite for life. It's no coincidence that, among the siblings, he has a special bond with Henrietta. Third and fourth in the surviving birth order as Ba and Bro are first and second, the pair share an analogous bond of temperament and age, relishing socialising, dancing and party-going. Characteristically, when Sam does finally return to England in November 1838, almost a year after his uncle's death, he takes in a tour of the eastern seaboard of the US, including a visit to New York, along the way. Indeed, even back in Britain he doesn't rush home, but goes first to old friends in Sidmouth.

By the time he arrives in London, the family will be settled in at Wimpole Street, and they see their new home's advantages and deficiencies through his eyes. Moving half a mile east from Gloucester Place means living in a yet more built-up area of London. Elizabeth has not been keen on the move, 'on account of the gloominesses of that street & of that part of the street—whose walls look so much like Newgate's turned inside out'. Wimpole Street, which runs parallel with Harley Street, isn't an arterial thoroughfare like Gloucester Place. If a little quieter, it's also less imposing: Sam is 'in some measure disappointed at the width of the Street; to this however I am reconciled, for the house is delightful in every respect'. (He also notices the London cold after the warmth of Montego Bay: 'My room as warm as I could wish it when in bed, but as cold as my *bitterest* enemy could desire when out.') But number 50 itself is if anything grander than the old house. Though constructed of plain brick – apart from the stone-faced ground and lower floor – it's triple-fronted, comprising a basement plus four storeys; five if you include the rooms in the mansard roof. A wide stone bridge leads to a front door with a magnificent peacock's tail of statement fanlight.

The Barrett men arrive at Wimpole Street in mid-April 1838. Elizabeth and her sisters follow after a few days because, 'The house was so unfinished, that we were obliged & glad to accept the charities of a kind friend & go to Crawford Street until the ghost of paint had been sufficiently exorcised.' But once there, 'We like the house very much indeed!' she tells Miss Mitford. 'The doves & my books & I have a little slip of sitting room to ourselves, —& dearest Papa in his abundant kindness surprised me in it with a whole vision of majestic [plaster] heads from Brucciani's—busts of poets and philosophers.'

This 'little slip of sitting room' is a gift, an acknowledgement – and something of a gilded cage. It lays out a future that Elizabeth, of all the siblings, is expected to spend indoors, reading and writing. And her father's 'abundant kindness' in making this as pleasant as he can for her does in fact create the ideal conditions for work, since it's not entirely true that, as Virginia Woolf will put it, 'A woman must have money and a room of her own if she is to write.' The money, at least, needn't absolutely be her own: for now, Papa's wealth genuinely enables Elizabeth's writing life.

In fact Edward Barrett Moulton-Barrett will receive such a bad posthumous press from his daughter's admirers that it's worth reckoning up just how important he's been for her emergence as a poet. Ever since she was fourteen and he paid for her debut publication, *The Battle of Marathon*, he has encouraged Elizabeth's writing both practically and emotionally: his 'admonitions have guided my youthful muse, even from her earliest infancy', as that volume's dedication puts it. There's more to being born into the right family than financial comfort, access to the parental library, and decent home tutoring, essential though these are. Without Papa's consent, *An Essay on Mind* would not have been published when Elizabeth was twenty; if he hadn't urged her to submit the manuscript, *Prometheus Bound* wouldn't have appeared when she was twenty-seven.

In the first half of the nineteenth century, gifted women are dependent on fragile connectors of good fortune. It's Elizabeth's particular luck, for example, that her father isn't interested in rushing his daughters into dynastic marriages: perhaps his own empire-building father-in-law put him off. In any case a strong, almost fundamentalist religiosity has now combined with what he views as his own worldly failure to make him see prayerful morality as life's most important work. Like nothing so much as the founder of one of those Catholic religious orders of which the Nonconformist in him must disapprove, he sees a cloistered existence dedicated to study and prayer not as half-lived, but as the best of all possible lives. 'We are dying & all are dying around us daily, eternity is hastening, be it our study to prepare for it', as he notes in a characteristically cheery missive to George. For this Revivalist Christian, prayer is an active, even heroic, intervention in the world rather than a retreat from it. In making the virtually housebound Elizabeth a domestic repository for the Christian duty 'to watch and pray', he is allotting her what he sees as a pivotal role; albeit one with more than a passing resemblance to mediaeval anchoress, or village sin-eater.

In coming years Papa will get in the habit of coming to pray with Elizabeth every night. But religiosity is just one face of her culture's emerging obsession with the figure of an imprisoned woman. Beyond the immuring walls of the Barrett home this is becoming highly sexualised. One of Elizabeth's emerging poetic peers, Alfred Tennyson – three years her junior – has already published two poems, 'Mariana' (in 1830) and 'The Lady of Shalott' (in 1833), fetishising walled-up women. Mariana in her 'moated grange', pining for lost love, is one of Shakespeare's 'spare' characters from *Measure for Measure*; in coming decades, Tennyson's poem will inspire famous paintings by John Everett Millais and John William Waterhouse. In a tangentially Arthurian story which generates three further Waterhouse canvases, his Lady of Shalott is locked in a tower and cursed to weave perpetually – until she falls fatally in love with Sir Lancelot:

> She left the web, she left the loom,
> She made three paces thro' the room,
> She saw the water-lily bloom,
> She saw the helmet and the plume,
> > She look'd down to Camelot.

Thwarted sexuality suffocates these fantasy figures, and it is striking how much they resemble later stories about Elizabeth – which she herself will protest. In 1844 she will be hurt when someone who she by then thinks of as a friend, Richard Hengist Horne, presents her as a reclusive invalid in his encyclopaedic *A New Spirit of the Age*: their relationship will never fully recover. A year later she'll challenge even Robert Browning, 'Do *you* conjecture sometimes that I live all alone here like Mariana in the moated Grange?' Twentieth-century popular fiction will turn the indoor years of her thirties into a thrumming Oedipal drama; or else portray her as sexually unawakened, a dammed-up force ready to burst into creativity once she's roused with a kiss. But if the reality of authorship is much more quotidian, it's also more self-directed. For all her father's support, it's Elizabeth's own strong will that has driven her forward through her piecemeal poetic education, over the threshold of the banal and into writing of real literary merit. She is a big personality crammed into the small frame of a diminutive body – and of a restricted life.

That personality finds the space to emerge on the page. It's impossible to ignore the spikey intellectual charm of Elizabeth's letters, as when she beautifully folds doubled puns, reflexivity and reflection into a thank-you note to John Kenyon:

> I have not been asleep over Landor's [work]. It is easier to dream than to sleep over a volume of his: and perhaps very beautiful as these are in many parts, one of *my* dreams is, that they express coldly, & with a hard stiff stoney outline, what the Greeks were. There were living Greeks—were there not? as well as Greek statues.

Nor can we discount the simpler, warmer tone she uses to Arabella about:

> flannel waistcoats up to the throat—& next the skin—& most of the most disagreeable things you can think of besides .. provided that you happen to be particularly imaginative *while* you think!— […] Tell us everything about everybody—*us* meaning Henrietta & me. I never *show* your letters & so you may open your heart!

Yet these are both ways of writing in persona. It's not that the petite brunette at her writing desk is faking it or being manipulative when she writes as an effusive young lady. But she *is* trying to work out how to be herself.

She's afraid of turning into an intellectual woman, of the kind who 'used to—frighten me more than any woman I ever knew. There used to be fear for me even in the pure intellect of her eye.' In a way, what she fears is what she's always pictured as the masculinity within her own make-up: a poetic vocation that, ever since her tomboy childhood, has been muddled up with the almost exclusively male role models, from Homer to Byron, that are available to her. Later generations of writing women will be released from similar anxieties by realising that the intellect is gender-free. Or at least by recognising that male writers are simply the historically available models, and that with more history this will change. But becoming a writer always has to do with individuation: a matter of making, or failing to make, private sense of the writing task.

Elizabeth has always understood that developing as a writer is no accident; sharpening her technique, she treats even letters as compositions. Now this process of poetic self-invention is bearing fruit. When *The*

Seraphim appears in June 1838, its reception makes clear that this is a real achievement. Reviews start to appear immediately, and are substantial. *The Sunbeam's* coverage extends across ten pages and five issues – an honour it otherwise accords only to Thomas Carlyle's *Sartor Resartus* – framing her as an important new figure. Pieces appear in *The Atlas, The Examiner, The Athenaeum, Blackwood's, The Metropolitan Magazine, The Monthly Review, The Literary Gazette, The Quarterly Review* and *The Monthly Chronicle*. In short, *The Seraphim* is one of the year's must-review books.

This extensive critical reception will later be short-handed by scholars as 'mixed'. In fact, reviewers speak with practically one voice, repeating the terms 'extraordinary' and 'exceptional', a consensus best summed up by *The Athenaeum*:

> This is an extraordinary volume—especially welcome as an evidence of female genius and accomplishment—but it is hardly less disappointing than extraordinary.

Uneven, even controversial: but undeniably important. Some critics object to religious verse in principle, others complain that the collection's title poem is static and conceptually weak. But, as *The Atlas* points out, 'the author deprecates such criticism by declaring she has not "written a book but a suggestion"'. It does well to seize on this key line from her Preface, because *The Seraphim* marks Elizabeth's shift from linear thought – philosophical argumentation or narrative – to evocation, 'sublimity—suggested, but not developed' as *The Monthly Chronicle* says. *The Athenaeum* assumes that this is a loss of control – 'Miss Barrett's genius is of a high order: active, vigorous, and versatile, but unaccompanied by discriminating taste. A thousand strange and beautiful visions flit across her mind' – while *The Monthly Review* sees 'evidence of a singularly original mind […] that […] must be carefully directed and forcibly controlled', and *Blackwood's* concludes that 'there is an originality in the whole cast and conception of the strain that beyond all dispute proves the possession of genius. But they are all disfigured by much imperfect and some bad writing.' In short, autodidacticism is both Elizabeth's strength and her weakness. Its reward is to be compared to Percy Bysshe Shelley by both *The Metropolitan Magazine* and *The Literary Gazette*; its penalty, to be reminded that she is a woman: 'Especially, when considered as the compositions of a female, [these poems] must command admiration and awaken hope.'

Elizabeth may prefer *The Athenaeum*'s observation that 'she addresses herself to sacred song with a devotional ecstacy.' In 1838 religious poetry appears not dated but radical, even risky, because religion matters. Not for another eight years will the doctrinal unorthodoxy and radically modern technique of J. M. W. Turner's 'seraphim', his visionary *The Angel Standing in the Sun*, combine to confound viewers. In fact ironically, now that Marsh Chapel and its stimulating theological entanglements are in the past, Elizabeth's own faith seems to be settling down within conventional bounds. Just as it once replaced her obsession with Greek prosody, now doctrinal argument has in turn disappeared from her correspondence. Both have been stages in the accidental education from which she emerges as a poet of technical accuracy and ethical acuity; both are also responsible for slowing her literary development, at least compared to men emerging from the forcing houses of good schools and university. Forced to guide herself through the bibliographical highways – and sometimes getting stuck in byways – Elizabeth is developing on a feminine timescale.

Future admirers will imagine that, had Elizabeth only been able to escape the parental home for happy marriage earlier, she would have survived longer and written more: the immured woman fantasy, once again. The truth is that all the most-read women of the early nineteenth century – Jane Austen, the Brontë sisters, Mary Shelley (before marriage, in widowhood) – write while unmarried. Even George Eliot and George Sand both choose cohabitation, a lifestyle that allows freedom for literary work. If Elizabeth had married before she received the literary world's imprimatur, her talents, like those of most women of the era, would have disappeared into household management, social respectability, and the repeated pregnancies by which they may well have been snuffed out, as Charlotte Brontë's were. Only fame can ring-fence her writing time. Only late marriage will spare her already frail body the risks of numerous pregnancies.

Mary Russell Mitford, less well-known in the twenty-first century but in her lifetime bestselling – is unmarried too. Her letters to Elizabeth are noticeably more effusive than others she writes, and it's entirely possible that this isn't only because she wants to encourage her shy protégée. But that she might conceivably have a crush plainly doesn't occur to the younger woman, who's busy being in awe – 'Indeed it does seem to me like a vision [...] that I shd. know you and be allowed to love you and write to you & think of you as my friend' – and picturing herself as a mentee. Nor should we jump to this conclusion, for in 1838 being single or married says more about a woman's social and financial security than it does about her sexuality. The tension that Elizabeth would have to resolve if she were free to leave home isn't between heterosexual marriage and loving women, but between what marriage means for a woman's life, and her own desire to live and to write freely as men do. What matters for her story is simply that Miss Mitford's affection is discerning, deep and enduring. But at thirty-two Elizabeth has anxieties about how to be a literary woman all the same. Must she be a sacred monster? With conspicuous tactlessness she tells her friend of her fear that, 'In seeing Lady Dacre I should see *a woman of the masculine gender*, with her genius very prominent in eccentricity of manner & sentiment', because, apart from Miss Mitford, 'The only literary woman I ever knew [...] was Lady Mary Shepherd whose kindness & *terribleness* I equally remember.'

Elizabeth herself, of course, has proved all too feminine in her ability to fall damagingly for a male authority figure. But though she may look up to the literary friends she's making now, unlike Boyd – or indeed her father – they don't trap her in humiliating codependency, whatever their own feelings. It's not inconceivable, for example, that the twice-widowed John Kenyon is attracted to his pretty and gifted protégée. At least that's the complexion Henrietta puts on their friendship. 'How would you like him to be your *brother in law*?' she asks Sam. 'You must know that he is in great esteem of our dearest Ba—we torment her most terribly about him.' Kenyon, who has been alone since his wife died in 1835, is charismatic, sociable, kind – and wealthy. In short, he is a catch. But he's also a year older than Papa and, although she frequently speculates with Miss Mitford about his private life, Elizabeth never seems to put her own self in this romantic frame.

Instead, ill-health is returning to claim her for a second time. By summer 1838 she's coughing continually. Infection succeeds infection. In June, 'I have been sometimes very unwell & sometimes better […] A cold this week threw me back a little […] The lungs are said to be affected—they did not respond as satisfactorily as heretofore to the latest application of the stethoscope.' Struggling for breath, she's confined to bed again, '& my weakness increases of course under the remedies which successive attacks render necessary'.

But these remedies represent the very best treatment available. Papa has hired the personal physician to the young Queen Victoria. Dr Chambers is renowned for using the still very-modern stethoscope to diagnose the presence or absence of TB. He gives Elizabeth the all clear: 'Dr Chambers—the *sincerest* of physicians! has told me that there seems to be no *ulceration* of lungs, & that he has grounds for hoping for my ultimate complete recovery.' Yet by mid-August it's clear that she has chronic lung disease of some kind. In this era before antibiotics it's easy for a chest infection to become life-threatening bronchitis, pneumonia or pleurisy; especially in someone as unfit as Elizabeth. 'Consumption' is far from the only fatal pulmonary condition; indeed Elizabeth's unusually isolated lifestyle makes her a less likely candidate for this contagious disease, and we know of no sufferers in her circle apart from her late Uncle Sam, who was far away in Jamaica for the last decade of his life. But by now Elizabeth is 'a helpless being […] whose migrations have for so many months been from the bed to the sofa'. She's coughing up some blood, thought to be the result of breaking a blood vessel in a coughing fit, and Chambers 'has made an essential condition of my leaving this part of England for the winter […] to stay at the risk of my life wd be wilfulness & foolishness at once'.

And so at the end of August, turning her back on literary London and her unfolding success as a poet, Elizabeth leaves for Devon where (after the usual tortuous decision-making) her father has allowed her to overwinter. She's too unwell to manage the 200-mile journey by carriage, but 25 August sees her at the docks boarding the Saturday breakfast-time sailing for Plymouth. There she connects with the packet, a fast, stopping mail boat, which arrives in Torquay on the evening of 27 August 1838.

For all her frailty, Elizabeth is a good traveller, 'the only lady on board who did not suffer from seasickness'. Besides, she hasn't made the journey alone. She's accompanied by Bro and George; and by Henrietta, who's by now desperate to escape the heavily supervised domestic round at Wimpole Street. Henrietta's memories of the 'gay' months she spent with Bro at Torquay five years ago mix with guilt at leaving Arabella '*sisterless*' in Wimpole Street; but Arabel, as family mostly call her, does have the Revd Hunter's by now teenaged daughter Mary for company, and she and Henrietta have agreed to swap places at the turn of the year.

At first the siblings stay with their 'aunt and uncle Hedley who have resided at Torquay for the last two or three years under Dr Chambers's jurisdiction, on account of my uncle's being affected in some similar way to myself'. (Hedley, an uncle only by marriage, offers no clue to genetic predisposition; besides, he will go on to a long, healthy life, dying in his seventies.) But awkwardly, their house is too far from the sea for Elizabeth, who's by now confined to an invalid chair. It is also rather cold. So it's agreed that from 1 October she will take a terraced house on the seafront. The rent, at £180 per annum, is high: poor health represents good business for these south Devon towns, famed for their mild climate and unpolluted sea air. But Elizabeth pays, and agrees to share the financial and legal responsibility with Bummy, who is now closing up her own home in rural Frocester, Gloucestershire to resume the care of her eldest niece.

However the heavy lifting, literal as well as metaphorical, will be done by Elizabeth's new maid, a country girl from Lincolnshire called Elizabeth Crow. Just before they left London her predecessor, who had worked for the family for a couple of years, '& had professed her willingness to go anywhere with me', announced that she wasn't well enough to come to Devon. Elizabeth, who like all members of her class tends to treat servants as invisible necessities, manages briefly to make sympathetic noises – 'and indeed she is not well, poor thing, nor does she look so!' – that are conspicuously muted compared with, for example, the terms in which she worries over Miss Mitford's dog Dash. Although perhaps this is a symptom of scepticism: 'We have some reason for suspecting fear of the sea-voyage to have had a little to do with the change.'

Elizabeth Crow is altogether more robust. She is in her early twenties, strong and energetic, with a northerner's brisk manner. She's also intelligent, as her mistress gradually realises: 'She is an excellent young woman—intelligent bright-tempered & feeling-hearted,—more to me than a mere servant; since her heart works more than her hand in all she does for me! And her delight in [Miss Mitford's book] *Village* which I gave her to read, was as true a thing as ever was that of readers of higher degree.' But even Crow, as the Barretts call her, will be overruled by Elizabeth's new physician. Dr Barry of Torquay is 'a young man—full of energy—with a countenance seeming to look *towards life*—devoted to his profession & rising rapidly into professional eminence—a young man with a young wife & child, & baby unborn.' An advocate of fresh air and early rising, he's initially certain his methods are working for Elizabeth; a month after her arrival, he declares that 'the respiration is clearer on the affected side.'

In fact his regime leaves the patient 'haunted throughout by weakness, an oppressive *sense* of weakness, & [...] such lowness of spirits, that I could have cried all day if there were no *exertion* in crying! For Dr Barry forbids her 'London habit (very useful in enabling an invalid to get thro' a good deal of writing without fatigue) of lying in bed until two', and forces Elizabeth out daily in the invalid chair; with the result that she 'seldom failed to come back quite exhausted & fit for nothing better than reading nonsense.' Worse:

> On the occasion of my writing case being accidentally visible —'Have you been writing today Miss Barrett'. 'No'—'Did you write yesterday?' 'Yes'. 'You will be so good as not to do so any more'!!— And again—'You have observed my directions & been idle lately Miss Barrett?' 'Yes'. 'And within these last three weeks you have never written any poetry? [...] if you please to do this, neither I nor anyone else can do anything for you'.

Life has got stuck once again: it's as if she had never escaped from Gloucester. To be exiled in Torquay, away from her newly flourishing literary life and many of the people she loves, is bad enough. 'These partings are *dyings*', she tells Arabella on the eve of George's departure for London; and she means it literally, since despite the doctor's assurances it's not certain that she'll live to see absent friends and family again. But to be forbidden to write is to be denied what is by now the central purpose of her life, as well as her habitual coping mechanism.

Barry is just another in the long line of medics who ban writing women from the one activity that probably makes them feel better and stronger than any other. His idea that writing is over-stimulating for the female, but not the male, system isn't new; nor is it about to vanish. Seven years from now, Elizabeth will manage to be funny as well as furious about this:

> I had a doctor once who thought he had done everything because he had carried the inkstand out of the room—[…] He gravely thought poetry a sort of disease .. a sort of fungus of the brain—& held as a serious opinion, that nobody could be properly well who exercised it as an art—which was true (he maintained) even of men—[…] for women, it was a mortal malady & incompatible with any common show of health under any circumstances.

But at the moment it's simply depressing. She had hoped, 'Encouraged by Dr C's permission, to manage here without medical visits, & to trust simply to God's sun & air'. However, far from taking the patient off drugs, Barry has upped her dose of digitalis, and added 'the blister &c applied without any particular call for it', and inhalations of '*what*, Dr Barry WONT tell me for I asked him twice & was answered each time by an evasion'. Things seem to be getting worse instead of better.

The only bright spot in the autumnal gloom is that Papa has given permission for Bro to stay on in Devon, even though both men would prefer he returned to London. Father and daughter share not only the tendency to hole up, but a desire to keep their loved ones holed up with them. Keeping 'Brozie' in Torquay with nothing to do except chaperone his sister prevents his having to return to Jamaica, but it must also 'quench the energies of his life', to paraphrase Elizabeth's own perceptive phrase. Of course, there are compensations. Sheltered by 'the slant woods of Beacon hill', the siblings' new home at 3 Beacon Terrace stands 'immediately *upon* the lovely bay—a few paces dividing our door from its waves—& nothing but the "sweet south" & congenial west wind can reach us'. A handsome Regency mid-terrace, its frontage dressed with a wrought-iron balcony and double-height ornamental pilasters, it's roomy enough for as many family members as she can persuade her father to part with. But as 1838 turns into 1839 Elizabeth's coughing continues to interrupt every activity, its convulsive rhythm forming the soundtrack to thought, so that putting together lines of poetry – even without Dr Barry's permission – feels almost impossible. At night coughing destroys the very sleep that might give the body a chance to heal; propped on pillows, Elizabeth hacks her way through the insomniac small hours.

Not till early summer does some good news interrupt this dour routine. On 18 May 1839, 'RB' – Richard Barrett, the distant cousin who has been hounding the family through Chancery – dies suddenly at the age of fifty, 'after only one hour & a half's illness caused by a fit of Apoplexy', leaving the years-long dispute unsettled but putting a de facto end to his personal campaign. But in September death crosses Elizabeth's own threshold. Dr Barry – by now her 'able & most kind physician who for above a year has attended me almost every day' – is taken ill with what seems at first to be 'rheumatic & nervous fever'. He rallies, relapses, rallies and relapses a second time, and dies before the end of the month. The patient is left with survivor's guilt that, once again, takes somatic form – 'the physician was taken & the patient left—& left of course deeply affected & shaken' – exacerbated by the three weeks without medical care that follow. She suffers 'my old attack of fever & imperviousness to sleep'.

Having to move house on 1 October, after a year's tenancy at number 3, adds to the stress. Number 1 Beacon Terrace, three doors down, is a plainer, larger and, crucially, a cheaper house. It's here that Dr Barry's successor, Dr Scully, 'comes to see her every day not only medically it appears, but to *chat*, he seldom leaves her under an hour & tells her all the news & the scandal of the neighbourhood.' Despite these ministrations, by the end of the year Elizabeth is still bedbound, 'not any thinner, altho' perhaps not *fatter*' and is 'carried to her sofa for a short time every day, but her Coming into the drawing room has not been thought of yet', as Henrietta confides to Sam, who's been back in Jamaica for the last half year.

Late summer saw Arabella arrive in Torquay, and as 1839 gives way to 1840 the siblings settle in around Elizabeth's invalid routines. But in April a letter arrives with shocking news that changes everything. Their brother Sam has died. He contracted what's probably (mosquito-borne) Yellow Fever – so called because it can trigger jaundice – and died two months ago, on 17 February 1840. He had also fallen ill during his first Jamaican trip; but this time he knew he was dying, dictated his will, and asked for the last rites, which were refused him by Hope Waddell, a preacher whose ministry the family have enabled, in a fit of self-righteous Revivalism. During the young man's earlier stay on the island, Waddell had denounced him for sleeping around – and with enslaved women at that. Now he decided that Sam was saying he had 'never taken the sacrament' and – though lack of confirmation into the Anglican Church is no barrier to Nonconformist communion – refused the twenty-eight-year-old's dying request, choosing instead comfortlessly to read him the Bible.

In short, it's as bitter a death as possible and, though the family may not be aware of every detail, they understand the loneliness of it. In the grief that follows, everyone worries especially about the effect on Elizabeth. Sure enough, she's poleaxed: 'It was a heavy blow for all of us—and I, being weak you see, was struck down as by a *bodily* blow, in a moment, without having time for tears.' Just as at the death of her mother, she seems unable to cry. Once again, as when Uncle Sam died, her mourning is psychosomatic. 'Too weak to hold a pen', she goes into such a serious decline that Papa hurries to Torquay.

Of course, he's terrified of losing another child. But the prolonged emergency of Elizabeth's health seems to paralyse him. Late June sees him writing to Sette, back in town, that:

> it is a monstrous time since I left you, and I am wanted very much in London, but how to leave my beloved Ba, I know not, I fear the very mention of it, for she is indeed lamentably weak, & yet it is absolutely necessary I should go; I really know not how to act.

Such vacillation is hardly reassuring for a teenager who might prefer paternal confidence to confidences. At eighteen, Sette has effectively been left in charge at Wimpole Street, while his elder brother Alfred studies at the newly founded University College London and the younger Octavius continues at home with a tutor. (Left in charge, too, in preference to the family's rebel, twenty-two-year-old world traveller and wannabe commissioned officer Henry, the son who seems unable to pick an 'occupation which is *not* insurmountably objectionable to Papa'.)

But for once Papa has chosen well. Sette has always been one of his father's favourites, 'both my right & left hand', the child who slept in his bed and from whom he couldn't be parted during the move from Hope End. This seventh son has developed a precocious confidence the family boast fondly about to each other; they particularly love his 'assurance in costuming himself in a long tailed coat belonging to his elder brother' to gatecrash an Oxford University presentation to the Queen on her marriage. Now this same filial maturity allows Papa to remain at Elizabeth's bedside till the end of the year.

Despite their father's presence, it seems that in this period of grief and anxiety both Bro and Arabella manage, astonishingly, to seize the day and conduct romances. Arabella's scrape sounds as though it may involve a beloved pony rather than a young man: Elizabeth may be able to afford new riding habits, like the one she buys Henrietta, but actual mounts must be borrowed and relinquished when friends move away. 'Poor dearest Bella' seems to have gone on a wild expedition; she receives a 'scolding after the perils!—& [...] the real thorough fatigue of half running nearly eight miles!' But Bro's love affair appears to be the real thing. Last July he was frankly mooning; Henrietta reported that he spent his time 'between drawing, fishing & *smoking* [...] His hair remains as long and lanky as ever—there is no hope for it now, since [Monti] [Miss] Garden expressed her approbation of it—she is very anxious to return to Torquay, but not more so I suspect than Bro is to see her.' By June 1840 the moment seems to be passing. Elizabeth notes that her brother has stopped keeping his blind drawn, '& indeed ventures to show his whole face out of doors by twilight instead of waiting for the very pitch dark'. For all the sisters' teasing, though, Elizabeth will later imply that this love affair was so serious that she had wanted to settle money on her favourite brother so he could marry.

But all such hopes and intrigues are in vain, for the following month Bro goes sailing with friends of a Saturday, and never returns. 'Boating' is a Barrett family pleasure, one at which Bro is an old hand, and the weather on 11 July is fine. He goes out, as he has before, with 'two of his friends Mr Vanneck & Captn Clarke', both also experienced sailors, on Vanneck's well-equipped vessel the *La Belle Sauvage*, where they're aided by a professional crewman. All three 'gentlemen' can swim, and nothing is amiss with the weather. So what happens next is a shocking mystery. As Papa writes to Wimpole Street:

> They left at a little of the 12 o'clock it seems, & up to this time 11 o'clock Monday Night, they have not been heard of, further than that on Saturday afternoon about 1/2 after 3 o'clock, a Gentleman in his Catch, about 4 miles to the East of Teingmouth [*sic*], saw a Boat exactly corresponding to the one they went in [...] about a mile from him, when he observed it go down; He set sail immediately to the spot, which he says he reached in 4 or 5 minutes, but nothing whatever could he see belo[n]ging to her or the Party in her [...] altho he remained about the place for nearly four hours—& what is extraordinary it does not appear that she upset, for he saw the point of her mast above the water last so that I cannot understand, how some one did not keep upon the surface.

The weekend drags on without either reassurance or confirmation of their worst fears. 'Henrietta, I think, scarcely can believe it, but weeps, Arabel does, & weeps, but her faith bears her up well' while:

> On Sunday afternoon, Mrs Vanneck & two others went over to Teingmouth [*sic*] & there they heard that a Boat containing two Ladies & I think two Men or Boys [...] had been lost off Dawlish now it is supposed that two of dear Bro's party may have taken their Coats off, & hence from their shirt sleeves supposing they were taken for women. Up to the arrival of the Mail we caught as a straw at the possibility of their having gone to the Land Ship near Lyme or to Weymouth, where Mr Vanneck the day before talked of going.

By Tuesday, Henrietta does believe the worst, and she has hysterics. Elizabeth has from the outset been neither optimistic nor consoled by faith. Her last words to her favourite brother were petulant; now that momentary irritation will remain with her forever. Once again her health collapses under the shock. 'Scarcely conscious, her mind wanders.' She comes even closer to dying than she did at the news of Sam's death. Love and grief lodge in the body, making the immune system, the hormones, buckle and rev. As Papa says, 'It is a wonder to me that she lives, for her love for [Bro] was truely great, & [...] uninterrupted, it began in infancy & has gone on growing with their growth—He was always the adytum of all her secrets & plans.'

The family are left hanging for three weeks until at last, on 4 August, Bro's body is washed up at nearby Babbacombe, along with the remains of Captain Clarke and of the sailor. Cruelly decomposed, all three are hastily buried just two days later in the local parish churchyard. The whole thing is both horrifying and uncanny. Until they had Bro's body, the family couldn't be absolutely certain he was dead, whatever common sense told them. But even once it *is* returned to them by the water they don't in a sense *have* it, because it's too destroyed to be viewed. And in the coming months Elizabeth must live on constantly in earshot of the sea that killed her brother. Now the breakers outside her window sound less like breathing than fighting for breath. In October she tells Miss Mitford, 'These walls—& the sound of what is very fearful a few yards from them—that perpetual dashing sound, have preyed on me. I have been crushed trodden down.'

Not till December does her father feel that she's well enough for him to leave her and resume his London responsibilities: the meetings with bankers, lawyers, middlemen and dealers that make up a life of international trade. Yet what she herself wants is for everyone just to go away and leave her alone: 'She cannot hear of any one coming near her, indeed she would have us all to leave her, as she associates in her mind every one & every thing with her loss.' As continuing ill-health, intensified now by grief, forces her to overwinter once more in 'this dreadful place', 'Months roll over months. I know it is for good—but *very hard to bear.*'

Incredibly, in the spring of 1841 life does resume. Arabella, by now twenty-seven and full of energy, gets involved in charitable work with the local school. She organises 'Tea & cake & a run in the grass' for the children, just like the old days at Hope End. Henrietta, now turning thirty-two, disapproves because the clergyman involved is High Church. Still, she herself escapes the sickroom as often as she can: her own grief, for her own intimate Sam as much as for Bro, goes relatively unacknowledged, and even a walk around the block must offer some relief from constantly ministering to Elizabeth's health and feelings. Friendship would be more restorative still. 'Henrietta had a luncheon party here today. She goes out a good deal', Elizabeth confides to George in April, 'But one heart can't judge for another.' Indeed. She herself is not so stricken that she cannot sit for her portrait, though she enjoins her brother, 'Say nothing of this— nor indeed of any thing else spoken by me today.'

'Any thing else' is Papa's latest scheme to buy sight unseen an estate 'reigning alone at the top of a mountain', across the Herefordshire border in the Black Mountains of Wales, rather than free up assets to establish his sons in their own lives. Such a hilltop exile would be 'the knell of [...] perpetual exile' for Elizabeth too: cut off from 'medical advice' and, perhaps even more importantly, literary London. Luckily the moment passes. So does a threatened worst of all worlds compromise by which she would forfeit Devonshire's healthy air yet remain in provincial exile at Clifton on the edge of Bristol.

Exile matters particularly because, encouraged by her literary friends, Elizabeth is starting to write again. She's missed the deadline for contributing to Miss Mitford's 1840 *Findens' Tableaux*, but now she acquires a new author-correspondent who also provokes her to put pen to paper. Richard Hengist Horne, just three years her senior, has lived an absurdly adventurous life. Having failed to get into the East India Company, he joined the Mexican Navy in his early twenties, survived shipwreck, mutiny and on-board fire, and managed to break two ribs while swimming at Niagara Falls. Back in London, he writes all this up for magazines, then parlays it into a literary career, producing fiction, drama, history and epic verse, and editing periodicals. It's all a far cry from Elizabeth's seaside sickroom; yet the two develop a flourishing if mismatched friendship. It was a former Hope End governess, Mrs Orme, who put them in touch, forwarding a letter to Horne from Elizabeth; possibly she painted an alluring portrait of the invalid – or else stressed 'the straightness of [her] prison'. But by now Elizabeth is widely published: peers like Horne are interested in what she's doing anyway.

In 1841 the two even try to collaborate on a verse-drama, *Psyche Apoc-alypté*, though this project loses momentum in the aftermath of Bro's death. Nevertheless, Horne is a typically rackety literary male, and the friendship worries Miss Mitford. Responding to what may be either pure protectiveness or just a touch of jealousy, Elizabeth justifies it to her older friend in ways that strikingly prefigure how she'll frame her relationship with Robert Browning:

> What claim had I in my solitude & sadness & helpless hopeless sickness, such as he believed it to be, upon a literary man overwhelmed with occupation & surrounded by friends & fitnesses of all sorts in London? Nevertheless from the first kind little note which he sent to me [...] to ask me to allow him to help in amusing me, he has never forgotten or seemed to forget me.

Miss Mitford is happier with – indeed she's the instigator of – another new relationship; one of the most enduring of Elizabeth's life, and a real turning point in her recovery. In December 1840 she offers the invalid a six-month-old spaniel from a litter sired by her own pet Flush. Elizabeth, who's just as capable of havering self-sabotage as her father, does her characteristic one step forward and two steps back of shyness and renunciation: the puppy, bred *'for sporting* purposes' would be 'exposed to a martyrdom, whether in this room, or hereafter, in [...] the London Streets prison'. And yet ... and yet. She's already taking advice from the local coaching inn:

> Send him by the railroad to Basingstoke, with a direction on the card .. 'to be forwarded by the first Exeter coach'—& the coachman both there & at Exeter will be commissioned to feed him & see to his comfort generally. There is no danger [...]—that is, if he is packed carefully in a *hamper*.

Which is modern indeed of her – the narrow-gauge Basingstoke line is a primitive affair, barely eighteen months old – but also impractical, since there is as yet no station at Reading.

Not surprisingly, when he finally arrives in Torquay at the start of 1841, Flush junior seems shaken by his journey. Additionally, a local panic about mad dogs makes it dangerous to let him out. So he starts by messing round the house. But soon:

A shawl thrown upon a chair by my fireside, is his favorite place—& there he sits most of the day .. coming down occasionally to be patted or enjoy a round of leaps. Such a quiet, loving intelligent little dog—& so very very pretty!

Spaniels of all breeds are highly strung. But Flush, cutely long-eared, with a white blazon on his chest and a mismatched head too dark for his ears, seems surprisingly docile. He will end up as one of the most widely travelled dogs of the nineteenth century, and by April is already becoming a domestic personality:

> He wants to lie on my bed—& most particularly objects to being shut up at night all by himself in the dark. [...] & whenever a door down stairs has happened to be left unclosed, up he comes to this door in the middle of the night, shaking the handle with his two paws until Arabel, who sleeps on a sofa by my side, gets up to let him in.

It's a dog's life. At the end of April Flush goes adventuring in the Torquay woods, gets lost, and is found again; in July he acquires 'a kitten for a playmate! [...] Think of his carrying this little white, snowball of a kitten, no larger than his head, *carrying* it about the room in his mouth—& playing with it for hours together!' He's become a charmer who 'creeps up in his usual irresistible way, & lays his head down on my pillow', and cocky with it:

> He is fond of milk—& when any is brought to me in a cup he wont let me drink a whole half without a hint that the rest belongs to him. He waits till his turn comes, till he thinks it *is* come—and then if I loiter, as I do sometimes pretend to do, Mr Flush tries to take possession of the cup by main force.

Confident at home, outdoors he has 'not, in fact, reached the point of heroism':

> if a cat stands & stares at us, we retreat prudently—if it runs our way by accident however free of hostile intention, we cry out piteously— if a stranger tries to pat our pretty head, we shrink away.

If Elizabeth, who feels rather the same about strangers herself, seems to be overinvolved with her new pet, that's partly because her isolated life still lacks incident. But things are changing. Her letters are once again alert and intellectual. She's ardently re-engaged with writing, and is reading widely. In July 1841 when not one but two mutual friends, Miss Mitford and John Kenyon, send her Robert Browning's new poem, 'Pippa Passes', it behoves her to be tactful. But she can't resist noting 'an occasional *manner*,' even though:

> There are fine things in it—& the presence of genius, never to be denied!—At the same time it is hard .. *to understand*—is'nt it?—Too hard?—I think so!—And the fault of Paracelsus,—the defect in harmony, is here too. After all, Browning is a true poet—[...] and if any critics *have*, as your critical friend wrote to you, 'flattered him into a wilderness & left him' they left him alone with his *genius* [...] the genius—the genius—it is undeniable—

All this adds up to a startling resurrection. Best of all, at long last Elizabeth is to leave Torquay. After the usual to and fro – 'Delay—delay— delay!—[...] We cant go on at all without stopping short' – Papa finally lets her chose where she wants to live and, desperate not to spend another winter in Devon, she decides to gamble on coming back to London – and by road. After all, the special 'patent' carriage her father has ordered – he will join the travellers himself at Exeter – has a bed in it, 'and its springs are numberless'. Dr Scully has set a deadline for safe travel before the autumn closes in and so on 1 September Elizabeth, Arabella, Crow and Flush set out for home.

They arrive in Wimpole Street on the afternoon of 11 September 1841. It is 'the loosening of chains whose iron entered into the soul', a chance for Elizabeth to break with everything that has happened to her in Torquay: bereavement, depression, and three years of isolation and illness. 'It was the opening of the dungeon to the captive! I looked at the chimney pots & at the smoke-issuing of this London .. all I cd see from my bed .. with the sort of exaltation & half-incredulity with which you have looked at the Alps!' The patient is probably almost as frail as when she left London but, though still spitting a little blood, she seems to have shaken off her cough. As after the Gloucester interlude, at least some of her weakness must simply be the result of being kept virtually bedbound.

Only Flush has a bad beginning. He dislikes the Barrett men:

> and, what was rather worse, he thought it necessary (being a moralist
> & a traveller) to express his disapprobation most loudly & tumultu-
> ously—starting up, whether by night or day, everytime he heard a
> footstep, throwing himself upon my shoulder & barking like a pack
> of hounds […] I was in despair—not so much for myself as for Papa
> who is not perhaps very particularly fond of dogs & most particu-
> larly, of silence.

Luckily, he calms down before Papa can ban him and decides that, like
his mistress, 'He likes London, he says, very much indeed.' And Elizabeth settles in to the delicious task of catching up with London literary
gossip. Less than a fortnight after her arrival she's already up to speed,
and is filling in Miss Mitford on the marriage breakdown suffered by
Poet Laureate Robert Southey. As 1841 ends, Elizabeth is retrieving the
central part of herself.

[*Tain*]

The *tain* of a mirror is the obstruction – traditionally a silvering – that stops the glass giving you a clear view through to the other side, and instead throws you back your own reflection. We could say that the obstruction in a two-way hospital mirror is the secrecy in which the people on one side of the glass – the staff – keep themselves in order not to be seen by the people on the other side.

The staff on the dark side of the two-way mirror can't see their own selves at all. For them, unlike for the people they're studying, there is no reflection, only observation. When I worked in mental healthcare units I particularly disliked using these mirrors. If a gaze must be met in order for us to encounter another person, I used to wonder, how on earth can we get to know them while we're hiding behind blacked-out glass?

From the staff side of the glass I could see the people I'd just been working with, in the room I'd just left, as clearly as if they were on stage. Yet they weren't acting. Actors direct their actions towards us as we sit in the darkness beyond the fourth wall of the footlights; the two-way mirror claimed paradoxically to prevent this happening. Actors consent to our sitting there in the dark; the two-way mirror did not feel consensual. On the contrary, it seemed to break the carefully worked-out group contract in which everyone was involved in an equal level of self-disclosure and what went on inside the group room stayed inside the group room. I felt I was failing the group, that I was a cheat, a voyeur, because they couldn't see me watching them.

What made it worse was that I was getting the people in the room to write poetry, that intimate gesture of self-disclosure and trust. The power of the lyric tradition comes from the way it explodes the distinction between the poet and her reader, the poem and its auditor, often using the first person singular as a kind of collective pronoun; a shared viewpoint. *I* says the poem, stepping forward to speak on behalf of us all.

That's a huge risk for the poet to take, because who *is* to speak for everyone? In the mid-nineteenth century Elizabeth Barrett Browning took this risk by writing and publishing as a woman. She exposed herself to misunderstanding, criticism and ridicule. In the day room, group members were taking a risk by writing as the repeatedly marginalised individuals many of them were; exposing themselves and their writing to being thought of as symptomatic cases, not poets.

What could possibly make up for this? In writing about Elizabeth I feel as though I'm at her service, just as I used to feel I was at the service of my hospital writers. I used to picture myself as a tabula rasa, the blank page for them to write on. Of course, that wasn't true. I was bringing all sorts of things into the group room with me: I just couldn't *see myself* when I was in there. The odd paradox I had slowly to learn was that, far from being self-indulgent, self-examination made me more useful to the group members. Which is true of biography, too. However hard we think about Elizabeth, we only know what we *can* know about her. I may be at my subject's service, but she herself is not here.

Book Six:
How to be dutiful

*'Male poets are preferable, straining less
And telling more.'* – LADY WALDEMAR

When Elizabeth shuts the door to her 'little slip of sitting room', she shuts out much of the imperfect world. Those she loves and depends on come in and out, of course: Crow, Flush, Papa, her brothers and sisters. But the battle of wills over who can stay with her is finished. No more wheedling and bribing: no more ponies or riding habits. Above all nobody to be responsible for, as she feels she was responsible for Bro's presence, and death, in Torquay. At thirty-six Elizabeth has absolutely no longing for a household of her own, like the one Mary Russell Mitford struggles to maintain.

Her unexpected recovery from the near-fatal illness which followed those catastrophic losses at Torquay has left her grateful for much less than her child self would have settled for. Actual domestic comfort and care replace dreams of Balkan adventure; settled family life frees her to write. And so she has every reason to be complicit in Papa's increasingly apparent desire to keep his children close. Her surviving brothers are busy working – Charles away in Jamaica, George as a barrister – travelling (in Henry's case), or studying: Sette to become a barrister, Occy an architect.

Her sisters have a home to run. Only Elizabeth, set aside by illness, is uniquely free to do as she wishes. It turns out that 'the duties belonging to my femineity' don't even include sewing. 'You can scarcely imagine, my awkwardness when I pretent to work! Such pricking of fingers, & knotting of thread, & sowing backwards in certain evolutions, instead of forwards!'

The busy household beyond her door blurs to a consoling thrum she's known since childhood. 'Domestic love only seemed to buzz gently around, like the bees about the grass', as she later puts it. Besides, through the imagined worlds of poetry Elizabeth not only escapes but feels she transcends the slight dullness of daily life. It's small wonder her recent work has tended to revisit that 'sacred song with a devotional ecstacy' which *The Athenaeum* noted of *The Seraphim*. The way this poetry turns repeatedly from the often burdensome embodied self to an uplift of spiritual feeling can seem awkward and dated to the twenty-first-century reader; for the women who's doing it, it is an act of will, a lift-off from life.

At the same time she can't deny the highly material facts of living in Wimpole Street, at the heart of one of London's smartest residential districts. The capital surrounds her with its rattle and hum. Writing friends surround her too. Suddenly easily accessible, she no longer needs to cook up projects like the ill-fated *Psyche Apocalypté* in order to keep in touch. They can visit. If ill-health prevents her from visiting in return – well, that's a useful fig leaf for the twin obstacles of Papa's protectiveness and her own shyness. And the writing world seems to scent out this new proximity, as if simply being in London makes her altogether more real. Predictably, Mary Russell Mitford is among the first to visit, just six weeks after Elizabeth's return, staying in Wimpole Street for two nights at the end of October 1841. The two enjoy a good catch-up – though disappointingly without Flush senior, who wasn't allowed on the train: 'How uncivilized the world is still!'

Miss Mitford's friendship and support, including annual commissions for *Findens' Tableaux*, has almost exclusively sustained Elizabeth's writing through her Torquay exile. But now, as that writing continues to develop, Elizabeth begins to spread her wings by almost imperceptible degrees beyond this loving mentorship. By autumn 1841 the success of

The Seraphim is established fact and, three years on from its appearance, Elizabeth is beginning to receive substantial commissions. *The Athenaeum* has published a couple of her poems and now its energetic and literary-minded editor Charles Wentworth Dilke agrees her pitch for a feature on Greek Christian poets, '(only begging me to keep away from *theology* —) & suggesting a subsequent reviewal of English poetical literature, from Chaucer down to our times', as she tells Mr Boyd, who remains willy-nilly her go-to for things classical. The resulting long essay is published in three parts in February and March 1842, and it is followed between June and August by a five-part survey of English verse, which Elizabeth titles 'The Book of the Poets'.

The 'Book' is, she realises, a crack at canon forming, and in an influential publication too. So she takes it seriously. The ideal anthology she pictures excludes more drama, but includes more religious poetry, than its predecessors. She manages to slip in a vignette of 'Robert' (today usually held to be 'William') Langland, mediaeval author of *Piers Plowman*, as a Malvern poet, which allows her to claim her own home ground at Hope End as the birthplace of English poetry:

> It is well for thinkers of England to remember reverently, while, taking thought of her poetry, they stand among the gorse,—that if we may boast now of more honoured localities, of Shakespeare's 'rocky Avon,' and Spenser's 'soft-streaming Thames,' and Wordsworth's 'Rydal Mere,' still our first holy poet-ground is there.

After this glimpse of personal foundation myth, Elizabeth goes on to outline a pantheon built from a tripod of Geoffrey Chaucer (Dilke's parameter), William Shakespeare (of course), and the currently unfashionable William Wordsworth. She mounts a spirited, *ad hominem* defence of the seventy-two-year-old, not yet Poet Laureate, whose masterpiece *The Prelude* will remain unknown until it is posthumously published eight years from now. Along the way she names Alfred Tennyson and Robert Browning as coming men, arguing that too many poets:

> do not live by their truth, but hold back their full strength from Art because they do not *reverence* it fully; and all booksellers cry aloud [...] that poetry will not sell; and certain critics utter melancholy

frenzies, that poetry is worn out for ever [...] In the meantime [...] the Tennysons and the Brownings, and other high-gifted spirits, will work, wait on.

By contrast, her vision of the 'heroic life of poetic duty', which she elides with the figure of Wordworth, has an almost Revivalist fervour:

the long life's work for its sake—the work of observation, of meditation, of reaching past models into nature, of reaching past nature unto God; and the early life's loss for its sake—the loss of the popular cheer, of the critical assent, and of the 'money in the purse'.

Critical intelligence, however idealistic, needs to keep engaging. Elizabeth's next piece for *The Athenaeum*, at the end of August, is a review of Wordsworth's *Poems, Chiefly of Early and Late Years*. The book's publisher is Edward Moxon, a driven, ambitious editor who's also recently published Mary Shelley's first posthumous *Poems* of Percy Bysshe Shelley (the swiftly withdrawn 1839 edition), Alfred Tennyson's reputation-making *Poems* of 1842, and Robert Browning's *Sordello* (1840), as well as a series of leading dramatists. He is, in short, the publisher of choice, and by the end of the year Elizabeth is proposing a volume of her own poems to him. Or rather, she sends her brother George to intercede on her behalf.

The meeting doesn't go well. 'No—Moxon wont have my poems', Elizabeth tells Miss Mitford. This is a rude awakening. She'd been planning to collect her 'fugitive poetry to make a volume' that might ensure a positive reception for the long poem she wants to work on next. But the business-like editor:

'did protest' like a bookseller, his 'respect for Miss Barrett's genius,'— the only drawback being that he preferred having nothing to do with her. He said that he happened to be personally connected with several poets, & from mere personal motives had been drawn in to publish their poems—that they did not sell .. [...] that Mr Tennyson's sold the best—indeed he might almost say that his last volume had succeeded —that Wordsworth's were only beginning to sell.

When Moxon changes his mind the following spring Elizabeth will be delighted, though it's really only editorial common sense: her poetry is appearing regularly in all the right places. But his acceptance will arrive via John Kenyon, who had expressed surprise at the initial brush-off, suggesting that her old friend may have had once again to be her advocate.

It also suggests that, however modern his literary tastes, Moxon is capable of old-fashioned gender prejudice. After all, it's not just illness that stops Elizabeth going out and about to literary launches, opening nights, and dinners; from schmoozing, in short, like the other leading poets of what's becoming her writing generation, Tennyson and Browning among them. It's also that she's a woman. She has to make her relationships on the page. In October 1842 the painter Benjamin Robert Haydon, a new friend Miss Mitford has introduced by letter, lends Elizabeth his just-completed portrait of 'Wordsworth on Helvellyn'. At just over three foot by four foot, the striking canvas is nearly life-size; it portrays the old man with arms crossed, deep in thought, a pose both heroic and reflective (though apparently the old man kept nodding off during the actual sitting). Small wonder: this is the painter's homage to Wordsworth's 1840 sonnet, 'On a portrait of the Duke of Wellington on the Field of Waterloo, by Haydon', which itself responds to Haydon's 1839 canvas 'Wellington musing on the Field of Waterloo' in which the Duke takes up a not dissimilar stance, his back to us but craggy profile visible, gazing out over a dramatically lit landscape. Elizabeth, having herself already framed Wordsworth as a poet-hero in her *Athenaeum* essay, sends Haydon a sonnet of her own, 'On a Portrait of Wordsworth by B. R. Haydon', on 17 October. It appears in *The Athenauem* less than a fortnight later.

Elizabeth tells the artist, 'You have brought me Wordsworth & Helvellyn into this dark & solitary room.' Yet she refuses to meet him, remaining to his frustration, 'My dear Invisible Friend [...] always to correspond & [...] never to descend to the Vulgarity of speaking.' She's still exasperatingly susceptible to a self-harming shyness. But everything's different on paper, a world she can control. Perhaps that's one reason that she's so interested in America, still a place almost entirely of the imagination for most Britons. (Another reason may well be that the Barretts are among the few for whom family life also goes on across the Atlantic.) When the *New-York Daily Tribune* and the *New-York Weekly Tribune* reprint her Haydon sonnet, it jump-starts her reputation there.

She begins to appear repeatedly in *The Boston Miscellany* and *The United States Magazine and Democratic Review*.

Mid-century, North America still has an exaggerated postcolonial respect for British writers. But Elizabeth is also repeatedly published by *Graham's Magazine*, which is edited by Cornelius Mathews, a young New York-based activist for a home-grown literature. In 1845 Mathews will explicitly align himself with anti-aristocratic Young America politics, named in part after the Young Italy movement (of which Elizabeth will herself become a passionate advocate, even a kind of celebrity supporter). Young America, based largely in the cities of the north, will be pro-immigration and in favour of rights for all, free trade, and international republicanism; making it a more radical version of the British Whig thought espoused by the Barretts.

But in 1842 Mathews is still working with colleagues to create the North American literary culture that will enable the careers of George Bancroft, Nathaniel Hawthorne, Herman Melville and others. Elizabeth's poetry is welcomed in these circles, despite her nationality, because she shares their political and poetic ideas. To American peers her writing is fresh and modern. And Elizabeth, ever the idealist, responds to both political appeal and personal friendship. Mathews, eleven years her junior, is perhaps her ideal correspondent, safely on the other side of the Atlantic and unlikely to drop in unannounced. She praises his writing's 'vital sinewy vigour' in print; and tells James Russell Lowell, another member of his circle, 'I love the Americans & America for the sake of national brotherhood & a common literature & I honor them for the sake of liberty & noble aspiration—& I am grateful to them, .. very grateful, .. for their kindness to me personally as a poet.'

For despite her growing international reputation, as 1844 opens Elizabeth is feeling isolated in the 'dark and solitary room' where her most frequent companion is her maid: she claims a '"fine madness" for turning servants into friends'. Traces remain of depressive guilt about Bro's death, that 'Bitter anguish of bestowing evil, unmitigated evil, where you wd only cause good'. She's also suffering from chronic pain, and has begun corresponding with fellow-Northumbrian Harriet Martineau, the distinguished feminist social theorist who in the same year publishes her autobiographical collection of essays, *Life in the Sickroom: Essays by an Invalid*. Also housebound, and suffering from what's believed to be an incurable uterine tumour, Martineau is one of the few able to understand how Elizabeth feels *physically*:

> How entirely I agree with you about severe pain!—about its lowering & perverting influences! Nobody who ever was familiar with very severe pain cd say the good of it that one sees said in books. How it does baffle one's will! […] Your picture of yourself *looks* cheerful & pretty; but I am not one to be deceived by your religious cheerfulness into an oversight of the suffering wh. lies beneath.

The women, who moreover share a free-thinking religious Noncon-formism, discuss a topic of absorbing interest to them both: mesmerism – hypnotherapy – and its possible use as a cure for physical illness. In November, Martineau, apparently miraculously cured of years of suffering, will publish a controversial series of letters in *The Athenaeum* advocating it as a cure. Though Elizabeth experiences no such radical improvement, she remains longingly enthusiastic about this and all things supernatural, and will support her friend in the face of widespread public scepticism.

At times, she even seems to float into a psychological twilight. In her room, drawn blinds and insomnia blur the difference between dream-like days and nights, and colour her imagination: 'I dare to perceive or imagine the grandeur of spiritual subjects—spirits & angels—spreading their faint shadowless glories over a vast surface.' She's still taking opium, ostensibly for difficulty sleeping – it's likely the dose was increased in Torquay – and admits to Martineau that it produces 'fairy visions'. Since her return home there's been a distinctly opiate flavour to her at times near-daily correspondence with Miss Mitford, with its disinhibited self-disclosure and obsessional working over of details. Besides, not all her visions are 'fairy'. Fretting over John Kenyon – who for weeks exchanges visits with the rest of the family while somehow failing to make it to her own room – Elizabeth worries about possible scandal in his private life, and is yet more concerned by his plan to buy a villa in Torquay, which she depicts as locked in a grotesque *danse macabre*:

> There is not such a dancing, fiddling cardplaying gossiping place

in all the rest of England as Torquay is—there is not such a dissipated place, in the strongest sense. And it's a ghastly merriment. Almost every family has a member either threatened with illness or ill. Whoever is merry, is so in a hospital. They carry away the dead, to take in benches for the company. [...] [T]he ghastliness of the collision there between life & death, merriment & wailing [...] has made my flesh creep sometimes. [...] A woman in the last agony in one house—a corpse laid out in another—& the whole of surviving Torquay dancing intermediately!

Since her return to Wimpole Street, an odd mixture of superstition and religious mysticism, 'Mr Haydon's mystical way of talking of the "poetry of dark"', has started to overtake the appeal of transcendence:

I have recognized again & again the charm of the mystical which is in fact the voice of our own souls calling to us thro' the dark of our ignorance [...] listening to those rustling sounds of what may be verities, beyond the shell of the body.

This highly active imagination is badly in need of an outlet. Elizabeth starts to contemplate a long narrative poem. Yet here too her mind turns first to Napoleon but then to Joan of Arc and, 'I turn myself wistfully towards Joan. Perhaps my original sin of mysticism is struggling towards her visions', she tells Miss Mitford, 'My belief is that she was *true*.' She goes on, 'Did you ever hear of Stilling, the German's, book upon Pneumatology? [...] you & I—believe everything—and Heinrich Stilling wants us to believe more than everything—.' For some weeks she fixates on this work arguing for the existence of a spirit world, Johann Heinrich Jung-Stilling's *Theory of Pneumatology*, loaning her own copy first to Miss Mitford, and then to Miss Mitford's friend Mrs Niven.

Not surprisingly, the poems she's currently writing increasingly explore this new territory. In 'Rhapsody of Life's Progress',

We are borne into life—it is sweet, it is strange.
We lie still on the knee of a mild Mystery.

Despite all this, Elizabeth's actual poetic voice is becoming steadily clearer and fresher. Gone are the contorted pseudo-Greek metrics, replaced in poems like 'Wine of Cyprus' and 'A Lay of the Early Rose' by newly fashionable ballad and song forms familiar from popular culture. More modern still is her use of her female narrators. Of course, women as protagonists in verse – from Penelope in Homer's *Odyssey* to Geoffrey Chaucer's fourteenth-century 'The Wife of Bath' or, two centuries later, Edmund Spenser's *The Faerie Queene* – are nothing new. But the female lyric voice is a radical departure. Lyric poetry's persona is necessarily both personal and universal: when I read a poem, I step into that poem's 'I'. Creating an illusion of plunging into intimacy with the female psyche, Elizabeth's new narrative poems are 'spoken' by women characters, like the lover of the great sixteenth-century Portuguese poet Luís de Camões ('Catarina to Camoens') or the eponymous 'Bertha in the Lane', whose stories highlight the *female* identity of their 'voice', and of the poet's voice too: after all, they aren't being ventriloquised by male poets. And of course sometimes she also simply writes in the female first person without 'dressing up' in character.

In the twenty-first-century none of this is new. We've seen the female lyric *I* be prayerful with Emily Dickinson, self-flagellating with Sylvia Plath, witness to history with Anna Akhmatova. But radical writers change their own *zeitgeist*, not ours. Or rather: they already changed ours, back when they changed their own. In the 1840s, when none of these poets has yet started work, Elizabeth's voice is radical and exciting. And without the changes she's effecting, none of their poetry might have been written.

Led by description and story, the newly narrative verse that she and fellow poets like Tennyson and Browning are writing is freshly founded in the lived world of interpersonal experience. These innovative Victorian fables in verse aren't only more emotionally and intellectually accessible than Romantic poetry, they're also a great deal more respectable. Lord Byron's narrative epics, *Childe Harold's Pilgrimage* and *Don Juan*, turned him into an international literary celebrity in the early decades of the century; but neither is exactly suitable matter for the new domestic habits that see reading aloud become family entertainment. Elizabeth's mid-century generation are making poetry accessible to a society being rapidly reshaped by the 'family values' the new queen has brought to public life since her accession in 1837. And so, as Moxon publishes Elizabeth's *Poems*

(1844), and she returns to planning the verse novel that will become *Aurora Leigh*, she specifically envisages a cleaned-up *Don Juan* to 'touch this real everyday life of our age, & hold it with my two hands':

> I want to write a poem of a new class, in a measure—a Don Juan, without the mockery & impurity [...]—& admitting of as much philosophical dreaming & digression (which is in fact a characteristic of the age) as I like to use.

Being 'characteristic of the age' is a form of social responsibility. Reading is no longer a hobby only of the elite. Literacy is slowly increasing as primary-level education for all gradually turns into first a church and then a state concern. In April of this year, at a private prayer meeting on Grays Inn Road, four ordinary Londoners create the Ragged School Union which, chaired by the 7th Earl of Shaftesbury, will found more than two hundred schools for destitute children over the next eight years – including some that Arabella will dedicate herself to. And so, although what Richard Hoggart a century from now will call the 'massification' of (pulp, tabloid) reading matter that shapes working-class culture is still in the future, fiction and poetry are beginning to find mass audiences. Charles Dickens, for example, though six years younger than Elizabeth, is already enjoying huge popular success and royal approval.

Writing for this emerging readership doesn't mean dumbing down. But it works best when mainstream values are genuinely shared. Elizabeth and her poetic peers are thoroughgoing Victorians in turning their back on the Romantic vision of poets as prophetic exceptions, Shelley's 'unacknowledged legislators of the world'. Instead, they view poetry as speaking to the special, quasi-spiritual, part of *every* individual, 'reaching past nature unto God', as Elizabeth put it in *The Athenaeum*. Poetry is still exceptional, but it plays its special part within *each* life. The democratising, flattening effect of this has more than a little in common with the congregational, Nonconformist Christianity that the Barretts by now thoroughly espouse.

As a result, Elizabeth and the poets like her are explicitly trying to give their everyman and everywoman reader a taste of beauty. (There are some striking parallels with how, at the 'other end' of the religious revival, Victorian High Anglicanism is using liturgical 'smells and bells', or extravagantly ornamented new builds by Gothic Revivalist prodigy Augustus Pugin, to draw in worshippers.) In both verse and prose, this is the era of the adjective. Poetry flirts with glamorously evocative settings, some orientalising, others historical. Elizabeth draws all these vibrating strings simultaneously tight in poems like 'The Lay of the Brown Rosary' where – in a perfect storm of symbolism and purple prosody – the haunted bride Onora fatally embraces her groom in a ruined chapel somewhere that's both foreign and Roman Catholic; ethics having got muddled up with the old Barrett anti-Catholicism:

> The grey owl on the ruined wall shut both his eyes to hide thee,
> And ever he flapped his heavy wing all brokenly and weak,
> And the long grass waved against the sky, around his gasping beak.
> I sate beside thee all the night, while the moonlight lay forlorn
> Strewn round us like a dead world's shroud in ghastly fragments torn.

Elsewhere, the new poetry preaches an explicitly social morality, licensing such fantasies by tying up scenes of sensual bliss with moral closure. Until its austere conclusion that, 'KNOWLEDGE BY SUFFERING ENTERETH, / AND LIFE IS PERFECTED BY DEATH', Elizabeth's own 'A Vision of Poets' is vividly sensual as it pictures the archetypal living poet. Sometimes, though, the moral is 'slant'. As raw economic 'progress' is slowly recognised as a source of social ills, romantic nostalgic – whether it's in Tennyson's 'The Lady of Shalott' or in Elizabeth's 'The Romaunt of the Page' – offers a comforting counter-fantasy. Precisely through its quaint mediaevalisms and far-flung settings, such poetry turns towards the changing society it serves, as even Elizabeth, writing among her plaster busts of the dead greats, is aware. After all, she is herself a daughter of the new mercantile class. And while there's nothing like London life for keeping you in the literary swim, there's also nothing like London for reminding you of the wider society on your doorstep.

Wimpole Street is smart, but it's no gated community. On 13 September 1843 Crow arrives home in floods of tears from walking Flush. Trotting loose behind her in busy Mortimer Street, a few blocks from home, the little dog has been pounced on and stolen. All the maid knows is that she heard his stranger-alarm bark, and when she turned round he had vanished. Elizabeth is distraught and, while she sobs herself into a fever, the three boys still at home – Sette, Alfred and Henry – get on the case. They have 'Missing' notices printed up within hours, and post them up all round the neighbourhood the same day. But there's no news, and Elizabeth passes a sleepless night.

The next day, however, the brothers make some more worldly-wise enquiries. It quickly becomes clear that they're dealing with organised crime. Sette meets 'dark men in dark alleys; & [derives] a fallacious hope from the ultra blackguardism of a certain Jim Green who talked pure Alsatian [a term for thieves' slang], & was just setting out for a dog-fight to meet "lots of dogstealers"'. Having barristers in the family is useful for tracing underworld contacts, and the correct intermediary turns out to be a gunmaker in New Bond Street. William Bishop 'is said to be "a highly respectable man", & keeps a petition against dogstealers in general' – something surely helpful for thieves looking for animals to steal. Nevertheless, he puts Alfred in touch with a *soi-disant* cobbler named Taylor. Taylor is the leader of The Fancy, a gang who kidnap the pets of the rich and 'who make four thousand a year by the trade'. He's already stolen 'Mrs Chichester's little black dog' from next door to the Barretts, and established the going rate for ransoming *feelings* is 'five pounds down'. He even announces to Henry that his gang have been 'two years on the watch for Flush'.

On the second evening of the emergency, Taylor arrives at number 50 while the family (apart, as usual, from Elizabeth) are sitting down to dinner. He claims to have 'found' Flush: for five pounds he will take Alfred to the dog. Unfortunately, Alfred knows Elizabeth has only two sovereigns to hand. Worse, Papa, overhearing the bargaining, storms into the hallway yelling that the family will 'not give a farthing more than two sovereigns', and that Taylor and the dog can go to hell. 'Papa said, "Say nothing of this to Ba"—but the voices were loud.' Upstairs in her little room, Elizabeth passes another sleepless night. But in the morning, once her father has left home on business, she sends the other three sovereigns to William Bishop's. It's enough to raise Taylor, who turns up again at Wimpole Street to demand a final half-sovereign and to agree a rendezvous with Henry that evening at the gun shop where, sure enough, Flush is waiting. Henry brings him home by cab.

The little dog is filthy and traumatised after two and a half days without food or water, but he turns out to have suffered no long-term ill effects. Almost as good, when Papa arrives home that evening, rather than interrogating the family about what he knows perfectly well must have happened, he is delighted. For this weak, anxious man the dual problem – of his favourite daughter losing her pet, and of having backed himself into a non-negotiable position – has been solved for him. Worldly-wise Henry had even arranged to be followed by a plain-clothed officer who would arrest Taylor the moment he had Flush; though this plan was foiled when the policeman got the time wrong. All in all, it's a joyous reunion, and when Taylor's gang steal Flush again, a year later, in October 1844, the Barrett siblings will swing into confident action, recovering him within forty-eight hours without letting their father know – although the ransom will have risen to seven pounds.

By then, though, the intimates of his doggy world will have changed. For in the middle of March 1844 Crow announces that she is leaving. She has married the Wimpole Street butler, William Treherne, a familiar face who's been with the family all his life – since his father was a Hope End tenant farmer – and who's risen from stable boy to head of the household servants. 'Quite above all aspersion', and 'honest, & good in the common way,' he's also 'a handsome young man, as perhaps you have observed,' Elizabeth comments, perhaps tartly, to Miss Mitford. But servants are expected to be unmarried and Elizabeth Treherne, as she now is, wed in secret at the end of 1843. More, she was already three months pregnant on her wedding day. Now the wedding is confessed – but not the preg-nancy – and Treherne leaves immediately upon this announcement to set up a bakery, which the Barretts promise to patronise, at a new home in Camden Town. Meanwhile 'Crow', as Elizabeth can't stop calling her, works out a protracted leave. She's already six months pregnant. In May, entering her eighth month, and on top of working the early hours of a bakery shift, she continues to walk the miles between Camden and Wimpole Street as part of a very gradual handover.

Which may in part express her own ambivalence. It's a shock to have to leave home and an absorbing, secure job just because you've married, especially as this was a shotgun wedding which left no time to prepare emotionally. Besides, pregnancy hormones keep the young mother-to-be emotional. She weeps copiously. Hers has been a demanding role. Elizabeth is always at home, has few other companions, and is never far from being bedbound. But nursing her successfully through a series of crises has made the two women's relationship unusually human. It has the intensity of absolute dependency on Elizabeth's side, while for Crow, a bright, opinionated woman, it has been an opportunity to access ideas and the books that Elizabeth lends or reads aloud to her – although this is probably less flattering than it seems, since Elizabeth also reads aloud to Flush and even tries to teach him to read.

To prevent her mistress getting worked up, Crow's final day passes unannounced, and 25 April 1844 is full of glorious chaos anyway, as Miss Mitford at last brings Flush senior to visit Elizabeth and Flush junior. But Elizabeth is upset all the same. She picks at the secrecy surrounding Crow's marriage, even though she must understand perfectly well that it's essential for people in service to get arrangements in place *before* they're dismissed into the world with no means of support. But if Crow ever had contemplated confiding in her, witnessing what happened when Miss Mitford's maid and groom got into a similar scrape at the start of this year would have put her off. Elizabeth's overreaction was the *cri de coeur* of someone who desperately wants those she has most to do with to *love* her:

> of the want of chastity,—I say nothing at all. I even can conceive of the chastest of women sacrificing her reputation to the love of one man. [...] But the train of deception [...] is a different matter—& the more I think of the *heart*, which could [...] so plot on, plot on, .. the wedding ring on the finger & the lover behind the door.

After the wedding ring is on Elizabeth Crow's finger, her successor, a fellow northerner, is chosen. Elizabeth Wilson has arrived from Northumberland in service to Susanna Maria, a Barrett cousin by marriage who's staying at Wimpole Street because her husband, Samuel Goodin Barrett, is in danger of arrest over another contested will. Henrietta, seeing someone 'gentle-voiced, & of a bright & kind countenance', responds to the emergency of Crow's departure by poaching Wilson on her sister's behalf. Elizabeth herself is a little less fulsome, though her reservations will prove unfounded: 'Very willing, very anxious, .. almost too anxious!

very gentle, .. almost too gentle! a little failing in the vivacity & cheerfulness I like about me. I am afraid I shall never like her as well as Crow.'

At which juncture we must pause to accuse one of these young women – Crow? Or Wilson? – over the development of Elizabeth's signature hairdo. In the 1840s barley curls, long vertical ringlets hanging over the ears, move from the nursery to the heads of grown women. So half of Elizabeth's hair is massed in a chignon low down at the nape of her neck, while the rest hangs in thick, dark curls either side of her face. It's a tumbling, girlish look, flattering to a woman in her late thirties who wishes to hide somewhat behind her coiffure. Its cheek-hugging also echoes the lacy side panels of invalid bonnets: perhaps Elizabeth finds the familiar feeling comforting. Unfortunately, though, while fashions continue to change, her hairstyle will not. By the time she's in her fifties it will long have ceased to be flattering, and will have come to look, if anything, like a homage to Flush.

In 1844 however, barley curls *are* fashionable. And so is Elizabeth herself, as a new collection of her work enjoys literary success. Edward Moxon publishes *Poems* on 13 August 1844, and this time the reviews are still more numerous and enthusiastic. She receives substantial coverage in sixteen British periodicals. Moxon's offprints are published simultaneously in New York by Henry G. Langley, who gives the book the title of its long opening poem, 'A Drama of Exile'. The young country is sensitive enough about its relationship with Britain for *The United States Magazine and Democratic Review* to quote from Elizabeth's dedication:

'My love and admiration have belonged to the great American people,' these are memorable words on the lips of Elizabeth Barrett [...] America is not marble nor stone that she should be insensible to a good will so earnest and true!

Other American reviews appear in *The Atlas*, *The Knickerbocker*, and *Godey's Lady's Book* – and in the 7 December issue of *Evening Mirror*, where a short piece thought to have been written by Edgar Allan Poe concludes: 'We do not believe that there is a poetical soul embodied in this world that [...] sees further out, toward the periphery permitted to angels, than Miss Barrett. Yet you would get a verdict of insanity upon her from any jury in Christendom.' This oddly mixed message comes from the same pen as an anonymous front-page rave a couple of months earlier:

> There will doubtless be criticism by Lowell and Poe—[...] of a certain new book, just published by the Langleys. It is, (as to style merely,) Tennyson, out-Tennysoned,—the last strain and tension of peculiarity and surprise—but withal brimfull of genius [...] Mrs. Barrett is worth a dozen of Tennyson, and six of Motherwell—equal perhaps in original genius to Keats and Shelley. We wish we knew more of her.

Poe, a complex individual with a reputation for invention of all kinds, may merely be trying to stoke literary controversy. But positioning Elizabeth's poetry *is* important. Something new is going on. Back in London, *The Spectator* makes its intelligent attempt in the month the book appears:

> Miss Barrett is of the school to which MR COVENTRY PATMORE belongs, but with a happier choice in the selection of her subjects, more of skill in the use of her materials, a healthier moral tone, and less affectation, unless in her style and the occasional choice of her meter. [...] The author whom MISS BARRETT immediately resembles is TENNYSON.

The piece goes on astutely to ascribe to her something close to the Picturesque culture with which she grew up:

> representing things not as they really are, or as they are supposed to be, but with a peculiarity derived from the writer's mind [her poems] excel in a species of quaint description, which is sometimes more effective than a natural style.

Other British reviews compare Elizabeth to Milton, Keats, Coleridge, Byron and Wordsworth. She's being read against the entire English canon as well as against her peers. Yet still she remains a special case, set apart by gender. 'We have no hesitation in saying that among the female poets of the day, MISS BARRETT stands at the head', pronounces *The Atlas*. Worse, in *Blackwood's*, Scottish metaphysician James Ferrier raps her over the knuckles for aspiring to the literary at all:

> If she will but wash her hands completely of Aeschylus and Milton,

and all other poets, […] and come before the public in the graces of her own feminine sensibilities […] her sway over human hearts will be more irresistible than ever, and she will have nothing to fear from a comparison with the most gifted and industrious of her sex.

Luckily, less antediluvian readers are to be found among her peers, the young poets who are giving each other a run for their money. A year ago John Kenyon let Elizabeth know that Robert Browning admired her poem 'The Dead Pan'. When *Poems* appears, Browning is travelling in Italy; he left London the day before it was published. But on 10 January 1845, after he's been home for just over a month, he reads a copy which Kenyon has sent to New Cross and writes to congratulate Elizabeth.

The letter he sends this short, dark winter day is an intimate expression of poetic kinship. Its 'Aha!' of recognising someone he's never seen through her words alone is the basis for everything that follows. That feeling might be asexual, but his language is intemperate:

I love your verses with all my heart, dear Miss Barrett,— […] I]nto me has it gone, and part of me has it become, this great living poetry of yours, not a flower of which but took root and grew. I can give a reason for my faith in one and another excellence, the fresh strange music, the affluent language, the exquisite pathos and true new brave thought—but in this addressing myself to you, your own self, and for the first time, my feeling rises altogether. I do, as I say, love these Books with all my heart—and I love you too.

For Elizabeth, no other kind of kinship could be more powerful. Her Preface to *Poems* restated how deeply personal her passion for poetry is:

Poetry has been as serious a thing to me as life itself; and life has been a very serious thing […] I never mistook pleasure for the final cause of poetry […] I have done my work […]—not as mere hand and head work, apart from the personal being,—but as the completest expression of that being to which I could attain.

Robert's letter makes clear that he's interested in her as a person too:

Do you know I was once not very far from seeing .. really seeing you? Mr Kenyon said to me one morning 'would you like to see

Miss Barrett?'—then he went to announce me,—then he returned ..
you were too unwell—and now it is years ago—and I feel as at some
untoward passage in my travels—as if I had been close, so close, to
some world's-wonder in chapel or crypt, ..

But it's his very first words that couldn't be better pitched to speak directly
to her poetic, which is to say her emotional, self. *I love your verses with
all my heart*: in fact he probably has her at *I love*. Eighteen months from
now, she will tell Robert that this word 'was a disguised angel & I should
have known it by its wings though they did not fly'. For, as she says to
Miss Mitford, quoting Percy Bysshe Shelley, 'Even when the object is not
poetry, "I love love."'

Elizabeth writes back to Robert the very next day, and her response
is perfectly pitched in turn to draw him in. She asks him to critique her
work: a lead none of her male correspondents has ever refused. And while
drawing back within the shelter of propriety she carefully chooses words
that mirror his own:

> I thank you, dear Mr Browning, from the bottom of my heart. [...]
> Such a letter from such a hand! Sympathy is dear—very dear to me:
> but the sympathy of a poet & of such a poet, is the quintessence of
> sympathy to me!

And though she havers, she finds herself, exceptionally, at least contemplating an actual meeting:

> Is it indeed true that I was so near to the pleasure & honour of
> making your acquaintance?—[...] I would rather hope (as I do) that
> what I lost by one chance I may recover by some future one. Winters
> shut me up as they do dormouse's eyes: in the spring, *we shall see*.

The next day is Sunday, so she has to calm her impatience for his response.
The wait is worth it. 'You make me very happy', Robert writes, on Monday
13 January, and he goes on to ask for her poetic companionship, even
guidance:

> your poetry must be, cannot but be, infinitely more to me than mine
> to you—for you *do* what I always wanted, hoped to do, and only seem
> now likely to do for the first time—you speak out, *you*, —I [...] fear

the pure white light, even if it is in me: but I am going to try .. so it will be no small comfort to have your company just now.

But Elizabeth doesn't hear the profound compliment in this. What she thinks is that she's being offered the worthy but tedious role of mentor. That fierce childhood shyness remains just as strong as the rest of her passionate nature. Immediately she retracts her suggest of meeting:

The fault was clearly with me & not with you.

When I had an Italian master, years ago, he told me that there was an unpronounceable English word which absolutely expressed me […] 'testa lunga.' Of course the signor meant *headlong!*—[…] Headlong I was at first, & headlong I continue—[…] guessing at the meaning of unknown words instead of looking into the diction- ary .. tearing open letters, & never untying a string,—& expecting everything to be done in a minute […]. And so, at your half word I flew at the whole one, with all its possible consequences, & wrote what you read.

In fact, hastiness has caused her to misread his *second* letter, not his first. Praising her poetry in terms of finding her own self present in it, Robert is finding a subtle way to keep open the possibility that he *is* inter- ested in that self – even though he can't know this, because the two have not yet met. He's just as idealistic as Elizabeth about poetry, and every bit as likely to fall in love through it. And, while protesting that he hates letter writing, he has already told her that she's the exception to this rule – and done so exquisitely, by quoting the epitaph to the great Renaissance poet Torquato Tasso, 'O *tu!*' – 'Ah, *you!*'

Now he waits a prideful fortnight before replying to Elizabeth's snip. These two weeks may also reflect a young man's self-absorption. For of course Robert *does* want this poet who has become a writerly touch- stone to help with his own poetry; but he doesn't seem nearly so eager to produce a detailed critique of hers. With charm and vagueness, when he does get in touch he tells her:

Your books lie on this table here, at arm's length from me, in this old room where I sit all day: and when my head aches or wanders or strikes work […] I […] read, read, read—and just as I have shut up the book and walked to the window, I recollect that you wanted me to find faults there.

Elizabeth manages to make herself wait a week before responding. She's struggling against powerful impulses, not just the draw of this particular correspondence. For her, letter writing is no chore: it's her social life: 'As for me, I have done most of my talking by the post of late years—'. Her response artfully coaches 'Dear Mr Browning' in the art of correspondence:

> Only *dont* let us have any constraint, any ceremony! *Dont* be civil to me when you feel rude,—nor loquacious, when you incline to silence,—nor yielding in the manners, when you are perverse in the mind. [...] .. & let us rest from the bowing & the curtseying, you & I, on each side. You will find me an honest man on the whole, if rather hasty & prejudging .. [...] And we have great sympathies in common, & I am inclined to look up to you in many things, & to learn as much of everything as you will teach me.

And so Robert realises that he has played it too cool. He writes back, after carefully observing the one-week rule:

> for reasons I know,—for other reasons I don't exactly know, but might if I chose to think a little, and for still other reasons, which, most likely, all the choosing and thinking in the world would not make me know, I had rather hear from you than see anybody else [...] Are not these fates written? There! Don't you answer this, please, but, mind it is on record.

Their *fates* are indeed *written*. When Robert posts this letter, on 11 February 1845, Elizabeth is about to turn thirty-nine, and established as one of the country's leading poets. Robert, six years her junior, is regarded as having lost his early gift, and his poetic way, with the rebarbative seven-part verse novel *Sordello*, published five years before. But reputational mismatch is balanced out by Elizabeth's loneliness, her gender – and something generous about her imagination. She has the ability to think the best of those she believes in, and believe she does in both Robert's attitude to poetry, and his 'genius' for it.

Right from the start she writes to him differently from the way she addresses Miss Mitford, hitherto her closest confidant beyond her sisters. It's as if there's no time to waste on gossip. She plunges straight into sharing her deepest self with Robert, telling him 'I am not desponding by nature', and that, 'I am *essentially better*, & have been for several winters', but 'a course of bitter mental discipline & long bodily seclusion' leaves her longing for life experience: 'If I live on & yet do not escape from this seclusion, do you not perceive that I labour under signal disadvantages .. that I am, in a manner, as a *blind poet*?' She seems unembarrassed to thus align herself with Homer – and Tiresias – rushing past the hubris with a pent-up frustration that leaps from every line:

> I have lived only inwardly [...] Before this seclusion of my illness, I was secluded still [...]. I grew up in the country .. had no social opportunities, .. had my heart in books & poetry, .. & my experience, in reveries. [...] And so time passed, & passed—and afterwards, when my illness came & I seemed to stand at the edge of the world with all done [...] I turned to thinking with some bitterness [...] that I had seen no Human nature [...] that I had beheld no great mountain or river—nothing in fact. [...] & it was too late!

In May, after four months and nearly thirty letters, Elizabeth finally lets Robert visit. The old social vertigo seems to have melted away. In the preceding weeks, as he starts to hint at meeting, she doesn't reject the idea. She even manages to restrain herself from rescheduling. It's almost as if being honest to him has forced her to be honest with herself about her longing 'for some experience of life & man, for some ...' – as she adds in a cheeky ellipsis.

So what does she expect at 3pm on 20 May 1845, as Wilson shows the visitor in? Kenyon has spoken 'warmly of his high cultivation & attainments, & singular humility of bearing', while also giving a some-what false impression that Robert suffers from ill health. Elizabeth already knows his long nose and youthful, vulnerable face framed by ample sideburns, the way he parts his hair to the side. She knows he's not handsome like that other rising young poet, Alfred Tennyson. She's had portraits of them both, along with matching engravings of Words-worth, Carlyle and Martineau, hanging on her walls for the last year. (Another link, though she doesn't yet know it, since all are taken from

A shoulder of Hope End parkland, 'Commanding the romantic scenery of the Malvern and the adjoining hills, with views… highly interesting and of great extent.'

The house Papa built: Hope End House in the mid-nineteenth century.

'I would give ten towns in Norfolk (if I had them) to own some purer lineage than that of the blood of the slave!—Cursed are we from generation to generation!' Cinnamon Hill Great House, Jamaica, where Ba's Papa was born.

Ba aged around eight with family pet Havannah in a drawing by Mamma.

At twelve, Ba displays 'an extraordinary genius... She has all the engenuous simplicity and airy volatility of spirits of the most sprightly of her age and sex,' according to the distinguished portraitist William Artaud, who paints her with Bro and Sam.

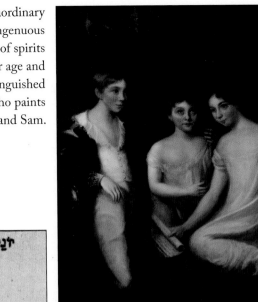

יוֹנַת אֵלֶם רְחֹקִים׃

This portrait of E.B.B was taken by *1821* her mother, – during the great illness, – and is given to me by Arabel. See also the faint outline on *R.B.* the otherside, which is even more like.

'The dove silenced in distant lands': Elizabeth, drawn by her mother, at the Gloucester Spa Hotel, where the fifteen-year-old is confined to a spinal sling and racked by spasms: 'The suffering is agony, and the paroxysms continue from a quarter of an hour to an hour and upwards.'

Daisy's watercolour of his sister with Flush, made a couple of years after Elizabeth's return from Torquay to the family home in Wimpole Street on 27 September 1843. This is the sofa in the foreground of the interior view at Casa Guidi.

Casa Guidi Windows:
'I heard last night a little
   child so singing
'Neath Casa Guidi windows,
   by the church,
O bella libertà, O bella!'

The Brownings' run of
first-floor windows and balcony
opposite the church.

'The sun strikes, through the windows, up the floor': view over the Wimpole
Street sofa through Casa Guidi from the extra room the Brownings rented when
Elizabeth was pregnant with what she hoped would be their second child.

Elizabeth and Robert in Florence in late 1853, in matching
portraits by Thomas Buchanan Read.

Via de Bocca di Leone,
in the fashionable
English quarter of Rome,
'which is considered
especially healthy'. The
Brownings' relatively
modest apartment was
on the third floor.

Elizabeth sits for Louis Cyrus Macaire and Jean Victor Macaire-Warnod in Le Havre on 17 September 1858, at the end of a tiring summer stay in the port. Understandably, this is not the image the Brownings chose for her publicity portrait.

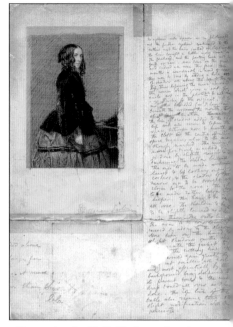

Engraving by T. O. Barlow after the most successful ambrotype from Elizabeth's Le Havre sitting. Dante Gabriel Rossetti has covered the proof with alteration notes for his celebrated portrait.

Elizabeth unedited. This photograph, by Elliott and Fry of London, is of a detail from the same Macaire brothers ambrotype that Rossetti used for his portrait.

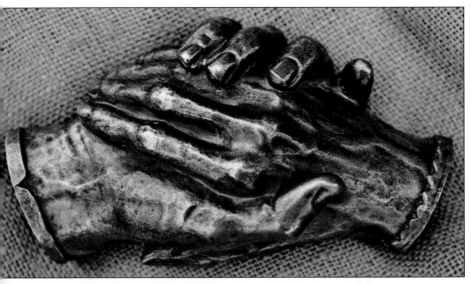

Elizabeth and Robert clasp hands in the seventh year of their marriage. A bronze cast in Rome by Harriet G. Hosmer.

At fifty-three, in this oil by Michele Gordigiani, the petite Mrs Browning has become heavy-set and looks at her most 'Portuguese'. Florence, July 1859.

Elizabeth and eleven-year-old Pen, photographed by Fratelli D'Alessandri in Rome in June 1860.

Elizabeth as a somewhat idealised fifty-four-year-old, drawn by Valentine Cameron Prinsep in Rome in February 1861.

Elizabeth a month before her death, photographed by Fratelli D'Alessandri in Rome on 27 May 1861.

Robert and Pen photographed by Constance Barclay on 14 November 1889, a fortnight before Robert died in his son's Venetian palazzo. By the time of this final trip to Italy he had been a widower for nearly three decades.

Horne's *A New Spirit of the Age*, to which both she and Robert have contributed.)

She puts Robert's portrait away for his visit. And the young man who steps into the room has a kindly, open, unformed appearance, the sort that invites confidences. His rather helpless, puppy-dog look is just the kind to draw out her protective side after a lifetime's lavishing of affection on younger brothers. Two years from now, in a comment in which jealousy is all but audible, and to which we'll return, Miss Mitford will describe the young Browning as emasculated: 'He resembled a girl drest in boy's clothes—[...] he seemed to me about the height & size of a boy of twelve years old.' She's remembering a twenty-four-year-old: now Robert is thirty-three and has filled out a little. But there's still something boyishly untried about him. Despite the bravura adventure of two trips to Italy, and one to the Baltic, he still lives at home with his parents, refusing to take up a profession and writing poetry all day.

To Elizabeth, this way of life looks like pure dedication. She finds other things to recognise in Robert too. Like Papa, he hated school and has been home-educated – as indeed has she. The Brownings, like the Barretts, are Whigs and religious Nonconformists. Like Elizabeth, Robert is the grandchild of a Caribbean plantation owner; also like her, he may have the suspicion that he has African-Caribbean heritage through his paternal grandmother. Not all of this common ground is apparent at first sight of course, but it's there in the ease with which the two poets talk to each other, in the little book-lined study-cum-sitting room hung with images of their distinguished literary mutual friends, and – as if demonstrating the succession – busts of the classical greats. And if the air around them is electric, well, since both are equally passionate in their determination to be the leading poets of their day, they share a sense that, simply by meeting, they're making literary history.

Robert stays for an hour and a half, 'And there was everything right—as how shd there not be?' Elizabeth's rigorous intellect and greater maturity is a perfect fit for his yielding uncertainty and emotional awareness. But both of them are evidently shaken by the realisation that something more than just the literary is going on, and both become defensive. Robert sends a note the same evening anxiously checking he didn't overstay his welcome, and Elizabeth responds with sudden formality. Whether she's protecting herself from a repetition of past effusiveness or simply from the sense that, as an invalid, she's shut out of the game of love, she resorts to frosty talk of 'kindness' and 'gratitude' for friendship from someone who inhabits a 'brilliant happy sphere'. And not a little self-pity, too: 'It is hard for you to understand what my mental position is after the peculiar experience I have suffered, & what a τι εμοι και σοι ['What have I to do with thee'] sort of feeling is irrepressible from me to you.'

Which works better, and more electrically, than she could have imagined. The next day, 22 May, Robert calls her bluff by making a declaration of love. Of course she repudiates this; as she must, in order for him to be able to continue to visit her – above all unchaperoned, and in what is in effect a bed-sitting room. Eighteen months from now, when she tells Mary Russell Mitford the truth about the relationship, she will say that, 'I would not listen—I could not believe even. […] I conceived it to be a mere poet's fancy .. an illusion of a confusion between the woman & the poetry.' For now, whether her disbelief is absolute or has something of a fig leaf about it, she italicises and uses a charming image to underline the fact that he must not breathe a word of this to anyone. The misstep must be forgotten and so 'will die out between *you & me alone*, like a misprint between you and the printer.' Realising that he risks losing access to Elizabeth altogether, Robert plays along, claiming in his response that he was just being hyperbolic.

With all this cleverly sorted – they're both intelligent as well as passionate, after all – the couple arrange to meet again, '*you & me alone*', and then again – a total of ninety-one times.

[*Sixth Frame*]

'Perception has an intellectual tail and is closely linked to insight', the artist Bridget Riley tells Paul Moorhouse in the course of a 2017 conversation. I'm reading her collected writings, *The Eye's Mind*, after seeing her work in a touring exhibition of prints. In the small, white-cube gallery where it had been hung her print sung and dazzled. Its colours were welcoming, related, generous: blue, red and green. Its plaited verticals – not stripes, unless stripes can wax and wane – teased and throbbed.

It's as if Riley has found the secret of chromatology, a secret as important as the invention of perspective for creating images to work upon eye and brain. The way Riley's colours react with each other, in the forms she gives them, go right into the mystery of perception – just as the rules of perspective do. She calls this *tonal organisation*, and says she learnt it from the post-impressionist Georges Seurat.

I still remember the sensation I had as a teenager – it was something like being hurled about – the first time I saw a Riley, one of her multiform, multicoloured acrylics from the 1970s. I also remember the force with which her name struck me: so this was a *woman's* mind. But I didn't yet realise the third dimension that is the magic of Riley's work. Usually, this third dimension resembles space: the eye makes what looks like a 3-D object appear backward or forward from the picture plane. Sometimes, though, the third dimension is time, and the image itself appears to move. The print I saw recently was like that; it appeared to flow up and down itself. It seemed as though the picture was in process: as though the artist's process was continuing with us, even *through* us. It would have been easy to imagine that we were watching Riley at work. And in a way, of course, we were. Riley is adamant that these effects aren't illusions or tricks, just part of what visible form *does*. 'That they will occur cannot be doubted, but precisely how can only be discovered in the context of picture making.'

It seems to me that the third dimension portraits want us to experience isn't space or time but narrative. It's the dimension of human encounter. Sometimes this dimension of encounter isn't just represented but *expressed*. Francis Bacon's portraits of George Dyer are statements of desire (and rage) as much as they are explorations of the irreducible corporeality of his muse. When Riley, an artist of the generation following his, says, 'Perception has an intellectual tail and is closely linked to insight', she reminds us that understanding and meaning-making are part of looking at every image, from a child's drawing stuck up on a fridge to a glossy perfume advert. They're also part of how we humans encounter each other. Looking at a person also 'has an intellectual tail and is closely linked to insight'.

Book Seven:
How to desire

While we two sate together, leaned that night
So close my very garments crept and thrilled
With strange electric life.

Monumental limestone harbour walls bleach in the October sun. They look lichened, though probably those discolourations are barnacles and the marks of Renaissance chisels. Livorno's Porto Mediceo has withstood the Ligurian Sea since the sixteenth century. Livorno, or Leghorn as Elizabeth and her compatriots call it, has long been Tuscany's only significant port. On 14 October 1846 its odd, long moles shelter arrivals on the morning tide, among them the little group of English passengers disembarking by tender from the Genoa night steamer. Seasick and faint after a stormy passage during which the engine broke down, they're looking 'as miserable as possible'. But not for long. After a reviving hotel breakfast they head for the railway station, eager to keep moving, for just fifteen miles north across a colourless, flat littoral lies their final destination, Pisa, that 'little city of great palaces, & the rolling, turbid Arno, striking its golden path betwixt them'.

Elizabeth has been dreaming about the Mediterranean since she was the child who pictured herself liberating the Balkans from Ottoman rule. She was just ten when her role model, Lord Byron, went into the

European exile that culminated in his attempt to do exactly this. Before that the poetic results of his earlier Grand Tour of the classical Mediterranean, including the first two cantos of *Childe Harold's Pilgrimage*, had already made him wildly famous, even in the sleepy Herefordshire valley where she was reading him. Her brothers, though, have made no such Grand Tours. In their short lives the pair she was closest too, Bro and Sam, were forced to substitute tours of family duty in Jamaica – and indeed Torquay. (Only Henry, always the family exception, started travelling when he was only eighteen, and recently managed to get Stormie to accompany him to Egypt.) But now here she is, the family invalid, walking in the footsteps of her Romantic heroes.

For it's not just Byron who came to live in Italy. Percy Bysshe Shelley emigrated here just as she was turning twelve; John Keats when she was fourteen. Byron died at Missolonghi in 1824; Shelley drowned here, off Livorno, in 1822; tuberculosis claimed Keats in Rome in 1821. But that all three perished in the classical Mediterranean doesn't diminish its attraction. You might even take the symbolic view that all three poets returned to their spiritual home to die. The south represents more than just a contemporary geography of therapeutic climate, or personal and political freedom. It's also the location of classical antiquity, which to Elizabeth has long represented the source of poetry: those allusions to the Pierian Spring in her youthful *An Essay on Mind* weren't entirely rhetorical. Historic Pisa, with its classical and Renaissance treasures and established English community, stands for *both* Italian culture *and* personal liberty. So it's not entirely surprising that last summer Elizabeth used her returning strength to fight for the chance to come to this city where, a quarter century ago, both Byron and Shelley spent substantial periods.

It rapidly became apparent that Robert Browning is the love of her life, but Elizabeth knew from the off that her father would forbid their romance. In Pisa though, away from parental scrutiny and the dangers of gossip, she could do more or less as she pleases without having to, in effect, choose between the two men she loves best. She also has a more pressing reason to get to Italy. In September 1845 Dr Chambers counsels strongly that she needs to go south for the winter if she is to survive. 'I was examined with that dreadful stethoscope, & received his command to go without fail *to Pisa by sea*. He said [...] that there was nothing for me but *warm air* .. no other possible remedy.' The stakes are high; and so explicit that Elizabeth's family actually explore a number of ways to make such a move. The patient could afford to run an independent household, as at Torquay, and her need to be chaperoned and supported seems to offer one or more of her siblings a chance of their own to escape the parental roof.

So the scheme she proposes later this month involves Arabel and George (who becomes her co-advocate) as travelling companions. Papa's reaction is, perhaps predictably, fury. It embarrasses him that the distinguished doctor he himself directed Elizabeth to consult has prescribed this trip as life-saving. It forces his moral hand and, like all weak men, Papa hates to have his hand forced. He can't refuse his ailing daughter permission to travel, so instead he punishes her emotionally: 'I was treated this morning as an undutiful daughter because I tried to put on my gloves.'

But Elizabeth can't quite yet accept that her beloved father is being selfish. She has trusted the family's difficult transitions as necessities, decisions much prayed over by a conscientious and loving parent; and has internalised her father's harsher judgements, alongside his encouragement and special attention, as corrective facts. The sternly Nonconformist Christianity he now practises aligns the head of the family with a God-the-Father whose infallible judgements must be obeyed. If her father proves pettier than this, then everything about family life must be reassessed: Sam's death in Jamaica and the pressure on Bro to return there, the curtailing of Henrietta's youthful fun, the uncompromising moves into smoggy central London, the truth or falsity of Papa's position over the contested will in the legal battle that lost him Hope End, even slave-owning itself. To throw all this in doubt would be overwhelming. It's no surprise that all the siblings – except that outlier Henry – resist losing faith in their father until long after the tipping point of evidence.

But while these emotional recalibrations are taking place, autumn marches on. The latest that Elizabeth could safely sail for Italy is early October; as the weeks tick by, discussion turns 'from steam-packet reasons' to departing for Malta on 3 October. Her father must realise that if uncertainty can be protracted past this date he won't have to shoulder the responsibility of directly refusing permission to travel. With a fortnight to go, the invalid tells Miss Mitford that she's 'very much in anxiety & tribulation about Pisa—It is all uncertain whether I shall go or not—& in the meantime I am vexed out of patience.' This uncharacteristic indiscretion reveals just how far her attitude is shifting. A month ago, she was still explaining her father to Robert in the old terms:

> what you *cannot* see, is the deep tender affection behind & below all those patriarchal ideas of governing grownup children 'in the way they *must* go!'—and there never was (under the strata) a truer affection in a father's heart [...]—he takes it to be his duty to rule like the Kings of Christendom, by divine right.

It's Robert himself, of course, who is producing this shift. However great Elizabeth's reluctance to see through her father, her 'first disobedience'– which, just as in John Milton's *Paradise Lost*, is falling in love – has made a crack in the edifice of paternal authority. And one crack quickly leads to another. For Robert offers a new model of love, a generosity learnt from his own family: 'I know as certainly as I know anything that if I could bring myself to ask them to give up everything in the world, they would do it and cheerfully', as he explains. If such generous, undestructive love is possible, Papa's is not the only way. Not every parent has to be like the Greek god Cronos, consuming his own children; not every love is fundamentally selfish. 'Yet each man kills the thing he loves', Oscar Wilde will write half a century from now, in *The Ballad of Reading Gaol*, his great poem of violence and betrayal. But this is the very lesson Elizabeth is now unlearning.

Gradually, her lover is replacing her father as her advisor. On 24 September, still grappling with what to do about Pisa, she asks Robert to 'Think for me. [...] Do think for me'. It's an acknowledgement of dependency very different from the apparent emotional assurance of her early letters. Yet she writes it on the very same day that, desperate to regain her belief in and intimacy with Papa, she has promised that she won't go to Italy against his wishes. Since staying in London is assumed by everyone around her to be life-threatening she's offering, in effect, to die for him. (Though she mentions 'future years', suggesting that she doesn't herself quite believe this.) Still, she has to make her sacrifice explicit in order to force the issue – and this, of course, her father can't accept:

> He would not even grant me the consolation of thinking that I sacrificed what I supposed to be a good, to HIM. I told him that [...] it was necessary to my self satisfaction in future years, to understand definitely that the sacrifice *was* exacted by him & *was* made to him, .. & not, thrown away blindly & by a misapprehension. And he would not answer *that*. I might do my own way, he said—[...] I had better do what I liked:—for his part, he washed his hands of me altogether—

It all seems so extreme. But if all the siblings have difficulty giving up their founding myth of the Barrett idyll, that's particularly true for the three women of the family, on whom restrictions now fall hardest but who, as the eldest surviving children, were most deeply formed by the paradise years at Hope End. The brothers at least have working lives, as they manage the family estates, but in an era when an upper-class woman's role is largely confined to wife- and motherhood (with charity work and religion the 'spinster' alternatives), to be denied marriage hollows out the sisters' existences.

It's no coincidence that this autumn sees both Henrietta and Elizabeth with serious suitors at ages that are for the times surprisingly advanced: Elizabeth is thirty-nine and Henrietta thirty-six. At the point of conventional 'last chances' they've been forced to realise that the permission they've been waiting for will never come. It's as if Papa has been relying on time to dribble away their chances for marriage, too. And this, in the end, is what brings the whole emotional edifice down. In the to and fro of the Pisa negotiations, Elizabeth finally recognises that her father is opposed to his children falling in love *at all*; at the same stroke she suddenly stops ascribing his convictions to religion. On the contrary, he 'is apt to take the world's measures of the means of life' and is refusing his offspring independence 'for the singular reason that he never *does* tolerate in his family (sons or daughters) the development of one class of feelings'.

For decades Elizabeth has misused her strong will to force herself to wear blinkers about the nature of this parental contract. Now that they're off she's impatient to make up for lost time. She and Robert will continue to meet in Wimpole Street roughly twice a week for another sixteen months after that first May afternoon. He calls in the afternoons when her father and brothers are at work, but the household's women – Wilson as well as Henrietta and Arabel – can't miss how often he's visiting. It is a headlong rush into experience. Three months after their first meeting, marriage – 'the *first subject*', Robert calls it – is once again being discussed. It's also the final subject, although Elizabeth hasn't yet accepted this. Still, this time she does acknowledge the proposition's serious. As indeed it must be: Breach of Promise litigation can be brought against any man who fails to carry through on a proposal; and even if most families might eschew such socially costly action, Papa is just the sort of man to sue.

As the summer ends she responds with a series of protests. First she fears that Robert would tire of an invalid wife. He responds that he would happily marry her even without sex – which is what he thinks she means: though it's not – 'I would marry you now and thus—I would come when you let me, and go when you bade me—I would be no more than one of your brothers—"*no more*"—.' For him this isn't weird. The society they live in forces young people to perfect the art of sublimation; being in love customarily *means* both acknowledging sexual desire and being unable to act on it, at least to begin with. The taboo on sex outside marriage is compounded by the long periods couples are often forced to wait for parental consent, or because they lack the financial independence to marry.

Money is no obstacle in this case, as Robert realises six months in, once Elizabeth tells him, on 25 September, that she has independent means: 'And if I *wished* to be very poor, in the world's sense of poverty, I *could not*, with three or four hundred a year of which no living will can dispossess me.' He responds, 'When you told me lately that "you could never be poor"—all my solicitude was at an end. I had but myself to care about, and [...] I can at any time amply provide for that.' Such confidence in his own earning ability may be misplaced: after all, he's still being supported by his father. But Elizabeth has no trouble believing him, and that belief is key to her love. Yet this in turn creates a further objection. She feels that, if they married, he would be wasted on sickroom duties instead of writing the important books that are his destiny. It would be 'an exchange of higher work for lower work .. & of the special work you are called to, for that which is work for anybody.'

A century from now the couple's love letters will be widely read even though they lack the sexy romance of, for example, those recently exchanged by their close contemporaries George Sand and Frédéric Chopin. But there's a great sweetness to such passages, in which the couple reveal the quality of their love by what they're prepared to sacrifice. Robert would leave friends and family for life in exile, and marry a woman with whom he imagines he'll never be able to make love or have children. Elizabeth is prepared to surrender romance for the sake of retaining Robert's friendship – 'You must leave me—these thoughts of me, I mean .. for [...] we may be friends always' – and ultimately even his company if he needs to move abroad for his own health.

For none of these is her fundamental reason for viewing their romance as ultimately impossible. As far as disability goes, she's simply worried that frequent illness makes her a liability. Of course she knows her own sexuality is functioning just fine. She also knows that she's not actually bedbound – she's no paraplegic, 'suffering from an incurable injury on the spine, which would prevent my ever standing up' – but simply resting up against the return of dangerous chest infections. Her fear is more profound, and profoundly superstitious; it survives even her new lessons in the beneficial effects of love. She fears letting Robert love and dedicate his life to her because of what happened the last time that someone did so. Bro's death is the palimpsest upon which this new love appears. 'And once *he* held my hand, .. how I remember! & said that he "loved me better than them all & that he *would not* leave me .. till I was well," he said!— how I remember *that*! And ten days from that day the boat had left the shore which never returned.'

Elizabeth finds this loss so hard to address that she writes to Robert about it only once. Yet buried experiences can be the most motivating. A thunderstorm on 11 July, the fifth anniversary of Bro's death, recalls to her a tree struck by lightning when she was a child:

> The whole trunk of that tree was bare & peeled—& up that new whiteness of it, ran the finger-mark of the lightning in a bright beautiful rose-colour [...] the fever-sign of the certain death [...] And,

in that same storm, two young women belonging to a festive party were killed on the Malvern hills—each, sealed to death in a moment.

These images of death and transfiguration are at one level a simple confession that the well-known thirty-nine-year-old author remains terrified of thunder. But they're also a dispatch from the morbid territory of complex grief.

It's not that Elizabeth consciously conflates Robert with Bro, who was in so many ways the partner of her early life. But her brother did prefigure her lover in a number of ways. Like Robert, he was younger than her: admittedly by just over a year to Robert's six, but this difference would still have felt substantial during their shared childhood; especially as Bro was not only junior but less precocious. She believed in her brother's relatively unproven talents, too, and has learnt from that first intimacy how simultaneously to frame a younger man as her soulmate and leave room for lesser actual achievement. It's a difficult trick made the more challenging now that she's a leading writer. Still, with imaginative ingenuity Elizabeth manages to turn Robert into the more 'successful' partner by emphasising his busy literary social life. Indeed, like many clever women, she spends a great deal of energy keeping herself tamped down:

> I never had […] a will in the common things of life […] in one's mere pleasures & fantasies, one wd rather be crossed & vexed a little than vex a person one loves .. & it is possible to get used to the harness & run easily in it at last—& there is a side-world to hide one's thoughts in […] 'literature' […] while in things not exactly *overt*, I & all of us are apt to act sometimes up to the limit of our means of acting, with shut doors & windows & no waiting for cognizance or permission.

Disingenuousness has its uses, in other words. And so it is that 1845's Italian plan appeals disingenuously: both because it doesn't commit her to marrying Robert and because she's able to convince herself that he's equally in need of a curative stay in the south.

Like her father, Elizabeth has internalised a Christianity that makes it hard for her to ask for what she wants. But there the resemblance ends. She is far from being controlling. On the contrary, she's turning Robert into her next male authority figure:

there *is* a natural inferiority of mind in women—of the intellect
[…] the history of Art & of genius testifies to this fact openly. […]
I believe women .. all of us in a mass .. to have minds of quicker
movement, but less power & depth .. & that we are under your feet,
because we cant stand upon our own.

Which is so evidently untrue, especially in her own case, that it's embarrassing. But maybe this is how, in the nineteenth century, a conservative
heterosexuality works: Elizabeth needs to frame Robert as *exceeding* her
in order to desire him. At the same time though, she undermines this very
paradigm by the mere fact of falling for a younger, less established man.
It's a muddle, a kind of *mauvaise foi*; Elizabeth isn't lying to herself, but
she has been conditioned into inauthenticity. Besides, a sheltered existence means that her ideas about masculinity are largely second-hand.
Recent friendships with writing men have been largely epistolary, and
there's only so much you can learn from younger brothers.

Yet this apparent contradiction at the heart of her love affair is the
turning point of her psychic life. The later twentieth century will invent
the trope of the suffering woman poet, either choosing to 'flay' herself
into authenticity, as critics like Germaine Greer in *Slip-Shod Sibyls* have
it, or else unable to escape from repeatedly going over her psychic wounds
instead of repairing them, as psychoanalytic literary critic Susan Kavaler-
Adler insists in *The Compulsion to Create*. Elizabeth certainly pushes
herself hard – in her writing, in her physical survival – and in the past
she's 'kissed the rod', internalising her adored father's authoritarianism
as love, and abasing herself before Boyd's cruelty. But she's outstripped
these early love-objects. Perhaps it's her good luck that they were, each in
their own way, second-rate. Had she met a great, established male artist
when she was younger, would she ever have brought herself to sever that
bond? Yet now she breaks absolutely with the old paternalistic pattern.
Everything that makes Robert an unconventional choice – his youth
and comparative lack of distinction, his feminine side, his explicit anti-
authoritarianism, even the way he will play the junior financial role in
their partnership – is what makes him the essential counter to the authority figure of her father. Little as she may realise this, it's an enormously
psychically healthy choice.

Just how narrowly Elizabeth understands even men she thinks she knows will be brought home the following June when Benjamin Haydon, desperate for money and exhausted by the struggle to sustain his artistic reputation, commits suicide. The old friends have fallen out of regular touch since her romance with Robert began, but Haydon will send her three notes just the week before he dies; to which, absorbed by her new life, she'll pay scant attention. His death will fill her with regret: 'I have been told again & again […] that to give money *there*, was to drop it into a hole of the ground. But if to have dropped it so, dust to dust, would have saved a living man—'

In general though, thinking through the consequences for others *is* Elizabeth's modus vivendi. When she finally abandons the Pisa plan in October 1845, it's partly because it risked having her father disown Arabel and George, who, like all the siblings except herself, are his financial dependents, 'Constrained *bodily* into submission .. apparent submission at least .. by that worst & most dishonoring of necessities, the necessity of *living* .. everyone of them all, except myself, being dependent in money-matters on the inflexible will.' Finally she acknowledges that 'The bitterest fact of all is, that I had believed Papa to have loved me more than he obviously does,' and tells Robert, 'I am—your own.' The long transition from daughter to partner and peer is complete.

Luckily for Papa's bluff – luckily for literature – the winter of 1845–46 turns out to be so exceptionally mild that still, two decades into the overheating twenty-first century, it's one of the dozen mildest since records began. Elizabeth survives it with ease. Indeed, she continues to get stronger. It helps that the summer which follows is also exceptionally warm. In July 1845 she was beginning to enjoy carriage rides to Regent's Park; in May 1846 she takes her first stroll there:

> Arabel & Flush & I were in the carriage—& the sun was shining with that green light through the trees […] .. & I wished so much to walk through a half open gate along a shaded path, that we stopped the carriage & got out & walked, & I put both my feet on the grass, .. which was the strangest feeling! .. […] Dearest, we shall walk together under the trees some day!

The intensity of this desire comes so recognisably from her country childhood that it's like a flashback to the flickering heat and green of a Hope End summer. Returning health, the love affair, and 'sun [...] shining with that green light through the trees' all belong to a psychical hinterland that she tells Robert is 'That Dreamland which is your especial dominion', where every element strengthens the others: 'How strong you make me, you who make me happy!'

By the next month she's even well enough to go visiting. It's like stepping back into life. In June alone she visits Mary Trepsack, John Kenyon and Hugh Stuart Boyd, the last of whom she hasn't seen for seven years. Kenyon takes her to see the Great Western Railway's new steam engine in action; she delights in the unfamiliar 'rush of the people & the earth-thunder of the engine'. She goes driving with the distinguished art historian Anna Jameson, a new friend who is also a friend of Robert's. Together they visit one of the great private art collections of London, belonging to Samuel Rogers, where Elizabeth sees a first edition of *Paradise Lost*, Michelangelo and Raphael cartoons, Rubens, Titian, Tintoretto and a late Rembrandt self-portrait, 'which if his landscapes, as they say, were "dug out of nature", looks as if it were dug out of humanity.' After years within the four walls of her own room, seeing these old masters first hand and close up is giddy-making, and Elizabeth has an artistically overwhelmed moment of Stendhal syndrome: 'Almost I could have run my head against the wall, I felt, with bewilderment.'

Something else is adding to the freshness of these experiences. In October 1845 she was still 'taking forty drops of laudanum a day' for her '*absolutely shattered*' 'nervous system'. But by February 1846, 'And that you should care so much about the opium—! Then *I* must care, & get to do with less .. at least—[...] But slowly & gradually something may be done—' For as she becomes stronger, so does Robert. He steps up to the plate, asking her to give up her opiate habit, urging marriage, and announcing that he will support them both and she can settle all her inheritance on her siblings. Elizabeth sensibly pooh-poohs this last impracticality – 'I shall refuse steadily [...] to put away from me God's gifts .. given perhaps in order to this very end' – while stepping up in turn. She cuts down the morphine, and tries gently to concentrate her lover's mind on how he *could* actually earn in Italy. A contract to write for a periodical would be good; or could they house-sit for one of his aristocratic friends? She also points out that her inheritance is useful but not limitless: 'Nearly two hundred a year of ship shares I never touch—Then there is the interest of six thousand pounds (not *less* at any rate) in the funds—& I referred to the principal of *that*, when I said yesterday, that when we had ceased to need it, it might return to my family […] if you chose.'

Perhaps every elopement needs a rehearsal. This summer a new Italian plan develops: the couple will run away together. They no longer pretend to each other that this trip would be primarily for health reasons, but, ironically, offers to act as travelling companion now arrive from friends anxious to rescue Elizabeth from another London winter. Fanny Dowglass, an Irish friend of almost Elizabeth's age and experienced in travelling for her own health, is put off with a fluent untruth: 'I cannot count on my courage—I have nerves like so many threads.' Anna Jameson, who is a highly experienced traveller, discusses routes through France while making her own plans. But when might the lovers leave, if they do? And where will they go? Elizabeth fancies Cava de' Tirreni, north of Salerno, whose Romanesque Benedictine abbey is an ancient seat of learning.

While they wait and plan in the privacy of her third-floor room in Wimpole Street, the lovers' shared world develops. Robert has known Elizabeth by her family diminutive since at least January, when she signed a couple of letters with a doodled 'Ba' instead of her usual 'EBB'. But it's not till July that she starts thinking of him as 'Robert' instead of a limitless 'you', that 'O, *tu*' he introduced at the very start of their correspondence. Now she learns about his background: parents, Robert senior and Sarah Anna, née Wiedemann, and sister Sarianna, two years his junior.

Like the Barrett family, the Brownings are Whigs. But they're also wholehearted abolitionists, whose lives have in no small measure been defined by their convictions. When he was twenty, Robert senior was sent to work on a St Kitts plantation belonging to his mother's family but, to his own father's fury, was so disgusted by the realities of slavery that he turned down the opportunity to run the estates and returned to London. 'Elizabeth's' Robert only learns the full extent of his father's sacrifice this August:

If we are poor, it is to my father's infinite glory, who, as my mother told me last night [...] 'conceived such a hatred to the slave-system in the West Indies', (where his mother was born, who died in his infancy,) that he relinquished every prospect,—supported himself, while there, in some other capacity, and came back, while yet a boy, to his father's profound astonishment and rage—[...] You may fancy, I am not ashamed of him.

Robert's cousin Cyrus Mason will later claim that this wasn't a question of principle but of an 'artistic nature' and 'refined instincts' that couldn't cope with rough and tumble plantation life. But to defend cruelty by calling objectors weak or ineffectual is an old trick – in twenty-first-century Britain the argot will be 'snowflakes' – and the son has no trouble turning around such verdicts. He tells Elizabeth how his father, 'tender-hearted to a fault', detests violence as a result of 'some abominable early experience' on the plantations, at the mere mention of which he 'shuts his eyes involuntarily and shows exactly the same marks of loathing that may be noticed while a piece of cruelty is mentioned.'

When Robert's grandfather 'Rob' Browning came to write his will in 1834, he left Robert senior and Margaret, the children of his first marriage, just token sums on the grounds that they 'have had by their uncle Tittle and aunt Mill much greater portion than can be left to my other dear children'. It was Robert senior's maternal grandfather, the Revd John Tittle, who owned the family plantations when he was a young man: Rob's will implies that he benefited from them after all. But there's no evidence corroborating what it so conveniently assumes. And even if the sacrifices Robert senior made *were* incomplete, perhaps this is as much as we can expect from one individual. For when he rejected the planter's life his own father in punishment demanded he pay back the money spent raising him. That one gesture has defined his life: even the comfortable family home at New Cross in Surrey is within commuting distance of the City of London because he's forced to work there in a bank.

Despite being prevented from following what is in fact his artistic vocation by the need to earn a living, Robert senior has filled this family home with art and books. He will draw – particularly satirical cartoons – all his life, and he collects engravings and drawings, notably by William Hogarth and artists from the Low Countries. He especially enjoys David

Teniers the Younger. He has a 6,000-volume library; treasures of his rare book collection include first editions of Sir Thomas Browne's *Works*, Ben Jonson's *First Folio*, John Milton's *Paradise Regain'd* and *Poems on Several Occasions*, Thomas More's *Utopia*, and – demonstrating genuine intellectual eclecticism in a Nonconformist household – *Eikon Basilike*, the book of meditations supposedly written by Charles I during his final imprisonment.

All this reveals a creative, wide-ranging mind that must have been at least partly formed by his schooldays at Cheshunt, where he befriended John Kenyon, later Elizabeth and Robert's 'dear Mr Kenyon, with whom we began'. But his son is largely home-educated, brought up on this astonishing library. Like Elizabeth, Robert has been thoroughly encouraged by both parents. His artistic mother Sarah Anna is an accomplished pianist and a creator of beautiful gardens. Her German ship-owning father met and married her mother in Dundee: this northern background powers the family's Nonconformism, and Sarah Anna is devout. Yet, life-loving rather than austere, she's altogether less fundamentalist than many of her fellow worshippers at York Street Chapel.

She also offers a template for Robert's relationship with a woman six years older than himself. Elizabeth's mother was four older than her father; her sister Henrietta is also four years older than the man she's fallen for. But Robert's mother is a full decade years older than his father. When they married in 1811 she was thirty-eight, the same age Elizabeth is when Robert starts writing to her, and gave birth to the poet, her first child, at just a month shy of her fortieth birthday. Her age is probably the reason Robert's parents stopped at just two children. Perhaps it is also what makes her family view her as frail, even though she seems to suffer no underlying condition and will live to seventy-six. Nevertheless, Robert learns early on to associate femininity with fragility, and with the beauty of an older woman. To some extent he even identifies with this principle, sharing his mother's susceptibility to migraine – something his early letters to Elizabeth harp on somewhat. Indeed in April 1845 Elizabeth feels constrained to defend him from Miss Mitford's accusations of 'silver forkism', and to argue for the 'masculinity' of his intellect: 'With all his darknesses, & charades of light, he is a very masculine writer &

thinker, & as remote as possible from Balzac's type of the *femmelette*: in doing so supplying the very term her friend will later use to abuse him.

Elizabeth is becoming more forceful in general. By April 1846, after more than a year of Browning idealism, she understands the British Empire as a violent aberration. The horrifying loss of life in the First Sikh War, concluded the previous month by the Battle of Sobraon, which killed 320 Brits but 10,000 Sikhs, shows her conclusively that empire subjugates rather than 'civilizes'. She takes this insight and runs:

> Some of these days our 'great Indian Empire' will stand up on its own legs, & make use of our own rope to scourge us to a distance. What right has England to an Indian empire? No more than the Duke of Sutherland, to his broad estates. Wait a little, & we shall see it all arranged according to a better justice, on the small scale & the large.

To foresee independence, and how subjugation itself will power the liberation struggle, is all the more remarkable because Elizabeth is writing two years before Karl Marx and Friedrich Engels will publish their theory of revolution in *The Communist Manifesto*, and indeed seventy before Vladimir Lenin's *Imperialism, the Highest Stage of Capitalism* – not to mention the powerful postcolonial critique the latter will go on to unlock in Frantz Fanon's *The Wretched of the Earth* (1961), Edward Said's *Orientalism* (1978) and beyond. None of this thinking has happened yet. In London in 1846 abolitionism is popular; anti-imperialism all but unknown. It will be another thirty years, and after Elizabeth's death, before the term 'imperialist' gains currency – and then only narrowly, as a criticism of Disraeli's foreign policy.

But this isn't the first time that Elizabeth has pointed out how subjugation works. In August 1843 she published 'The Cry of the Children', a response to 1842's *Report of the Children's Employment Commission*, in the mass circulation *Blackwood's Magazine*:

> Will you stand, to move the world, on a child's heart—
> Stifle down with a mailed heel its palpitation,
> And tread onward to your throne amid the mart?
> Our blood splashes upward, O gold-heaper

Here too she pictures oppression rebounding on the oppressor – *blood splashing upward* – though her poem ends by releasing the tension of that insight. The child in the poem, 'weeping in the playtime of the others, / In the country of the free' has been indentured, a system that enslaves children in plain sight in mines and mills like those owned by Elizabeth's own grandfather in Newcastle. Published forty years after William Blake's 'Jerusalem', 'The Cry of the Children' is less visionary but more political about the actual workings of Britain's 'dark Satanic Mills'. It makes explicit the links between child labour, child mortality, lack of education, hopelessness and the 'mart' of unchecked, laissez-faire capitalism.

This understanding of nineteenth-century industrial practice will seem obvious to the point of cliché in the twenty-first century, but in the 1840s much of what's going on has simply never been named. By adding to what mainstream society can find words for, 'The Cry of the Children' helps shift popular opinion against such practices, and in 1844 the second in a sequence of Factory Acts will further shorten children's working hours, increase their compulsory schooling hours, and institute major safety reforms in factories.

As a result, in spring 1845 Elizabeth is asked for a poem by the Anti-Corn Law League, which campaigns against the protectionist legal tariffs on wheat imports that, along with cartel-type arrangements between domestic landowners, keep the price of this staple so high that people are starving. Under pressure from her father and brothers Elizabeth declines, instead donating money to the cause. But she does so with regret, her excuses – 'as a woman you will know that women are subject to various influences' – audibly contorted by the inimical impulses of domestic probity and a passionate desire to 'lift my voice in my poetry, as high as my heart'.

In December 1845, however, she starts work on another political poem. 'The Runaway Slave at Pilgrim's Point' tells the story of an enslaved woman who is raped by her owner(s) after they've killed her partner. The woman murders the resulting child, whose colour betrays the rape, and is hunted down and flogged to death. Here too Elizabeth makes oppression turn itself into the engine of resistance, pitching the status quo upside down: the narrator is as revolted by her baby's 'white' face as her persecutors are dismissive of 'my black face, my black hand'. Given Elizabeth's family background this is a revolutionary vision – which is perhaps why it takes her a year to write – and she doesn't publish the poem while living under her father's roof. But it demonstrates how, in giving up her belief in him, she's free at last to give up believing in slavery. And perhaps it *is* easier to be publicly abolitionist than to oppose Britain's Corn Laws since, now that the country has outlawed slavery, it can be 'distanced' as a purely American crime.

'The Runaway Slave' will first be published in an American abolitionist anthology, *The Liberty Bell*, in 1848, although Elizabeth sends it to James Russell Lowell in New England at the end of 1846. This is verse as public speech, aiming to create a moral catharsis when shared emotion leads to shared moral insight. Such an elevated view of poetry's social role comes, like so much in Elizabeth's work and thought, from her classical education: after all, Homeric epic celebrates public, political ethics. This places poetry excitingly at the heart of contemporary debates. But it can also be inhibiting. Morally necessary conclusions may leave little room for poetic ambiguity; the effort to be persuasive can make a poem over-rhetorical or simplistic.

Yet the fiercely inhabited psyche of the 'Runaway Slave', together with the poem's obsessional iteration of 'black' and 'white' – first as colours in the non-human natural world, but then also as racist constructions of human identity – create a genuine feeling of terror and hyper-reality:

> I look at the sky.
> The clouds are breaking on my brain;
> I am floated along, as if I should die
> Of liberty's exquisite pain.
> In the name of the white child waiting for me
> In the death-dark.

It works so well indeed that this is sometimes taken as evidence of Elizabeth's anxiety about her own possible African-Caribbean heritage. After all, it's in December 1845, while working on this poem, that she sends Robert her famous 'blood of a slave' letter. But the assumption is reductive. Elizabeth is turning such prevailing prejudices on their head. In her poem it is *whiteness* and all that it means – the abuses, the power-relations – that is disgusting.

That the possibility of mixed heritage haunts the West Indian planto-cracy is poetic justice, of course. But it *is* a haunting, and, just as it can't be proved in Elizabeth's case, it's no more than rumour in Robert's. Claims that his maternal grandmother Margaret Tittle was the daughter of an enslaved woman are simply untrue. Her mother Margaret Strachan was the daughter of a St Kitts surgeon, Dr George Strachan, while her father, the Revd John Tittle, was an estate manager and legal representative for the Society for the Propagation of the Gospel.

In fact, during 1846 Elizabeth is also secretly working on what will become a famous marker not of African-Caribbean but of her possible Portuguese heritage: the forty-four love poems that will eventually be pub-lished as *Sonnets from the Portuguese*. In both this sequence and, in a differ-ent way, in 'The Runaway Slave', it's as if she has finally caught her breath enough to speak out, producing personal, political poetry that isn't just con-cerned with art for art's sake, but takes part in the world around her. Yet she remains uncertain about the confessional character of this verse, which she knows Robert disdains, as she'll later tell Arabella: 'I never showed them to Robert [...] I felt shy about them altogether [...] I had heard him express himself strongly against "personal" poetry & I shrank back.'

Besides, she's still hesitating over giving herself away, one way or another. All summer the lovers' correspondence has yawed between the impossibility and the necessity of eloping. Elizabeth's panics are in proportion to the size of this step. She's particularly worried that John Kenyon, who understands both her and Robert well, will winkle out their secret. She hates lying to him, and all her friends: it makes her feel she's 'swindling' them. But preoccupation is itself a giveaway. By early Septem-ber 1846, both Mr Boyd and Treppy, who's visiting Wimpole Street, seem to guess what's afoot. As Treppy says, 'Secrets indeed! You think that nobody can see & hear except yourselves, I suppose,—& there are two circumstances going on in the house, plain for any eyes to see!'

That second 'circumstance' is Henrietta's love affair with an army ensign the family call Surtees: full name, William Surtees Cook. (He's actually a second cousin, whose mother and Elizabeth's maternal grand-mother were sisters.) Henrietta's courtship, unlike Elizabeth's, is an open secret not least because Surtees has seen off two other suitors since 1844 by laying siege at Wimpole Street. The siblings and their servants close ranks to protect the romance as he takes up residence in the drawing room during visiting hours, breaks down in tears, and generally outlasts his rivals' stores of time, patience and dignity. It's dramatic stuff, which quite possibly helps distract everyone from the equally intense affair being conducted altogether more discreetly on the third floor.

In July 1846 Elizabeth's maternal aunt, Jane Hedley, staying at Wimpole Street for her own daughter Arabella's marriage, conjectures that if Henrietta and Surtees were to elope to Italy they could take Elizabeth with them. But elopement is a radical step, even for these more able-bodied lovers. Besides, Surtees lacks the money to marry. He's hoping against hope for promotion: things have become so desperate that he has even written a novel in hopes of making money from fiction. As many an aspirant has discovered, this isn't as easy as it looks, even if, like him, you have Elizabeth Barrett as personal editor. *Johnny Cheerful* is submitted to Colburn but turned down, and remains unpublished. Besides, when Surtees *is* promoted to captain at the end of 1845, he almost immediately retires from his regiment on half pay, cancelling out the rise.

Still, all this adds to the general undertone of plotting with which, this summer, 50 Wimpole Street is seething; and Aunt Hedley, with her 'beaming affectionate face', keeps accidentally putting her foot in it. First she teases Elizabeth in front of Papa that an investment document is her marriage-settlement, then she reveals to him that Robert has been visiting her niece. Meanwhile Robert himself is feeling compromised in another way. He's desperate to tell his beloved parents everything:

> Why should not my father & mother know? What possible harm can follow from their knowing? Why should I wound them to the very soul and for ever […] For in any case they will take my feeling for their own with implicit trust.

It would all be so much easier out of Papa's punitive reach in cheap, sunny, southern Europe. So the summer of 1846 comes to an end with a vertiginous feeling of now or never. If the lovers really are to sail south, and Elizabeth to escape another London winter, they must do so before the weather closes in. Something has to change. And suddenly, on 9 September, it does. As if to force their hand, Papa announces, with characteristic lack of consultation, that he's moving the entire family out to the countryside because, he says, Wimpole Street needs to be refurbished. Less than a fortnight later, on 21 September, the Barretts have relocated to the small Surrey village of Little Bookham.

But Elizabeth isn't with them. 'Therefore decide!' she challenges Robert when she gets the news. 'It seems quite too soon & too sudden for us to set out on our Italian adventure now—.' But her lover is tired of waiting. He understands quite well that if Elizabeth goes off to the countryside now, the window for European escape will close for another year. And maybe forever. Even if she does survive the winter cold, a relationship can only endure stasis for so long before it becomes fixed in unreality. So he takes her at her word, and decides: 'If you *do* go on Monday, our marriage will be impossible for another year—the misery! You see what we have gained by waiting. We must be *married directly* and go to Italy—I will go for a licence today and we can be married on Saturday.'

It's not entirely out of the blue. In recent weeks things have been getting increasingly practical. On 5 August Elizabeth detailed her money. The interest on her nest egg of £8,000 produces an annual income of around £160 to £180, which her father doles out to her quarterly; the shares Uncle Sam left her in the *David Lyon* generate another £200 per annum. The next day, she discovered that she has around a third more than this to play with. Papa has been keeping back around £120 of her interest every year:

> Stormie told me this morning, in answer to an enquiry of mine, that certainly I did not receive the whole interest of the fund-money, .. could not .. making ever so much allowance for the income-tax. And now, upon consideration, I seem to see that I cannot have done so—[…] Stormie said 'There must be three hundred a year of interest from the fund-money—even at the low rate of interest paid there.'

It will be enough to live on. Even so, Robert borrows £100 from his father to meet the cost of the journey. He has finally told his parents the plan, which is to be scrupulously honourable. The lovers won't elope, which would bring scandal on their families, but will marry *first* and only then travel abroad as a respectably married couple – albeit secretly. Their secrecy will also protect siblings and friends from being punished by Elizabeth's father for any presumed complicity. One reason Elizabeth now decides to travel with her maid is indeed that she needs lots of practical help. She's never even learnt to do her own hair: those barley curls! But it's also a way to protect Elizabeth Wilson from the consequences of her connivance. 'If I left her behind she would be turned into the street before sunset', Elizabeth tells Robert – while at the same time noting shrewdly that, 'She is an expensive servant—she has sixteen pounds a year'.

Shrewd or no, there's real affection between Elizabeth and Wilson, who 'has professed herself willing "to go anywhere in the world with me",' and whose loyalty now proves indispensable. Just three days after Papa's announcement about the country move, Robert and Elizabeth are indeed 'married on Saturday', at eleven o'clock on the morning of 12 September 1846. The witnesses are Robert's cousin James Silverthorne and, taking a huge risk, Elizabeth Wilson. She has only Elizabeth's loyalty to protect her from the consequences of disobeying her powerful employer. 'Remember to thank Wilson for me,' Robert injuncts his new bride that evening and again the next day, 'It was kind, very kind of Wilson.'

However quiet the actual ceremony, it takes place in the smart Regency parish church of St Marylebone, which, with its impressive pediment and broad flight of steps giving right onto the Marylebone Road, could hardly be less discreet. The couple are in a sense hiding in plain sight. They're also taking care to shield the community of Nonconformist Paddington Chapel, their natural spiritual home and the more obvious place for them to marry. Its minister, the Revd James Stratten, is a Congregational appointment who, unlike the Anglican clergy of St Marylebone, could be driven out by a furious Barrett paterfamilias. Besides, the Chapel is a lifeline they mustn't endanger for the by now deeply religious Arabella.

The logistics of the day itself are delicate. Elizabeth can only leave home unchallenged between ten and five, when the men are out and about. Today she waits discreetly till half past ten. That leaves her and Wilson only half an hour to get to St Marylebone Church. It's a distance of just a third of a mile, no more than ten minutes at a normal stroll. But Elizabeth isn't a strong walker at the best of times and this morning, having not slept all night, she's in such a state that she nearly faints. In her fluster she's left home without smelling salts; but she has the presence of mind to go into a chemist's to buy some. She revives, and with Wilson's help makes it to the cab rank on Marylebone High Street, where she takes a fly to the church.

This is going the long way round. Church and fly stand are roughly equidistant from 50 Wimpole Street. But the fly is a crucial alibi, because last night Elizabeth told Arabella she would be taking one to call on Mr Boyd. The ride to St Marylebone is short indeed, a matter of two or three minutes, but worth the cabbie's while because Elizabeth retains him to wait outside the church. These are the days of the *Book of Common Prayer*, so she and Robert make their vows using the same words as innumerable couples before them. Spoken, the Marriage Service takes no more than half an hour. But, especially in this era when marriage is a matter of material survival as well as social identity, that half hour is life-changing.

For no one is that more true than for Elizabeth and Robert. The pews of St Marylebone, where tablet monuments are already starting to crowd the walls, are empty as they speak their lines. But the elegant neoclassical building, still barely thirty years old, is full of the sense of the particular, monied central London community it serves: and from which the new Mr and Mrs Browning are now expelling themselves vow by vow. This is not Robert's community but it is – socially, if not spiritually – Elizabeth's. Her feelings as they emerge from the church and she makes it down the porticoed steps to the waiting cab must be dizzying. A year on, she recalls:

> it *does* make us laugh, for instance, to think of the official's […] atti-
> tude & gesture of astonishment, as he stood at the churchdoor & saw
> bride & bridegroom part on the best terms possible & go off in sepa-
> rate flies. Robert was very generous & threw about his gold to clerk,
> pew openers &c &c in a way to convict us of being in a condition of
> incognito .. and […] "Never had he seen anything more remarkable
> than *that*, in the whole course of his practice!"

But at the time, full of 'emotion & confusion', it's not funny at all. (It even looks as though Elizabeth has had to supply her own ring. Two days before the wedding, she's asked Robert to call, 'And then, you shall have the ring .. soon enough, and safer.')

Now her immediate worry is that sensationalist journalists, who scan church registers looking for scandal, may 'out' the wedding. Still, she sends Wilson home and, as planned, directs the cab to nearby St John's Wood, where she calls on 'poor Mr Boyd' in his 'dark little room'. She's arranged for her sisters to join her here so they'll witness her alibi. But they seem to take forever to arrive, and Elizabeth gets in such a state that Boyd, who's in on the truth, persuades her to drink some Cyprus wine and eat some bread and butter to keep her strength up. It's the last time she'll see her old friend, now sixty-five, who will die less than two years from now; this time at least, he does right by her. At last Arabella and Henrietta turn up in a panic, '& with such grave faces!' – because Arabella had forgotten the arrangement. And once they have arrived the sisters prolong the agony. As the day's holding fair, they decide to take the carriage on for a drive to Hampstead Heath.

But half past four sees Elizabeth finally back in her own room and writing to Robert as usual. Only it is no longer as usual. This time she's writing to her husband, and from the home she has renounced by marrying him. Besides, the risks of discovery and separation still aren't over, and won't be till they're out of the country. Recently, Flush was kidnapped for the third time; as her brothers and lover held back, Elizabeth herself went to Shoreditch where she saw the 'immense female bandit' Mrs Taylor and negotiated his release. Now the same practical determination drives her travel planning. Papa has announced Monday 21 September as moving day. Is it really possible to leave before then, getting everything done in just a week? But on Thursday, with just two days to go, the lovers agree. Since Elizabeth can't leave the house on a Friday or Sunday, they will set out for Europe on Saturday 19 September.

Packing, in this intensely scrutinising household, is almost out of the question. Robert urges Elizabeth to bring as little as possible; she can buy clothes en route. She promises, 'I will be docile about the books, dearest': no mean feat for a writer, especially one whose entire waking life has relied so disproportionately on the page. In the event she and Wilson pack just two smallish bags, 'a light box and a carpet bag' containing only the basics, including most of her jewellery, Robert's letters, and the manuscript of *Sonnets from the Portuguese*. On Friday, Wilson smuggles these out of the house and round the corner to the cab stand, where she dispatches them to the railway company's offices 'care of Robert Browning'.

In fact Wilson is responsible for many of these arrangements. Robert has got in such an excited muddle that he fails to realise that there are two different Channel crossing services offered by rival companies, each with their own connecting trains. The night before their departure, Elizabeth has to correct his timing for their rendezvous, reminding him that the express train leaves Vauxhall at 5pm and gets to Southampton at 8pm. As *The Railway Times* for 19 September records, the 'South Western Steam Packet Company's splendid and powerful ships' depart from Southampton for Le Havre via Portsmouth on a scheduled twice-weekly sailing at 9pm that day.

Under the pressure of remaining practical Elizabeth's writing slants and staggers down the page. Robert is being unreliable just when she needs to rely on him. It's as if, believing his long wait is over, he's taken his eye off the ball. A disproportionate amount of his energy seems to be absorbed by wording the newspaper notice of the marriage, and of joint calling cards. These matter to Elizabeth too, but for purely practical reasons: public announcement tells the world that the Brownings are legally married, not unwed lovers running away together. She's so stressed she even snaps at Robert:

> You have acted throughout too much 'the woman's part', as that is considered—You loved me because I was lower than others, that you might be generous & raise me up:—[…] quite wrong for a man, as again & again I used to signify to you, Robert—but you went on & did it all the same. And now, you still go on—[…] You are to do everything I like, instead of my doing what *you* like, .. and to 'honour & obey' *me*, in spite of what was in the vows last Saturday.

Never again will she be as vulnerable as she is during these last hours alone at Wimpole Street, surrounded by everything she's giving up. Robert's delighted family share his sense that the romance is on the home straight, and send loving messages. But her own people are very different, and in these final moments she must write the letters she will leave for them: confession, explanation, messages of farewell. Overwhelmed in advance by homesickness and loneliness, she pleads with her siblings and father to write poste restante to Orléans, where the couple plan to stop on their way south. The tone of her surviving letter to her old ally is heartbreaking:

> My dearest George I throw myself on your affection for me & beseech of God that it may hold under the weight—[...] I bless you, I love you—I am your Ba—.

Hardly thinking straight, she alludes only in passing to the parental prohibition that's impelled her deception: 'I knew, & *you know*, what the consequence of that application [for Papa's permission] would have been—we should have been separated from that moment.'

At last, leaving the house between half part three and four 'precisely' while her father and siblings are eating, Elizabeth, Wilson and Flush make their way round the corner to Hodgson's British and Foreign Subscription Library, at what is now 45 New Cavendish Street; where behind the smart ionic columns of the façade Robert is waiting in the Reading Room.

The following morning they're in France, and there's suddenly no more need for secrecy, adrenaline or headlong flight. But it's as if nothing feels quite real yet. Elizabeth sets an unrealistic pace, as she will admit to Arabel:

> After the Havre passage which was a miserable thing in all ways [...] We were all three of us exhausted either by the sea or the sorrow, & Wilson & I lay down for a few hours, & had coffee & what else we could take—this, till nine oclock in the evening when the diligence set out for Rouen.

The railway line is only open beyond Rouen, so this dream-like progress continues by diligence:

> now five horses, now seven .. all looking wild & loosely harnessed, .. some of them white, some brown, some black, with the manes leaping as they gallopped, & the white reins dripping down over their heads .. such a fantastic scene it was in the moonlight!—& I who was a little feverish [...] began to see it all as in a vision & to doubt whether I was in or out of the body.

But at Rouen they come abruptly back to earth. There's a mix-up with the luggage, which has been already been loaded onto the overnight train and so:

> I prevailed over all the fears [and] after a rest of twenty minutes at the Rouen Hotel .. coffee & the breaking of bread […] Robert in his infinite tenderness would insist on carrying me, between the lines of strange foreign faces & in the travellers' room, .. back again to the coupè of the diligence which was placed on the railway, .. & so we rolled on towards Paris.

At the terminus, the following morning:

> we were deposited in the Messagerie Hotel, in a great noisy court— taking & not choosing that Hotel .. […] Still we had good coffee, & everything was clean, & everybody courteous to the top of courtesy—& while I lay resting, Robert went to speak to Mrs Jameson […] She was not at home. He left a note […By now] he was so thoroughly worn out with the anxiety, agitation, fatigue, & effect of the sea voyage together with that of having scarcely eaten anything for three weeks, that he quite staggered.

This makes good sense. Anna Jameson is an old friend and woman of the world. Robert's note, 'Come & see your friend & my wife EBB—', asks her to continue the interplay of friendship and social nicety that creates the texture of normal life. And she is the right person to ask. Sure enough, that very evening:

> She came with her hands stretched out, & eyes opened as wide as Flush's .. 'Can it be possible? is it possible? You wild, dear creature! You dear, abominable poets! Why what a ménage you will make!— […] But he is a wise man .. in choosing *so* .. & you are a wise woman, let the world say as it pleases!'

Better still, their much-travelled friend is used to looking after herself, and is as practical as she is intellectual. She moves the Brownings to the much more comfortable Hôtel aux Armes de la Ville de Paris, where she and a seventeen-year-old travelling companion, her orphaned niece Gerardine Bate, are staying. Having settled them in, she persuades the couple to spend a week in Paris gathering their strength; meanwhile she uses personal contacts to sort out a problem with their passport. Best of all, she arranges to accompany them on their onward journey.

In truth, this may be partly self-interest. Gerardine isn't the most scintillating company for the sophisticated art historian:

> just a pretty accomplished, gentle little girl [...] thinking how to please herself, and loving 'aunt Nina' in a sort of indolent fashion, (enough to wish to please her too, if it could be done without much exertion) .. but who was no more fitted to be what Mrs Jameson desired, a *laborious artist*, than to fly up to heaven like a lark. For ever & ever there were discussions about Gerardine's indolence, who had been besought to do this drawing or that, instead of which she lay in bed in the morning & played with Flush at night.

But whatever Anna Jameson's reasons, on 28 September the oddly assorted party of five travellers, plus dog, arrive in Orléans. It's here that, next day, Elizabeth reads her family's responses to her departure: 'my "death warrant" I called it at the time [...]. Robert brought in a great packet of letters .. & I held them in my hands, not able to open one, & growing paler & colder every moment.'

In the event, it's both better and worse than she'd feared. Her sisters' reactions to both her marriage and the secrecy it entailed are joyfully supportive. But her brothers are furious. 'They were very hard letters [...] I thought it hard, I confess, that [George] should [...] use his love for me to half break my heart with such a letter—Only he wrote in excitement & in ignorance.' Papa's reaction is exactly the extreme she predicted to Robert two days after their marriage: 'He will wish [...] that I had died years ago!' He writes that he considers her dead.

This is heartbreaking for Elizabeth, who has spent forty years being a compliant, often adoring daughter. Yet in the same bundle are letters of congratulation from friends. Sarianna Browning sends her new sister-in-law a portable writing desk. There are congratulations from Nelly Bordman, Elizabeth's doctor Mr Jago, Miss Mitford, and John Kenyon, who writes that 'the very peculiar circumstances of your case have transmuted what might have been otherwise called "Imprudence" into "Prudence," [...] if the thing had been asked of me I should have advised it.' A month from now, mail sent poste restante to Pisa will bring more good wishes, from literary friends in particular. 'We hear everyday kind speeches & messages from people .. such as Mr Chorley of the Athenæum who "has tears in his eyes" .. Mon[c]kton Milnes, Barry Cornwall & other friends of my husband's .. but who only know *me* by my books,' as Elizabeth tells Julia Martin, back in a Herefordshire that must seem increasingly remote. This is all excellent as far as it goes, but not quite comforting enough: 'I want the love & sympathy of those who love me & whom I love.' And so a pattern is set. Literary and artistic contemporaries, and readers in the decades to come, will welcome, and even romanticise, the marriage. But even while they embrace this public version, the couple themselves will have to struggle for years to recreate normal family relationships.

Now, whether vindicated or condemned, they need to keep moving south ahead of the weather. At Bourges they admire the cathedral's thirteenth-century stained glass. In the middle of a rainstorm they travel down the Rhone from Lyon to Avignon, where Elizabeth misses seeing the Palais des Papes but joins a trip to Petrarch's Fontaine de Vaucluse. Despite objections from Robert – and Flush – she clambers across slippery stones in the 'boiling water' to sit on a rock midstream, enjoying the spray. 'R. said "Ba, are you losing your senses?"' but 'The change of air appeared to act on me like a charm.' And she's not the only one thriving. She's able to reassure Miss Mitford that, 'Nearly as much attention has been paid to Flush as to me from the beginning, so that he is perfectly reconciled, & would be happy, if the people at the railroads were not barbarians & immoveable in their evil designs of shutting him up in a box when we travel that way.'

On to Aix-en-Provence, and then 'glittering, roaring Marseilles .. *coloured* even down into its puddles', from where, on 11 October, the party sail to Genoa. They leave in hot sun, but pass a stormy night. Everyone is seasick. But the next morning, wrapped in a warm cloak – and quickly joined by Robert – Elizabeth takes her famously strong sea legs up alone on deck for her first look at Italy. It is love at first sight:

> a thousand mountains & their rocks leapt up against the morning-sun, & [I] counted the little Italian towns one after another. [...] The ship was near enough to shore for us to see the green blinds to the windows of the houses [...] In one place, I counted six mountains

(such mountains!) one behind another, colour behind colour, from black, or the most gorgeous purple, to that spectral white which the crowding of the olives gives. [...] & sometimes fragments of cloud hung on the rocks, shining as if the sun himself had broken it. It was all glorious, & past speaking of.

The enchantment continues at Genoa, where the lovers sleep in the frescoed chamber of a dilapidated palazzo. 'Beautiful Genoa—what a vision it is!—& our first sight of Italy beside.' At last, after one more stormy night in the steamer, they arrive at Livorno on 14 October 1846.

'And now this is Pisa—beautiful Pisa! [...] All tranquil & grand.' Here the travellers part: Anna and Gerardine are going on to Rome. After three nights in the Hotel Tre Donzelli, Robert and Elizabeth rent a furnished three-bedroom apartment in the sixteenth-century Collegio Di Ferdinando, one short block from the Duomo, the Baptistery and the Leaning Tower, and with a good view of all three. They're the only tenants of this stuccoed Renaissance palazzo in 'the very "most eligible situation in Pisa"', which boasts a 'grand marble entrance, marble steps & pillars' restored by Giorgio Vasari, whose *Lives* introduced generations of Europeans like the Brownings to Italy's Renaissance artists. Better still, it has hot water thrown in with the rent, which Elizabeth and Robert believe is cheap – though it turns out to be above the going rate.

But after all they're a new couple, and there's going to be as much play as seriousness as they embark on their first, quixotic stabs at married life:

You would certainly smile to see how we set about housekeeping. R. brought home white sugar in his pocket—[...] & our general councils with Wilson .. "What *is* a pound? what *is* an ounce?" .. would amuse you if you could hear them.

Impracticality settles into joyous pattern as the lovers embrace new habits:

We have our dinners from the Trattoria at two oclock, & can dine our favorite way on thrushes & Chianti with a miraculous cheapness—& no trouble, no cook, no kitchen, .. [...] which exactly suits us—It is a continental fashion, which we never cease commending. Then at six we have coffee & rolls of milk—made of milk, I mean: & at nine, our supper (call it supper, if you please) of roast chestnuts &

grapes—So you see how primitive we are, & how I forget to praise the eggs at breakfast.

And why not? The six months they'll live here are an extended honeymoon. Robert 'rises on my admiration, and is better & dearer to my affections every day & hour. […] And we have been together a whole month now, & he professes to love me "infinitely more", instead of the dreadful "less" which was to have been expected.'

We can picture the newlyweds pottering about their emerging routines like a pair of clockwork mice. 'How large a part of the real world, I wonder, are those two small people?—taking meanwhile so little room in any railway carriage, & hardly needing a double bed at the inn', as Dante Gabriel Rossetti will speculate affectionately, ten years from now. But in fact there are three people – and a dog – on this adventure, and it's Wilson who must interact with the world to make it all happen. From getting baggage delivered to providing 'the coffee & milk & bread' on which the household appears to run, she's forced to be intrepid, learning languages with impressive rapidity: 'Just when she had succeeded so well in French as to be able to ask for various things, [she has] to merge all the new knowledge in the Italian "which seems to her harder still".' Far from becoming homesick, the formerly shy northern lass is blossoming: 'Wilson is an oracle—very useful too & very kind.'

Perhaps it helps that there's a separation of powers. Elizabeth has no desire to be a domestic goddess. Her ideal home life is literary, 'We are going to be busy—we are full of literary plans', as she announces on day one, and she's more than happy to hand over household responsibilities:

> the ordering of the dinner is quite out of my hands. As for me, when I am so good as to let myself be carried upstairs, & so angelical as to sit still on the sofa, & so considerate moreover as *not* to put my foot into a puddle, why *my* duty is considered done to a perfection.

Meanwhile, despite or because of this spoiling, she is 'renewed to the point of being able to throw off most of my invalid habits, & of walking quite like a woman'. Less than a month after arriving, 'everyday I am out walking while the golden oranges look at me over the walls, .. & when I am tired R. & I sit down on a stone to watch the lizards', she tells Julia

Martin. To Miss Mitford she boasts that, 'Mrs Jameson says, she "wont call me *improved*, but *transformed* rather." [...] .. my spirits rise: I live—I can adapt myself.'

She can indeed adapt herself. At the beginning of 1847 Wilson collapses with stomach pains that she's been alternately ignoring and treating with quack medicines for weeks. Elizabeth sends for a doctor, puts the maid to bed for ten days, and nurses her back to health. Close up, the invalid whom Robert married is proving unexpectedly resilient. In fact, so little does she notice physical discomfort that when she falls pregnant in October she doesn't even realise it. She suffers no morning sickness, and, even when miscarriage threatens, she remains partially in denial. But on 21 March 1847 her pregnancy becomes undeniable and she miscarries what the attending doctor identifies as a five months' pregnancy.

The day-long labour can't but be a huge shock. Yet Elizabeth doesn't grieve; on the contrary. She is forty-one, and this unexpected pregnancy feels like another marvel of her new life. She reports it carefully to her unmarried sisters:

> Towards evening however regular pains came on, every five minutes .. & these lasted for above four & twenty hours, much as in an ordinary confinement—Oh, not so very violent! I have had worse pain, I assure you—It did not continue long enough at once to exhaust one! and when my eyes were open to the truth, I was as little frightened or agitated as at this moment, & bore it all so well (I mean with so much bodily vigour) as to surprise Wilson .. & Dr Cook, too indeed—

She is, truth be told, rather proud of what she takes as a new achievement; even though she's also angry with herself for not having realised what was going on. She believes she lost the child through taking morphine (probably correct) and keeping too warm (perhaps incorrect). Robert is less sanguine. He 'was so dreadfully affected by my illness, as to be quite overset, overcome—only never *too* much so, to spend every moment he was allowed to spend, by my bedside .. rubbing me, talking to me, reading to me .. and all with such tenderness, such goodness!' and afterwards, 'In the first moment of his readmission into this room he threw himself down on the bed in a passion of tears, sobbing like a child.'

Elizabeth is touched and delighted by this too, even as she can't help noticing 'Wilson shaking her head behind the curtain.' Visceral reality replaces the fine words of nearly two years of courtship, and the first great test of their marriage has brought the couple closer still. Chianti and milk rolls, sunshine and mediaeval city streets: the embodied life takes its place at the heart of their partnership.

[*Seventh Frame*]

'It has been *within the philosophical tradition,* which for me includes social, political and religious thought, that I have found the resources for the exploration of this identity and lack of identity, this independence and dependence, this power and powerlessness', wrote the brilliant British philosopher Gillian Rose, introducing her often self-reflexive essays on *Judaism and Modernity* in 1993.

Elizabeth uses the poetic tradition in a similar way. Of course, *Aurora Leigh* isn't a self-portrait as such. But its author's lifelong relationship with poetry, from precocious obsession to the literary homage that is her final poem, starts and ends with a fierce credo of *art for art's sake* that has nothing to do with an ivory tower but everything to do with poetry in the world. It is poetry as political action, as prayer, as a way of life; and what *Aurora Leigh* captures is this notion of a life *as* and *for* writing. Like Gillian Rose, Elizabeth asks and resolves her life's questions through the tradition she practises. Like Rose, she does this not by stepping outside it to reflect, but in the very process of contributing to it.

Her poems may not be autobiographical or largely confessional, but because they are the record of becoming herself, they record her life. Stephen Spender encapsulates this two-way, mirroring relationship between the poet's self and their work in his 1964 poem 'One More New Botched Beginning'. It's a memorial to lost friends, the phenomenologist Maurice Merleau-Ponty and fellow poets Louis MacNeice and Bernard Spencer. That all three were writers, and famous ones at that, is also to the point of this strange, touching and rather wandering poem. Life stories get drafted and redrafted, interrupted and lost, just like poems, it says. Our own continual process of rehearsal is carried on after death by our friends, and – for famous writers – by a posterity of strangers.

Book Eight:
How to be autonomous

Inward evermore
To outward,—so in life, and so in art
Which still is life.

The auspiciously named Via delle Belle Donne, near the Piazza di Santa Maria Novella in Florence, is a cool chasm into which the bright April sun only just makes it between the wide eaves of Renaissance town houses. But less than 200 metres away are the giant chess pieces of the Duomo, Baptistery and Giotto's tower. It's here, just a month after Elizabeth's miscarriage, that she, Robert and Wilson settle into comfortable new lodgings. They're in search of a better climate, closer to where the action is. Happiness, it seems, is infinitely perfectible:

> I persuaded Robert to get a piano—and we have a good one, a grand [...] including the hire of music, for about ten shillings a month. [...] Our payment for the apartment includes everything [...]—we have real cups instead of the famous mugs of Pisa, & a complement of spoons & knives & forks, nay, we have decanters & champagne glasses [...] As Wilson says succinctly, "*it is something like*".

Once again the couple order in their meals from a trattoria, and they acquire a "'*donna di faccenda*' [...] who comes for a few hours everyday to make the beds, clean the rooms, brush Robert's clothes, wash up the cups & saucers &c &c.' In 1847 Florence is crisscrossed by English households and the network of tradespeople attuned to their needs. It attracts English visitors too. A couple of days after their arrival, the Brownings find themselves hosting Anna Jameson and Gerardine, homeward bound and eager to toast 23 April, Shakespeare's birthday, with 'a bottle of wine from Arezzo'. The runaways seem to have set young Geddie a poor example: in Rome she's fallen in love with 'A bad artist,! an unrefined gentleman,!! a Roman catholic! (converted from Protestantism!) a poor man!! with a red beard!!!' as Elizabeth notes with amusement. Nevertheless, the women stay a week, celebrating the '*matrimonio miracoloso*, with as much love at the end of nearly eight months as at the beginning', of which Mrs Jameson is such a key witness for literary London.

And literary London signals its approval. In May, 'Mr Forster of the *Examiner*' sends greetings, while news arrives that John Abraham Heraud, editor of *The Christian's Monthly Magazine*, is lecturing 'on the poems of Robert & Elizabeth Barrett Browning "now joined together in the bonds of holy matrimony."' 'Certainly if ever there was a union indicated by the finger of Heaven itself, and sanctioned & prescribed by the Eternal Laws […] it seemed to me […] to be this!' purrs Robert's literary mentor Thomas Carlyle. Fashionable callers at the Via delle Belle Donne range from American artists – writer George William Curtis, and sculptor Hiram Powers – to old neighbours from among the English gentry.

Elizabeth's flattering 'Hiram Powers' "Greek Slave"' will appear in her *Poems (1850)*. The Brownings respond differently to Hope End acquaintances Compton John Hanford and his sister Fanny, getting them to witness the marriage property settlement that Robert has asked John Kenyon to have drawn up. And it doesn't hurt one bit to have such well-connected visitors witness this legal agreement, by which Robert returns to Elizabeth all the wealth that otherwise passed automatically to him on their marriage, and in so doing proves he's no bounty hunter. Elizabeth seems to come over all aflutter at this, telling Arabella:

> It was half past ten oclock, & Robert said .. "Now, Ba, do you lie down on the sofa, and I will read this to you"—"Oh," I exclaimed, throwing myself down in utter prostration of body & soul, .. "if you

read a page of it to me, I shall be fast asleep! [...] It's *your* Deed, you will please to remember, yours & Mr Kenyon's, & not mine by any manner of means. [...]—Well & how do you think the discussion ended? *He would'nt read it either—*

Don't believe a word of it. This is a scenario staged by a woman as determined as she is intelligent. Elizabeth wants to give Robert all she possesses, and also to put that impulse in writing. But at the same time she's determined to make his renunciation as public as possible.

The sisters are corresponding regularly now, though Elizabeth still gets homesick: 'I dream of you all often & cry in my sleep.' Three of her brothers also write: George sends a package of magazines and a book he's careful to inscribe 'Mrs R Browning'. Henry, long the most resistant to their father's sway, mails a letter; and so does Stormie, settled this spring back in Jamaica away from Papa. Treppy sends loving greetings. But in a way their father is right. Elizabeth's departure has gone to the heart of the family's sense of itself. Now the sisters openly criticise Papa to each other – 'It really does at this distance, appear to me a quite *monstrous* state of things' – and Elizabeth unapologetically includes Henrietta's unofficial fiancé Captain Surtees in family greetings.

She leaves out Bummy, though. When their unmarried aunt shouldered the 'wicked stepmother' role after her sister's death in 1828, she sometimes crossed swords with the strong-willed eldest Barrett daughter. Even in the Torquay years, according to Henrietta, 'She has sometimes been disposed to scold me a little, & *sometimes* to look coldly upon Ba which has made her feel nervous & fidgetey.' Perhaps caring work is simply not Bummy's nature. But what she feels about her brother-in-law, whom she's known since they were both teenagers, is an intriguing blank. Presumably she found him likeable enough when she became his confidant during the difficult departure from Hope End. Fifteen years later, this impression of intimacy is reinforced as she takes his side against the newlyweds. It's entirely possible that she expects to gain absolutely nothing by this. Marrying a dead wife's sister has been illegal since 1835; it was 'voidable' and attracted social opprobrium even before then. But feelings can't be legislated for, perhaps. We shouldn't forget that back in 1828 Bummy was only a couple of years older than Elizabeth is now; plenty young enough to feel the push and pull of flattery and desire.

Or perhaps her motives are purely principled. After all the family sense of what's possible, even morally permissible, *has* been shaken. It will take Surtees and Henrietta another four years to follow Elizabeth's precedent, but this is rapid progress by Barrett standards. Besides, three more unofficial liaisons are to follow. Sixth son Alfred, the unfortunately nicknamed Daisy, having celebrated Henrietta's 1850 marriage with a seventy-two-stanza epic, will go on to marry against Papa's wishes in 1855. Even after their father's death the Barrett boys seem to associate romance with the clandestine. Stormie's two daughters, born out of wedlock in Jamaica (Eva, the first, just before Papa dies), are educated on the island by a governess – whom Stormie briefly marries – and later in France. The girls, their mother and the governess all have mixed heritage, and it's noticeable that Stormie never brings them home to his Montgomeryshire estate. But then neither, in the previous generation, did everyone's favourite, Uncle Sam: and it is his illegitimate daughter Elizabeth – Stormie's and indeed Elizabeth's first cousin – who will be the mother of Stormie's children. Finally, after joining his brother in Jamaica, in 1864 Sette too will have a mixed-heritage daughter by his 'housekeeper'. All these illegitimate Barrett children, whose pasts and futures uncomfortably straddle both sides of the Caribbean's violent racial divide, face lives destabilised by their fathers' clandestine behaviour. And so damage passes down through the Barrett family.

But these ripple effects are in the future. Summer 1847 sees Elizabeth increasingly out and about, exploring Florence's tawny-stuccoed neighbourhoods and its art treasures. 'It is so delightful to see her enjoyment, everything that is beautiful from sentiment or form or colour she seizes directly, but particularly in sentiment', Fanny Hanford reports. Michelangelo's tomb and Galileo's villa are trumped by a tea party with a couple who actually knew some of Elizabeth's literary heroes. The Hoppners befriended Byron and the Shelleys in Venice, when Mr Hoppner was vice consul there. Though Elizabeth is thrilled by the connection, she doesn't quite seem to realise that these were no casual acquaintances, but the family who fostered Byron's daughter Allegra and took in the distraught Shelleys when their daughter Clara died in 1818. Apparently:

> On their arrival they ate nothing except water gruel & boiled cabbages & cherries, because it was a principle of Shelley's not to touch animal food, & [...] Mrs Hoppner did, as she said, 'seduce' him into taking roast beef & puddings .. 'Dear Mr Shelley, you are so thin['].
> (Fancy all this said with a pretty foreign accent.) 'Now if you wd take my advice, you would have a very little slice of beef today—You are an Englishman & you ought to like beef—A very little slice of this beef, dear Mr Shelley'—And so, she said, by degrees, he took a little beef & immediately confessed that 'he did feel a great deal better'.

As literary gossip this is astonishingly incomplete. Yet for Elizabeth it establishes continuity, across the intervening quarter century, between her own and the Romantic poets' lives. After all, she and Robert have also fled to Italy in search of freedom to live as they choose. And her belief that their relationship is profoundly more authentic than mere convention – 'we could not lead the abominable lives of "married people" all round— you *know* we could not' – is innocently, but undeniably, Shelleyan.

The couple's own literary life is continuing. They're both at work, Elizabeth composing *Poems (1850)* and Robert polishing *Poems 1849*, and Elizabeth's poems appear regularly in *Blackwood's*. In July they upsize to a comfortable, seven-roomed apartment on the *piano nobile* of Palazzo Guidi, 'which belonged to the Guidi who intermarried with Dante's Ugolino family of Pisa'. It will become their permanent home, and inspire one of Elizabeth's most important poems, but they don't know that yet. For now, they've simply taken a three-month lease on furnished rooms recently vacated by 'a Russian prince'. The Palazzo is 'In THE situation of Florence' on Piazza San Felice, a hundred yards from the Pitti Palace; admission to the green maze of the Boboli Gardens beyond is included in the rent:

> The eight windows which are very large [...] open on a sort of balcony-terrace [...] which is built out from the house, giving it an antique & picturesque appearance to the exterior—And you may suppose what a pleasure it is to have such a place to walk up & down in, when we are not inclined to go into the streets. Opposite

is the grey wall of a church, San Felice, and we walk on the balcony listening to the organ & choir—

They fall into a happy routine. 'At about eight in the evening we walk in the comparative cool .. stand on the bridge of Santa Trinita, & go eat an ice at Dony's .. then return to supper, & dont sit up three m[inutes] afterwards'. Elizabeth develops a delight in clothes, 'the green plaid which is Robert's favorite & which I just begin to wear every day [...] the silk shot, [the] blue barége, [the] prettiest of possible slippers, which Henrietta has made for me!' Wilson, freed from the heavy duties of travel – and by the 'donna di faccenda' Annunziata, who has followed them across town – is once again a proper lady's maid, busy sewing Elizabeth:

> little front-caps [...] very prettily of net in the old fashion, but with a worsted edge, as slight as possible to be embroidered at all—[...] & very pretty, at the expense of a few pennies—[...] Robert likes them so, that I scarcely wear anything else, & have them in various colours, blue, green, lilac, purple, with my hair done in the old Grecian plait behind, which Wilson sighs in the doing of.

Only Flush is not quite his usual self. Like his mistress, he finds the heat hard to sleep through. Like Wilson, he suffers from stomach upsets and constipation. These troubles pass; but it's plain he needs worming: 'He is in great spirits & as full of caprices as ever .. only thin. Why shd he be thin, I wonder.'

Now the little household takes its front-row seats for the drama of Italian Republicanism. They've arrived on the peninsula at almost the tipping point of the Risorgimento, the cultural and political 'resurgence' that will eventually culminate in the creation of the Kingdom of Italy in 1861. The three decades since the 1815 Congress of Vienna reimposed Habsburg Austria's control of the fractured territory – especially through its rule of the northern Italian states – have seen guerrilla action and sporadic insurrections, and the foundation of the secretive Carboneria in the south and of *La Giovine Italia* north of the border in Marseille. On 12 September, their first wedding anniversary, Elizabeth and Robert watch and wave as 'for above three hours an infinite procession' of citizens and 'forty thousand [...] inhabitants of the different Tuscan states, deputations and companies of various kinds [pass] under our windows with all their various flags & symbols, into the Piazza Pitti where the Duke & his family stood in tears at the window to receive the thanks of his people'. By granting the right to form a civic guard, Austrian Grand Duke Leopold II seems to have taken a first step towards offering Tuscan independence from the Habsburg empire.

The excitement is contagious:

> The windows dropping down their glittering draperies, seemed to grow larger with the multitude of pretty heads, & of hands which threw out flowers & waved white handkerchiefs—There was not an inch of wall, not alive, if the eye might judge—Clouds of flowers & laurel leaves came fluttering down on the advancing procession—and the clapping of hands, & the frenetic shouting, and the music which came in gushes […] and the exulting faces, and the kisses given for very exultation.

Even Flush gets carried away, and goes missing while being walked. Robert, who has a nasty cold, spends the anniversary evening searching for him; only for the little dog to return next day none the worse for wear. But the couple don't forget their own celebration in all the excitement. As an anniversary thank-you they give Wilson a turquoise brooch, bought the night before on the Ponte Vecchio; in return, she makes Yorkshire Knead Cakes for tea.

Next February, when Leopold grants Tuscany its own constitution, Elizabeth and Robert will have a still closer view of his triumphant arrival at the Pitti Palace 'in the midst of a "milky way" of waxen torchlights—you wd have thought that all the stars out of Heaven had fallen into the piazza'. By then they will have left Palazzo Guidi, where the rent doubles in high season. Here it's not winter that's cheap but summer, with its risk of cholera and typhoid, its almost unmanageable heat. After much agonising, on 19 October they move just up Via Maggio, to rooms so cold and uncomfortable that they almost immediately move again to a 'little baby-house' actually on the Piazza de' Pitti. And here, from the double windows of their cramped new drawing room, they share a grandstand view of history with numerous visitors: 'In came Wilson to announce Count & Countess Cottrell, Mr Tulk, Mr & Mrs Ley: Mrs Ley's nurse

& two children, & Dr Allnutt [*sic*], .. all come to crowd into our little drawingroom to see the "festa" in the piazza.'

Sometimes this is just all a bit too much. February 1848 sees both Brownings preoccupied. Robert worries about paying two rents, which has made leaving Palazzo Guidi a false economy. Elizabeth is busy writing a long, political poem and is also pregnant again, full of hopeful anticipation despite continuing to have periods: 'I have had my usual health, *as regularly as possible* [...] I have both laughed & cried, in one or another crisis of this fatal uncertainty.' Although she knows that 'the habit of miscarriages is hard to break', she can't resist dropping a hint about morning sickness to Henrietta: 'Very well I am [...] The exception is a sickness in the morning, which is'nt the pleasantest thing in the world, on first getting up.'

But the habit of miscarriages is indeed hard to break. A fortnight after she's mailed the letter Elizabeth loses the baby. Possibly the bleeding she'd experienced was a sign that the pregnancy was already lost or unviable. Yet, again, she seems not quite bereft. Possibly she still can't imagine a new kind of love to rival her grand *amour*. As she wrote to Miss Mitford while she was still pregnant, 'Of course, it is natural to be rather anxious—one is not more nor less than a woman. Still, it strikes me often, that I have no right to ask for more [...] Robert has the dear goodness to say that he never cd love his child as he loves his wife [...] Perhaps, God should keep his gifts of children, for such women as have missed something of the ideal of love.'

And there's always poetry to absorb her energy and emotion. 'A Meditation in Tuscany', the long political poem she's been working on and now sends to *Blackwood's*, includes impressions recycled from her letters:

> And all the thousand windows which had cast
>   A ripple of silks in blue and scarlet down
> (As if the houses overflowed at last),
>   Seemed growing larger with fair heads and eyes
> [...]
> At which the stones seemed breaking into thanks
>   And rattling up the sky, such sounds in proof
> Arose; the very house-walls seemed to bend;

The very windows, up from door to roof,
Flashed out a rapture of bright heads [...]

This is politics as crowd scene: even the writing is crowded. In its trans-
ferred epithets, their fluidity mimicking the fast-changing revolutionary
scene, we see the *idea* of 'Italy' – abstract, historical – brought to life by
the people, 'IL POPOLO—/ The word means dukedom, empire, majesty'.
For Elizabeth, the ideal of a free Italy is inseparable from the vibrant
physicality of daily Florentine life.

Revolutionary enthusiasm is all mixed up with personal experience.
These initial eighteen months in Italy are her first sustained chance to
enjoy bodily autonomy and the vivid sensuality of an outdoor life since
she was a fourteen-year-old tomboy; even her pregnancies a sign that
she's 'not more or less than a woman' than the 'black-eyed' mothers with
their children in the streets. Warm climate, Italian food, novel surround-
ings and the sexiness of new marriage have all contributed to a bodily
resurrection. Elizabeth's gift for passionate imaginative identification has
always been attractive: as Uncle Sam remarked decades ago, she has a
gift for love. Now her ardent, optimistic 'A Meditation' reverberates with
the poet's own Risorgimento as it portrays emptied tombs and compares
the ruined architecture of Italy's historical reputation with a resurrected
national future.

Blackwood's eventually turns down this 'grand' poem on the insular
British grounds that these are foreign affairs, incomprehensible without
extensive footnotes. But Elizabeth's own attitude is changing anyway
as she and Robert become increasingly anxious about the influence of
French revolutionary politics on the Italian quest for independence. It's
all very well that the leaders of the French Second Republic, declared on
26 February, include their fellow poet Alphonse de Lamartine. But the
Brownings are liberals, not socialists. For them, France's 1848 Revolution
is frightening. It realises some of the socialist philosopher Charles Fourier
and anarchist Pierre-Joseph Proudhon's utopian ideas about cooperative
organisations along with Louis Blanc's *droit au travail* (the right to work);
and 'Really we are not communists', Elizabeth finds herself reassuring
Kenyon. 'Nothing can be more hateful to me than this communist idea
of quenching individualities in the mass.'

Revolution as self-determination does appeal, and Elizabeth understands individuation not least because she herself has laboured to achieve it. 'Life develops from within', as she'll put it in *Aurora Leigh*, seven years from now. She knows at first hand how easily individual human flowering can be blocked, 'As if the hope of the world did not always consist in the eliciting of the individual man.. But like most people who don't have to earn their living, she doesn't understand economic bondage. Unless what Elizabeth calls 'matters of material life' are arranged differently, whoever rules Italy the labouring poor will remain desperate, the small traders worse off than bankers and bishops. Sure enough, in *The Communist Manifesto*, which is published in London this very month, February 1848, Karl Marx and Friedrich Engels aim their critique not at grand dukes but at exploitative business owners like her own family.

Elizabeth rather resembles the second-generation Romantics, in whose steps she so admiringly treads, in being moved by the idea of 'liberty' but failing to see that her own privilege is complicit in denying it to the many. It remains ineluctably the case that her escape from Wimpole Street was made possible by slavery money. And in the twenty-first century, 'A Meditation in Tuscany', which eventually appears in 1851 as Part One of *Casa Guidi Windows*, feels lacking in intellectual underpinning. Yet at the midpoint of the nineteenth century it *is* radical; forcing a British readership otherwise protected from these proto-revolutionary scenes into imaginative complicity with ordinary Italians. Elizabeth turns the reader into a fellow revolutionary participant by evoking her own enthusiasm in all its vulnerability rather than hiding behind the conceit of an omniscient narrator; she puts her own self in the frame as advocate. As *The Globe and Traveller* will write, on the poem's eventual appearance, 'when the exponent of Italian feelings is the most gifted of England's poetic daughters [...] the claim on her own country's hearing becomes paramount'.

Meanwhile the Browning household is undergoing its own revolutions. Lateral thinking saves the day when Robert realises that renting unfurnished is much cheaper than a furnished let. Political crises keep property prices low: he manages to resecure the apartment at Palazzo Guidi for just twenty-five guineas per annum, and the household returns there on 9 May 1848. As Elizabeth tells Arabel, 'Next summer we shall [sub-]let our apartment for at least eight pounds a month […] & return here in the winter to a rent-free residence.' With canny furniture-shopping they can create a smart asset and fund their travel:

> The carpet is down in the drawingroom & looks very well. The walls are green, the chairs crimson, with white & gold frames, & the carpet mixes up all colours. The ceiling has a good deal of gilding in Italian fashion, .. and the little sittingroom at the end of the suite, a very pretty room, has a cloud full of angels looking down on you […]. Of course you are to understand that our furniture is not *new*—but it is in good taste & characteristic.

But this is also Elizabeth's first opportunity to nest-build:

> we wanted linen & plate, & then our rooms being immense, yearned for more & more filling—& then again, we grew ambitious, & instead of four legs to every chair we looked to gilding & spring seats, .. & so, we have passed sixty pounds & still want curtains.

Six months on, the pleasure – and expenditure – are unabated:

> The bedrooms & Wilson's room […] are to have the curtains altogether of white muslin, checked in rather a large pattern—two to each window, very full. And the bed in my room is hung with the same […] there's a new carpet laid down in my bedroom—I wanted a drugget, but the carpet was as cheap, & very thick & rich looking it is. […] we had bought for that room a beautiful chest of drawers […] Robert bought the other day a companion-chest, infinitely more beautiful—in fact far too good for any bedroom—ebony & ivory inlaid, with the curiosest gilt handles […] & he gave two pounds for it.

Furnishings can be resold, but they represent a considerable investment of money and imagination, especially given the 'panic' of war nearby – about the dangers of which Elizabeth seems strangely relaxed. But then her emotional reactions have always been somewhat disassociated. Around her, much of Europe is being shaken by the fear and promise of revolution, and there have been democratic uprisings in Vienna and Berlin as well as in Paris. In March, King Charles Albert of Piedmont-Sardinia had declared his intention to unite divided Italy under the Pope. He built on a local revolt against Habsburg rule in Lombardy-Venetia by attacking the Austrians' military headquarters in the Quadrilatero, a set of four city fortresses centred on Verona and Mantua and just 125 miles from Florence. Joined by papal, Tuscan and Sicilian forces, for a while his campaign went well: two fortresses fell. But in May the Pope, Pius IX, became nervous about challenging the mighty Austrian Empire (which is also Catholic) and withdrew his support, as did Ferdinand II of the Two Sicilies. Austrian Field Marshal Count Radetzky will finally defeat the Italian forces in August, after a three-month siege of Venice, and become Viceroy of Lombardy-Venetia for almost a decade.

These are bloody battles, not just street demonstrations, and it's hard to avoid the feeling that Elizabeth's determination to build a new life willy-nilly in such a time and place is not just wilful, but irrational. For there's another fly in the ointment: Robert isn't writing. For him, marriage has exchanged an extended adolescence, at his writing desk day and night, for adult, practical – even if not financial – household responsibilities. Also, neither Browning is under any illusion that he's currently the more distinguished partner and, while it's exciting to be adored by the author of poems you *love with all your heart*, it's altogether different to make a *life* as the lesser writer. Robert is, in effect, playing The Partner, that conflicted role to which, traditionally, artistic and literary partnerships relegate the women.

But however unorthodox the couple's domestic roles, bodies are still bodies. In June 1848, just after their return to Palazzo Guidi, Elizabeth falls pregnant again. Once again she feels so well that she carries on as usual. In mid-July, she and Robert escape the city on '*un bel giro*' alone together, first to the coast at Fano and then, when that proves altogether dreary, south down the Adriatic coast to Ancona. Here they stay for a week, and Robert at last writes a poem. But even this signals that all is not well. The depressive narrator of 'The Guardian Angel: A picture at Fano' is accompanied, like Robert himself, by a lover. Despite this he identifies with Guercino the 'Little Squinter', painter of a sentimental seventeenth-century altarpiece in the town, and prays for the angelic guardianship it portrays. Eight stanzas conclude by breaking the 'fourth wall' of fictional

conceit to appeal to someone from real life, the long-lashed, baby-faced
Alfred Domett, who was Robert's pal about (literary) town before emi-
grating to New Zealand in 1842:

> Where are you, dear old friend?
> How rolls the Wairoa at your world's far end?
> This is Ancona, yonder is the sea.

So what's going on here? In later years Domett will publish a verse
epic, *Ranolf and Amohia*, celebrating Maori culture, but his real skill is in
public office. He has the restless, slightly misfit energy that does well in
new enterprises, and will become New Zealand's fourth premier in 1862–
63. When he retires to England, more than two decades from now, the
old friends will reunite after an emotional message from Robert: 'I never
could bear to answer the letter you sent me years ago, though I carried it
always about with me.' Feelings which turn out to have been deep-seated
for when Domett left England Robert declared:

> I cannot well say *nothing* of my constant thoughts about you, most
> pleasant remembrances of you, earnest desires for you—yet I will
> [...] *write* freely what, I dare say, I *said* niggardly enough—my real
> love for you—better love than I had supposed I was fit for: [...]
> There! And now, let that lie, till we meet again.

Even though his friend didn't respond for a year and a half, Robert continued to send long, affectionate missives whose intensity only abated
after he met Elizabeth. Which would matter little by 1848; except that
another figure from Robert's bachelor days is about to enter Elizabeth's
life and, for a while, 'turn her evenings to ashes'.

The Fano poem may well be triggered by post-viral depression.
Robert hasn't completely shaken off a summer flu even as the couple
complete their three-week trip by visiting Rimini and Ravenna, where
they spend a pre-dawn hour at Dante's tomb. The tour gives Elizabeth yet more Italy to fall in love with: 'the exquisite, almost visionary scenery of the Apennines, the wonderful variety of shape & colour,
the sudden transitions, & vital individuality of those mountains .. the
chestnut forests dropping by their own weight into the deep ravines'.
Flush enjoys himself too, especially in towns: 'He looked east, he looked

west .. you would conclude that he was taking notes or preparing them. His eagerness to get into the carriage first used to amuse the Italians.' But Robert remains under par. Back home he develops a severe throat infection. For three weeks he has a high fever and, as pain keeps him awake and it becomes increasingly painful to take anything by mouth, gradually loses strength; yet he refuses to see a doctor. So it seems like sheer luck when, in the third week of September, a literary bachelor friend, the Revd Fr Francis Sylvester Mahony, calls unexpectedly. Seeing the state Robert's in, Mahony forces him to drink an improvised concoction of egg yolks and heated port wine, that, in helping the feverish patient to sleep, is key to his cure.

At least, this is the story according to Mahony, who styles himself 'Father Prout' and encourages the belief that 'he is one of [the Jesuit order's] most active members & in constant employment, .. holding high trusts', but who has actually been working as the Rome correspondent of the *Daily News* since 1846. In fact, Elizabeth records of Mahony's famous hot drink merely that her husband 'was the better' for sleeping after it. Robert's actual recovery from what his symptoms suggest is a quinsy comes when this abscess behind the tonsils bursts: 'Relief came at last by the breaking of something in the throat, & by nearly a wineglass full of matter coming up.' No matter. The talkative and energetic, but also vulgar and cynical, 'Revd Father' now invites himself to the Palazzo Guidi drawing room to smoke 'everyday [...], sometimes twice a day, & generally for two hours at a time [...] walking up & down in the room & performing an alternation of expectorations now in the fireplace & now on [...] our new carpet.'

This would be revolting at the best of times. But Robert is breathing the smoke through an infected throat, and a pregnant Elizabeth is nauseated, 'catastrophe as nearly occurring as possible [...] through an ascend<ing>of the personal incommodity':

> he plants himself close to my sofa, smokes at leisure two or three cigars, takes one of our Raffael-basins for a spitting convenience, & last night, not for the first time by any means, both Robert & I were fairly *sick*. [...] When he had gone .. between ten & eleve<n> [we opened] windows & doors & relieved ourselves by swearing gently.

By 22 November, after two months of this performance every night but one, Mahony's 'disagreeableness is beginning to pass his agreebleness'. He calls Elizabeth 'a regular child .. a *bambino*, my dear'. She is his '"Little dear" in his first visit, and "Dearest" on the second, so that, as I told Robert, I fully expected to be kissed on the third—[…] I shant be asked […] whether I *allow* it or not—'. He hijacks the intimate nickname 'Ba', and mocks his hostess for having shyly pulled down her travelling veil when he intercepted the couple as they first arrived in Livorno. The evenings are spent in conversation primarily between the men, and there's an undercurrent of misogyny to this dismissal of someone who is increasingly being seen as Britain's greatest living woman poet; a sense, almost, of trying to recruit Robert back to a bachelor cause.

Mahony is just two years older than Elizabeth, and lives precisely the kind of literary life from which gender excludes her. Since the 1830s he's been a prolific columnist, for example in *Fraser's Magazine*. There he hobnobbed with *le tout monde*, including surviving second-generation Romantics Thomas Jefferson Hogg and Thomas Medwin. Another 'Fraserian' is Robert's mentor William Makepeace Thackeray, whose masterpiece *Vanity Fair*, 'Very clever, very effective, but cruel to human nature–', has just recently finished lengthy serialisation in *Punch*. It will be apparent to everyone at Palazzo Guidi that, if there is a 'Vanity Fair' of the literary world, Mahony belongs there.

But does Robert belong there too? Elizabeth's writing life has been disproportionately inner, as her occasional sententiousness reveals. She's sheltered and high-minded; in fact this is just what she represents to Robert. 'I want to be a Poet […] dear angel of my life', as he wrote to her towards the culmination of their courtship, when he was finding 'the dullness […] mortal' at the kind of literary soirée he'd hitherto enjoyed. 'I am far from my ordinary self […] oh, to be with you, Ba'. Onlookers, Mahony possibly among them, will assume this difference is a fault line in the marriage. But the couple aren't young ingénues. They understand each other. And perhaps they recognise how each can help the other experience a fuller writing life, as Elizabeth, formerly so shy, now falls easily into literary socialising – 'Society *by flashes* is the brightest way of having it' – and Robert picks up her poetic techniques.

Still, Mahony's arrival at Palazzo Guidi is a signal of some kind. It's the fourth in what would be a quite remarkable chain of coincidences:

> [Robert] laughed a little as he told me that in crossing Poland Street with our passport, just at that crisis, he met .. Father Prout—[…] I said, 'Curious', & the conversation changed. On our landing at Leghorn, at nine oclock in the morning, our boat which was rowed from the steamer to the shore, passed close to a bare jutting piece of rock on which stood a man wrapt in a cloak, he also having just landed […] Robert cried out, 'Good Heavens, there he is again! there's Father Prout!' We went to the inn & breakfasted, & after breakfast the reverend Lion came into the room.

This already seems almost too good to be true. Then there's a third 'coincidence', the day last November when Robert, full of flirtatious high spirits, came bounding back to the Via delle Belle Donne to announce that Mahony had bumped into him in the street, taken him for coffee, and kissed him full on the mouth. Now the journalist-priest has turned up at Palazzo Guidi, where someone – who? – has given him the address.

'Mrs Jameson says he is the bitterest of clever talkers, and that Robert is nearly the only man in the world whom he speaks well of—.' Perhaps being based in Rome means that Mahony is starved of English literary talk. But at this point we need to cock an ear to Mary Russell Mitford's gossip. In 1847 she thought back eleven years to 1836 and that opening-night party for Noon Talfourd's *Ion*. There, as she confided to the travel writer Charles Boner, she met 'Mr Browning':

> & remember thinking how exactly he resembled a girl drest in boy's clothes—[…] he had long ringlets & no neckcloth—& […] seemed to me about the height & size of a boy of twelve years old— Femmelette—is a word made for him. A strange sort of person to carry such a woman as Elizabeth Barrett off her feet.

Every generation misreads the dandyism of the next, and as an ambitious young poet Robert tried hard to establish a Bohemian persona. But Mitford is making a stronger claim than this, 'in malice' as she admits. By the 1880s *femmelette* will be pre-eminently used – in French, which she speaks fluently – to indicate sexuality, rather like English twentieth-century uses of 'effeminate'. But in the first half of the nine-teenth century desire of all kinds is much less socially acknowledged than it will become, and 'sodomy' in particular is illegal – which is why the 1816 legal separation case divulging Byron's proclivities led to his exile. Prohibition creates an innocence around same-sex friendships that allows them to include behaviour, like declarations of love and bed-sharing, that could be anachronistically misinterpreted as sexual. For exactly the same reason, it also allows same-sex love to be acted out in plain sight despite social conventions – and whether or not both participants realise it.

So might Robert the *femmelette* ever have experimented with bisexu-ality, or attracted crushes? The possibility will traditionally be ignored: after all, the Brownings share a passion that's clearly sexual as well as romantic. But bisexuality isn't disproved by a great love affair with an individual of either sex. Also, Robert is long held to have condemned Shakespeare's bisexuality. In fact his much-cited debate is with William Wordsworth not Shakespeare, concerns literary biography not sexu-ality, and goes like this. In 1827 Wordsworth's eponymous 'Scorn not the Sonnet' called Shakespeare's notoriously sexually ambiguous sonnets a 'key' with which he 'unlocked his heart'. But this is a conventional charac-terisation of sonnet form itself, not of any particular sexuality, and nearly four decades later Robert's 1876 poem 'House' will retort that it's wrong to read any poetry as confessional:

> 'Tis the fall of its frontage permits you feast
> On the inside arrangement you praise or blame.
> Outside should suffice for evidence:
> [...] *'With this same key*
> *Shakespeare unlocked his heart,'* [...]
> Did Shakespeare? If so, the less Shakespeare he!

This is a reflection on literary celebrity by a sixty-four-year-old whose life has been marked by it for thirty years, not writing about desire of any kind.

All of which matters because of what it leaves open, in late 1848, in the background of the Palazzo Guidi drawing room. The young Alfred Domett can't have missed the strength of feelings that the young Robert waited till his departure to the ends of the earth to declare, but that proves nothing. Best-friendship can be intense, addictive. Mahony is another matter altogether. Bon viveur yet a life-long celibate when it comes to women, a priest ordained against his spiritual advisors' counsels, the formerly brilliant seminarian expelled for drunken socialising with his students: he seems likely to know *exactly* what and whom he desires.

Does this cross Elizabeth's mind as she sits in the green drawing room, watching the clock and making sure a spittoon is to hand? Probably not. With her father's literal-mindedness about religion, she takes Mahony's alleged priesthood as guarantee that he must be a better man than he appears. Besides, she's pregnant, just two years married and very much in love, with a certainty that's helped her to brave parental abandonment, storms at sea, miscarriage, and the risk of social stigma. Compared to all this, someone flirting with the man who loves her is just the faint buzz of a Florentine mosquito. And of course in the end she wins: eventually, Mahony leaves.

Elizabeth may be naïve but she's tough. She has coped well with Robert's illness. Her respect for his refusal to call a doctor isn't hand-wringing weakness, but self-denial by someone who understands intimately a patient's right to self-determination: 'I wd have sent to Dr Harding without asking him [but] he never wd do such things to me .. often saying to me that he cd not treat me *so*, without confidence, whatever his own feelings might be:—' She looks after her husband in other ways too. On 9 October, kneeling on a fauteuil to pray, she has a nasty, and slightly ridiculous, fall on to the tiled apartment floor. Her nose and forehead bleed, but she's quick to reassure the recuperating Robert, confining her true feelings of anxiety that this may have endangered her pregnancy to letters home.

Such wifeliness is part of a burgeoning strength. By November the baby is kicking:

> the *second life*—[...] is distinctly appreciable now [...] the insertion of new gores & the letting out of waist-bands goes on steadily .. & the appetite is good, & the strength keeping up, & the morphine diminishing!

Times change, and while some changes, including Hugh Stuart Boyd's death in May, are sad – most are exciting. Elizabeth is cutting out morphine after nearly thirty years of dependency. The household has acquired a cook, Alessandro, whose snobbery drives Wilson mad; but the maid herself, 'our friend rather than our servant', has become engaged to a member of the ducal guard who plans to take a palace clerkship in order to marry her (though in fact he will open a shop). Tall and good-looking, Signor Righi is the educated younger son of a doctor; his brother a wealthy merchant in nearby Prato 'with town and country house'. It's a relationship across religious lines, but if Wilson were to become Signora Righi she'd be almost as well off as the Brownings themselves.

Palazzo Guidi has become a real home, as full of life as any soap-opera set: shortly, when the household is completed, Elizabeth will rename it Casa Guidi. As she turns forty-three she's in her prime, and to cap it all on 9 March 1849, three days after her birthday, she gives birth to a healthy little boy. Though the labour is fairly long – twenty-one hours 'during the whole of which time she never once cried out, or shed a tear' – it's shorter than her first miscarriage, and Elizabeth's years of struggle with her body have prepared her for it. At a quarter past two in the morning 'the very model of a beautiful boy' is born. 'The nurse says of the babe "e stato ben nutrito", "how well nourished he has been".'

Robert has stayed with Elizabeth holding her hand for as much of the labour as Dr Harding, the midwife Madame Biondi and Wilson, who are all in attendance, will allow '& I comforted myself by pulling his head nearly off.' For her, 'The first cry came to me in the rapture of a surprise! [...] it had always seemed to me *reasonable* to expect some evil about the child—malformation if nothing else.' But Robert, whose proud announcement of the birth appears in *The Times* on 19 March, is in no doubt that it's the reward 'for her perfect goodness, patience, selfdenial and general rationality. That resolution of leaving off the morphine, for instance—' In fact, healthy late childbearing is also in the family genes: soon Henrietta too will give birth three times between the ages of forty-two and forty-seven, to two sons and a daughter.

The 'little fellow grows prettier and bigger visibly' daily, and the new mother thrives too, as Robert records with exuberance. Though her milk has come in, she follows custom by choosing not to breast-feed. In the first week three *balie*, or wet nurses, don't work out, but by 18 March a fourth, Tecla Celavini, has been engaged. This 'mighty woman, that would cut up into twenty Bas, aged 26, with a child of not yet a month old— good-natured, and intelligent spite of her fat cheeks which overflow her neck as she bends down' will remain with the Brownings for over two years. But the date she arrives has a double significance. Early in the pregnancy, when Robert was ill, Elizabeth had written to Miss Mitford, 'Nobody was ever born to be happier & unhappier than I—the "mingled yarn" is black & white.' Now the 'mingled yarn' knots tight, for on the day Tecla arrives, Robert's beloved mother dies of a heart attack without having ever met her daughter-in-law or known she has a grandchild. From elation at the birth, Robert crashes into a depressive grief: 'Just because he was *too happy* when the child was born, the pain was overwhelming afterwards. [...] While he was full of joy for the child,—his mother was dying at a distance, and the very thought of accepting that new affection for the old, became a thing to recoil from.'

There may in any case have been something fragile about this slightly hyperactive joy, for Robert's sense of his own self continues to take a battering. In January Chapman and Hall published his selected *Poems*, omitting both *Strafford*, the drama he wrote for Macready, and *Sordello*, the long poem which in 1840 destroyed his precociously brilliant reputation. As Miss Mitford says (behind Elizabeth's back), his poetry is now regularly dismissed as 'one heap of obscurity confusion & weakness [...] book upon book all bad [...] the first edition of each having gone off in the form of waste paper'. Critics are slow to change a pigeonhole, and *Poems*'s reception is poor. The *Eclectic Review* rakes up *Sordello* to review alongside it, while *The Atlas* opens with that 'prodigious mistake' before going on to dedicate its review to a nit-picking appraisal of Robert's revisions. *The English Review* claims the poems are immoral (and that, for example, 'Pippa Passes' advocates suicide) and, while the book receives serious, glowing reviews from John Forster in *The Examiner* and, among several positive notices in the US, Edwin Percy Whipple in *Graham's American Monthly*, the *Morning Post* is swingeing:

> We have searched in vain [...] for a single passage that would place our author in a favourable light before the public, and we feel no

small degree of mortification in having wasted so much profitable time in a pursuit which has proved so unpleasant and abortive.

Small wonder perhaps that the loss of his mother, that loving, unconditional admirer, overwhelms Robert. Worries about Elizabeth giving birth abroad have been triumphantly assuaged, but this sudden bereavement underscores the couple's distance from home. That distance helped Sarianna keep back the bad news until the baby was safely born, but now it breaks apart familial support structures. Elizabeth advises her own sisters not to visit their sister-in-law with support and condolences, lest Papa create a row and intensify Sarianna's suffering. Robert no longer wants to take a planned trip to England, because his mother 'was so longingly anxious to have us back again .. and we waiting till it was just too late for our return to make her happy'.

The new mother swallows down her disappointment: she won't be able to show off her baby to her sisters. Things are so bad that by early May that she's relieved when Robert is still going through the motions with his baby, '& goes to see him bathed every morning & walks up & down on the terrace with him in his arms'. As she tells Sarianna, 'If your dear father can toss & rock babies, as Robert can, he will be a nurse in great favour.' It seems only logical to help her husband by reinforcing the positive, so she decides the baby should take her late mother-in-law's maiden name. He's christened Robert Wiedeman Barrett Browning on 26 June in the Evangelical Church, and Elizabeth insists he's to be known as Wiedeman – though before he turns three, the irrepressible Barrett habit of nicknames will have transformed this to Pen, a name which sticks for the rest of his life.

Four days after the christening, the household – including Wilson, who's become the baby's nursemaid, the *balia* and Flush – set out for Bagni di Lucca, where they've rented an apartment in Casa Valeri, on hills above Bagni Caldi. They've decamped for the summer in the Italian style, but also because Robert is still in a bad way. In fact he's so depressed that Elizabeth has had to force the issue. 'The truth was, there was a necessity for our going. His nerves were unstrung, and [...] he began to leave off eating altogether.'

They're following where the Shelleys summered a quarter century ago. Indeed earlier in June they also checked out Percy Bysshe Shelley's last home, La Spezia, on the Ligurian coast north of Leghorn, but despite 'the most exquisite and various country [...] found the prices *enormous.*' In any case, Bagni di Lucca is beautiful in ways that speak touchingly of Hope End:

> You may take some suggestion of it from Malvern [...]. There is a throng of mountains, much higher of course & more romantic than the Worcestershire hills, .. the chesnut woods running up them perpendicularly, and the pretty, bright village, with a scattering of villa residences, burrowing, like rabbits, in the clefts of the rocks.

Life up here is good. Wiedeman thrives, 'plays with Flush's ears & talks to him. By the way, I forgot to tell you that I cant help calling him Flush, and Flush, Baby—& Robert is apt to make the same mistake—'. Elizabeth has put on so much weight that she's 'grown the image of Henrietta', and is enjoying long walks in the surrounding hills. Before they leave Bagni di Lucca she has fallen pregnant again. So restored is she that she now finally does something she has resisted for years, revealing to Robert the sonnet sequence she wrote during their courtship. Relaxed and sure of herself, perhaps she no longer sees the point of keeping them secret in a relationship that's inevitably more or less 'warts and all'. Or maybe she wants gently to remind her partner of the love at the heart of their great adventure. Romance can't heal bereavement, but Robert seems to need a fresh injection of joy.

In the twenty-first century, these immaculate sonnets will be her best-known legacy. But in 1849 Elizabeth has nothing but instinct to go on as to whether they work, and the emotional risk she's running is considerable. If they fail as *poetry* then something fundamental to this poets' love match will be damaged. For in them Elizabeth is again being radical: this time by stepping into the first person to speak in the literary masculine. In the nineteenth century the sonnet is still a form expressing *male* desire, even if that's not always heterosexual – think Michelangelo, if not, indeed, Shakespeare. Can it adapt itself to female experience? And what could adopting this form do to the balance of her femininity and Robert's masculinity?

Of course Elizabeth isn't the first woman to write a sonnet. Her

English precursors include the sixteenth-century Lady Mary Wroth, also famous for *The Countess of Montgomery's Urania* (the first prose romance known to be by a woman), and poet-novelist Charlotte Turner Smith, who died the year Elizabeth was born. But this sustained investigation of form and feeling is unique. The most famous, penultimate poem of the sequence transforms long literary tradition into intimate immediacy:

> How do I love thee? Let me count the ways.
> I love thee to the depth and breadth and height
> My soul can reach [...]
> I love thee to the level of everyday's
> Most quiet need, by sun and candlelight.

Luckily, Robert is enthusiastic; indeed he urges her to include the sequence in her next collection. All the same, he has a canny idea. He suggests using a title to signal that this isn't to be read as scandalous confession but as a serious literary project. Elizabeth first thinks of 'Sonnets translated from the Bosnian', but 'Sonnets from the Portuguese' has the additional virtue of deflecting attention onto her poem on 'Catarina to Camoens', Portugal's national poet, which immediately precedes the sonnets in her manuscript. It also alludes to a rich tradition of homage to the seventeenth-century French *Lettres Portuguese*, a 'woman's' love letters supposedly by a Portuguese nun, a literary sensation that in the mid-nineteenth century is still attracting wide readership and distinguished translations. Last and not least, buried among these literary allusions is Robert's nickname for Elizabeth: his 'little Portuguese'.

Perhaps it's the injection of joy that works. Gradually Robert recovers from his long funk. About a month after the family's return to Casa Guidi, in mid-October, he starts writing the diptych *Christmas-Eve and Easter-Day*. At the start of March 1850 he sends this manuscript to Chapman and Hall, who turn it round quickly, publishing on 1 April. At last, the critical response is respectful, substantial and close-reading; though there are no raves and sales remain poor. Meanwhile in February Elizabeth has sent in her own manuscript. A substantial volume, including heavily revised versions of *Prometheus Bound* and *The Seraphim*, most of *Poems (1844)*, recent poems, and the *Sonnets*, it appears as *Poems (1850)*.

The critical response will be, by her standards, muted; several critics assume that this is largely a reissue plus some new translations. It will also be the first time that she's widely characterised as a 'poetess': as if marriage has gendered her, removing her liberty to be pure ungendered mind. *The Christian Register* will dismiss her work as 'deficient in that weight and breadth of thought—that enlarged view of life, which is as essential to the highest poetry as to the highest philosophy.' *The English Review* will wheel out Arthur Thompson Gurney for a hatchet job, which starts with a 1,300-word rant on the 'endless twaddle' of 'Female Poetry' and gratuitously brings in Robert as 'Upon the whole [...] the higher and the master spirit'. *The Morning Post* has graciously 'ALWAYS been of opinion that Elizabeth Browning is the best English poetess [...] since the days of Felicia Hemans [...] The grace and sensibility which are so charmingly characteristic of female genius are found throughout her poetry.' And so on. Even *The Athenaeum* will crystalise the double-edged compliment: 'Mrs. Browning is probably, of her sex, the first imaginative writer England has produced in any age:—she is, beyond comparison, the first poetess of her own.'

And yet: she's arrived at a canonical moment. In 1850 there is, as *Harper's* will put it, 'a wide circle which has learned to venerate Mrs. Browning's genius, [...] the most remarkable poetess of modern times.' Her body of work isn't huge and she's not yet a bestseller, but almost by stealth she has become one of the undeniable poets. Gurney is right in one way, though: she *is* undeniably a woman. 1849's summer pregnancy had been ended in the second half of October by a bleed bad enough to make Elizabeth faint. And there is one final throw of the dice: this spring, at the age of forty-four, she falls pregnant for the fifth and final time.

Spring 1850 is an exciting time in general. On 6 April Henrietta and Surtees finally marry, after a wait of six years. Money is still a worry but to delay any longer would be folly: at forty-one, the bride is even older than Elizabeth was on her wedding day. Like her older sister, Henrietta tries her best not to elope. She and Surtees ask her father's permission, which he refuses on the perverse grounds that she's a hypocrite because she'll go ahead and marry whatever his response. But this time the Barrett brothers 'though generally obtuse on such matters', Elizabeth drily observes, are more supportive. Treppy even braves the wedding itself. Only Bummy, 'whose conduct has been, I do think, shameful & most treacherous', as Arabella says, betrays her niece by sending Papa the letter in which Henrietta confided her plans, commenting, 'I grieve for you dearest Edward—.' The match holds up a mirror to Elizabeth's own hard-won happiness:

> what emotion this [...] has stirred me to! How I have felt every line of it, gone with you through the whole trial .. no less bitter indeed, because, if God pleases, happiness & love catch up the ends of it for ever.

But now the literary world holds up a mirror too. This same month, shortly after his eightieth birthday, William Wordsworth dies (symbolically, on Shakespeare's birthday). Almost immediately the question arises of who will succeed him as Poet Laureate. On 1 June *The Athenaeum* publishes its opinion that, 'There is no living poet of either sex who can prefer a higher claim than that of Mrs Elizabeth Barrett Browning', and that to have a female laureate 'would be at once an honourable testimony to the individual, a fitting recognition of the remarkable place which the women of England have taken in literature of the day, and a graceful compliment to the Sovereign herself.'

As Elizabeth tells Arabel, 'Somebody of the name of Langley suggested it first, in the Daily News—The Globe took it up—& Robert saw it in two or three other English papers, besides Galignani', we glimpse, fascinatingly, her pragmatism:

> it's curious to myself that I should seem to have a chance—a faint one though, because the gallantry of Englishmen always takes care, carefully taking off its hat, to push a woman against the wall, upon principle. Besides, even *among the candidates named*, both Leigh Hunt & Tennyson are worthier than I .. & except as a proof that women have made some way against prejudice, I should shrink from the very thought of appearing in the competition.

In fact, of course, it will take another century and a half for Britain to create its first woman Poet Laureate. It is Tennyson who is finally appointed in November, just three weeks after Elizabeth's *Poems (1850)* has appeared. If she's disappointed, her correspondence gives no suggestion of it. Instead, reading Tennyson's *In Memoriam* in December, she finds it 'appeals, heart to heart, directly as from his own to the universal heart'.

Besides, there has been a more critical disappointment in her personal life. On 28 July she suffered a near-fatal miscarriage, losing 'above a hundred ounces of blood within the twenty four hours' as Robert overshares with John Kenyon. A month later she was still pale – 'when I look in the glass [...] I see nothing but a perfectly white & black face, the eyes being obliterated by large blots of blackness' – when the family moved to the countryside for the summer cool. They had rented the Villa Poggio al Vento outside Siena, which, as its name suggests, sits on a sunny, windy knoll with a 'vineyard up to the door, with the purple of grapes caught sight of down the vistas of vines—& magnificent views beyond all'. Little Wiedeman had also been ill, with heatstroke turning to fever, but both patients recovered quickly in the country air; even though 'except the blackberries & grapes, .. yes, & except the donkey, & the pigeons, & the pig, & the great yellow dog [Baby] does'nt particularly enjoy a rural life'.

The trip ended with a week in Siena and, for Wilson, the crushing disappointment of a disappearing act by Signor Righi, who broke their engagement with this cruelly practical expedient. But once they're home, in the second week of October, Elizabeth got down to work. She started writing the second part to what will become *Casa Guidi Windows*, almost as a riposte to Part One, as 'A Meditation in Tuscany' now becomes. She also composed a prefatory 'Advertisement', drawing attention to the eponymous 'Windows' as framing, limiting device. 'No continuous narrative nor exposition of political philosophy is attempted. It is a simple story of personal impressions', she claimed, distancing herself from her own first response to the Tuscan dream of independence, and underlining her poem's radically subjective approach.

Perhaps we should remember that as she wrote she was waiting for her previous book to come out, and anticipating the critical reception of the *Sonnets* in particular. All the same her caution now reminds us how thoroughly she's a cultural Victorian, aiming to speak not for an intellectual avant-garde but from the heart of consensus morality. By the time *Casa Guidi Windows* is published next May, Elizabeth will know both the muted verdict on *Poems (1850)*, and which way the tide of British public opinion is turning over Italy. At first her political caution seems to have been rewarded. When the book appears on 21 May 1851 it receives more than two dozen reviews in Britain, America and Europe. From *The Literary Gazette* and *The Athenaeum* to *The Scotsman* most chorus applause for both her sentiments and the poetry itself, especially in Part Two: critics seem to find it hard to separate poetics from politics. *The Liberator* praises her 'relentless insight, into the heart of Italian strength and weakness, and [...] the cardinal principles of all reform', reminding its readers, 'she is the only poet of the first rank in England, except Campbell, who has made a direct offering on the altar of American Anti-Slavery'. For *Revista Britannica*, the poem offers a riposte to Goethe's dismissal of political poetry; for *The Monthly Christian Spectator* a principled response to despotism; and for *Die Grenzboten* proof of why Elizabeth 'is revered as a prophet by all the ambitious minds of her race in England'.

But the feminising continues apace, some of it as a backhanded compliment: *The Morning Chronicle* 'We will not call her poetess, for Mrs. Barrett Browning's mind is masculine'; *Fraser's* 'altogether manlike'; and the *The Eclectic Review*, which grumbles that 'her otherwise manly and prominent progression' advocates violence. Much is negative: 'Mrs. Browning [...] presents us with a pleasant little volume of extracts from a journal of her residence in Florence', sneers *The Prospective Review*. The *Manchester Guardian*'s complaint about 'diffuse and rather commonplace reflection and regret. She is really not at home in politics and social philosophy' becomes understandable when it declares its own political allegiance: 'She must get better heroes than Mazzini and Garibaldi.' Worst of all, *The English Review* – 'Woe to relate! Mrs. Browning is not contented with being Elizabeth Barrett Browning; she will be Robert Browning also' – starts the long trend in Browning reception for ignoring chronology, and poetic record, to claim that Elizabeth imitates her husband.

By the time these notices appear the Brownings themselves have left Casa Guidi. The eighteen months they'll stay away, from 3 May 1851 to mid-November 1852, illustrate starkly the dilemma posed by Elizabeth's health. In sunny Italy she appears as strong as anyone; it is Robert who suffers from the lack of social and cutting-edge cultural stimulation. But now, as they travel north to rejoin the cultural world, Elizabeth starts to cough. Something is on the turn. Still, it doesn't look that way at first. Leaving Pen's *balia* behind in a rainy Florence they set out for Paris, visiting Bologna, Modena, Parma, Mantua – and Venice, where they rent rooms on the Grand Canal for a month, and Elizabeth falls for 'the mystery of the rippling streets & soundless gondolas'. But while she and Pen thrive in the watery city, and the toddler's Italian vocabulary comes on apace, Wilson feels constantly bilious and Robert 'cant eat or sleep, .. & suffers from continual nervous irritability'. He even overrules Elizabeth on how to dress their son:

> Robert & I had a quarrel about it yesterday & Robert had the upper-hand. Robert wants to make the child like *a boy*, he says—(because he is a man)—and I […] like him to be a baby as long as possible. […] The truth is that the child is not 'like a boy,' and that if you put him into a coat & waistcoat forthwith, he only would look like a small angel travestied. For he is'nt exactly like a girl either—no, not a bit. He's a sort of neutral creature, so far. But it vexes Robert when people ask if he is a boy or a girl—(oh, man's pride!).

This is ironic. It's not so long ago that Robert was himself the ring-letted one, rather than the high-handed husband of this cameo; a little earlier still and Elizabeth was that 'sort of neutral creature', the child Ba. Certainly, enough of the literary dreamer remains in both Brownings for them to retrace Lord Byron's routes through city and lagoon three decades ago. They visit the Lido, and the Armenian Mekhitarist Monastery on San Lazzaro degli Armeni where, as part of his anti-Ottoman crusade, Byron had studied Armenian with the Superior, Haroutiun Aukerian, and collaborated on an English–Armenian dictionary and grammar that contributed to the Armenian Renaissance. Thrillingly, they even bump into Aukerian himself, 'an old man with a white beard long below his waist, sitting under a rose-tree in full bloom'.

The third week of June sees more cultural pilgrimage. The family continues north via Padua, Petrarch's house at Arquà, Milan Cathedral and Leonardo da Vinci's *The Last Supper*, the Italian Lakes, the St Gotthard Pass, and Lucerne. Here, on 24 June, they discover the reason that Elizabeth's annual 'ship money' has been delayed: the *David Lyon* has only generated one quarter its usual profit. This shortfall puts an abrupt end to further sightseeing. They take the quickest, cheapest route to Paris, where they arrive on 30 June, and, as on their honeymoon journey, take rooms in the Hôtel aux Armes de la Ville de Paris.

A highlight of their three-week stopover in the French capital is meeting the Tennysons. Alfred already knows Robert, though neither he nor his wife Emily has met Elizabeth. Now the couples meet up three times in quick succession, getting on so well that Alfred even offers the use of his Twickenham home. But Robert has suddenly got cold feet about crossing the Channel. Apparently he remains his mother's boy, still more concerned by his own grief than the needs of his widowed father, sister or wife:

> The idea of taking his wife & child to New Cross & putting them into the place of his mother, was haunting him day & night, & I was afraid to think how it might end. As soon as we had decided not to go, the imagination became quieted & he was better at once. Then, [...] suddenly 'he could'nt bear to disappoint Arabel', and 'he would go to a lodging in London near her, &, so, visit his own home by himself & get it over'.

The couple finally arrive in London on 23 July, and take a rental at 26 Devonshire Street, less than five minutes on foot from 50 Wimpole Street. It's so very close, yet not quite home. 'It is a position on a thickset hedge—I cant make a movement to right or left without pain', as Elizabeth puts it. The two months here will be a time of emotional struggle for both her and Robert, who goes almost immediately to New Cross to see his family. 'Thank God it is not to be looked forward to anymore. He is himself again', Elizabeth records.

The decision made with such difficulty proves a good one. Soon, exciting plans are being laid. Henrietta brings her husband and first child up by train from Taunton to spend the beginning of August in Bentinck Street, equally close to Wimpole Street and Arabella. Of the brothers, 'Henry has been very kind in coming not infrequently,—he has a kind, good heart. Occy, too, I have seen three or four times—Alfred & Sette, once'. Meanwhile, 'dear George [...] was very good & kind & feeling to me at last—it has made me really happier'. Only Papa remains obdurate, refusing to see even his first grandchild, writing 'a very violent and unsparing letter' in response to Robert's overture. Indeed he returns Elizabeth's letters 'all with their unbroken seals testifying to the sealed up heart which refused to be opened by me'. 'It is so very disastrous & hopeless', his daughter grieves.

But by contrast, artistic and literary London embraces the couple. They see old friends like Mary Russell Mitford and John Kenyon. Through the American artist Thomas Buchanan Read they befriend Dante Gabriel Rossetti. Moreover:

> Mr Arnauld [*sic*] the chancery barrister, has begged us to go and live <in his> town house—! [...] Mrs Fanny Kemble called on us & left us tickets for her Shakespeare reading—[...] Mr Forster of the Examiner gave us a magnificent dinner at Thames Ditton in sight of the swans, & we breakfast on saturday with Mr Rogers. Then we have seen the Literary Guild actors at the Hanover Square rooms,—& we have passed an evening with *Carlyle* [...] It's a great dazzling heap of things new & strange. Barry Cornwall (Mr Procter) came to see us every day, till business swept him out of town, & dear Mrs Jameson left her Madonna for us in despite of the printers. Such kindness, on all sides.

Still, now it's Elizabeth's turn to falter. 'There's kindness in England after all. Yet I grew cold to the heart as I set foot on the ground of it, & wished myself away.' As well as griefs that remain too immediate – she can't bear to visit Julia Martin in Herefordshire, which reminds her of Bro – she's falling ill. It's still summer, but London is a polluted city, set in a basin nearly at sea level where dust and industrial dirt hang in the air and in the lungs. 'The quality of the air does *not* agree with me .. that's evident. For nearly five years I have had no such cough nor difficulty of breathing, & [...] I get so much paler every day.' And so, 'We pass this winter in Paris, in the hope of my being able to bear the climate—for indeed Italy is too far. And if the winter does not disagree with me too much we mean to take a house & settle in Paris, so as to be close.'

Low-lying and northern European, Paris has a climate not much better than London's, and even this compromise will prove unworkable. Nevertheless, it seems the couple's best hope of a life among friends and loved ones. They cut short their London stay and leave for France on 25

September, travelling this time with Thomas Carlyle. After a rough crossing and a night in Dieppe, they're back at the Hôtel aux Armes, where
they rest for a fortnight before moving into a second-floor apartment,
'flooded with sunshine', at 138 Avenue des Champs-Élysées: ample reward
for Robert's 'miseries in house-hunting'. The 'pretty cheerful, carpeted
rooms' comprise 'a drawing room, a dressing & writing room for Robert,
a small dining room, two comfortable bedrooms & a third bedroom up
stairs for the femme de service,—kitchen &c—for two hundred francs a
month'. The address is gloriously fashionable too, and they'll remain here
till they return to London next July. In fact, they like it so much that, in
spring 1853, Robert's father and sister will move in.

One shortcoming seems obvious: there's no writing room for Elizabeth. But within two days of moving in, Robert, who's preparing an
edition for Moxon of what will unfortunately prove to be forged letters
by Shelley:

> has taken to his new room with green curtains, & sits there half
> in sun & half in shade, 'doing' his Shelley to his heart's content.
> 'Monday,' he said, 'was the happiest day he had had since he left
> England; and we *never* have lived in a house, he likes so well as this.'!
> So 'Casa Guidi' is slighted you see—dear Casa Guidi.

It's a moment of what seems like masculine ascendancy. In the same
week 'Baby', now two and a half, invents his family nickname: 'He has
now taken to call himself *Peninni*—by an extraordinary revolution of
syllables: he means *Wiedeman* [...] Peninni can do this, Peninni can do
that, Peninni wants this & that, all day long'. This autumn, the small
boy obsessed with soldiers graduates to trousers: 'Such ridiculous tiny
trowsers up to his knees!—and long, white knit gaiters. It's a beautiful costume, & he is much admired', his mother boasts. She still loves
dressing him up in 'a white felt hat, white satin ribbons & feathers ..
really the prettiest hat I ever saw, & he looks lovely in it—with a trim-
ming of blue satin ribbon inside at each cheek!' But, odd though this
sounds in the twenty-first century, she's doing nothing unusual. Even in
sleepy Taunton, Henrietta contemplates a black felt hat for her first son
Altham, while Parisians go altogether further: 'Do you know, in Paris,
they even put the boys into curlpapers? boys ten years old, Wilson has

seen curled up regularly in the morning, .. a process which I could not approve of.'

It's nothing to do with gender: only with privilege and ostentation. For appearances matter. Soon after moving in, Elizabeth has to sack the cook-housekeeper, caught three times with her lover coming out of her room, because 'the facts were known in the house, & we could not keep a woman of a disreputable character'. Her replacement is Desirée, 'a little brisk laughing creature, who tumbles about everything .. "has no method," Wilson says, but who cooks extremely well & is as good natured as possible'.

But scandal turns up nonetheless. Desirée is installed in mid-October, just in time for the arrival of Robert's father and sister on a three-week visit, during which Robert senior divulges that back in New Cross he's got involved with a widow called Minny von Müller. Under the misapprehension that she's bothering his father, Robert writes the lady a stern letter. Unfortunately, the old man hasn't been entirely honest. Scandalously, on 1 July the following year huge damages of £800 – about twenty-five times an agricultural labourer's annual salary – will be awarded against him for both breach of promise and defamation of Mrs von Müller's character: on evidence which includes over fifty love letters plus a (false) accusation of bigamy, and Robert's own shot across her bows. Three weeks after the court ruling, Robert's father and sister will flee the country. The case is shocking enough to make the papers and Robert, who escorts them to Paris, will feel it 'to the heart of his heart'.

But these personal embarrassments are to come. Meanwhile, the old year ends with darkness and drama. On 2 December 1851 Charles-Louis-Napoléon Bonaparte leads a coup in the streets of Paris. Elizabeth is sanguine in letters home: she's used to European revolutions going on around her. But she has battles of her own. This month she's once again seriously ill with bronchitis, perhaps even pneumonia; and in January, as she sits coughing in the Champs-Élysées apartment, she is deeply hurt to discover that Mary Russell Mitford has betrayed her confidence by writing about the death of Bro in a memoir, *Recollections of a Literary Life*.

Robert, on the other hand, is thriving in Paris. His New Year's resolution for 1852, to write a poem a day, will result eventually in *Men and Women*, the book with which he takes his great step forward. He's being encouraged in his work by a new friend, the critic Joseph Milsand, who, back in August, published a highly complimentary essay dedicated to his work, 'English Poetry after Byron II', in *La Revue des deux mondes*. On 15 January Milsand's follow-up three-hander, covering Elizabeth alongside John Reade and Henry Taylor, is positive enough; but certainly no rave. Still, by the spring, Milsand is spending every Tuesday evening at the Brownings'.

Their cultural milieu is tilting towards Robert; this tilt increases as Elizabeth's illness allows him to resume the conventionally male literary life. While she's confined at home by pulmonary disease he goes out alone, though with her blessing, for intellectual chat and writerly gossip. But she is determined to meet George Sand, the brilliant Frenchwoman who is her near contemporary. Almost as soon as they had arrived in Paris, she had persuaded Robert to ask Carlyle for a letter of introduction to Sand from Italian activist Giuseppe Mazzini. Robert, who himself meets Sand several times, seems offhand virtually to the point of obstructiveness. It's almost as if the diminutive 'Ba' has replaced the major talent who is 'Elizabeth Barrett Browning' in his mind. Or perhaps he's simply not quite as Bohemian as he thinks: Sand has a scandalous reputation as a sexual free spirit. And as a woman writer and thinker too; when all three do eventually meet, on 15 February 1852, Elizabeth encounters once more that *other* way of being a female intellectual:

> she seemed to be in fact *the man* in that company, & the profound respect with which she was listened to, a good deal impressed me [...] scorn of pleasing, she evidently had—there never could have been a colour of coquetry in that woman. [...] I liked her .. I did not love her .. but I felt the burning soul through all that quietness, & was not disappointed.

Life seems a little easier come the summer. From 6 July till 12 October 1852 the Brownings are back in London, renting at 58 Welbeck Street, again roughly a hundred yards from 50 Wimpole Street. Again they see Henrietta and Surtees Cook, who again come to stay nearby; again they also meet old friends and new. Through Jane Carlyle, they meet Mazzini in person; the wealthy, hop-farming Paines of Farnham introduce clergyman-novelist Charles Kingsley; through Coventry Patmore they meet

John and Effie Ruskin, lunch with the couple and view Ruskin's collection of Turners; and at the christening of Hallam Tennyson, Robert meets F. T. Palgrave, later the famous anthologist. After escorting his disgraced father into French exile, Robert is back in town with Sarianna to help dispose of Robert senior's home; Elizabeth's intelligent, self-effacing sister-in-law spends the rest of the summer with the couple.

Their only other disruption comes in August, when Wilson asks for a pay rise from £16 to £20. The Brownings, short of money, refuse; Wilson responds that she needs to find better-paying employers. But in fact she and the Brownings are by now friends and housemates as much as employers and employee. By the time she goes north on 3 September to spend three weeks with her family, she has already agreed to stay on. The relief is huge. The household relies on her: while she was away on the equivalent trip last year, Elizabeth found herself in a 'dreadful state of slavery, with Wiedeman hanging to the skirts of my garment whatever way I turned'.

On 16 October the household is back in Paris. From the Hôtel de la Ville l'Évêque they watch Louis-Napoléon's triumphalist return from the tour that set in motion his process of becoming emperor. A week later they set off south. This is abrupt, but Elizabeth has been coughing since September, and John Kenyon has given them the money for a swift return to Florence. They travel overland via Lyon, Turin and Genoa, where Elizabeth is so weak that they rest up for ten days. 'I was no longer flesh of Robert's flesh, only bone of his bone. Fever and cough every night had completely wasted me away', Elizabeth tells Mrs Jameson later. They arrive home on 10 or 11 November:

> To my deep joy .. I cant tell you how pleased I felt. Dear Florence, I do love it certainly, though Robert (demoralized man that he is by the too enchanting Paris) maintains that it's dead & dull [...] I feel myself back in my nest again, and cant enjoy it too much.

Within a couple of days, even her cough is better: 'We have no fires on this fourteenth of November, nor think of fires .. and I have half forgotten my cough .. it's all but gone .. and the chest is as free as a bird.'

This time, though, individual bodily autonomy will not be confused with civic liberty: 'Neither I nor Baby can be said to flourish less for the revolutions and counter-revolutions, the putting up & pulling down of liberty trees, & the invasions of Austrian & French armies.' Back in Paris, on 2 December Louis-Napoléon is crowned Emperor Napoleon III. But here in socially and economically depressed Florence, life is altogether quieter. Pen's old *balia* visits, 'kissing [Pen] again & again [...] She almost knocked out all my front teeth with her energetic kisses—'. Though Alessandro has found another job, his children come over. 'Madame Biondi [...] and Mr Stuart .. and the Cottrells & heaps of other people' come through the door. The frightening decline in Elizabeth's health has been halted, and it's the start of 'a very happy winter, with nothing from without to vex us much'. By the spring, revising *Poems* for its third (1853) edition, and with Robert deep in *Men and Women*, Elizabeth has also started work on that project she's had so long in mind: the new, narrative poem that will become *Aurora Leigh*.

[*Eighth Frame*]

Could you look me in the eye? In the biblical tradition from which that compassionate philosopher Emmanuel Levinas comes, the encounter with the other person isn't a response to the entire face. It's only the eyes that are 'the light of the soul', where personhood sees and is seen. And surely this is why people who are going to be executed are blindfolded or hooded: not really to protect them from seeing their fate, but to protect the executioner from seeing them and being seen by them. To protect the executioner from seeing himself fail his primary duty – that of recognising, and preserving, the other person.

In photographs taken by the highly accomplished Fratelli D'Alessandri in the last two years of her life, we see Elizabeth trying to look her photographer in the eye. Posing with and without Pen, her chin is ever so slightly down and she glances ever so slightly upward. It's the pose that Lady Diana Spencer made famous: as a shy young royal fiancée, Diana looked dazzled by the world's gaze.

Elizabeth too has been a shy young woman. Now she simply seems worn out. Success and illness have both worn down her defences. She looks towards Father Antonio D'Alessandri – towards this figure whose face, as she tries to find it, is hidden under a blackout hood – as if the camera's inspection is something she must bear. (She's trying to stay still too, of course.) On 27 May 1861, four weeks before her death, she looks at the camera that will deliver its final verdict, and her eyes seem to express an undefended acceptance. She looks at the lens with sincerity and expectation.

Book Nine:
How to lose a body

It is the hour for souls.

Now things begin to speed up. In September 1853, Elizabeth and Robert spend their seventh wedding anniversary in Bagni di Lucca, 'this green, cool, bright, quiet, noisy place', as Robert calls it, where they've once again rented a house for the summer. Seven-year relationships are notoriously 'itchy', as inner and outer stories shift, a shared history beginning to obscure the initial connection, but the couple seem happy enough: 'Well—here's the wedding-day. Robert told me this morning that he should love me still more the next seven years—but I shall be satisfied with the old love.'

Staying this time right in town on Piazza Tolomei, they're more worried about other people, 'Likely indeed to infest us, but we have made it public [...] that we mean to be private'. But at just £11 for over thirteen weeks, and with more rooms than they can use, Casa Tolomei is too good to miss. 'Our little Penini [Elizabeth is still varying the spelling] is in paradise with the garden & the mountains, & the donkeys.' Robert is busy with poems in his own 'cheerful little blue room with two windows'. And Elizabeth is at work on *Aurora Leigh*.

She knows she needs privacy to write: 'An artist must, I fancy, either find or *make* a solitude to work in .. if it is to be good work at all.' Yet strangely, as in Paris and despite all those spare rooms, she again has no study of her own and, though she can always leave Penini with Wilson, there's a lingering sense of her fitting work around family life in ways Robert does not.

Still, things work out well enough. Florence was far more distracting:

> there was something painful in breaking the thread & letting our pleasant friends roll off like lost beads. Mr Tennyson [...] used to come to us every few days & take coffee & smoke [...] & commune about books, men & spirits till past midnight. [...] He was with us the last night. So was Count Cottrell [...] So was the American minister from the court of Turin, Mr Kinney and his wife.

Besides, distractions do furnish a life. In Bagni di Lucca the Brownings are deepening their friendship with a younger couple, the American writer-sculptor William Wetmore Story and his wife Emelyn: 'She & I go backward & forward on donkeyback to tea drinking & gossiping at one another's houses, & our husbands hold the reins.'

One interest they all share is spiritualism, something that dominates this summer's correspondence. Séances aren't just entertaining or philosophically interesting 'happenings'. As possible proof of life after death their stakes couldn't be higher. But the Brownings are bashful, uncertain. In their world Christian belief is socially fundamental; being Nonconformists, they know well that even the wrong kind of Christianity is problematic. Since Wimpole Street days Elizabeth has counted several Swedenborgians among her acquaintances, and she'll remain attracted to the sect's idea of the perfectible self passing through a series of purely spiritual reincarnations after death. However, she must perform some mental juggling to manage both her faith and the untheological possibility that the dead can speak to us: she's careful not to expose four-year-old Pen to something she recognises may be mere superstition.

Yet she writes persuasively to her siblings about what, if true, could hugely ameliorate the family's painful losses. She both believes, and does not, in table-rapping. Communicating with the dead is tantamount to heresy. But if this were not pseudo-religion but simply an undiscovered, biomechanical fact about the status of the thinking self after bodily death, it would be enormously reassuring, especially for the bereaved and those at particular risk of dying prematurely. Elizabeth is both these things. Perhaps, too, a life of struggle with a bodily 'machine' that keeps letting her down makes it intuitively easier for her to accept the mind as separate from the body. Illness can make Cartesians of us all. She's eager for Robert to share spiritualism's message of hope. But, though thrilled by the uncanny theatricality of séances, he struggles to reconcile this last gasp of gothic Romanticism with his sense of himself as a man of the modern world.

In fact it's Elizabeth who is once again attuned to the *zeitgeist*, caught up by a vogue that, in the coming decade, will gain huge traction as it comforts the bereaved of the American Civil War (not to mention President Abraham Lincoln and his wife), and intrigues British public figures including Charles Dickens, the social reformer Robert Owen, and another of the Brownings' younger friends, the diplomat and writer Robert Bulwer-Lytton. It's easy to dismiss this craze as morbid; but the Victorians are in some ways condemned to morbidity. For the upper and rapidly expanding middle classes, modernity means increased leisure to ponder the big questions; yet life can still be cut short at any moment. Medical knowledge remains quasi-mediaeval, as Elizabeth's own experience testifies. Spiritualism addresses both death's ubiquity and the desire for radical advances in understanding. With its public demonstrations and do-it-yourself 'experiments' mimicking the rise of empirical science earlier in the century, it appeals strongly to the Brownings' community of Nonconformists and outliers. 'The subject deepens & deepens with us all', Elizabeth tells Miss Mitford, and, 'Everybody is apt to be "mad" who gets beyond the conventions'.

It's with fellow enthusiasts Bulwer-Lytton and the Storys that Robert and Elizabeth take a day trip to the hamlet of Prato Fiorito a few days after their wedding anniversary. Among the surrounding hills they come across a ruined chapel, which Robert shortly recreates in 'By the Fireside', a poem that's quite remarkably elegiac, not to mention ghostly, especially for an anniversary. It pictures a wife 'Reading by fire-light, that great brow / And the spirit-small hand propping it'; among the shadows, her 'dark hair' and 'dark grey eyes' match the 'Blackish-grey' stone ruins. Ostensibly a celebration of how constancy deepens love, 'By the Fireside' couldn't be blunter about the end of the honeymoon, and of youth itself, 'A turn, and we stand in the heart of things [...] Youth, flowery all the way, there stops—'.

Not quite an itch; but it's certainly a seven-year reckoning. The honeymoon years, with their sense of steadily opening possibilities – the excitements of discovering Italy and choosing where to live, Elizabeth's continually developing work and reputation, her greatly improved health taking shape above all with Pen's arrival, even the gradual mending of many Barrett family bridges – are over. Now comes the *tristesse* of having arrived where the couple had hoped to arrive; of being at the top of the hill – and seeing over the other side. Elizabeth is only forty-seven; but she's disproportionately aged by repeated grave illness. There are clearly going to be no more children. These will be the years when her looks fade in conventional terms, and when illness grows more risky still for her.

Yet work remains exciting. By the time they return to Casa Guidi on 10 October, Elizabeth is able to tell her brother George that her new long poem 'is growing heavy on my hands, .. & will be considerably longer than [Tennyson's] the "Princess" when finished. I mean it to be, beyond all question, my best work—' She's ambitious for it, and 'For the sake of this poem I should prefer staying at Florence this winter', but 'to see Rome is a necessity'. And this too is exciting. A month later they leave for the city, where on 22 November – after calling at Perugia, Assisi and its Basilica, and Terni, famous for waterfalls – they settle in to the third floor of 43 Via Bocca di Leone, an apartment reserved for them by their new friends the Storys.

Elizabeth's letters home claim that living high above this narrow mediaeval street is healthier than being at ground level. In fact the reservations she expresses to Emelyn Story – 'remember unless by miraculous interposition something better (that is lower) shall offer itself we accept thankfully your third piano' – reveal that Rome is both expensive and full-up. This small-windowed upper floor is the only affordable way to live in the fashionable English quarter 'which is considered especially healthy'. Just round the corner from the famous Caffè Greco, once frequented by Byron and the Shelleys, this new residence is also midway between the famous shopping parades of the Corso and the Spanish Steps – opposite which the Storys are already installed at 93 Piazza di Spagna.

But what should be a happy continuation of the summer suddenly becomes the opposite. As soon as the Browning household – Elizabeth, Robert, Pen, Wilson, Ferdinando the cook, and of course Flush – arrive, the couple themselves head straight round to the Storys'. The women go for coffee, while the men check out the new apartment. Emelyn Story tells Elizabeth that her six-year-old, Joe, has gone to bed early with a slight cold; she arranges a playdate with Pen for next day. But in the morning before breakfast the Story's nine-year-old daughter Edith arrives suddenly and dramatically at Via Bocca di Leone. She's been sent over for safe-keeping because her little brother is seriously ill.

> Robert & I, leaving Edith with Wilson & Penini, set out instantly of course to see what the evil was. Oh—Arabel, it was death's own evil! The child had a succession of convulsions .. never recovered consciousness, & before the night had set in, was dead [...] A boy six years old, & beloved by its mother above all her loves—[...] I shall not forget the destraction in which she threw herself down, beside the empty little chair.

The diagnosis is gastric flu, which the doctor assures everyone is noncontagious. But by now both the Storys' nursemaid and, back in Via Bocca di Leone, Edith are also gravely ill. The doctor now claims that all three caught cold in a fierce tramontana two days earlier. By nightfall, the little girl is too sick to be taken home and so is carried down the stairs to the second-floor apartment that the Storys' other friends, American artist William Page and his family, are renting:

> "She may not live till morning" was the medical apprehension. So the poor mother & father quitted their own house, with the still unburied little body of their boy in it, and came here to wait & tremble before the possibility of another blow.

Though Edith does recover, much has been made since of Elizabeth's fear, at this juncture, for her own child. 'I look at him with a tremble at the heart! These treasures,—which at once are ours, & not ours!!' Of course. The doctor is clearly a charlatan. Elizabeth is a loving mother, and exposing Pen to infection won't help Edith, or her grieving parents, in any way. Yet the reason she gives for moving the feverish little girl, that 'we had no night-room to give her', is probably not entirely an excuse either. The Brownings had camped the first night in their new home, where the furniture is all 'just as I had pushed [it], when interrupted, in the middle of the floor' and it's ill-equipped and comfortless for a very sick child.

But when Elizabeth refuses to have anything to do with Joe's dead body, this isn't logic but visceral recoil. Unlike most of her generation, she has no experience of laying out the dead: by coincidence all her loved ones have been buried without her seeing them: her mother died away from home in Cheltenham, Sam and Uncle Sam in distant Jamaica, and Bro's body was too far gone when it was retrieved. Her horrified exclamation now to Arabel, 'This dust is not my beloved. I recoil from this paddling with clay', is the other face of her spiritualist search; the same fierce need to believe that personhood can outlast the vulnerable mortal body.

Death, though it remains at one remove, has come to join Elizabeth in Italy. Yet it cedes the foreground to a number of friends soon enough. December and January see William Makepeace Thackeray make several visits, accompanied by the two daughters of whom he's had care since his wife succumbed to postpartum psychosis. The elder girl, future writer Anne, keeps a journal that lets us glimpse the Brownings as physically tiny but effervescing with warmth. Robert appears as 'a dark, short man, slightly, but nervously built, with [...] a large mouth which opens widely when he speaks, white teeth, a dark beard and a loud voice with a slight lisp, and the best and kindest heart in the world.' Elizabeth is:

> the greatest woman I ever knew in my life. She is very very small, not more than four feet eight inches I should think. She is brown, with dark eyes and dead brown hair, and she has white teeth and a low harsh voice, her eyes are bright and full of life, she has a manner full of charm and kindness. She rarely laughs, but is always cheerful and smiling.

The couple's 'charm and kindness' draws them into the social whirl. In February they join the Prince of Prussia at a musical soirée run by the Secretary to the German Archaeological Institute. Robert goes out and about with Frederic Leighton, Bulwer-Lytton, Scottish writer John Gibson Lockhart, and the power couple of landowner and future MP Edward John Sartoris and his wife Adelaide, a well-known opera singer until her marriage. By April the weather is mild enough for concerts and picnics in the Roman Campagna, the famous local countryside that's become an indispensable stop on the Grand Tour. Both Adelaide's sister, the actress Fanny Kemble, and Elizabeth herself join in these entertainments, where 'the talk was almost too brilliant for the sentiment of the scenery, but it harmonized entirely with the mayonnaise & champagne.'

Yet sadness haunts the Brownings' six months in Rome. The poems Robert is writing return to themes of unachievable or misplaced love. His 'Two in the Campagna', while it echoes the plethora of landscape paintings that have made the area famous, records not parties but the fleeting nature of intimacy:

> […] I yearn upward, touch you close,
> Then stand away. I kiss your cheek,
> Catch your soul's warmth,—[…]
> Then the good minute goes.

It almost sounds like an accusation:

> I would that you were all to me,
> You that are just so much, no more.
> […]
> Where does the fault lie? What the core
> O' the wound, since wound must be?

The dramatic monologues and persona poems that will soon contribute so much to his reputation are the work of someone still in love with theatre, and they are fiction. But it's striking that so many of these personae have ambivalent relationships with women. Of course probably the most famous among them, the murderous narrator of 'My Last Duchess', appeared in print three years before Robert had even met Elizabeth, in 1842's *Dramatic Lyrics*. And it would be simplistic to reduce the unhappy speakers of *Men and Women*, or indeed of any poems, to sublimated wish fulfilment: writing doesn't work like that. But they must certainly cast, as much as capture, a psychic shadow in the Via Bocca di Leone. What is

Robert's mood as he works on them – and what does Elizabeth feel when she reads them?

Whatever the mood in the apartment, outside it the Roman climate is casting a real shadow – over the children's health. In March 1854 Edith Story falls gravely ill once more – though she again survives – and by May Pen has become 'a delicate, pale little creature'. And even the couple's writing lives aren't going particularly smoothly. *Two Poems by Elizabeth Barrett and Robert Browning*, which Chapman and Hall publish at the couple's expense this spring in aid of Arabella's work with the Ragged Schools, doesn't sell well; and a hundred copies of *Casa Guidi Windows* remain unsold, meaning that there are no earnings to speak of. Altogether, when they leave for home on 28 May Elizabeth is relieved: 'I have'nt taken to [Rome] as a poet should [...] the associations of the place have not been personally favorable to me.'

Yet things don't improve greatly back in Florence, where they'll spend the next twelve months, unable even to escape the summer heat, due to lack of funds. This year Elizabeth receives no annual bonus from the *David Lyon*; while John Kenyon, who has generously given the couple £50 every six months since Pen was born, but who's ageing – he's now seventy-one – forgets to send his cheque. Flush has been getting old too, and three weeks after their return, on 16 June 1854, he dies. He was thirteen, and had been in poor shape for a while:

He died quite quietly [...] He was old you know—though dogs of his kind have lived much longer—and the climate acted unfavorably upon him. He had scarcely a hair on his back—everyone thought it was the mange, and the smell made his presence in the drawingroom a difficult thing. In spite of all however, it has been quite a shock to me & a sadness—A dear dog he was.

Elizabeth's reasoned reaction seems very far indeed from her earlier passionate affection for the little creature. But what makes Flush's going bearable is probably not only the passage of time, but unspeakable relief that it isn't Pen they have lost; for 'our own child became affected by the climate a week or two before we left [Rome], and frightened us considerably', as Robert tells William Story.

But as August turns into September Elizabeth becomes frantic with fresh worry. Her father has been run over in Wimpole Street. His leg is broken, and by mid-September George is reporting that 'permanent lameness' with 'one leg shorter than the other' is 'probable'. Elizabeth, entertaining the fantasy that the accident 'may bring him closer to his children [...] & more cognizant of their attachment & tenderness', sends a note. The gesture's rebuffed, even though she adopts the precautionary disguise of having Penini address the envelope: at five, the boy already has handsome handwriting. Still, the 'beautiful and singularly intelligent little boy who promises to prove worthy of his parents' can always raise the mood at Casa Guidi. Indeed he has already received his own first press notice from the Italian correspondent of *The Critic*, who now, in a precursor to twenty-first-century celebrity magazine spreads, visits the Brownings 'at home in that Casa Guidi which has become classic in English poetry'. A further fillip comes when the *David Lyon* at last yields a dividend, and it proves the largest in five years.

But at the start of 1855 life closes in again. That dear friend and one-time close confidant Mary Russell Mitford dies on 10 January, and over the winter Elizabeth suffers 'the worst attack on the chest I ever suffered from in Italy', which she blames on 'more frost & a bitterer wind than are common to us':

> The cough was very wearing, & the night-fever most depressing ..
> & by the time there was a possibility of sleep for either me or poor
> Robert (who passed his nights in keeping up the fire & warming the
> coffee) of course I had become very weak & thin.

Meanwhile, back in London it's not only Papa who needs nursing. Treppy, by now eighty-six, won't die for another two years. But she's becoming paranoid, perhaps actually suffering from dementia. Arabella, who undertakes the family visiting duties, is one of the few people she usually tolerates. But the old lady:

> constantly supposes that people mean to poison her [...] and now she
> has begun to distrust Arabel! [...] What Arabel has to go through
> you may suppose. Only she has a nature great enough in its affections
> [...] however at the cost of many & bitter tears—

Arabella's life may indeed be feeling bitter. At forty-two she's still just young enough to escape Wimpole Street, as her sisters have at similar ages, for marriage, children and a home of her own. But unlike them she has no one waiting in the wings. She has become one of those convenient women with no life of their own, ceaselessly available in the nineteenth century to hold upper-class families – and wider society – together. Rather like Bummy, in fact. Her famous sister is among many who takes this free labour for granted, viewing care work as 'not [...] the best use to which we can put a gifted & accomplished woman'.

Even before her current high-profile work in the military hospitals of the Crimean War, Florence Nightingale has been professionalising and dignifying nursing. Elizabeth has met and liked the younger, Florence-born woman but, despite admiring her work, believes encouraging women into caring roles is 'retrograde—a revival of old virtues!' as she tells Anna Jameson:

> Since the siege of Troy & earlier, we have had princesses binding wounds with their hands—it's strictly the woman's part .. & men understand it so [...]. Every man is on his knees before ladies carrying lint,—calling them 'angelical she's,' .. whereas, if they stir an inch as thinkers or artists from the beaten line, [....] the very same men would curse the impudence of the very same women & stop there!—

As this swift return to her own preoccupations reveals, Elizabeth is never quite able to face what her sister's life must be. Later, when Arabella announces plans to adopt a foundling, she'll comment with excruciating tactlessness that having one's 'own' child is much better. But it's no coincidence that Elizabeth is reflecting on women's roles. She's now deeply involved in writing her exploration of how women are shaped by what they're allowed to do – *Aurora Leigh*. In January:

> Robert & I do work every day—[...] I have some four thousand five hundred lines towards [the book]. I am afraid that six thousand lines will not finish it. I shall be ready, at any rate—for I work on regularly.

But by early March summer publication is looking much more likely for Robert's 'large volume of short poems' than for her verse novel:

here are between five & six thousand lines *in blots* .. not one copied out .. & I am not nearly at an end of the composition even—

In fact she won't complete *Aurora Leigh* until the following summer. By the time she does so, in June 1856 in Paris, it will have sprouted into nine books and more than eleven thousand lines.

That draft *in blots* takes her to about the halfway mark, which is the brilliantly metafictional 570 lines, roughly a twentieth of the entire work, that constitutes one long *ars poetica*. In this relentless first half of Book Five the poem's narrator, who so closely resembles Elizabeth in her dedication to becoming a woman poet, agonises over the work of poetry that could and will be – inside Elizabeth's own tour de force – her masterpiece. Long before postmodernism, *Aurora Leigh*'s first readers must have had an especially vertiginous sense at this point of falling into the poem they were reading: even today, the effect is of a curious lip-synching or feedback as Elizabeth and Aurora, author and character, chorus their lines.

Elizabeth starts by rehearsing the usual put-downs women writers internalise: our writing can't achieve artistic greatness because we don't care enough about it, being preoccupied by masculine approbation and our private lives, which trap us in confessional mode. It's tediously familiar stuff, to poets at least, even in the twenty-first century:

Too light a book for a grave man's reading!
[…]
We women […] strain our natures at doing something great,
Far less because it's something great to do,
Than haply that we, so, commend ourselves
[…]
To some one friend. […]
We miss the abstract when we comprehend.
We miss it most when we aspire,—and fail.
Yet, so, I will not.—This vile woman's way
Of trailing garments, shall not trip me up:
I'll have no traffic with the personal thought
In art's pure temple. Must I work in vain,
Without the approbation of a man?
It cannot be; it shall not. Fame itself

[...]
Presents a poor end [...] Art for art
[...]
Although our woman-hands should shake and fail;
And if we fail.. But must we?—
              Shall I fail?

In 1855, when most leading British women writers conceal themselves with anonymity ('A Lady', 'the author of *Frankenstein*') or a masculine pseudonym ('George Eliot', the 'Bells'), it seems daring for Elizabeth to address this problem so directly under her own name – or Aurora's. But she's better placed than most to make the case with some impunity. Unusually for a woman, she has emerged from the same literary training as her male peers – an education in translating classical verse – so her project makes sense to them. Besides, she's insulated from the usual social and familial pressures to conform by financial independence, and by living abroad.

All the same, as Elizabeth makes light work of hurts that must still be fresh from the reception of *Casa Guidi Windows* and *Poems (1850)*, twenty-first-century readers can find themselves asking whom this passage addresses. Does it matter how a woman becomes a poet? Who exactly is *Aurora Leigh* for? But in the mid-nineteenth century poetry is culturally central, poets are cultural superstars who make attractive fictional protagonists, and what they feel and do is of real popular interest. Indeed, as *The Critic*'s feature writer has shown, there is popular appetite for details of Elizabeth's own life. And so it's neither a surprise, nor cheating, when scenes from her own experience are woven through her novel, whose protagonist Aurora, born in Elizabeth's beloved Italy, is orphaned and sent to live with an aunt in a rural setting remarkably similar to Hope End.

This *paternal* relative turns out to be (it *is* somewhat schematic) a cold disciplinarian; nevertheless the teenager develops into a poet. Her cousin and neighbour Romney falls in love with her and proposes. He's wealthy and loving, but he doesn't see the point of Aurora's newly discovered vocation: so she refuses to marry him. Romney goes on to a sublimated life of good works on which he spends his fortune, despite never managing entirely to turn the social tide, only (as we learn eventually) to lose everything and be blinded in a fire. Aurora moves to London and writes successful verse but is blocked when it comes to Real Art: she can never quite produce her masterpiece. One day a wealthy socialite, Lady Waldemar, turns up to enlist her help in dislodging Marian Erle, one of Romney's charity cases to whom he's become engaged in an overflow of feeling. Lady Waldemar wants to secure him for herself. Though Aurora and Romney now meet again they still don't understand each other's life choices; it's the titled lady herself who manages to dislodge Marian Erle ('Marry an Earl'!) by having her abducted to Paris and sold into prostitution.

Marian is living there in destitution with the child who is the result of this rape when by shameless authorial contrivance Aurora – travelling south in search of poetic inspiration – chances to encounter the pair and takes them in. In another tangle with reality, the fictional ménage travel on to Elizabeth's own home city, Florence, where they settle and where Aurora learns that the semi-autobiographical poetry manuscript she sold to fund her travel has been published and has achieved huge artistic success. Back in England, Romney reads it with admiration and understands her at last. Believing that Marian jilted him at the altar, he has become engaged to Lady Waldemar; but this relationship sours when a letter from Aurora forces her to admit all. Eventually Romney comes to Florence in search of his first fiancée, by whom he plans to do the right thing, but, luckily for the gradually converging protagonists, Marian wishes to devote herself to the joys of motherhood, and anyway realises that her own love was just hero worship. After 11,000 lines, Romney and Aurora are able to unite their social and poetic vocations: in the concluding symbolism of their story, 'last, an amethyst'.

None of this is quite as whistle-stop as it sounds: *Aurora Leigh* comprises a lengthy nine books. But it does manage to be simultaneously a page-turner and a radical read. After publication Elizabeth will admit that she 'expected to be put in the stocks & pelted with the eggs of the last twenty years' singing birds, as a disorderly woman & free thinking poet'. Instead, 'People have been so kind, that […] I really come to modify my opinions somewhat upon their conventionality, .. to see the progress made in freedom of thought—Think of quite decent women taking the part of the book.'

This wider readership from 'decent' society will make the book a best-seller whose first edition sells out in a fortnight. But Elizabeth's Ideal Reader remains her alter ego. There's a sense in many passages that she's trying to pass on a baton to an as yet unknown, perhaps even greater, woman poet. Did she but know it, this is exactly what she's managed. Among the many women readers *Aurora Leigh* will influence around the world and who subsequently become poets, from 'Michael Field' to Charlotte Mew, is Emily Dickinson, who will write her a number of memorial praise poems:

> Silver – perished – with her Tongue –
> Not on Record – bubbled other,
> Flute – or Woman –
> So divine –

All this, though, is in the future. In 1855, Elizabeth is working away steadily at her epic *Künstlerroman*. That brilliant riff on ways to dismiss women's poetry comes immediately after a passage (in Book Four) in which one particular man, future partner Romney, dismisses Aurora's own poetry in particular. *Aurora Leigh* will become a highly influential book, and here it tells us that there is an asymmetry at the heart of heterosexuality:

> I held him in respect.
> I comprehended what he was […] but he
> Supposed me a thing too small, to deign to know:
> He blew me, plainly, from the crucible
> As some intruding, interrupting fly,
> Not worth the pains of his analysis.

A man treating the woman he loves like an insect makes an arresting, even disgusting, image; this is going much further than simple enquiry into women's writing. Once again, we should beware assuming that a poet is being autobiographical, especially because women poets are so readily assumed to be confessional in that 'vile woman's way / Of trailing […] the personal thought'. But nor should we assume that either Browning is incapable of dramatising ambivalences within their own life as fiction. As Elizabeth completes *Aurora Leigh* things *are* changing, at any rate beneath the surface, in the apparently happy Browning household.

By consorting with one of Britain's leading poets, Robert has gained social entry into her literary and poetic league: at which point it would be easy to forget, as many a muse has done, that he isn't there in his own right. Now he increasingly replaces his wife at literary events. Back in January 1855, while she was ill, 'Mr Frederick Tennyson gave "punch" on the twelfth night to those whom Mr Lytton designates as "the brethren" .. viz Robert, Mr Norton, & Isa Blagden': only Elizabeth's name is missing from the list. And her growing isolation takes several forms. Though she knows other women writers – whether good friends like Anna Jameson or esteemed acquaintances like George Sand – Elizabeth has no other serious women *poets* in her life. Florentine acquaintances include ladies like Mrs Kinney, whose amateur verse is everything that Elizabeth (and Aurora Leigh) reject. Still, she throws herself into inspiring and encouraging younger women who *will* become serious writers: Anne Thackeray, or Isa Blagden, 'a single lady, with black hair, black eyes, yet somehow not pretty, who does literature, leads a London life among the "litterateurs" when she is in England'. And not only writers: last spring the Brownings made 'a great pet' of 'a perfectly "emancipated female"', sculptor Harriet Hosmer, a young American who 'lives here all alone [...] dines & breakfasts at the caffés precisely as a young man would,—works from six oclock in the morning till night, as a great artist must'. This could be an exciting new role for the woman who remained a tyro herself for so long. But it's being performed against the perhaps similar background of mothering little Penini – as well as of the Italian machismo that infects even him:

> he feels his advantage of belonging to the male sex, to a degree that quite startles me—there's a sort of instinct in it—I suppose. One morning [...] Ferdinando spoke of some tradesman in Florence who would only employ men. Penini broke out suddenly with .. "Benissimo! Tutte le donne sono cattive, eccetto mia mamma—Mamma solamente e buona." ['*Very good! All ladies are wicked except my mama – only Mama is good.*']

'Ferdinando' is Ferdinando Romagnoli, the Brownings' cook, who is making his presence felt in more ways than one. It's not only Penini who adores him. On 12 June 1855, the day before the ménage leaves for Paris and London, he marries Wilson – now clearly recovered from her chagrin at the disappearance of the prosperous Signor Righi – at the British Embassy. As this simplifies the household to two married couples with just the six-year-old Pen to look after, many things including travel should now be easier than in previous years. Yet the party manage to miss the boat at Livorno, and have to set out all over again a week later – when accidental delay turns into happy accident. Travelling via Corsica, at Marseille they bump into Elizabeth's brother Daisy, in France 'On His Majesty's Business'.

On 24 June they arrive in Paris for three weeks at 138 Avenue des Champs-Élysées with Sarianna and Robert Senior, whose disgrace causes no embarrassment here. This is a happy visit; one highlight a party where Elizabeth and Robert meet Prosper Mérimée, François-Auguste Mignet, the leading tragedienne Adelaide Ristori, and philosopher Victor Cousin. On 10 July Elizabeth Wilson becomes Mrs Romagnoli according to the Catholic rite as well as the Anglican one. Now legal under Tuscan as well as British law, the Romagnolis set out next day with their employers for three London months at 13 Dorset Street, less than half a mile from Wimpole Street.

Right from the off it's a sociable stay. Adelaide Sartoris calls on the day they arrive; two days later, breakfasting with John Kenyon, the Brownings meet 'half America & a quarter of London'. They may be visitors, but they're at the heart of the artistic and intellectual establishment. They spend time with John Ruskin, Thomas Carlyle, Frederic Leighton, Dante Gabriel Rossetti and Alfred Tennyson. It's a summer of artistic collegiality among distinguished peers, the personal and the artistic integrating not only within the poetry that both Brownings are writing, but in their joint outer life. When, one late September evening, Robert joins Tennyson in reading aloud to friends – though Elizabeth does not – the circle gathered to listen includes the painters Ford Madox Brown and William Holman Hunt.

But privately things are more complicated. In Wimpole Street, Papa's strength is beginning to decline. He turned seventy in May, and is now having daily healing sessions with a 'mesmerizer'. Still, he's no spent force. In August he catches Pen playing with his uncle George at Wimpole Street and, though he doesn't quite order the child out, demands, 'And what is he doing here, pray?' before freezing the topic shut and, later in the month, moving his household out of reach to Eastbourne on the excuse of another Wimpole Street redecoration. The Brownings' own household is changing shape too. By late August it's apparent that Wilson is pregnant, and she's planning to go home to Lincolnshire to have the baby.

Elizabeth experiences again the separation anxiety she felt when Crow left to start a family; and indeed the circumstances *are* similar. Orestes Wilson Romagnoli will be born on 13 October 1855, so Wilson must have fallen pregnant early in the year. Apparently, like Crow, she felt unable to admit to her mistress that both summer ceremonies were shotgun weddings; also like Crow, she had her reasons. After all, it's only four years since the Brownings dismissed their Parisian cook because of her 'reputation'.

Or perhaps Elizabeth knows – or at least guesses – the truth all along, and is covering for a loved and trusted intimate. Her own five pregnancies mean she's no longer innocent about the physical symptoms, and as the Casa Guidi apartment isn't huge she may well have an inkling of sleeping arrangements. She and Robert fight, with real protective urgency, to get the marriage correctly solemnised in Paris (although Ferdinando is clearly not contemplating abandonment: he even offers to convert to Protestant-ism) and, writing to Arabella on the Romagnolis' second wedding day, Elizabeth seems to imply that she knows more than she can for respect-ability's sake admit to: 'She has shed tears enough, as it is [...] I will tell you all.' As this is July, Wilson is by now six months pregnant and must show, but everyone has their fig leaf. She's married, and her mistress can claim ignorance.

Wilson (as Elizabeth continues to call her: Pen calls her Lily) will return to work the following July. Meanwhile, the Brownings return south four days after baby Orestes's safe arrival. There's cholera in Flor-ence, so they will over-winter in Paris. A Left Bank apartment found for them by friends is too small, though it may be the one Anne Thackeray will remember as a 'little warm, sunny, shabby, happy apartment, with a wood fire always burning, and a big sofa, where [Elizabeth] sat and wrote her books out of a tiny inkstand, in her beautiful delicate handwriting'. In fact it's not for a further two months, until they move back to the

neighbourhood of the Champs-Élysées at 3 rue du Colisée, that Elizabeth is able to resume work on *Aurora Leigh*. Now Paris, itself, whose 'old
charm [...] has siezed [*sic*] on me—nothing in the world (except Venice)
is so beautiful as a city' enters her story:

> the terraced streets,
> The glittering boulevards, the white colonnades
> Of fair fantastic Paris who wears trees
> Like plumes, as if man made them, spire and tower
> As if they had grown by nature, tossing up
> Her fountains in the sunshine of the squares.

And in the real-life city in which these lines are being written, the
opening three months of 1856 are spent fair-copying the verse novel's first
six books, Robert reading them as she goes.

His own *Men and Women* has just been published, to widespread but
mixed reception. *The Literary Gazette* finds 'all that complication of crude-
ness, obscurity, and disorder, by which the mystical and spasmodic school
of poetry is marked'; *Blackwood's* follows remarks on Elizabeth by noting
that 'Robert Browning is the wild boy of the household—the boisterous
noisy shouting voice which the elder people shake their heads to hear'; *The
Athenaeum* laments, 'Who will not grieve over energy wasted and power
misspent,—over fancies [...] so overhung by the "seven veils" of obscurity, [...] there is an amount of extravagant licence'. Elizabeth's protective instincts are aroused. Understandably perhaps, she feels that this time
it's personal: three years ago several of these same publications panned
Robert's ill-fated edition of forged Shelley letters, issued by Moxon to the
'unseemly merriment' of critics. But now their influential friends, including Carlyle, Rossetti – who comes to Paris and visits the Louvre with
Robert – and Ruskin (in the magisterial prose of *Modern Painters* volume
4) come to the rescue with positive reviews and good company. Throughout the spring, as Elizabeth works through the last third of *Aurora Leigh*
and proofs her *Poems (1856)*, Robert's social life continues to blossom. He
goes to the theatre with Charles Dickens and the actor William Macready
and dines with Camillo Benso, Count of Cavour, the modernising prime
minister of Piedmont-Sardinia known everywhere as Cavour.

At the end of June 1856 the Brownings return to London, this time to John Kenyon's home at 39 Devonshire Place. Each of these family summers costs Elizabeth: last time she told Henrietta, 'There's always a weight on my heart when I arrive. The land-sickness is worse than the sea's.' This year she feels additionally overpowered by the sustained effort of writing *Aurora Leigh*, which she had finally delivered to the publishers by the first week of August. And Devonshire Place is unusually gloomy. The couple's old mentor isn't there with them, but is seriously ill at his house on the Isle of Wight. Papa, as usual dispatching his household to the south coast for the weeks when Elizabeth is in England, has this year by coincidence picked Ventnor, on the island's dramatic, leafy, south-east coast. It feels only sensible for the Brownings to follow them here for a fortnight, before spending a further two weeks with Kenyon in his home on the Solent shore at 3 the Parade, West Cowes.

The Wight's mild, countrified climate and sea air can only do Elizabeth good. She relaxes. Proofs follow her across the Solent in batches, and Arabella and George join Robert in reading her revisions as she goes. But this interval is bittersweet. Kenyon has in many ways been the father figure that Papa ceased to be once Elizabeth grew up, and that her younger husband can never be. It's his support, financial as well as emotional, that has made her mature achievement possible; indeed it will continue posthumously in the form of a generous bequest totalling £10,500, which, invested, gives the couple a secure income for life. Back in London at the start of October, she will dedicate *Aurora Leigh*, this story of a cousin's love, to him:

> The words 'cousin' and 'friend' are constantly recurring in this poem, the last pages of which have been finished under the hospitality of your roof, my own dearest cousin and friend [...] therefore [... I venture to leave in your hands this book [...] that as, through my various efforts in literature and steps in life, you have believed in me, borne with me, and been generous to me, far beyond the common uses of mere relationship or sympathy of mind, so you may kindly accept, in sight of the public., this poor sign of esteem, gratitude, and affection from your unforgetting E.B.B.

This is the public acknowledgement that fame allows. It's also a personal farewell. When Elizabeth leaves Cowes on 22 September, she and

Kenyon must know that they won't see each other again. For all the pleasure with which she goes on to Taunton to spend a week with Henrietta,
that sadness – and a linked sense of her own mortality – colour the book's
final revisions. Her 'dearest cousin and friend' will die on 3 December, but
he lives just long enough to see and celebrate the masterpiece his protégée
has dedicated to him. He even manages to send friends several copies of
the achievement she calls 'the most mature of my works, and the one into
which my highest convictions upon Life and Art have entered'.

Elizabeth's *Poems (Fourth Edition)* is published on 1 November; a
fortnight later, on 15 November, *Aurora Leigh* appears. It's issued simultaneously in New York by C. S. Francis, who has in the past pirated her
work and 'is said to have shed tears over the proofs .. (perhaps in reference to the hundred pounds he had to pay for them)', as she mordantly
comments. The book is an instant success. 'All the best people shout [...]
rapturously', as John Ruskin notes in the course of two letters buzzing
with enthusiasm:

> I think Aurora Leigh the greatest *poem* in the English language:
> unsurpassed by anything but Shakespeare—*not* surpassed by Shake-
> speare[']s *sonnets*—& therefore the greatest poem in the language.

Which may be a touch overstated, but puts a finger on why *Aurora Leigh*
is so important: it is 'the first perfect poetical expression of the Age'. This
is not just down to the fresh Victorian language (not yet a contradiction
in terms). The story of conflicting models of duty and vocation speaks
to contemporary concerns. It's also a vivid exploration of changing ideas
about womanhood. Both its dramatisation of forced prostitution, refusing, like 'The Runaway Slave', to blame the victim of rape, and its advocacy of an unconventional but stable family unit in which to bring up
the child of that rape, are provocatively up to the minute. Its final vision
of building a new Jerusalem is deeply, fashionably Christian – yet also
the contemporary secular vernacular in a Britain still proud of the novel
feats of manufacture and engineering that its Industrial Revolution has
ushered in.

Leigh Hunt, too, sends Elizabeth twenty admiring pages. Though
many of the nearly eighty reviews the book receives – in France, Italy, and

Ireland as well as in Britain and America – comment on the rarity of the verse novel genre, they're mostly enthusiastic. First out of the gate, five days after publication, *The Globe and Traveller* decides, '"AURORA LEIGH," Mrs. Browning's new poem, is a wealthy world of beauty, truth, and the noblest thoughts, faiths, hopes, and charities that can inform and sanctify our human nature', while the *Edinburgh Weekly Review* sees it 'marking an epoch in literature, for it is, in many respects, an innovation on long-accepted uses in poetry.' In *The Athenaeum*, H. F. Chorley says that 'our greatest English poetess of any time has essayed [...] to blend the epic with the didactic novel' in:

> her contribution to the chorus of protest and mutual exhortation, which Woman is now raising, in hope of gaining the due place and sympathy which, it is held, have been denied to her.

Although declaring the book's advocacy of women writers 'unnatural', he concludes that for some readers it will afford 'almost a scriptural revelation' – and so it proves, particularly among writing women.

Elsewhere, the *New-York Daily Times* calls Elizabeth's blank verse 'a phenomenon. Pure, simple, lively, flexible, it is such verse as no living pen can command in greater perfection.' But it's that new fictional form blending epic poetry with the novel that is *Aurora Leigh*'s most radical adventure and greatest achievement. Coventry Patmore, in a lengthy essay in the *North British Review* making clear his reservations about both this genre and what he sees as a great deal of hasty, under-polished writing throughout the poet's oeuvre, clarifies the nature of this accomplishment: 'There is a vital continuity, through the whole of this immensely long work.' This sense of 'disciplined energy, that unflagging imagination, which were necessary for the composition of the greatest poem ever written by woman', is taken up by the *Daily News*. *The Albion* is 'mastered [...] by the form and beauty of the whole'. And so on.

Perhaps predictably, it's George Eliot, writing in the *Westminster Review*, who best *gets* the 'grand source of the profound impression produced in us' by *Aurora Leigh*'s integration of form with content: 'the idea of *ample being*'. Turning the role of 'poetess' from a handicap to a strength, Elizabeth is:

perhaps, the first woman who has produced a work which exhibits all the peculiar powers without the negations of her sex; which superadds to masculine vigour, breadth, and culture, feminine subtlety of perception, feminine quickness of sensibility, and feminine tenderness.[…] Mrs. Browning has shown herself all the greater poet because she is intensely a poetess.

What is the high tide of a life, and how do we know when we're afloat on it? By the time *Aurora Leigh* appears, the Brownings are back in Casa Guidi. Travelling their usual route via Paris, Dijon, Marseille, Genoa and Livorno, they arrived home on 30 October. The first months of 1857 are defined by the book's continued success. It's in its third edition by March. Harriet Beecher Stowe visits Casa Guidi in April; the meeting of these two famous literary women abolitionists another confirmation of Elizabeth's international standing. But as ever the private human experience is different. There's artistic *esprit de l'escalier*:

> There has been an enormous quantity of extravagance talked & written on [*Aurora Leigh*…]. I wish it were all true. But I see too distinctly what I *ought* to have written—Still, it is nearer the mark than my former efforts .. fuller, stronger, more sustained, .. and one may be encouraged to push on to something worthier: for I dont feel as if I had done yet—no indeed.

And there's the ever-present threat of mortality. Treppy dies on 9 March. Though she was eighty-eight, and dementia had made her increasingly remote, Elizabeth's mourning for her is heartfelt.

But it is upstaged five weeks later when she endures a far more complex loss. On 17 April 1857 Edward Barrett Moulton-Barrett dies, and takes with him any hope of reconciliation. For the last couple of years Elizabeth has understood it would end this way. When Papa rebuffed her in summer 1855 she told Henrietta, 'I shall try nothing more—[…] It is absolutely useless—& it is irritating on one side & painful on the other.' But emotions run deeper than understanding: 'Yet when it came, it seemed insufferable as if unforseen.' This is 'closure' of the wrong kind, as Elizabeth writes to Arabella: 'Without a word, without a sign—Its like slamming a door on me as he went out—'

There are consolations. Julia Martin tells her that Papa had written of 'forgiving' Elizabeth, Henrietta and Alfred, his married, disinherited children. Stormie, who as the oldest surviving son is his father's heir, makes over a total of £15,000 out of his inheritance to the trio. And maybe the long wait for resolution of any kind has muted the intensity of Elizabeth's feeling, or allowed her to grieve already. For though in the first days after her father's death she can't even write a letter, Robert is surprised how well she bears up. Unlike at earlier bereavements there is no physical collapse; instead she even manages to weep.

But still the losses aren't done. This summer, a month into their stay at Bagni di Lucca, Wilson's second pregnancy starts to go wrong. Premature labour or miscarriage threaten and she's ordered to bed. Once a replacement is found she has to go back to Florence; she will never return to work for the Brownings, though Ferdinando stays in their service. Instead, with a loan from the Brownings, she rents a lodging house right by Casa Guidi, where she can stay in touch with the household, keep an eye on Ferdinando – and make more money than she did as a maid. Later, she'll move to better accommodation still, as Robert arranges for the elderly Walter Savage Landor, now suffering from dementia, to become a paying guest when his confusion and violence cause Mrs Landor to throw him out. Though this is perhaps a mixed blessing, it's this extra income that will allow Wilson to pay for Orestes to join her in Italy.

In mid-September 1857, Wilson's place with the family at Bagni di Lucca is taken by Annunziata Lena, a local woman of just under thirty, who has experience in working for the very particular constituency of Englishwomen. Robert and Elizabeth remain at the spa town until the second week in October, but this summer is haunted by a gastric fever that Robert Bulwer-Lytton brought with him from Florence in early August; Annunziata falls ill with it almost immediately. Worse, Pen is ill for much of the second half of September. All three recover, but on top of new bereavement this mortal maternal terror is almost too much for Elizabeth: 'When I wanted repose to recover from a great shock, I could'nt get it [...]—& Peni's illness ended by breaking me to pieces when I was peculiarly brittle—.'

It's all driving her closer to a new friend, an amateur medium called Sophie Eckley. By now spiritualism divides the Brownings. In London last summer they attended a séance in Ealing at which the famous Scottish medium Daniel Dunglas Home 'manifested' Robert's 'dead infant son' – which turned out to be Home's bare foot. (One can see why Robert would seize on such 'evidence' with fury, with its niggling implication of an earlier child, abandonment, and infidelity added to sheer clumsy cheek.) Famously, in 1864's *Dramatis Personae* Robert will make his feelings clear with the excoriating poem 'Mr Sludge, "The Medium"'. Now he suspects Mrs Eckley of manipulating his wife. Yet he doesn't resist when more distinguished visitors turn to the subject, for example on the June evening at Casa Guidi when they're joined by the American poet William Cullen Bryant, Robert's old friend the poet Fanny Haworth, and Nathaniel and Sophia Hawthorne.

Hawthorne will record that he finds this visit haunting in another way: his hostess is kind, but so small and frail she seems 'scarcely embodied at all'. As Elizabeth tells Arabella:

> A bad winter have I had? In some ways, but not with my chest. [...] Altogether I am not as strong as usual [...] I have a horrible vibrating body—If I am uneasy in mind for half an hour, I am unwell,—& then, being unwell makes one uneasy again. It acts, & reacts.

At fifty-two, she's probably coping with the wear and tear of menopausal symptoms on top of her usual weakness. But even Robert, who's bought a skeleton and a chest of homeopathic remedies, seems newly preoccupied by the body and its ills.

Altogether it's a subdued party that leaves Casa Guidi for France on 1 July 1858. This year they'll spend just two weeks in Paris catching up with old friends: Anna Jameson, 'Father Prout', and Lady Elgin, now horribly disabled by a series of strokes. On 19 July they move out to the Normandy port of Le Havre. The idea is to take a halfway house for a family summer. In many ways this works. Sarianna and Robert Senior house-share, Arabella, George and Henry (with his new wife Amelia) cross the Channel to visit, and Robert's best friend Joseph Milsand comes to stay. And it's at the end of this busy stay that Elizabeth sits for Cyrus Macaire for the photograph that will become Dante Gabriel Rossetti's famous portrait. But 'hideous' 2 rue du Perrey, destined to disappear under twentieth-century apartment blocks, is a quite astonishingly bad choice for all this activity. Le Havre, by the 1870s confirmed as the European capital for tuberculosis deaths, is already being mapped street by street for infection rates, and it's the low-lying harbour-side areas like this that are worst affected. Do Robert and Elizabeth not notice that, despite the handsome eighteenth-century houses, the neighbourhood is poor and unsanitary? Are they simply blinded by the English dogma of healthy sea air? There will be no radical symptomatic changes in Elizabeth's subsequent health to suggest that she does get infected. But it's a foolish place to stay for any invalid, particularly one already suffering from respiratory disease.

The very day after Elizabeth's photographic session with the Macaire brothers the Brownings return to Paris, where they rent at 6 rue de Castiglione for a month before setting off for home. En route to Italy, storms turn the Genoa to Livorno sea-leg into an eighteen-hour nightmare, a brutal reminder that these are the very waters where Shelley drowned. But this time home, when they finally get there, offers no safety either. Elizabeth's health has deteriorated so much that the Florentine winter is simply not warm and dry enough for her any more. She must go further south. Travelling with the Eckley household, the Brownings set out straight away for Rome, whose winter climate seems healthier than its summers, and by 26 November are reinstalled at Via Bocca di Leone. Here Robert resumes his social life, while Elizabeth rests up after all the travel, and assiduously revises *Aurora Leigh*: she has her changes for what becomes the fourth edition sent off by the middle of January 1859.

The couple now seem to be leading almost parallel lives. While Elizabeth sits for her portrait thrice – in March to Field Talfourd and Eliza Bridell Fox, and in May to Rudolf Lehmann (who also paints Robert) – her husband is learning to draw, tutored by a young lady, Mary Mackenzie. He has also become a particular fan of Adelaide Ristori's acting, and, in the first week of January 1859 alone, he goes to three productions in which she stars. The artist Frederic Leighton and actress Charlotte Cushman are among the many acquaintances, often celebrated, that Robert now sees 'sometimes two or three times deep in a one night's engagements'; so are older friends like Nathaniel Hawthorne, William Page, and the Storys. 'So plenty of distraction, and no *Men and Women*',

Elizabeth frets. Political turmoil is intensifying, and Robert also meets up with 'the really instructed people': former ambassador Lord Stratford de Redcliffe, diplomat Odo Russell, and *Times* correspondent Henry Wreford. In mid-March, he even briefs the Prince of Wales on the Italian situation over a dinner.

Elizabeth, equally riveted by the political events unfolding around them, tries to get Robert writing by proposing that they publish together again: this time, poems celebrating the end of Austrian rule. But Austrian rule is not at an end. On 3 May 1859, roughly a week after Austria sends troops into Piedmont-Sardinia, France declares war on Austria; by the end of the month, when Elizabeth and Robert return home to Florence, French troops are in the city and the Austrian Grand Duke has fled. In June, the French ally with the Piedmontese to defeat the Austrians twice, at Magenta and Solferino. But they suffer such heavy losses that they throw away the liberation they've won at so much cost. On 11 July, at Villafranca, they make a peace, which, while it unites Lombardy with Piedmont, returns much of northern Italy to Austrian control.

This shocking decision has wide-reaching effects. The end of the 'beautiful dream' of a free Italy is felt within the Brownings' relationship too. Robert destroys his celebratory poem; Elizabeth keeps hers, 'Napoleon III in Italy', but as usual when she's faced with a grief too big for expression, her health collapses. She's in bed for nearly three weeks. When the time comes for the usual summer move to the country – this time to Marciano, a hilltop village that's almost a satellite of Siena – she has to be carried from the train, and is confined to bed for her first ten days at 'grim square' Villa Alberti. Advised by Elizabeth's Roman doctor E. G. T. Grisanowsky to seek a healthier climate, the Brownings won't return to Florence this year till mid-October.

The air in Siena is undeniably fresher than it is in Rome: it is out of the Tiber basin and a little further north, while not as northerly as Florence. The Brownings squeeze in just six weeks at home in Casa Guidi before setting out once more for Rome on 28 November, harried south by the approaching winter. For Elizabeth, life itself is feeling increasingly unsustainable; travel is the most exhausting of remedies. Yet through all the comings and goings she continues to write. The enormous set-piece efforts of her achievement – elopement, child-bearing, the compositions culminating in *Aurora Leigh*, not to mention the sheer effort of surviving chronic illness – all demonstrate her fierce will to embrace life. Possibly writing helps concentrate that will by narrowing its focus. Morphine has certainly helped, though if this were widely known it could cause a scandal. Already at the start of this year Robert called on Louisa Crawford to protest about her sister Julia Ward Howe's allegations, in a spitefully slanderous poem baldly titled 'One Word More with E.B.B.', that Elizabeth's 'unearthly' verse, her 'ill-directed flight / And sentence, mystical, and hard', is the result of a 'nameless draught […] a drug'. Elizabeth's own response was to admit ruefully to Sophie Eckley that morphine was indeed her lifeline.

But now even this isn't quite enough to manage her symptoms, though her imagination is certainly undimmed as she writes 'An August Voice', 'A Tale of Villafranca' – and 'Where's Agnes?', a grief-struck debunking of spiritualism. Here, as she has before, she approaches autobiographical material 'slant', through fiction. The poem's narrator has lost a dear friend, Agnes, who cannot come back from the dead because she's too good to have any truck with things hellish. Her ghostly 'manifestation' must therefore be a fake; which means that Agnes is now nothing more than 'That sort of worm in the clay'. Embodiment, the 'worm in the clay', *means* mortality for all of us – the poem's speaker and its reader too. 'And my mouth is full of dust / Till I cannot speak', Elizabeth concludes.

For by late 1859 the hope that spiritualism held out to her, of transcending the mortal body, is itself dying. At the end of the summer she sends Sophie a letter questioning some of the supernatural experiences that seemed especially staged by the younger woman. What is it that prompts Elizabeth to do so? Has the devil in some detail finally changed her mind? Or is it just that, away from her friend's charm and faced with the increasingly grim realities of trying to stay alive, she at last sees things clearly? Whatever her reasons, just as when she finally relinquished her belief in her father, she now rips off her own blinkers. But this time the reward of clarity is a gathering gloom. And as the Brownings settle in for their Roman winter and the turn of the decade – finding accommodation suddenly cheap due to the threat of impending war – their friendship with the Eckleys melts away to mere formality.

Everything is becoming difficult now. In mid-January 1860 Elizabeth ventures on a rare outing. She and Robert go to Castellani the jeweller's, to see a fashionable exhibition of presentation swords for Napoleon III and Victor Emmanuel. One popular cause meets another: the Brownings are mobbed for autographs. Fun though this might have been in the past, now it leaves Elizabeth coughing, breathless and suffering an arrhythmic heartbeat for days. Still, she's managed to send Chapman and Hall her *Poems Before Congress*, and proofs of the new book arrive this month. Her title, advertising the collection's highly political content, comes from an abandoned congress on Italian sovereignty that had been due to take place at this very time. In February she composes a Preface in which she implies that Britain, preoccupied with free trade, has failed properly to support Italian unification:

> Non-intervention in the affairs of neighbouring states is a high polit-
> ical virtue; but non-intervention does not mean, passing by on the
> other side when your neighbour falls among thieves.

Not surprisingly, when *Congress* appears in print in March it brings down a storm of hostile reviews, mostly accusing Elizabeth of being unpatriotic. In *The Athenaeum*, her old literary ally but political opponent H. F. Chorley even misreads 'A Curse for a Nation', as being directed at 'perfidious Albion' rather than American slavery (although he has a point, since the poem is fierce in its injunctions, but vague about what exactly it means by 'Freedom' and 'writhing bond-slaves'). Reviews in *Bell's Weekly Messenger*, *The Examiner*, *The Critic*, *The Bookseller*, *The Atlas*, the *Daily News*, *The Press*, *The Spectator*, *The Saturday Review* and the *Manchester Guardian* are among those that follow, and *Blackwood's* verdict that 'women should not interfere with politics' is typical. Elizabeth's profile ensures the very breadth of coverage that makes this criticism so insistent. She feels besieged, and moves the fight to Robert's work, fuming to Sarianna about the 'blindness, deafness, and stupidity of the English public to Robert', who she says is appreciated in Britain by only 'a small knot of pre-Rafaellite men', though in America 'he's a power, a writer, a poet [...] he lives in the hearts of the people'.

It's a projection, but perhaps a healthy one, of the anger and abandonment she must feel. It can't help that the staunchly intelligent and Italophile Anna Jameson, that good friend, dies this same month. Now the sense of political abandonment intensifies too. Tuscany has come under Victor Emmanuel's rule after a plebiscite on 11 March, but French 'liberation' troops enter Savoy before the vote there has even been held. Elizabeth isn't well enough to join the crowds in the streets who witness 'King Victor Emmanuel Entering Florence, April 1860' – though she writes about it in her poem of this title as if she were. Or as if she were reminded of that first, triumphant procession in 1847 below Casa Guidi's windows: 'And thousands of faces, in wild exultation, / Burn over the windows to feel him near—' In May, Garibaldi gambles by invading Sicily with such small forces that he could have cost the country its slowly cohering political solution, 'the soil beneath my feet / In valour's act [...] forfeited', as Elizabeth writes in 'Garibaldi'; though the gamble does pay off. Robert is working on persona poems again, but Italian political themes continue to dominate her own new work, which is still appearing regularly in Britain (*Cornhill Magazine*) and America (*The Independent*).

Elizabeth manages to engage eleven-year-old Pen's emerging sensibilities in progressive realpolitik: she tells Henrietta that he cried when he read the political poems in *Congress*. But political stress is attritional. In June 1860 a fifth edition of *Aurora Leigh* appears without further revisions. On 7 July the Brownings are once again installed in Villa Alberti, Marciano, where by September William Michael Rossetti (brother of their old friend Dante Gabriel) and Vernon Lushington witness the threads drawn thin. In their presence Elizabeth quarrels with Walter Savage Landor over Napoleon III, and Robert shows 'some slight symptom of approaching antagonism if Mrs Browning in talking came to the outskirts of the "spiritual" theme'. Apparently, 'Browning could express himself with some harshness to his wife when this subject was mooted'.

By 7 November though, when Garibaldi and Victor Emmanuel enter Naples together in triumph, Mrs Browning has other worries. After the usual six-week autumn in Casa Guidi, the household travel south for what is to be their final Roman winter. Arriving on 23 November, they pick a vertiginous, skinny house above the Spanish Steps at 126 Via Felice. But while this is happening Elizabeth is somewhat removed, and in a state of cruel suspense. Back in Somerset, Henrietta is dying slowly and agonisingly of cancer. She's been gravely ill since the summer, in the lovely old stone manor house of Stoke Court, Thurlbear, which Surtees has finally been able to afford. Arabella may be the place-marker who keeps the scattering family connected, but Henrietta is the sibling with whom, since Bro's death, Elizabeth has had most in common – especially once they both married. The dreaded news arrives on 3 December: she died on the day Elizabeth and Robert arrived in Rome. It seems against the natural order of things that she should predecease the family invalid, and perhaps Elizabeth's profound grief is intensified by survivor's guilt. By dark coincidence, her poem of grief written after Bro's death, 'De Profundis', appears in *The Independent* just three days later.

Yet as 1861 dawns, her poems, from 'Little Mattie' to 'Nature's Remorses', increasingly adopt the fictional, often persona form that will dominate her hugely successful *Last Poems* when it appears in 1862. This style is a pre-echo of Robert's *Dramatis Personae*, which will be published two years later; and it's he who will prepare the posthumous volume, apparently following 'a list drawn up' in June 1861. Widower-poets face a difficult choice between 'improving' an uncompleted legacy or letting it go, perhaps overexposed, into the world. A century from now, for example, conspiracy stories will surround Ted Hughes's attempts to do right by his late wife Sylvia Plath's work, though his choices will clearly be good ones, as Plath's posthumous reputation attests. No similar cloud of suspicion will hang over Robert's head, even though the posthumous Elizabeth is much more in his own poetic image than she ever was alive. But suspicion without evidence is just gossip. Better perhaps to remember how long Elizabeth *has* been writing in persona: even 1826's *An Essay on Mind* included 'Riga's Song' among its 'Other Poems'.

Now the living Elizabeth has a rare moment of cultural disconnect with 'Lord Walter's Wife', which Thackeray turns down for *Cornhill Magazine* on grounds of immodesty. Usually so acutely tuned in to the *zeitgeist*, she has perhaps let herself get out of touch, as she busies herself preparing Italian literals of her own poetry for Francesco Dall'Ongaro to turn into Italian verse. Elizabeth's heart is 'heavy' and Robert – 'not inclined to write this winter', as she tells Sarianna – is once again toying with visual art, this time modelling clay in William Story's studio. Yet the couple remain a magnet for writers and artists. In April they talk with Joseph Severn, now British consul, about how he nursed the dying Keats forty years ago, right here at the Spanish Steps. In late May they go to the studio of Father Antonio D'Alessandri to be photographed. This is Elizabeth's second sitting: last year he posed her with Pen. Now D'Alessandri records a face drawn by illness, and hair dyed jet-black like a disguise. This same month she also has a visit from Hans Christian Andersen. Her response is a homage, 'The North and The South', which she sends straight off to Thackeray for *Cornhill*.

It is 21 May 1861, and this is the last poem she will write. On 1 June, as if by a kind of instinct – though ostensibly because of the weather – the Brownings break the pattern of recent years and leave for Casa Guidi, arriving home on 5 June. The very next day, Cavour, that great statesman who was to unite Italy, dies. Elizabeth is shocked and grief-stricken; once again her 'horrible vibrating body' reacts. The death of her adored sister, and of what seems to be any hope of democracy and independence for her much-loved adopted country, bleed into each other. It feels as if nothing good can ever happen again.

Grief is a kind of yearning, and Elizabeth yearns from the apartment towards the sights and sounds of her beloved Florence, the elegant yet so-habitable city astride the River Arno that she has made her home, but which she has become too ill to go out into. Now even Casa Guidi has its ghosts: of old freedoms when her health was improving and she went out and about with Robert, of happy days with Wilson, lit up by the blossoming romance with Ferdinando, of Pen's infancy, of letters arriving from Henrietta, of those first civic parades. The unseasonably cool June means that even the apartment's tall windows let in less brightness than usual. On 20 June, Elizabeth, trapped in nostalgia and grief, has them opened – and catches cold.

Two nights later, on 22 June, Robert has to call the doctor. Dr Wilson diagnoses congestion and a possible abscess in the right lung. Although feverish, with a racking cough and sore throat, Elizabeth is sure he's wrong. She feels just the same as all the other times she's been ill and besides, she can feel that it's her *left* lung that's troubling her, as always.

Whether or not it *is* the same as usual, she spends the next five days coughing and, as a result, getting little sleep. She loses strength. Robert, too, passes these nights of coughing in a state of insomniac attention. It's as if they're keeping watch together to see whether the angel of death will pass over the house one more time.

Suddenly, on the evening of 28 June, there's an injection of hopefulness. Isa Blagden calls with the news that the new prime minister, Baron Ricasoli, shares Cavour's vision. Italy is going to be alright. It's a close call, but the news for the country is miraculously good. The angel of death seems to have passed over the city roofs – over the entire peninsula – leaving it untouched. And it means, perhaps, that there's no longer a battle for Elizabeth to brace herself against. Possibly she relaxes. At any rate, just after three in the morning of what is now 29 June, Robert notices that her feet have become very cold. He rouses Annunziata, and asks her to bring warm water and some jellied chicken, that soothing, sustaining food of invalids. He almost certainly administers some extra morphine, too. Elizabeth is confused as she half-wakes from a travel dream to exclaim 'What a fine steamer – how comfortable!'

Annunziata bathes Elizabeth's feet in the warm water, and feeds her some of the chicken. Robert sends the maid for more warm water and Elizabeth, with a trace of her old glitter, teases, 'You *are* determined to make an exaggerated case of it'. But she lets him take her in his arms. They rest like that together. Sometime after 4am, Robert asks her if she knows him and she reassures him, 'My Robert—My heavens, my beloved'. 'Our lives are held by God', she tells him. He lifts her and she kisses him repeatedly; when he moves his face away, she kisses her hands towards him, saying 'Beautiful... beautiful...' A few moments later, she has stopped breathing. It is, perhaps, an ideal death. Immensely moving and intensely intimate, it is also and essentially the death of a lover. Elizabeth, raised on the doctrine of family love and prepared to lose everything for romantic love, has ended her life with love's avowal.

According to her lover, at least. But perhaps he isn't absolutely the most reliable narrator. Sometimes we believe that what *should* be true really *was*. Could this ideal deathbed be even slightly idealised? For Robert, the catastrophic loss of the person on whom his life is built runs the risk, like the loss of his mother in 1849, of destroying not just a way of life, but his own sense of self. He needs desperately to hold onto his foundation myth, the story of twin poetic souls finding each other and building their own idyllic home together.

Still, what he says about these last moments in his letters home rings true in many ways. At great moments, people do often become their most loving selves; since 'what will survive of us is love' is much more wholly true than Philip Larkin asserts in that famous poem. The tiny, frail Elizabeth of 1861, her face drawn and crumpled by long illness, certainly seems physically ready to slip quickly away from life.

And something else. This quiet unmooring is not the desperate struggle of a fatal asthma attack, nor the agonised drowning in infected fluid of a burst abscess. It most resembles a breath-shallowing, heart-stopping morphine overdose. Combine the high doses that result from Elizabeth's lifetime dependency on the drug with the panicky human desire to relieve suffering and this is not inconceivable. And who's to say that it would not even be a kind of pragmatic, if unconscious, compassion?

Love takes many forms. And of course Elizabeth had another great love besides Robert. Twelve-year-old Pen still sports the long curls and fancy clothes that have been his mother's whim. Three years ago Nathaniel Hawthorne found him 'slender, fragile, and spirit-like [...] as if he had little or nothing to do with human flesh and blood'. Since then, a rather solitary childhood, as the only offspring of parents whose migratory lifestyle means he's acquired no close friends his own age, has given him an enjoyment of solitary amusements; sketching and riding his pony. Wilson, in effect his nanny, has been gone for a couple of years. Though sociable since birth, his reliance on his mother has been as great as any boy's. Where is he during this trance-like deathbed scene? What does he see or overhear – what does he understand has happened?

In the morning light Isa Blagden returns to Casa Guidi and takes Pen off to Villa Brichieri, her home in nearby Bellosguardo, an exclusive, wooded hill district. The next day but one, 1 July 1861, Pen is brought back into town for his mother's funeral. Elizabeth Barrett Browning is regarded as a heroine of Italian reunification, and all the shops near Casa Guidi have been closed in her honour. Indeed the whole city, hung with the black of official mourning for Cavour, seems to be grieving for her. Nor is this entirely an illusion. Next week a prominent government minister, Simone Luigi Peruzzi, will call at Casa Guidi to express the hopes of 'all Italians' that Robert and Pen will remain in Tuscany; within a couple of years 'grateful Florence' will erect a tablet on the house wall to memorialise Elizabeth 'whose poems forged a gold ring / Between Italy and England'. And today her coffin, crowned with white blossoms and laurel wreaths, is carried on a special ceremonial route allowed only to public figures through the city to the Protestant Cemetery.

At the graveside Pen's father reads from his mother's poem 'The Sleep':

And, friends, dear friends,—when it shall be
That this low breath is gone from me,
And round my bier ye come to weep,
Let One, most loving of you all,
Say, 'Not a tear must o'er her fall;
He giveth His belovèd, sleep.'

That night, he joins Pen at Isa Blagden's luxurious villa.

Now changes happen in quick succession. In less than a week, by 5 July, the boy has been shorn of his long hair and princeling style. 'Pen, the golden curls and fantastic dress, is gone just as Ba is gone', Robert tells Sarianna, and 'is a common boy all at once'. This is practical, making it possible to do without Annunziata living in (which would be scandalous now that theirs is an all-male household), but it also draws a line under the life that Elizabeth led. Even Casa Guidi is to be abandoned. Robert commissions a photographer to create a record of the household's extraordinary way of life, but, in the rooms darkened by the church wall immediately opposite, the daguerreotype process doesn't take. So instead the painter George Mignaty is commissioned to enshrine the drawing room just as Elizabeth 'disposed it and left it', and on 1 August Robert and Pen leave Florence – as it turns out, for good.

Pen has become a boy who can never go home. His immediate future holds a month in Paris, then five weeks with his father, Aunt Sarianna and grandfather in Brittany. Perhaps one small comfort and continuity in this headlong transition is that he's allowed to keep his little Giara mare, Stella. But all too soon Pen and his father – and Stella – are in London, and the boy is being enrolled with a tutor as the first stage of a years-long, ultimately unsuccessful struggle to cram him through an Oxford degree.

By next May, his father will be settled at 19 Warwick Crescent, where he'll stay for the next quarter century as he manages the legacy of those sixteen miraculous years of marriage, and as his reputation grows and grows. Robert Browning will become an extraordinary poet and an avid traveller. Eventually, after seventeen years, he'll even make return trips to Italy. Indeed he will die there, on 12 December 1889, while visiting his son in the splendid palazzo Ca' Rezzonico on the Grand Canal in Venice.

For Pen will never outgrow his mother's joyous legacy. Italy and art are his destiny. After an uncertain start on adulthood, he'll study fine art in Paris and Antwerp and become an accomplished, if never distinguished, professional sculptor and painter. His marriage to American heiress Fannie Coddington will do as much to enable his life in Italy as his father's active support will in establishing him as an artist. He will prove a devoted heir, assiduously collecting archival material and memorabilia of his parents' lives. He'll give a home for life to his aunt Sarianna (whom photographs reveal he closely resembles) and – albeit at separate addresses, since their marriage fails – to his childhood intimates, Wilson and Ferdinando. But he will die intestate in 1912, and at his death everything that this first, and most loving, witness of Elizabeth Barrett Browning's life has amassed will be auctioned off and dispersed.

And Elizabeth herself? She has undergone the transformation from living, breathing woman – fluent, motivated, sometimes self-absorbed but always pushing herself onwards, fighting for breath, determined to stay alive and to speak – into a figure in the stories other people tell about her. Her own 'low breath is gone' from the social matrix. Yet she hasn't fallen silent; far from it. Over the next century and a half her words will be read around the world. They continue to be heard today, in the third decade of the twenty-first century, changed into the currency of what's now become conventional political and social thought – about slavery, child labour, rape, women's rights – and transformed again into the more than two centuries of women's writing that has appeared since her first book, *The Battle of Marathon*, was published.

Societies around the world would doubtless have changed, and women emerged as writers and poets in increasing numbers, even if Elizabeth Barrett Browning had never lived. But these more recent writing women are her heirs nonetheless. What they write – the poets among them in particular – would have been different without her. The whole direction of poetry in English would have changed. Flexible, tender, intimate: Elizabeth's poetic voice, as she asks yet again, 'How do I love thee? Let me count the ways', comes back to us with a directness that seems startlingly modern. It's as if she's looking back over her shoulder at us, her wide, sensual mouth dipping and rising in a curly bracket.

[*Closing Frame*]

Like *Aurora Leigh*, this biography is a portrait, not a self-portrait. But the imagination is greedy: as Elizabeth's readers, we respond to elements of her life we feel mirror our own. Something that especially speaks to me, for example, is seeing what John Milton in his sonnet 'When I consider how my light is spent' calls 'that one Talent which is death to hide' squandered by family circumstance, ill-health, shyness, casual intellectual misogyny.

There's surely nothing wrong with such feelings – let's call them recognition, or complicity. It's how humans have always used stories, and biographies are in the first place stories, after all. Besides, how else can we encounter our biographical subject, except by coming to meet her? Writing can never be wholly innocent of the writing self, and slowly I'm coming to accept that a biographer's own self always frames her subject.

But Elizabeth's poetry too composes a kind of self-portrait, or rather mirror. As she became herself through writing, her writing reflected that developing self. And so her body of work creates a kind of looking glass in which, dimly, we make out the person who wrote it: her choices and opinions, what moved her, habits and characteristic turns of phrase.

Though this is true of all writers' work, it's especially true for Elizabeth because poetry isn't, to paraphrase that early hero Byron, 'of her life a thing apart', but her 'whole existence'. She makes a brilliant case study in writerly self-invention: in the self on the page. Besides, this is a self that overwhelmingly repays our attention. Barrett Browning shows us that the way into good, even great, writing goes step by step, *gradus ad Parnassum*. You could say that her story works like a practice mirror for writers, even today.

Seven years after his wife's death, in his four-volume verse novel *The Ring and the Book*, Robert describes the literal mirror in which Elizabeth saw her own face daily: the one with 'twin Cherubs in the tarnished frame' which hung in the drawing-room at Casa Guidi, 'tall [...] to the ceiling-top'. Today it hangs there once again, on the green wall above the red sofa, facing the windows, the balcony, and the side wall of San Felice; a shady view which it reflects only incompletely. Visitors to the apartment see their own reflections pass to and fro in the glass. Perhaps some even fantasise that they glimpse Elizabeth there too. But we don't need to visit Florence or to believe in ghosts to encounter her. To read Elizabeth Barrett Browning is to witness how, unaware that she's being observed, she reflects herself in her poetry. Which, with all its innovative brilliance, makes a fabulously ornate two-way mirror.

Notes

Both Elizabeth Barrett Browning's work and Robert Browning's writing is widely available, including online. So I've referenced only poem titles and (in longer poems) line numbers. However, an excellent Norton Critical Edition of *Aurora Leigh* is available, edited by Margaret Reynolds (New York & London: W. W. Norton, 1996); as is the comprehensive *The Works of Elizabeth Barrett Browning* (five volumes) edited by Sandra Donaldson et al. (London: Pickering and Chatto, 2010). The Norton Critical Edition of *Robert Browning's Poetry* is edited by James F. Loucks and Andrew M. Stauffer (New York & London: W. W. Norton, 2007). The Wedgestone Press multi-volume and online edition of *The Browning Correspondence*, edited by Philip Kelley et al., www.browningscorrespondence.com, includes not only letters (here given as # numbers) but supporting documents (here given as SD numbers), images and portraits, and contemporary critical responses to the Brownings, and is by far the best resource for research. So authoritative and comprehensive is it that I have adopted its numbering throughout these references. Also indispensible for any Browning scholar is *The Brownings: A Research Guide*, www. browningguide.org/, also prepared by Kelley et al. Published before much of this material had been made available, the last full-length solo biography is Margaret Forster's wonderfully readable and emotionally insightful *Elizabeth Barrett Browning* (London: Chatto & Windus, 1988). Robert is more recently and comprehensively served by Ian Finlayson's authoritative *Browning* (London: Harper Collins, 2004).

Key to abbreviations
EBB – Elizabeth Barrett Browning
Edward B MB – her father, Edward Barrett Moulton-Barrett
Samuel B MB – her 'Uncle Sam'
Edward MB – her brother 'Bro'
Samuel MB – her brother Sam
Mary MB – her mother
Henrietta MB and Arabella MB – her sisters Henrietta and Arabella
RB – Robert Browning
Mitford – Mary Russell Mitford

DEDICATION

p. v   The last line of *Aurora Leigh* [*AL*].

FRONTISPIECE

Epigraph   Elizabeth Barrett Browning, *AL* Bk 2, L. 485.

p. 1   C. S. Francis & Co. commission this cheap successor to daguerreotype, taken on 18 September 1858. RB to Charles Stephen Francis 19 September 1858, #4243; RB to Edward Law 19 September 1858, #4244.

p. 2   Barlow is selected by William Michael Rossetti. Barlow's offprint is held at the Armstrong Browning Library. Alicia Constant, 'Artefacts Relating to EBB's *Aurora Leigh*', http://blogs.baylor.edu/19crs/2016/01/21/artifacts-related-to-ebbs-aurora-leigh/ [retrieved 11 September 2018].

Rossetti's request for 'the shoulder & back to be slightly lowered' has been taken as evidence that EBB developed a humped back. D. A. B. Young, 'The illnesses of Elizabeth Barrett Browning' in *British Medical Journal* vol. 298 (18 February 1989), p. 441. Simpler and more likely is that she's hunched over by chronic pulmonary disease.

'An evening resort...' Dante Gabriel Rossetti to William Allingham 18 December 1856, SD2023. 'As unattractive a person...' Rossetti to Walter Howell Deverell 30 August 1851, SD1501.

p. 3   RB to Edward Chapman 19 September 1858, #4246.

The 'horrible libel', a medallion by the sculptor Marshall Wood, is reproduced in *The National Magazine* (14 February 1857), p. 313. RB retains the original ambrotype, 'so satisfactory that I keep it myself and only send a copy to Francis'. RB to Edward Chapman 19 September 1858, #4246. Sent via the *Fulton*. RB to Charles Stephen Francis 19 September 1858, #4243.

Brady advertised in the *New-York Daily Tribune*.

p. 4   *AL* Bk 8, Ll. 283, 285. As famously argued in Roland Barthes, 'The Death of the Author' in Phyllis Johnson, ed, *Aspen* vol. 5 + 6 (1967).

p. 5   Lionel Trilling and Harold Bloom in Frank Kermode, John Hollander, Harold Bloom, Martin Price, J. B. Trapp, Lionel Trilling, eds, *The Oxford Anthology of English Literature* (New York, London, Toronto: Oxford University Press, 1973), p. 1475.

p. 6   The 1980s also see the last full-length biography, Margaret Forster's *Elizabeth Barrett Browning* (London: Chatto & Windus, 1988). Important studies of EBB as a 'woman writer' published in this era include Angela Leighton, *Elizabeth Barrett Browning* (Brighton: The Harvester Press, 1986) in their Key Women Writers series; Marjorie Stone, *Elizabeth Barrett Browning* (Basingstoke: Macmillan, 1995) in their Women Writers series; and Germaine Greer, *Slip-Shod Sibyls: Recognition, Rejection and the Female Poet* (London: Viking, 1995), pp. 95–101, 394–400, 424.

Woolf misses the verse novel's grand narrative of becoming a woman poet.

Virginia Woolf, 'Aurora Leigh' in *The Second Common Reader* (New York: Harcourt Brace, 1932).

Virginia Woolf, *Flush: A Biography* (London: The Hogarth Press, 1932).

p. 8   Under the principle of coverture. Such non-professional occupations as governess or seamstress are open to unmarried women.

The father of Mary Ann Evans (1819–1880) invested in schooling because the future George Eliot was a plain child whose marriage prospects he considered poor.

EBB, 'Glimpses into My Own Life and Literary Character', in Philip Kelley and Ronald Hudson, eds, *The Brownings' Correspondence* (Winfield, Kansas: Wedgestone Press, 1984), vol. 1, pp. 348–56, p. 351.

p. 9   *AL* Bk 2, Ll. 494–97.

AL Bk 1, Ll. 959–61.

Michael Field is a pseudonym for Katharine Harris Bradley and Edith Emma Cooper.

p. 10   *AL* Bk 2, Ll. 33–34.

'The worthiest poets have remained uncrowned / Till death has bleached their foreheads to the bone', *AL* Bk 2, Ll. 28–29.

AL Bk 1, Ll. 1049–52.

p. 11   *AL* Bk 2, Ll. 232–36.

AL Bk 2, Ll. 240–43. Even in the year of Elizabeth's birth, when roughly 60 per cent of women (and 40 per cent of men) are illiterate, female literacy is not bizarre. David Mitch, 'Education and Skill of the British Labour Force', in Roderick Floud and Paul Johnson, eds, *The Cambridge Economic History of Modern Britain, vol. I: Industrialisation, 1700–1860* (Cambridge: Cambridge University Press, 2004), p. 344.

Virginia Woolf, *A Room of One's Own* (London: Hogarth Press, 1929), p. 6.

p. 12   Though EBB still hadn't read Godwin's *Memoir* in her forties. Charlotte Brontë, quoted in Elizabeth Gaskell, *The Life of Charlotte Brontë* (London: Smith, Elder, 1857), Bk 1, p. 140. By the time *Aurora Leigh* is published, biographies are bestsellers. Samuel Smiles's 1857 *The Life of George Stephenson and of his son Robert Stephenson* sells 25,500 copies in its first six years. Richard Altick, *The English Common Reader: A Social History of the Mass Reading Public 1800–1900* (Columbus: Ohio State University Press, 1998), p. 388.

BOOK ONE

Epigraph   *AL* Bk 1, Ll. 1139–40.

p. 14   *The Gentleman's Magazine* vol. 108 (September 1810), p. 202. 'Transactions of the Royal Irish Academy vol. XII' in *The Monthly Journal* vol. 93 (September–December 1820), pp. 161–62. Though still within the cool, thirty-year Dalton Minimum, in 1810, 'Summer was generally dry and hot': Lucy Veale, Georgina H. Endfield, 'Situating 1816, the "year without summer", in the UK', in *The Geographical Journal* vol. 182, no. 4 (10 August 2016), pp. 318–30.

AL, Bk 1, L. 1083. A local but also central-northern English place name, 'hope' comes from the Old English 'hop'. University of Nottingham *Key to English Place-names* http://kepn.nottingham.ac.uk/map/place/ Herefordshire/Hope%20under%20Dinmore [retrieved 29 July 2018].

Notice of Auction Sale on 25 August 1831, *London Morning Post* (4 August 1831), p. 4.

AL Bk 1, L. 630.

Edward B MB to EBB 5 September 1809, #1. He offers £24,000 against an asking price of £27,000.

p. 15   EBB to Elizabeth Moulton *c*.15 July 1810, #3. Elizabeth Moulton to EBB 18 July 1810, #4.

Bro started life as 'Buff', Edward B MB to EBB 5 September 1809, #1. As an unaccompanied seven-year-old, E B MB crossed the Atlantic on a ship auspiciously bearing his mother's name. The *Elizabeth*'s arrival in Bristol is recorded in *Felix Farley's Bristol Journal* 29 September 1792, cited in Kelley and Hudson, eds, *The Brownings' Correspondence*, fn. 2 to Elizabeth Moulton to EBB *c*.June 1826, #232. Elizabeth seems to have stayed behind because her youngest child, George Goodin, born at the end of 1789, was too young to travel; he died on 8 January 1793, just after his third birthday. R. A. Barrett, *The Barretts of Jamaica* (Winfield, Kansas: The Armstrong Browning Library of Baylor University, The Browning Society, Wedgestone Press, 2000), p. 184.

Pinkie is immortalised in Thomas Lawrence's 1794 oil portrait, now at Huntington Library, San Marino, California.

Edward B MB to EBB 5 September 1809, #1.

p. 16   Mary MB to Arabella Graham-Clarke 12 May 1809, SD123. In this letter sent four months earlier to her mother, Mary both describes 'a journey to the dear North, as the *Summit* of *happiness*' and praises Hope End: 'Nothing in short *Ever was* so picturesque and beautiful.'

Graham-Clarke co-owned the glassworks with executor, Joseph Lamb: https://www.ucl.ac.uk/lbs/person/view/42836 [retrieved 9 August 2018]. In 1774 he contributed to the subscription for a new Infirmary and in 1776 to that for the Assembly Rooms. John Charlton, *Hidden Chains: The Slavery Business and North East England 1600–1865* (Newcastle: Tyne Bridge Publishing, 2008), pp. 120, 124.

In 1750 sugar, not wheat, was 'the most valuable commodity in European trade – it made up a fifth of all European imports and in the last decades of the century four-fifths of the sugar came from the British and French colonies in the West Indies'. Clive Ponting, *World History: A New Perspective* (London: Chatto & Windus, 2000), p. 501.

The well-connected Arabella (b.1755) was the daughter of Roger Altham (b.1706). Called to the Bar in the year of her birth, his distinguished career included serving as Seal Keeper of the High Court of Admiralty, Registrar of the Archdeaconry of Middlesex, and for the Dean & Chapter of Westminster. In 1746 Roger married Mary Isaacson of Fenton in Northumberland; Fenton Hall later passed into John Graham-Clarke's hands (see Charlton, op. cit., p. 121). Arabella's elder sister Mary married Newcastle banker Aubone Surtees the Younger, and became sister-in-law to the Lord Chancellor.

Born John Graham in 1735/6, with Hull merchant relatives, Ba's maternal grandfather came to Newcastle with the East Yorkshire Grenadier Militia, http://hector.davie.ch/misc/Graham.html [retrieved 5 July 2018]. The Rutters were merchants, master bakers, brewers, church wardens and a High Sheriff. Elizabeth Rutter died 20 August 1772.

p. 17   *AL* Bk 1, Ll. 1129–31.

A lengthy legal battle will follow Graham-Clarke's death. The original will leaves his property to his wife and his two sons, and a cousin, Thomas Clarke. James Losh, a close friend although an abolitionist, testifies that he was mentally sound in 1817 when he created a codicil which added William Baker as an heir, and mentioned his five daughters. (Another son, John, takes on the running of both Newcastle business and his West Indian trade.)

The first Boulton & Watt steam-driven sugar-cane mill arrives in Jamaica in 1810; other steam mills have already been in use there for four decades. Veront M. Satchell, 'Early use of steam power in the Jamaican sugar industry, 1768–1810' in *Transactions of the Newcomen Society* vol. 67 no. 1 (1995), pp. 221–31.

Man-hours measured on the Indian subcontinent in 2003. R. N. S. Yadav, 1 Yadav, Raj Kumar Tejra, 'Labour saving and cost reduction machinery for sugarcane cultivation', *Sugar Tech* vol. 5, no. 1–2 (2003), pp. 7–10. Graham-Clarke's *Arabella* and *Mayflower* advertise 'excellent accommodations for Passengers'. *Newcastle Chronicle* (31 January 1794).

p. 18   Edward sent his mother a tear-stained glove as a keepsake. Elizabeth Moulton to EBB *c*.June 1826, #232.

p. 19   Edward B MB to Philip Scarlett 30 November 1807, SD74. Edward's father-in-law will never pay this debt; over half a century from now his own son George Goodin will be pursuing it. George Goodin Moulton-Barrett to John Altham Graham-Clarke Jr 7 January 1860, SD2317 et seq. 'A sweet, gentle nature…' EBB to RB 27 August 1846, #2565. 'I rejoice…' Mary Moulton-Barrett to EBB 4 April 1826, #229. To say nothing of modern slavery. *UCL Legacies of British Slave-ownership*, https://www.ucl.ac.uk/lbs/project/context [retrieved 19 September 2019].

p. 20   *AL* Bk 1, Ll. 1132–35, 1137–38, 1143–44.

The Rt Hon C. W. Radcliffe Cooke MP is the Member for Cider. Farm labourers receive on average less than half what building labourers are paid; in Herefordshire they earn less even than the national average.

If they have at least four children, as is usual, they can't support their families. Gregory Clark, 'The long march of history: farm laborers' wages in England 1208–1850' in *New Economics Papers* (24 September 2001), p. 10. https://EconPapers.repec.org/RePEc:cla:najeco:62501800000000238 [retrieved 29 July 2018].

The hop industry suffers particular transport difficulties. 'Out of sight / The lane was: sunk so deep, no foreign tramp / Nor drover of wild ponies out of Wales' could see out. *AL* Bk 1, Ll. 588–90.

p. 21   *London Morning Post*, 1831.

EBB 'Untitled Essay', *c.*early 1840s, Kelley and Hudson, eds, *The Brownings' Correspondence* vol. 1, pp. 360–62.

Elizabeth Moulton to EBB *c.*May 1817, #45.

To lose only one child is a remarkable achievement at a time when one child in three dies before the age of five: https://ourworldindata.org/child-mortality [retrieved 1 August 2018]. Mary is memorialised as a footnote to her parents' memorial tablet on the east wall of the north transept of Ledbury Parish Church.

p. 22   EBB identifies the poodle in 'Untitled Essay'. The miniaturist Charles Hayter paints Ba aged around nine. William Artaud paints the six eldest children in two groups of three.

William Artaud to Wager Tayler 29 March 1818, SD283.

'Poet-Laureat…' Edward B MB to EBB 24 April 1814, #11; EBB, 'Glimpses', pp. 348–56.

p. 23   EBB to E B MB 27 April 1814, #12; EBB to Mary MB 1 May 1814 #13; EBB to Henrietta MB 14 May 1814, #14; EBB to E B MB 28 May 1814, #15.

EBB, 'Glimpses', p. 350.

EBB, 'My Own Character', pp. 347–48.

p. 24   'Ardent…' EBB, 'My Character and Bro's Compared' in Kelley and Hudson, eds, *The Brownings' Correspondence* vol. 1, pp. 357–58. Precociously, Ba understands that even her desire to be truthful about herself is vanity. 'Theology… more mad!' EBB, 'Glimpses' p. 353. Artaud SD283. 'At eleven…' EBB, 'Glimpses', p. 351.

The Latin tutor is an Irishman called Daniel McSwiney. Letter, in my translation, is EBB to Samuel Moulton-Barrett *c.*July 1817, #50.

EBB, 'To Summer', 4 May 1819.

p. 25   Such stays briefly show promise of becoming a pattern in 1819, when they summer at Worthing: but then abruptly stop. From the age of four Arabella will spend nearly three years away at Ramsgate and Worthing, returning to Hope End in 1820.

'I don't like dancing…' in my translation, EBB to Mme Gordin *c.*July 1817, #47. 'House under the sideboard…' EBB to RB 15 January 1846, #2175. 'Steady indignation…' EBB to Mary Russell Mitford 22 July 1842, #988. 'One great misfortune…' EBB 'Untitled Essay', p. 361.

Though of course we can't rule dysphoria out, even as a phase, since there's no definite statement to the contrary.

p. 26   'I hate needlework...' EBB, 'My Own Character', p. 347. 'Admirer at thirteen...' EBB to Mitford 28–29 March 1842, #931. 'An old maid...' Mary MB to EBB c.September 1821, #135. If spinsterhood means rigidity, femininity must indeed mean, for Ba's Mama, flexibility.
'Coterie...' Artaud to Taylor SD283.
EBB, 'Essay on Woman', Ll. 33–34, *Studies in Browning and His Circle* vol. 12 (1984), pp. 11–12.
'Your Lordship is the only instrument of the ceaseless shame which now pollutes your name.' EBB to Lord Somers – draft c.September 1817, #51.

p. 27   Her first surviving poem, 'On the Cruelty of Forcement to Man', protests the Royal Navy's press-ganging of sailors. In 1812 this practice is debated in Parliament and the press, and becomes a catalyst for war between Britain and the United States.
The MS in the Berg Collection, New York Public Library (*Reconstruction* D666), is probably misdated as 1814. However, press coverage of the issue in 1812 accords with EBB's own version of herself as a poet from the age of six. EBB, 'Glimpses', p. 349.
'One little city...' Preface, *The Battle of Marathon*. 'Doubt clouds...' *Marathon* Bk I, Ll. 363–68.

p. 28   'Dear Ba seemed so unhappy at our going that it inspired my idea that it would be a material improvement to her to do so, and she jumped into the carriage with us.' Mary MB to Arabella Graham-Clarke 25 October 1815, SD236.
'Thuillerie Gardens...' EBB to Arabella Graham-Clarke 26 December 1815, #26. 'In spite of the romantic prospects...' EBB to E B MB c.November 1817, #53.

p. 29   'The blood of the slave...' EBB to RB 20 December 1845, #2144.

p. 30   George Goodin remembers his mixed-heritage illegitimate children in his will in much the same terms that white illegitimate children are customarily remembered. He leaves them the maximum amount allowed under racist laws of the time. Elissa is not free, and meaningful consent is lacking. Moreover, as she was herself of mixed heritage – she's described as 'mulatto' – something similar must have happened to her mother, or grandmother. 'To each of his quadroon children Goodin Barrett left "two thousand pounds Current money of Jamaica", the maximum allowed to colored offspring by law.' Jeannette Marks, *The Family of the Barrett: A Colonial Romance* (New York: Macmillan, 1938: p. 223). Elissa Peters receives an annuity, a house and three enslaved women as servants.
Cecilia A. Green, 'Hierarchies of whiteness in the geographies of empire: Thomas Thistlewood and the Barretts of Jamaica' in *NWIG: New West Indian Guide/Nieuwe West-Indische Gids* vol. 80, no. 1/2 (2006), pp. 5–43, 35.

UCL Legacies of British Slave-ownership https://www.ucl.ac.uk/lbs/person/view/2146642461 [retrieved 11 August 2018].

p. 31 'When we consider them…' 'An Impartial Review of New Publications' in *The London Magazine* vol. 42 (September 1773), p. 456. Wheatley fell out of fashion and died in poverty, albeit a free woman, two decades before Ba's birth. She would be republished in America in the 1830s by abolitionists.

W. T. J. Gun, ed, *Harrow School Register 1571–1800* (London, New York, Toronto: Longmans, 1934), p. 36.

RB, 'Prefatory Note', *The Collected Works of Elizabeth Barrett Browning* (London: George Routledge & Sons, 1887).

p. 32 E B MB seems to have lied about his age, since the *Alumni Cantabrigiensis* has him admitted as Fellow Commoner in October 1801 aged eighteen. When Robert Moulton surrendered his claim on the estates to Philip Scarlett on 20 February 1806 he was forced to give Ba's Uncle Sam more than £500; but Papa had to find £6,533/17/7½ to pay him off. R. A. Barrett, *The Barretts of Jamaica*, pp. 52–53.

The Epsom house had belonged to Charles Moulton's father-in-law's sister. Land Tax returns list him as occupant for this year only. Vere Langford Oliver, ed, *Caribbeana: being miscellaneous papers relating to the history, genealogy, topography, and antiquities of the British West Indies* (London: Mitchell, Hughes and Clarke, 1910). He is named as owner 1812–26 in *Epsom and Ewell Explorer*, http://www.epsomandewellhistoryexplorer.org.uk/TheCedars.html [retrieved 30 July 2018]. According to R. A. Barrett, in *The Barretts of Jamaica*, Moulton bought the house from the family, and resold it back to them.

The History of Parliament http://www.historyofparliamentonline.org/volume/1820-1832/member/moulton-barrett-samuel-1787-1837 [retrieved 3 July 2018].

The *London Chronicle* for 1761 records the *Truelove*, belonging to 'Moulton', sailing from Madeira for Barbados on 4 April. A. Arnaiz-Villena, R. Reguera, A. Ferri, L. Barbolla, S. Abd-El-Fatah-Khalil, N. Bakhtiyarova, P. Millan, J. Moscoso, A. Mafalda, J. I. Serrano-Vela, 'The peopling of Madeira archipelago (Portugal) according to HLA genes' in *International Journal of Immunogenetics* vol. 36, no. 1 (1 Feb 2009), p. 9. From 1768 the import of foreign-born slaves to Madeira was banned; but full emancipation was not achieved until 1858. Alberto Vieira, 'Slavery in Madeira in the XV and XVII Centuries: the Balance', in *Centro de Estudos de História do Atlantico*, 1996. http://www.madeira-edu.pt/Portals/31/CEHA/bdigital/hm-esc-2en.pdf [retrieved 22 August 2018].

'I fell into the habit…' EBB to RB 20 December 1845, #2144.

p. 33 For subsequent children there's a full year between a delivery and the next conception.

Marriage recorded in 'Provincial Occurrences' in *Monthly Magazine and Register* (1 June 1805).

Double christenings become the family pattern.
James Ramsay MacDonald, 'Rham, Willam Lewis' in *Dictionary of National Biography 1885–1900*, vol. 48, https://en.wikisource.org/wiki/Rham,_William_Lewis_(DNB00) [retrieved 2 July 2018].
Edward has enjoyed easy, informal access to the Graham-Clarke household.

p. 34   Orientalism becomes especially fashionable once India comes under crown control in 1858. The Royal Pavilion at Brighton doesn't acquire its famous, fantastical exoskeleton of cast-iron domes by John Nash till 1815–21, though the interior decor of Henry Holland's 1786 design, by John Crase and Sons, is in Chinese style.
C. A. Hewitt bought Hope End in 1867 from Thomas Heywood, chairman of the Worcester and Hereford Railway, an antiquary who, like Edward Barrett, became High Sheriff of Herefordshire.

OPENING FRAME

p. 35   Italo Calvino, quoted in Esther Calvino's 'Note' to Italo Calvino, *Under the Jaguar Sun* (Harmondsworth: Penguin, 2002), pp. 84–85.

BOOK TWO

Epigraph   *AL* Bk 7, Ll. 1306–308, 1311.
p. 38   EBB to Henrietta MB *c.*July 1821, #134.
Gloucester spa grew up round springs discovered in Ridley Stile in 1814. The following year, Sir James Jelf built a pump room, laid out gardens, and was bankrupted; under shareholder ownership it remained open. The Spa Hotel was completed in 1818. *Gloucester Journal* (5 & 12 September & 21 November 1814, 24 April & 8 May 1815). 'Bath and Cheltenham occupy the toy and dissipation trade; indeed the latter is a very shouldering, unpleasant neighbour.' Thomas Dudley Fosbrooke, *An original history of the city of Gloucester, almost wholly compiled from new materials; supplying the numerous deficiencies, and correcting the errors, of preceding accounts; including also the original papers of the late Ralph Bigland, esq.* (London: John Nichols and Son, 1819), p. 31. http://www.pascalbonenfant.com/18c/weather.html https://www.booty.org.uk/booty.weather/climate/histclimat.htm [retrieved 9 October 2019].

p. 39   Engraving *c.*1820 by W. Holl after Henry Room, http://www.artfinder.com/work/john-baron-engraved-by-w-holl-from-the-national-portrait-gallery/ [retrieved 30 August 2018].
'Penchant for the pillow...' #134. 'Out in my chair...' EBB to Mary MB *c.*June 1821, #131.
Born in Jamaica at nearly the same time as Ba's father, Nuttall is close in age to Uncle Sam. There is no record of the Nuttalls as plantocracy, but one Thomas Nuttall was Master of the last Liverpool slaving ship,

the *Kitty's Amelia*. https://www.hslc.org.uk/wp-content/uploads/140-5-Behrendt.pdf [retrieved 4 September 2018], *Gentleman's Magazine and Historical Chronicle*, vol. 101 (January–June 1831) (London: Nichols and Son, 1831), p. 186. George Ricketts Nuttall is listed as a Licentiate of the Royal College of Physicians in *The Royal Kalendar: and Court and City Register for England, Scotland, Ireland and the Colonies, for the year 1822* (London: Hansard, 1822), p. 282.

Diagnostic letter: William Cother to Edward B MB, 24 June 1821, SD389. 'You have a description of it from her own eloquent pen', Cother reminds Nuttall, who has not actually examined EBB but commends her for 'deliver[ing] so clear a description of the symptoms which necessarily obtruded themselves on your own observation'. William Cother to George Ricketts Nuttall 24 June 1821, SD389.1 Nuttall to EBB 31 May 1821, #130.

p. 40   'The right side...' SD389.1. Nuttall hasn't prescribed opium; simply a purgative (jalap root, extract of aloes, submuriate of mercury). 'Motions... Your active turn of mind...' #130. 'Derangement... I do not wish...' #131.

p. 41   'A young lady on her back...' EBB to Henrietta MB *c.*November 1821, #138. 'Often entertained...' EBB to Arabella Graham-Clarke early 1822, #146.

p. 42   'Long weary sickness...' EBB to Lady Margaret Cocks *c.*13 March 1838, #619. Bro's been with Ba in Gloucester since at least 7 August: EBB to Henrietta MB 5 October 1821, #137 and Edward MB to Henrietta MB 9 August 1821, SD396. He's still there in September: EBB to Henrietta MB 12 September 1821, #136. Papa visits Ba: Edward MB to EBB 31 December 1821, #145; EBB to Lady Margaret Cocks, March 1838, #619. No later letters by Bro from Gloucester survive and by 23 December he's writing from home: Edward MB to EBB 23 December 1821, #142; Mary MB to Henrietta MB October 1821, SD410.

'Little Tommy Cooke...' #137. Cooke will later encounter the Barrett boys socially. R. Dingwall, *An Introduction to the Social History of Nursing* (London: Routledge, 1988), p. 17. Cf. literary London's snobbery about 'Cockney rhymester' John Keats.

'Medical skill' makes Cooke Dr Baron's 'illustrious coadjutor'. #138. Florence Nightingale to Sir Thomas Watson, Bart, London 19 January 1867, quoted in Robert Gaffney, 'Women as Doctors and Nurses' in Olive Checkland, Margaret Lamb, eds, *Health Care as Social History: The Glasgow Case* (Aberdeen: Elsevier Science, 1982), pp. 134–48, 139.

p. 43   Dr John Carden to Edward BMB 8 May 1821, SD379. Valerian is especially prescribed today for insomnia, anxiety and depression, period pain and other cramps and tremors, chronic fatigue syndrome and fits. An elm bark decoction is prescribed for scurvy in Hugh Smythson, *The Compleat Family Physician or Universal Medical Repository* (London: Harrison and Co., 1785), p. 321. An astringent bark draught for bloody urine in smallpox is prescribed in G. G. and J. Robinson, R. Baldwin, J. Walker and T. N.

London, *London Practice of Physic: The Sixth Edition* (London: Longman, 1797), pp. 93–94. https://www.wood-database.com/wood-articles/wood-allergies-and-toxicity/#npc [retrieved 4 September 2018].
'Opium... The mind... Only a relish...' SD389.1. 'Daily dispatches...' #130.

p. 44   https://www.nature.com/articles/sc200919 [retrieved 18 January 2019]. In letters to the *BMJ* editor, J. N. Milnes and J. G. Weir weigh in to Young's debate on the side of encephalomyelitis because of some of EBB's secondary symptoms, including sensory abnormalities and paroxysms. But both admit that this doesn't explain her illness *before* the measles: Weir, J. G., 'The illnesses of Elizabeth Barrett Browning', in *British Medical Journal* vol. 298 (18 March 1989); J. N. Milnes, 'The illnesses of Elizabeth Barrett Browning' in *British Medical Journal* vol. 298 (22 April 1989); D. A. B. Young, 'The illnesses of Elizabeth Barrett Browning' in *British Medical Journal* vol. 298 (18 February 1989) pp. 439–43, p. 441. Young discusses how the adult Ba's clothes and even hairstyle may disguise crooked shoulders or a humped back. But no contemporary mention of any such deformity survives. Anne Buchanan, Ellen Buchanan Weiss, 'Of Sad and Wished-For Years: Ba Barrett Browning's lifelong illness' in *Perspectives in Biology and Medicine* vol. 54, no. 4 (Autumn 2011), pp. 479–503. 'Honokiol and magnolol have been identified as modulators of the GABA(A) receptors in vitro (Squires et al. 1999, Ai et al., 2001)': Jiri Patocka, Jiri Jakl, and Anna Strunecka, 'Expectations of biologically active compounds of the genus *Magnolia* in biomedicine' in *Journal of Applied Biomedicine* vol. 4 (2006), pp. 171–78, p. 174. J. K. Crellin, Jane Philpott, A. L. Tommie Bass, *Herbal Medicine Past and Present: A Reference Guide to Medicinal Plants* (Durham and London: Duke University Press, 1990), pp. 75, 182, 352–53. EBB's triggers also match those for ME, rheumatoid arthritis and opportunistic infections.

p. 45   Today, clinicians sometimes diagnose remotely or collaboratively or by remote video examination.
'The suffering is agony...' SD389.1.

SECOND FRAME

Emmanuel Levinas, trans. Alphonso Lingis, *Totality and Infinity: An Essay on Exteriority* (Pittsburgh, Pennsylvania: Duquesne University Press, 1969), p. 297.

BOOK THREE

Epigraph   *AL* Bk 8, Ll. 830–32.

p. 48   Since 1576 sexual activity with 'any woman child under the age of ten years' has been viewed legally as more heinous. Stephen Robertson, 'Age of Consent Laws' in *Children and Youth in History* no. 230, http://chnm.gmu.edu/cyh/items/show/230 [retrieved 9 September 2018].

Septimus is born 11 February 1822. Birthday poems arrive from Mamma, Henrietta and Arabella. Henrietta MB to EBB 6 March 1822, #154.

p. 49   EBB, Diary 1831–32; 6 July 1831.

AL Bk 1, Ll. 578, 581–88, 594–95, 600.

p. 50   'Conversed, read, studied...' EBB, 'My Character and Bro's Compared'.

'George & Stormy...' Mary MB to EBB 5 July 1824, #195.

p. 51   Henrietta MB to Mary MB 1 May 1822, SD430.

'My dear Miss Bazy...' Edward MB to EBB 2 November 1822, #169. 'M is also cut off...' Edward MB to EBB 22 June 1823, #186. Emotional support: Edward MB to EBB 17 June 1822, #158. EMB to EBB 18 June 1822, #159. Treppy's postscript says Bro is 'melancholy', suffering from 'the disease of Silence' and missing EBB. Charterhouse is still near Smithfield Market, London. 'For the third time I have come home by myself without poor Sam, he stopped on account of having been reported irregular.' Edward MB to EBB 22 February 1823, #174. 'Those hundred lines...' Edward MB to EBB 10 November 1824, #204.

p. 52   Percy Bysshe Shelley, *Adonais*, st. VIII, Ll. 1–3.

p. 53   'Very much in love...' EBB, 'Untitled Essay'. '*Silver remember...*' Edward MB to EBB 26 March 1825, #217.

'Who should walk in but little Tommy Cooky, he had a dish of tea with us and said the reason he had come to town was that during his illness a gentleman had given him a carriage & he had come to see about it.' Edward MB to EBB 20 June 1822, #160.

'Stanzas on the Death of Lord Byron' in *The Globe and Traveller* no. 6733 (30 June 1824). The form requires unusually sustained work with rhyme: ABABBCBCC makes it hard to find rhymes and keep word choice lively. It also requires the ninth line of each stanza to break out of pentameter and make an alexandrine – that is, to have an extra metrical foot.

p. 54   Mary MB to EBB 5 July 1824, #195.

Cf. 'The Tempest', 'A Sea-Side Meditation', 'Life and Death', 'To a Poet's Child'.

Charles Knight is the newly fashionable publisher of *Knight's Quarterly*, 'If Knight delays giving you an answer soon I would beg Sam to remove your Poem into some other hand.' Edward B MB to EBB 16 August 1825, #220. *The Jewish Expositor*, produced by the London Society for Promoting Christianity Among the Jews, publishes one of Elizabeth's poems in January.

p. 55   In Greek mythology, the Pierian spring is the Macedonian fount of knowledge and playground of infant muses. EBB, *An Essay on Mind* Bk II, Ll. 908–11, 914–15 and Notes to Bk II (i). For more on Irving, see http://ebbarchive.org/poems/who_art_thou_of_the_veiled_countenance.php [retrieved 9 January 2019].

'Along the banks of the Danube...' EBB, 'Untitled Essay'.

p. 56   EBB to Edward B MB *c.*March 1821, #119.

p. 57   Coventry Patmore, 'The Dean's Consent' in *The Angel in the House*, 1854, Ll. 65–66.

McSwiney matriculated at St Patrick's Maynooth, and the likelihood is that his MA in Classics is from the college.

'Miss Sauce-box…' Edward MB and Daniel McSwiney to EBB 18 March 1821, #125. McSwiney teases EBB that 'instead of *eulogizing* my recent Heroism you […] assimilate it to the most ordinary rencontre among *ordinary men*'. EBB to Samuel MB 16 June 1814, #16; EBB to Samuel MB November 1818, #77; McSwiney 'does not quite detest a glass of wine' in EBB's unpublished poem 'Visions' dated 17 January 1819, *Reconstruction*, D1097.

p. 58   John Kenyon to EBB 12 July 1826, #237.

p. 59   William Gilpin, *An Essay on the Picturesque* (London: J. Robson, 1794). Gilpin first articulated the idea in 1768 in his at the time anonymous *Essay on Prints*. His identity was revealed in the third edition: William Gilpin, *An Essay on Prints* (London: R. Blamire, 1781). In the French tradition, 'The ground is like the canvas of the picture' according to C. H. Watelet in 1774 in *Essay on Gardens: A Chapter in the French Picturesque* (republished Philadelphia: University of Pennsylvannia Press, 2003). See also Réné Girardin, *An Essay on Landscape* (London, 1783).

Another friend of Price is fellow Herefordian exponent Richard Payne Knight of Downton Castle, in the north of the county.

William Wordsworth, 'Lines Composed a Few Miles above Tintern Abbey, On Revisiting the Banks of the Wye during a Tour, July 13, 1798', Ll. 15–19. *AL*, Bk 1, Ll. 594–600.

p. 60   Sir Uvedale Price to EBB 1 July 1826, #236.

EBB Diary, 7 June 1831.

p. 61   Papa's verdict: 'Untitled Essay' 4 February 1827: '"I advise you to burn the wretched thing." […] I have hardly ever been mortified as I was mortified last night—but perhaps this also will do me good.'

'I regret…' EBB to Hugh Stuart Boyd 2 March 1827, #253. Boyd was born 23 March 1781.

'The Conversation was down five degrees below *freezing*. Every body thinking what to say next—except Mrs Waddington who does not seem to think *at all*.' EBB to Henrietta MB *c.*November 1826, #240.

p. 62   'Mama was on the lawn…' Henrietta MB to EBB 24 February 1827, #250.

'As I have taken the liberty of calling you *Ba*, I shall not be more ceremonious in writing than in speaking', Price to EBB 17 November 1826, #241; '"Ba" is *much* better pleased to hear from you than "Miss Barrett" *could* be', EBB to Price *c.*December 1826, #242.

'As a female…' EBB to Boyd 3 November 1827, #275. EBB explains her mother was unwell: EBB to Boyd 15 March 1828, #288. 'I was the cause…' EBB to Elizabeth Moulton and Mary Trepsack 17 March 1828, #290.

p. 63   Boyd has published a number of translations of classical Greek and the

Church Fathers since his debut, *Luceria, A Tragedy*, in the year of EBB's birth. Elizabeth sometimes tests him on long passages of classical Greek verse he has memorised.

'Awhile they sailed...': Boyd writes two poems on this theme, 'A Day of Pleasure at Malvern' and 'A Malvern Tale'.

The *Gentleman's Magazine* reviewed Boyd's *Thoughts on an Illustrious Exile, Occasioned by the Persecution of the Protestants in 1815, with other Poems*: 'Mr Boyd is a Greek scholar; and energetic poet (as most blank-verse men are); and we are truly glad to see once more the unimprovable classical style, recently neglected for the rhymed prose which was brought into vogue by Lord Byron.' *Gentleman's Magazine and Historical Chronicle* vol. 96 (London: John Nichols & Son, February 1826), p. 156. EBB lends Boyd Price's *Essay on the Modern Pronunciation of Greek and Latin*, hot off the press, and passes back his praise to the author.

p. 64
Boyd married the eldest child of influential, polymathic and self-made engraver Wilson Lowry in 1805. Raised by a stepmother from the age of eight, she may not have had the happiest of lives.

'Rather young looking than otherwise...' EBB to Elizabeth Moulton and Mary Trepsack 17 March 1828, #290. 'Really all the young ladies...' EBB Diary, 22 June 1831. 'Miss Steers...' EBB Diary, 18 June 1831. Reading *Tom Jones*: EBB Diary, 24 June 1831. Henry Fielding, *The History of Tom Jones, a Foundling* (London: A. Millar, 1749).

p. 65
'Alfieri' of B— T— to EBB *c.*February 1829, #332. 'I suspect...' EBB Diary, 4 June 1831. 'Kissing the rod...' EBB Diary, 1 July 1831.

p. 66
Misses Bordman and Mushet: EBB Diary, 15 November 1831 and 29 December 1831. 'Put his hat...' EBB Diary, 19 July 1831. 'Attacked me... Ought to love him...' EBB Diary, 21 June 1831. 'Adam made fig leaves... Thoughts of my heart...' EBB Diary, 4 June 1831. 'On opening my drawer...' EBB Diary, 25 June 1831.

p. 67
The Athenaeum vol. 456 (23 July 1836). 'Nothing else... I feel *bitterly*...' EBB Diary, 29 June 1831.

A full account of the inheritance dispute appears in Robert A. Barrett, 'Note on Barrett v Barrett' in Michael Meredith, ed, *Browning Society Notes* vol. 22 (December 1994), pp. 61–68.

'Empty minded...' EBB Diary, 7 July 1831. On 23 April 1832, 'Mrs Boyd is certainly an extraordinary woman, to be Mrs Boyd'. 'I am quite aware that in your late removal I had no right or shadow of right, to be considered; & I sincerely hope that both you & Annie may gain from it as much happiness as you expect, – & as I have lost.' EBB to Boyd and Ann Lowry Boyd 17 May 1832, #451.

p. 68
'How very very very unkindly...' EBB Diary, 4 June 1831. 'Some talking...' EBB Diary, 14 June 1831.

Boyd had published *The Fathers not Papists, with Select Passages and Tributes to the Dead* just two years earlier. Elizabeth's report that, 'The bride looked very lovely, & behaved very well—I mean, without *demonstrating* in any unbecoming manner, the agitation which was within her evidently', implies a continued and shared low opinion of Annie. EBB to Boyd 2 August 1837, #578. Annie's unhappy, childless marriage may be a mere match of financial convenience for Henry William Hayes, who turns out a bankrupt (twice) and an adulterer. In 1855 Annie divorces him for adultery. He has a number of illegitimate children before dying intestate. Annie's revenge is to live till ninety. https://www.wikitree.com/wiki/Hayes-2303 [retrieved 3 March 2019].

'Driving to church...' EBB Diary, 5 June 1831.

Nonconformist adherents number some 56,000 in 1791, 360,000 in 1836, and 1,463,000 in 1851. Numbers of Congregationalists and Baptists also swelled. John Cannon and Robert Crowcroft, eds, *The Oxford Companion to British History* (Oxford: Oxford University Press, 2015), p. 1040.

'To make me *glow*...' EBB Diary, 5 June 1831.

p. 69   'Seven chapters...' EBB Diary, 16 June 1831. Elizabeth dislikes Anglicanism's '"*holy mysteries*" &c. What mystery is there, can there be, in this simple rite?' EBB Diary, 25 September 1831. But she records, 'Bummy expressed a general dislike towards the *Methodists*' EBB Diary, 8 June 1831. Bummy requests confidentiality: EBB Diary, 4 July 1831.

EBB tells Julia Martin of her mother's 'first agony of grief' and of her subsequent 'frequent bursts of tears'. EBB to Julia Martin 15 November 1827, #276.

p. 70   'Not quite so gay...' Mary MB to EBB 1 October 1828, #321. E B MB's raw grief: E B MB to his children 3 January 1831, #393. 'I dare say God...' EBB to Henrietta MB *c*.10 October 1828, #324. 'She read...' Edward MB to Julia Martin *c*.9 October 1828, SD674.

p. 71   EBB, 'Glimpses'.

BOOK FOUR

Epigraph   *AL* Bk 7, L. 411.

p. 74   EBB to Julia Martin 28 August 1832, #462.

p. 75   Papa 'shrinks' and even afterwards, 'never up to this moment, has he even alluded to the subject [...] he had not power to say *one word*'. #462.

'The drawing room's four windows...' #462.

Cricket in Jamaica: https://en.wikipedia.org/wiki/History_of_cricket_in_the_West_Indies_to_1918

Henrietta's sketch is collected in *The Brownings' Correspondence*, vol. 3, facing p. 256.

Sunset was at 19.18 in Hereford on 23 August 1832. The moon in its last quarter: https://www.timeanddate.com/calendar/?year=1832&country=9 [retrieved 3 Feb 2019].

p. 76   'A broken down man...' Mary Russell Mitford to Lady Dacre 3 July 1836, SD804.

'I cannot dwell...' #462. Julia Martin's father was Revd John Vignoles of Portarlington, County Laois. James was third son of the Martins banking family of Overbury Court, a little over twenty miles away. They married on 20 Sept 1819. https://www.stirnet.com/genie/data/british/mm4ae/martin07.php [retrieved 3 Feb 2019].

p. 77 EBB guessed on the previous Monday, 14 May 1832, that the Boyds would move 'the next day or the one after'. So they left on Tuesday 15 May. EBB to Boyd, 17 May 1832 #451. The diary breaks off before this farewell; wilder entries after 1 January 1832 were posthumously excised by her brother George, who had possession of the second volume.

'I never could apprehend...' EBB to Boyd 26 May 1832, #452.

'Looking back...' is quoted in EBB to Boyd 17 May 1832, #451.

Correspondence with the Revd Commeline lapses: 'The conjunction of so much talent & so much indolence always appears to me a minor miracle.' EBB to Lady Margaret Cocks 15 November 1833, #483. EBB to Boyd 27 January 1832, #439.

p. 78 EBB to Julia Martin 14 December 1832, #470. 'They are incredulous here in my *really thinking* that you will not come to Sidmouth. But I *do* think so.' EBB to Boyd 2 November 1832, #468; EBB to Boyd 22 November 1832, #469. EBB to Lady Margaret Cocks 15 May 1833, #478.

John Ruskin, *Modern Painters* (London: Smith, Elder & Co., 1856) vol. 3, Part 4.

'A footstep...' *AL* Bk. 6, Ll. 391–92.

'I have been riding a donkey two or three times, & enjoy very much going to the edge of the sea', EBB to Julia Martin 28 August 1832, #462. EBB to Julia Martin 27 May 1833, #479.

'We are all squeezed...' Arabella MB to Ann Henrietta Boyd, 22 November 1832, #SD756. 'We have had one chimney pulled down to prevent it from tumbling down; and have received especial injunctions from the bricklayers, not to lean too much out of the windows, for fear the walls should follow the destiny of the chimney.' EBB to Julia Martin 7 September 1833, #481.

p. 79 'No ties...' EBB to Lady Margaret Cocks 14 September 1834, #488.

'A pretty villa...' EBB to Lady Margaret Cocks 15 November 1833, #483. Since extended, the house, now 'Cedar Shade', became first a hotel and then an old people's home.

'*On dit*...' EBB to Julia Martin, 28 August 1832, #462. In fairness, Papa also sends Henrietta, escorted by Bro, to Torquay, where she is 'far gayer than I should like to be, tho' not I believe gayer than *she* liked to be', #478.

'Very full...' #488.

Sixteen-year-old Henry has joined his father and, 'Henrietta & Arabella & I are the only guardians just now of the three youngest boys the only ones at home', EBB to Julia Martin 19 December 1834 #493. The brothers in Glasgow studied under an 'Independent minister', Dr Wardlaw, of whom Edward Barrett approved. 'Georgie [...] was examined in Logic, Moral philosophy, Greek & Latin [...] his answers were more pertinent than those of any other of the examined, & elicited much applause. [...] Stormie shrank from the public examination, on account of the hesitation in his speech. He would not go up,—altho', according to report, as well qualified as Georgie. Mr Groube says that the ladies of Glasgow are preparing to break their hearts for Georgie's departure.' EBB to Boyd 21 April 1835, #504. https://www.universitystory.gla.ac.uk/ biography/?id=WH8409&type=P and https://www.universitystory.gla. ac.uk/browse-graduates/?start=280&max=20&o=&l=b [retrieved 9 Oct 2019]

p. 80   'Papa took him...' #483.

'A party led by Mr. Barrett would have prohibited the use of the cattle whip in the field, and the flogging of women under any circumstances, but they were overruled. Even a modified amendment, to substitute the military cat for the atrocious cattle whip, and to prevent unnecessary exposure when women were whipped, was rejected by twenty-four against seventeen.' William James Gardner, *A History of Jamaica* (London: Elliot Stock, 1873), p. 263. Responding to Uncle Sam, Howick agreed that the hardliner plantocracy were, 'Only putting arms into the hands of the extreme Anti-Slavery party, & making it more difficult to prevent the adoption of some violent course.' Lord Howick to Samuel Barrett Moulton-Barrett 7 October 1831, SD745. Uncle Sam was MP for Richmond, Yorkshire 1820–28.

The Assembly's estimate: March 1832 report quoted in Mary Turner, *Slaves and Missionaries: The Disintegration of Jamaican Slave Society, 1787–1834* (Champaign, Illinois: University of Illinois Press, 1982), p. 121.

p. 81   'All her negroes...' Joseph Shore in John Stewart, ed, *In Old St James (Jamaica)* (Kingston, Jamaica: Aston W. Gardner & Co., 1911), p. 98. Uncle Sam would remarry within two years, to Anne Elizabeth Gordon, daughter of plantation owners.

Papa agreed arrangements that Knibb proposed. Marks, *The Family of the Barrett*, p. 411.

In January 1831 the Colonial Church Union was founded, allegedly to support the established church, and in practice to try to force the closure of Nonconformist chapels by any means, including false imprisonment and arson.

Sharpe was hanged on 23 May 1832. He was buried in the sands of Montego Bay Harbour and later reinterred beneath the pulpit of Burchell Baptist Church.

Uncle Sam decreed Saturdays should be taken off: 'Even during crop time.' Marks, *The Family of the Barrett*, p. 410.

'*Highly disapprove...*' Mr McDonald, Custos of Trelawny, to the Governor of Jamaica, quoted in R. A. Barrett, *The Barretts of Jamaica*, p. 85.

p. 82   Sending in troops: R. A. Barrett, *The Barretts of Jamaica*, p. 86. Marks, *The Family of the Barrett*, pp. 406–407. The timing of Bro's arrival in Jamaica: by 1833 the Atlantic crossing takes twenty-two days; Bro left Gravesend on 13 November 1833. 'An exile…' #488. 'The West Indians…' #479.
The scandal of the Baptist War is uncovered by two governmental inquiries within two years. Henry Belby, *Death Struggles of Slavery: Being a Narrative of Facts and Incidents, Which Occurred in a British Colony, During the Two Years Immediately preceding Negro Emancipation* (London: Hamilton & Adams and Co., 1853), Chapter IV 'Blood', pp. 25–36.
The Society for the Mitigation and Gradual Abolition of Slavery Throughout the British Dominions, founded by William Wilberforce, Thomas Clarkson et al., was succeeded in 1839 by the *British and Foreign Anti-Slavery Society*, which campaigned for worldwide abolition. The book triggered competing defamation suits. Mary Prince, *The History of Mary Prince, a West Indian Slave, Related by Herself. With a Supplement by the Editor* (London and Edinburgh: F. Westley and A. H. Davis, and Waugh & Innes, 1831), pp. 22–23.

p. 83   The Office of Commissioners of Compensation announced compensation conditions with a set of General Rules governing ownership of slaves on 31 March 1834, and the compensation pot in the *London Gazette* on 18 April 1834. Marks, *The Family of the Barrett*, p. 444.
'Of course you know…' #481.

p. 84   'Veneering…' EBB to Mitford 5 April 1845, #1880.
For a full account of 'Handsome Sam''s case, see Robert A. Barrett, 'Note on Barrett v Barrett' in *Browning Society Notes*, vol. 22 (December 1994), pp. 61–68.
'A cousin came…' Mitford to Lady Dacre 3 July 1836, SD804. 'Papa has been away from us in London, six weeks this summer. I was glad of it, as it seemed to bring him a pleasant variety to what I fear he sometimes feels as monotony.' #488.

p. 85   'Without him…' EBB to Julia Martin 19 December 1834, #493.
Treppy uses the term 'black': for example, a letter from her and Elizabeth's brother Sam to Henrietta MB 20 July 1828, SD667.
'She has nursed…' EBB to RB 2 June 1846 (2), #2395. *UCL Legacies of British Slave-ownership* https://www.ucl.ac.uk/lbs/person/view/23359 [retrieved 27 September 2019].

p. 86   For nuanced discussion of EBB's Congregationalism see Karen Dieleman, *Religious Imaginaries: The Liturgical and Poetic Practices of Elizabeth Barrett Browning* (Athens, Ohio: Ohio University Press, 2012), pp. 25–29.
'Madness!…' EBB to Miss Mitford 12 November 1842, #1047. Soliciting letters: EBB to Lady Margaret Cocks 14 September 1834, #488; EBB to Julia Martin 19 December 1834, #493.
Friendship with Hunter: this time it may even be Elizabeth who holds the upper hand. As her relationship with RB is beginning, EBB will write:

'Half the acidities arise from the cream of his affection for me turning sour in a thunderstorm of jealousy, ... not of *me* ... but of others in relation to me! [...] Poor Mr Hunter is irritable, as persons of great sensibility under adverse circumstances, are apt to be.' EBB to Mitford 5 April 1845, #1880.

p. 87 'My poem on the cholera. I think I like it, & shall send it to the Times tomorrow.' Papa calls it 'beautiful, most beautiful'. EBB Diary, 9 January and 22 January 1832.

Boyd, in usual passive-aggressive style, first pours cold water on the idea of publishing *Prometheus Unbound*, then two days later denies doing so. EBB Diary, 2–18 February 1832. Review in *The Athenaeum Journal of Literature, Science and the Fine Arts* (London: J. Francis, 1833) p. 362. The accompanying poems are pretty much ignored. Elizabeth retains them as 'Juvenilia' in collected editions of her *Poetical Works*, but comes to see 'Prometheus' as, in the words of a future editor, 'an offence against Aeschylus', eventually retranslating. 'The second translation was deliberately intended to efface the first.' Frederic G. Kenyon, 'Editor's Preface, 1887', in *The Poetical Works of Elizabeth Barrett Browning* (London: John Murray, 1914), p. vi.

Boyd leaves Sidmouth in May 1834, almost exactly a year after *Prometheus Unbound* had appeared.

'A nest...' EBB to Miss Commeline 14 September 1834, #489.

Three more poems appear in *The New Monthly* and three in *The Athenaeum*. Reprinted, some with modified titles, in *The Seraphim*.

p. 88 Poetic homage is itself a feminine tradition: Hemans wrote 'The Grave of a Poetess' after the death of Mary Tighe (1772–1810).

'I shall not be pained in leaving Sidmouth, as some time ago, I should have been. [...] And after all, I would rather go to London, than to an hundred places I could mention.' EBB to Lady Margaret Cocks c.4 November 1835, #513.

Dating Bro's return: in #513, his return is 'lately'. EBB to Boyd c.October 1825, #511, which records his arrival, is the second letter after Annie Boyd's July 1835 visit to Sidmouth and also the second to mention a possible move to London.

p. 89 'Capacities for living... The sea shore...' EBB to Lady Margaret Cocks 9 December 1835, #516. 'Mummy...' EBB to Julia Martin, 1 January 1836, #519. Chimney: EBB to Julia Martin 7 December 1836, #546. Doves: EBB to Mitford 10 August 1836, #534. We learn that they're from Jamaica in EBB to Mitford 8 November 1837, #596.

p. 90 Coughs: EBB to Boyd 7 January 1836, #520; EBB to Boyd 15 March 1836, #524.

Kenyon: 'References to him occur in Southey's Life, Ticknor's Life, Letters, and Journals, L'Estrange's Life of Mary Russell Mitford, Horne's Letters of Elizabeth Barrett Browning, Ingram's Life of Elizabeth Barrett Browning, Crabb Robinson's Diary, Clayden's Rogers and his

Contemporaries, Macready's Reminiscences, Field's Old Acquaintance ...'
James McMullen Rigg, 'John Kenyon' in *Dictionary of National Biography
1885–1900*, vol. 31 https://en.wikisource.org/wiki/Kenyon,_John_(DNB00)
[retrieved 5 March 2019]. Later, he also helped Coleridge's family
financially.
Robinson: Charles R. Mack, Ilona Schulze Mack, eds, *Like a Sponge
Thrown Into Water: Francis Lieber's European Travel Journal of 1844–1845: a
Lively Tour Through England, France, Belgium, Holland, Germany, Austria,
and Bohemia: with Observations on Politics, the Visual and Performing
Arts, Economics, Religion, Penology, Technology, History, Literature, Social
Customs, Travel, Geography, Jurisprudence, Linguistics, Personalities, and
Numerous Other Matters* (Columbia, South Carolina: University of South
Carolina Press, 2002), p. 121. Barred from Oxbridge as a Nonconformist,
Robinson helped found the University of London. Thomas Sadler, ed,
Diary, Reminiscences, and Correspondence of Henry Crabb Robinson (London
and New York: Macmillan & Co., 3rd Edition with Corrections and
Additions, 1872), vol. 2, chapter XXXII, '3 May 1828', p. 54.

p. 91   'Lions...' Sadler, ed, *Diary, Reminiscences*, vol. 3, p. 451, fn.
Talfourd is at Middle and George at Inner Temple. Talfourd has just
been created a serjeant, a member of a juridical order dating back to the
fourteenth century, and elected the MP for Reading: like George, he's a
barrister. Indeed, the two men will become friends.

p. 91   Talfourd's first night, on 26 May 1836: Sadler, ed, *Diary, Reminiscences*, vol.
2, Chapter XXXIX, p. 176. The same group dined at 56 Russell Square the
night before: 'Mr. Wordsworth, Mr. Landor, and Mr. White dined here.
I like Mr. Wordsworth of all things; he is a most venerable-looking old
man, delightfully mild and placid, and most kind to me. Mr. Landor is a
very striking-looking person, and exceedingly clever. Also we had a Mr.
Browning, a young poet (author of "Paracelsus"), and Mr. Proctor, and
Mr. Chorley, and quantities more of poets.' Mitford to George Mitford 26
May 1836, SD798. *Paracelsus*, the first work published by Browning under
his own name, was published by Effingham Wilson on 15 August 1835,
paid for by RB's father.
'Dare I...' EBB to Thomas Noon Talfourd 21 January 1836, #523. 'I wrote as
if writing for my private conscience, & privately repented writing in a day';
EBB to RB 7 December 1845, #2131.

p. 92   'A Tragedy...' RB to William Charles Macready 28 May 1836, #526. But
they fall out over revisions.
'Wd wish for more harmony...' EBB to Mitford 10 August 1836, #534.
The Athenaeum vol. 454 (1836), p. 491.

p. 93   'You might think me...' EBB to Julia Martin 7 December 1836, #546.
Mary Russell Mitford, *Our Village* (London: Whittaker & Co.),
vol. 1 1824, vol. 2 1826, vol. 3 1828, vol. 4 1830, vol. 5 1832, followed by a
new edition in three volumes (London: Whittaker & Co., 1835), with

engravings by Baxter. *Belford Regis* (1835) was also based on life in Three Mile Cross. In 1851 she moved to nearby Swallowfield.

Mitford's portrait: 1853 oil by John Lucas after Benjamin Robert Haydon 1824, National Portrait Gallery 404; 1852 chalk drawing by John Lucas, NPG 4045.

p. 94   Mitford repackages work to maximise sales, edits annuals, and writes for non-literary magazines.

'Sweet young woman...' Mitford to George Mitford 27 May 1836, SD799. 'The most difficult of the Greek plays...' Mitford to George Mitford 28 & 29 May 1836, SD801.

When it's published, *The Literary Gazette* singles out Elizabeth's 'A Romance of the Ganges' from the *Tableaux* for praise.

p. 95   'All that is painful in her shyness...' Mitford to Lady Dacre 3 July 1836, SD804. 'Small neighbourhood...' quoted from 'Introduction', by Anne Thackeray Ritchie, to Mary Russell Mitford's *Our Village* (London: Macmillan, 1893), p. 1.

Lady Dacre's circle: Harriet Kramer Linkin, 'Mary Tighe and the Coterie of Women Poets in *Psyche*' in Jacqueline M. Labbe, ed, *The History of British Women's Writing, 1750–1830*, vol. 5 (London: Palgrave, 2010), pp. 303–304. Cambridge University database bizarrely states that Lady Dacre (1768–1854) 'wrote as an amateur in the Romantic period': as if a respectable woman could then write in any other way. http://orlando.cambridge.org/public/svPeople?formname=r&person_id=dacrba&heading=c [retrieved 7 March 2019]. This network also has connections with literary men including Mary Tighe's cousin George, by now a friend of the Shelleys and living in Italy with Mary Wollstonecraft's mentee Lady Mountcashell.

'Depend upon it...' Mitford to William Harness July 1836, SD803. 'Of course the poverty...' Mitford to Lady Dacre 3 July 1836, SD804.

p. 96   'If events lead her...' SD804.

FOURTH FRAME

p. 98   Luce Irigaray, *Speculum of the Other Woman*, trans. Gillian G. Gill (Ithaca, New York: Cornell University Press, 1985), p. 125.

BOOK FIVE

Epigraph   *AL* Bk 8, L. 44.

p. 99   Coughs: EBB to Mitford, a Tuesday in January 1838, #606; EBB to Boyd mid-January 1838, #609; EBB to Lady Margaret Cocks, *c.*29 Jan 1838, #611.

p. 100   'Chimneys...' EBB to Lady Margaret Cocks, 29 September 1837, #590. An egg on 22 July 1837, the chick hatches on 16 August 1837. EBB to Mitford 22 July 1837, #577; EBB to Julia Martin 16 August 1837, #583. #606. Critique: EBB to Kenyon *c.*February 1838, #614. Civil List: in 1835, EBB's cousin Arabella Butler married Ralph Gosset, son of recently knighted Sir William, a former MP. 'My dear Love...' Mitford to EBB 1 February 1838, #612.

p. 101   'I have already *had* two proof sheets...' EBB to Boyd 26 March 1838, #620. 'Valpy is giving up...' EBB to Boyd 27 February 1838, #615. 'No more mss...' EBB to Kenyon, Wednesday c.March 1838, #616. 'Late remorse...' EBB to Mitford, a Monday in early April 1838, #621. 'Rather a dramatic lyric...' EBB to Mitford, a Monday in March 1838, #617. She's particularly proud that she managed to reconstruct the whole first part after it was lost by the publisher Colburn. 'Then, would come...' #616. 'Incapable...' EBB to Lady Margaret Cocks c.13 March 1838, #619. 'Grand angelic sin...' #616.

p. 102   Henrietta informs Sam about the move: Henrietta Moulton-Barrett to Sam Moulton-Barrett 14 & 15 November 1837, SD835. 'How the waves...' #619. 'My strength flags...' #617.

'Had no idea...' The Atlantic barrier, so useful in concealing the disgusting reality of the Jamaican planter ship, also prevents genuine personal contact: an exchange of letters takes roughly two months. A month before his brother's death, Edward's letters to him are full of trivia about shipping him gifts: Edward B MB to Samuel B MB 15 November 1837, SD836; Edward B MB to Samuel B MB c.20 November 1837, SD837.

The legal conveyance of Uncle Sam's gift to EBB was completed posthumously. Edward B MB to Samuel B MB 24 October 1837, SD832. Boddingtons wrote to Uncle Sam a week after his death, asking for his signature on the Bill of Sale: Boddington & Co. to Samuel B MB 30 December 1837, SD844.

'Uncle brother friend & nurse...' #619. 'Kindness melted...' Henrietta MB to Samuel MB 14–15 November 1837, SD835.

Value calculated according to the Office for National Statistics composite price index. http://www.in2013dollars.com/uk/inflation/1838?amount=200; http://www.nationalarchives.gov.uk/currency-converter/#currency-result [retrieved 11 March 2019].

Sam is coming home 'for a few months' only; #619.

p. 103   Sam tells his favourite sister his itinerary: Samuel MB to Henrietta MB 21 November 1838, SD956. 'On account of the gloominess...' EBB to Julia Martin 7 December 1836, #546. 'Disappointed... reconciled...' SD956. 'Ghost of paint...' EBB to Mitford 23–24 April 1838, #627. 'Little slip of sitting room...' EBB to Mitford 1 June 1838, #636. They stay at number 129 with Ann Smith, daughter of Dr Adam Clarke and a friend of Mr Boyd's.

p. 104   'We are dying...' is admittedly the letter in which Papa announces Bro's probable drowning. Edward B MB to George Goodin MB 13 July 1840, SD1129.

p. 105   'Do *you* conjecture...' EBB to RB 11 August 1845, #1996.

p. 106   'I have not been asleep...' EBB to Kenyon c.January 1838, #607. 'Flannel waistcoats…' EBB to Arabella MB and Mary Hunter 27 September 1838, #666. 'Used to—frighten me…' EBB to Mitford 8 June 1836, #528.

p. 107   'Consensus…' *The Athenaeum* 7 July 1838 pp. 466–68. The other reviews appear in: *The Atlas* (23 June 1838), p. 395; *The Examiner* (24 June 1838), pp. 387–88; *Blackwood's* (August 1838), pp. 279–84; *The Metropolitan Magazine* (August 1838), pp. 97–101; *The Monthly Chronicle* (August 1838), p.195; *The Monthly Review* (September 1838), pp. 125–30; *The Sunbeam* (1 September 1838), pp. 243 & 245, (8 September), pp. 254–55, (23 September), pp. 269–70, (6 October) p. 287, (13 October), pp. 293–95; *The Literary Gazette* (1 December 1838), pp. 759–60; and *The Quarterly Review* (September 1840), pp. 382–89. *The Metropolitan Magazine* and *The Examiner* concede that *The Divine Comedy* and *Paradise Lost* also pose the problem of religious poetry.

p. 108   'Elizabeth's own faith…' The Revd Hunter and his daughter Mary remain in the family's life.
'Forcing houses…' Both Byron and Shelley first published books of poetry at seventeen: respectively, *Fugitive Pieces* (1805) and *Original Poetry; By Victor and Cazire* (1810); unlike Elizabeth, they followed these up promptly.

p. 109   'Indeed it does seem…' EBB to Mitford 8 June 1836, #528. 'Let me apply my theory about "spoiling children" to your practice of spoiling *me*—& go on to maintain that nobody is injured by too much love!' EBB to Mitford 30 October 1838, #669.
'In seeing Lady Dacre…' EBB to Mitford 3 July 1838, #651. 'The most eloquent woman I ever heard speak, certainly—and the vainest in speaking of herself': EBB to Mitford 27 September 1839, #713.
'*Brother in law…*' SD835.

p. 110   'I have been…' EBB to Mitford 1 June 1838, #636. '& my weakness…' EBB to Boyd 21 June 1838, #645.
According to Forster, *Elizabeth Barrett Browning*, note 1 to chapter 6, pp. 378–79, 'At a meeting of the Browning Society in 1985, two eminent doctors' agreed on Dr Chambers's proficiency, and that therefore EBB doesn't suffer from TB at this point.
'A helpless being…' EBB to Lady Margaret Cocks 4 August 1838, #658. With 'only a too great fullness of the blood vessels upon them': EBB to Mitford 10 August 1838, #660.

p. 111   '*Sisterless…*' Henrietta MB to Sam MB 15 September 1838, SD943: 'I was in a most terrible state of inquietude & anxiety, about the probability that existed of not obtaining permission to accompany our dearest Ba to these genial shores, but Papa very kindly gave it to me at *last*.'
The Hedleys' elegant Regency hilltop house is 'The Braddens'. This move is 'The difference between the coldest situation in Torquay & the warmest'. EBB to Mitford 10 October 1838, #668.
Bummy arrives from Frocester: SD943.

Crow's mother will be living in Caistor when Crow returns to her for the birth of her first child.

'And indeed…' EBB to Mitford 14 August 1838, #662.

p. 112   'She is an excellent…' EBB to Mitford 9 August 1841, #841. 'A young man…' EBB to Mitford ?25 October 1839, #715, makes clear this sequence of events. 'Haunted… London habit…' EBB to Mitford 25 September 1838, #664. 'On the occasion… These partings…' EBB to Arabella MB and Mary Hunter, 27 September 1838, #666.

p. 113   'I had a doctor…' EBB to RB 11 August 1845, #1996. 'Encouraged… the blister &c…' #666. Inhalations like Tincture of Benzoin have been around since the 1760s.

'Dear Bro's individual opinion was that he would do better in returning to London': #666. Her brothers will 'quench the energies of their lives in hunting & fishing' if the family retreats to a Welsh estate where they cannot practise their professions. EBB to George Goodin MB 15 April 1841, #805.

'The lovely bay…' #668.

p. 114   'After only one hour…' Samuel Goodin Barrett to R. W. Appleton 23 May 1839, SD1005.

'Able and most kind…' EBB to Mitford ?14 September 1839, #710. 'He has taken a great interest in her which is also very much in his favor—as he has not received as yet a farthing for his attendance, she wrote to him the other day requesting he would let her know "the *pecuniary* part of her obligations to him" he sent in his account £125—a moderate charge I think for so long a time': Henrietta MB to Samuel MB 14 September 1839, SD1042. #715.

'Comes to see her…' Henrietta MB to Samuel MB 14 December 1839, SD1090. 'Not any thinner…' SD1090.

Sam and Stormie were sent to Jamaica together on the 26 June 1839. After Sam's death, Stormie returned in December 1840: Henrietta MB to Samuel MB 14–15 July 1839, SD1018.

p. 115   Sleeping around: Forster, *Elizabeth Barrett Browning*, p. 97, no ref given. 'Never taken the sacrament…' Hope Waddell to Edward B MB 20 February 1840, SD1116. 'It was a heavy blow…' EBB to Richard Hengist Horne 15 May 1840, #756. Papa hurries to Torquay: 'When I saw her she appeared crushed by the intelligence; she has never wept, nor has ever alluded to the distressing subject': Edward B MB to Septimus MB 4 May 1840, SD1121. 'It is a monstrous time…' Edward B MB to Septimus MB 24 June 1840, SD1127.

p. 116   'Occupation…' EBB to George Goodin MB 17 June 1840, #766. Gatecrashing: Edward B MB to EBB 9 March 1840, #741; EBB to Mitford 28 March 1840, #748.

The family are enthusiastically pro-monarchy. EBB publishes verses on the royal marriage in *The Athenaeum*; Miss Mitford conspires to get them to the Queen via a lady-in-waiting.

Bro's romance: Henrietta MB to Samuel MB 14–15 July 1839, SD1018; #766; EBB to RB 12 December 1845, #2136.

p. 117   Edward B MB to George Goodin MB 13 July 1840, SD1129.

p. 118   'It is a wonder…' Edward B MB to Septimus MB 1 August 1840, SD1131. 'These walls…' EBB to Mitford early October 1840, #772.   'If I dont return soon, my affairs will be so enta[n]gled that I shall never be able to unravel them'; Edward B MB to Septimus MB 26 August 1840, SD1132. 'She cannot hear…' SD1131. 'Months roll…' EBB to Mitford, a Monday in November 1840, #773; #772. 'Tea & cake…' EBB to George Goodin MB 20 July 1841, #830.

p. 119   'One heart… Say nothing…' EBB to George Goodin MB 15 April 1841, #805. Matilda Carter is painting her miniature. It won't turn out well, to EBB's amusement; EBB to Mitford 14 June 1841, #819. 'Prison…' EBB to Mitford 18 July 1841, #829.

p. 120   'What claim had I…' #829. '*For sporting* purposes…' EBB to Mitford 28 December 1840, #783. 'Send him by the railroad…' EBB to Mitford mid-December 1840, #779. No station: https://www.railscot.co.uk/London_ and_South_Western_Railway/ [retrieved 22 March 2019].

p. 121   'A shawl thrown…' EBB to Mitford 9 February 1841, #797. He is due Thursday (7 January, if letter #787 is dated correctly, but this dating is itself taken from reference to his arrival). EBB to Mitford 16 April 1841, #806; EBB to Mitford 5 August 1841, #840; EBB to Mitford late July 1841, #835; EBB to Mitford 15 July 1841, #827; #840.

p. 122   'An occasional *manner*…' EBB to Mitford 17 July 1841, #828. 'There are fine things…' #827.

That John Kenyon is house-hunting in Torquay she finds incomprehensible. He will eventually buy after she's left town, according to the *Dictionary of National Biography*, https://en.wikisource.org/wiki/ Kenyon,_John_(DNB00) [retrieved 21 May 2020]. EBB to Mitford 12 November 1841, #872.

'Delay…' #830. 'Patent…' EBB to Mitford 25 August 1841, #845. 'Loosening the chains…' EBB to Kenyon 10 November 1841, #871.

'The opening of the dungeon…' EBB to Fanny Dowglass 31 March 1842, #935: 'Ten days we spent upon the road. I suffered in the manner that was apprehended by renewed & increased spitting of blood, but not to the extent—& altho' exhausted day after day to fainting & speechlessness I came into London perfectly alive & inclined to remain so.'

EBB also reports this spitting of blood to Miss Mitford: EBB to Mitford 13 September 1841, #851.

p. 123   'And what was worse…' EBB to Mitford 21 September 1841, #853. 'He likes London…' EBB to Mitford 23 September 1841, #854. Literary gossip: EBB to Mitford 24 September 1841, #855.

BOOK SIX

Epigraph Spoken by the wicked Lady Waldemar in *AL* Bk 9, Ll. 65–66.

p. 126 Miss Mitford handles everything from domestic finance to runaway horses.

p. 127 EBB blames reading Wollstonecraft at twelve for her 'awkwardness…': EBB to Mitford 22 July 1842, #988. 'Domestic love…' EBB to RB 20 March 1845, #1870. 'How uncivilized…' EBB to Mitford 19 October 1841, #863.

p. 128 EBB to Boyd 12 January 1842, #898. The poems are 'The House of Clouds' in August and 'Lessons from the Gorse' in October. The essays are posthumously published together as a freestanding volume in 1863. 'It is well…' *The Athenaeum*, 4 June 1842. 'Do not live by…' *The Athenaeum*, 27 August 1842.

p. 129 'The long life's work…' *The Athenaeum*, 27 August 1842. 'No—…' EBB to Mitford 30 December 1842, #1105.

p. 130 The right places: *The Athenaeum*, *Blackwood's*, *Schloss's Bijou Almanac*. Kenyon 'was a good deal surprised, he said, that Moxon shd have answered so decidedly.' EBB to Mitford 2 January 1843, #1110. Wordsworth composed his poetic tribute to Haydon while climbing Helvellyn at seventy, a decade after promising to write something for the 1829 piece portraying Napoleon Bonaparte to which his portrait is a companion. 'If I can command my thoughts I will write something about your Picture, in prose for the Muse has forsaken me.' William Wordsworth to Haydon 23 April 1831: https://www.npg.org.uk/collections/ search/portraitExtended/mw04614/Napolon-Bonaparte? https://www. npg.org.uk/collections/search/portrait/mw06661 'You have brought me…' EBB to B. R. Haydon 17 October 1842, #1026. 'Invisible Friend…' Benjamin Robert Haydon to EBB 9 January 1843, #1121. The American reprints of EBB's Haydon sonnet appear on 26 November and 3 December 1842.

p. 131 EBB commends and quotes from Mathews's *Poems on Man* in the epigraph to 'A Rhapsody of Life's Progress' in *Poems (1850)*. EBB to James Russell Lowell, 4 January 1843, #1112. Mathews publishes, and would like to be published by, Edward Moxon: 'I mentioned, I think, in a former hasty note that […] you might, perhaps, be waited on with regard to a little volume of Poems ("Poems on Man") with some proposition as to its re-production in London. […] I beg also to offer a copy for the acceptance of Mr. Browning, in token of the pleasure I have derived from his writings which you were good enough to send me.' Cornelius Mathews to Edward Moxon 27 February 1844, SD1201.1. 'Dark…' EBB to Mitford 16 January 1844, #1505. 'Bitter anguish…' EBB to Mitford 9 November 1841, #870.

p. 132 Harriet Martineau, *Life in the Sickroom: Essays by an Invalid* (London: Edward Moxon, 1844).

'How entirely…' Martineau to EBB 6 March 1844, #1564. 'I dare…' EBB to Mitford 8 November 1841, #869. 'Fairy visions…' #1564.

p. 133   'Torquay dancing…' EBB to Mitford 12 November 1841, #872. 'Mr Haydon's mystical…' #869. 'I have recognized…' EBB to Mitford 25 November 1841, #874. 'Did you hear of…' EBB to Mitford 18 November 1841, #873.

p. 134   Contemporaries found that the lack of moral template, and use of archaisms, made Samuel Taylor Coleridge's 'The Rime of the Ancient Mariner' a difficult read. The Barretts are typical in being excited by the 1837 accession of eighteen-year-old Victoria and subsequent palace affairs, from the Lady Flora Hastings scandal to the Queen's marriage to Prince Albert and the births of her nine children.

p. 135   'I want to write…' EBB to Mitford 30 December 1844, #1797.
Education: Anglican National Schools have appeared since 1811, their Nonconformist equivalents in the Lancasterian System since 1808. By 1831, 1.25 million children attend Sunday school. In 1833 the government voted annual sums for state education; in 1840 the Grammar Schools Act expanded the state secondary curriculum to include literature and science. Richard Hoggart, *The Uses of Literacy: Aspects of Working Class Life* (London, Chatto & Windus: 1957). 'On April 11th, in 1844, Mr Locke, a wollen-draper; Mr. Moulton, a dealer in second-hand tools; Mr. Morrison, a City Missionary, and Mr Starey formed the beginnings of the Ragged Schools Union.' https://www.raggeduniversity.co.uk/2012/08/08/history-ragged-schools-2/ [retrieved 15 March 2020].
Like EBB, Dickens is developing a reputation in North America, where he has already been given his first lecture tour. In 1844 he lives in Europe, working on the great novels of his middle period, but is about to take on the editorship of the London *Daily News*.

p. 136   'The Lay of the Brown Rosary' Pt Three, Ll. 181–85.

p. 137   William Bishop in *The Brownings' Correspondence*, note 2 of #1380. EBB to Mitford 16 September 1843, #1380; EBB to Mitford 15 September 1843, #1379. 'Five pounds down…' EBB to Mitford 20 September 1843, #1383.

p. 138   'My dear Papa was delighted to come home & find Flush, & has not put me on an inquest for the means': #1380. The second time, Flush is stolen from the doorstep as Arabella returns from walking him, and is recovered by Alfred. 'Quite above…' EBB to Mitford 29 March 1844, #1585.

p. 139   'Shedding abundant tears when the time came for leaving me. She said, it was as great a deprivation to her as it cd be to me,—[…]. I earnestly hope she may be happy, poor thing,—and, so far, the business seems flourishing, & he is very attentive & apparently fond of her. She goes to her mother's to be confined,—& *then*, will come the full loss to *me*!' EBB to Mitford 7 May 1844, #1607. This has been unfairly scrutinised for selfishness. EBB is being both honest and emotionally intelligent. Crow's life as a baker's wife *will* be less comfortable and secure than service in Wimpole Street;

and dependent on her husband's personality. If he's violent or drinks, for example, she'll have no escape. And once her baby is born, she will indeed have to surrender care for Elizabeth. Acknowledging this doesn't mean that Elizabeth is putting herself *ahead* of the coming baby, or suggesting it should be otherwise. And, 'She was with me when I was very ill & weak—& something of the gentle authority of nurse to patient, remained in her manner & ways.' #1607. However, 'Of the want of chastity...' EBB to Mitford 3 February 1844, #1517. Contested will: EBB to Mitford 1 February 1844, #1516. 'Gentle-voiced...' #1585.

p. 140   'Very willing...' #1607.

EBB's hairdo can be seen in the May 1843 sketch and 27 September 1843 watercolour portraits by her brother Alfred.

Substantial coverage: *The Globe and Traveller, The Athenaeum, The Spectator, John Bull, Ainsworth's Magazine, The Metropolitan Magazine, The Monthly Review, The New Monthly Magazine and Humorist, The New Quarterly Review, The Examiner, Blackwood's, Tait's Edinburgh Magazine, The Critic, The Sun, The Westminster Review* and *The League*.

'We do not believe...' *Evening Mirror* (New York) 7 December 1844, p. 2.

p. 141   'There will doubtless...' *Evening Mirror* (New York) 8 October 1844, p. 1.

The Spectator 24 August 1844, pp. 809–10.

The Atlas 31 August 1844, pp. 593–94.

Blackwood's Edinburgh Magazine November 1844, pp. 621–39.

p. 142   'I love...' RB to EBB 10 January 1845, #1811.

'Preface' in *The Poetical Works of Elizabeth Barrett* (London: John Murray), 1914, p. xiv.

p. 143   'A disguised angel...' EBB to RB 16 June 1846, #2421. 'I love love...' EBB to Mitford 8 November 1841, #869. 'I thank you... Is it indeed...' EBB to RB 11 January 1845, #1812. 'You make me... Your poetry must be...' RB to EBB 13 January 1845, #1814.

p. 144   'The fault..' EBB to RB 15 January 1845, #1816. 'Your books...' RB to EBB 27 January 1845, #1825.

p. 145   'As for me... Only *don't* let us...' EBB to RB 3 February 1845, #1829.

'For reasons I know...' RB to EBB 11 February 1845, #1837. He goes on: 'Your talking of "tiring me," "being too curious," &c. &c [...] I should never have heard of had the plain truth looked out of my letter with its unmistakeable eyes.'

'Genius..' EBB to Mitford 19 October 1842 #1028. She goes on: 'There is a unity & nobleness of conception in "Pippa passes" [...] Pippa, dark as she is, is worth all those rhymes you speak of—in my eyes.'

p. 146   'I am *essentially better*... EBB to RB 5 March 1845, #1857. 'Bitter mental discipline... Blind poet... I have lived only inwardly...' EBB to RB 20 March 1845, #1870. Robert hints in RB to EBB 15 April 1845, #1888. 'For some experience...' #1870. On Kenyon on RB: EBB to Mitford 19 October 1842 #1028.

p. 147   'He resembled a girl…' Mitford to Charles Boner, 22 February 1847, SD1310. RB travelled at twenty-one, as Private Secretary to a Russian consul general, Chevalier George de Benkhausen. 'And there was everything right…' EBB to RB 21 May 1845, #1922.

p. 148   'My mental position…' #1922. 'I would not listen…' EBB to Mitford 18 September 1846, #2617. 'Like a misprint…' EBB to RB 23 May 1845, #1925.

SIXTH FRAME

p. 149   Bridget Riley interview with Paul Moorhouse, 'In the Studio', in *The Eye's Mind: Bridget Riley Collected Writings 1965–2019* (London: The Bridget Riley Art Foundation and Thames & Hudson, 2019), p. 247.

BOOK SEVEN

Epigraph   *AL* Bk 9, Ll. 820–22.

p. 151   'Little city…' EBB to Arabella MB, 16–19 October 1846, #2624.

p. 152   Orientalist poems like 'The Giaour: A Turkish Tale' also resulted from Byron's travels.

Elizabeth's brothers travelled in 1844.

EBB is fretting because of a casual remark by Richard Hengist Horne: '"Your envelope reminds me of"—*you*, he said […] he *cant* have heard of your having been here, & it *must* have been a chance-remark— altogether!—taking an imaginary emphasis from my evil conscience perhaps.' EBB to RB 7 July 1845, #1968.

'I was examined…' EBB to Mitford 13 September 1845, #2028.

p. 153   'I was treated… From steam-packet reasons…' EBB to RB 24 September 1845, #2042.

p. 154   'Very much…' EBB to Mitford *c*.20 September 1845, #2039. 'What you cannot see…' EBB to RB *c*.20 August 1845, #2007. 'I know as certainly…' RB to EBB 12 June 1846, #2411. 'Think for me…' #2042.

p. 155   'He would not even…' #2042. 'The singular reason…' EBB to RB 16 September 1845, #2030.

p. 156   'The *first subject*…' RB to EBB 30 August 1845, #2014. 'I would marry you…' RB to EBB 25 September 1845, #2043. 'And if I…' #2030. 'When you told me…' #2043.

p. 157   'An exchange…' EBB to RB 17 September 1845, #2034. 'You must leave me…' #2030. 'Suffering from…' EBB to George Goodin MB 17–18 September 1846, #2616. 'And once he…' #2007. 'Lightning…' EBB to RB 11 July 1845, #1971.

p. 158   'I never had…' #2007.

p. 159   'Natural inferiority…' EBB to RB 2–3 July 1845 #1965. Her letters at this time ask repeatedly after Robert's health.

He knows he's the junior partner: RB to EBB 3 March 1846, #2238.

Germaine Greer, *Slip-Shod Sibyls: Recognition, Rejection and the Woman*

Poet (London and New York: Viking Penguin, 1995); Susan Kavaler-Adler, *The Compulsion to Create: A Psychoanalytic Study of Women Artists* (London: Routledge, 1993).

p. 160 'Saved a living man...' EBB to RB 23 June 1846, #2433. 'Constrained bodily...' #2007. 'I am...' EBB to RB 11 October 1845, #2062.
1845 is in the top five warm summers since records began: http://www.pascalbonenfant.com/18c/geography/weather.html [retrieved 30 April 2019].
EBB's first carriage rides: EBB to RB 7 July 1845, #1968. Her first stroll: EBB to RB 11 May 1846, #2355.

p. 161 'That Dreamland...' EBB to RB 27 June 1846, #2441. EBB goes visiting: EBB to RB 30 June 1846, #2446. To the GWR: EBB to RB 13 June 1846, #2414. To look at art: EBB to RB 22 June 1846, #2430. On taking laudanum: EBB to Julia Martin *c.*7 October 1845, #2057. On cutting down: EBB to RB 4 Feb 1846, #2197. 'I shall refuse steadily...' EBB to RB 12 June 1846, #2412.

p. 162 'Nearly two hundred...' #2414. 'Courage...' EBB to Fanny Dowglass *c.*23 July 1846, #2500. For Cava de' Tirreni, EBB's guide uses the Neopolitan name, 'La Cava': EBB to RB 30 June 1846, #2444.
'I have not been in the *habit* of saying "Robert", speaking of you. You have only been The One. No word ever stood for you—' EBB to RB 2 July 1846, #2455.
'If we are poor...' RB to EBB 26 August 1846, #2561. W. Craig Turner, ed, *The Poet Robert Browning and his Kinsfolk by his Cousin Cyrus Mason* (Waco, Texas: Baylor University Press, 1983), p. 63.

p. 163 'Tender-hearted... Shuts his eyes...' RB to EBB 27 August 1846, #2564. Grandfather 'Rob' Browning's will is cited in *UCL Legacies of British Slave-ownership*, https://www.ucl.ac.uk/lbs/person/view/2146646289 [retrieved 26 April 2019].
Even if there were a bequest from Tittle, Robert senior may well have refused it.
Paying back: *The Brownings' Correspondence*, vol. 3, p 308. Banking is also practised by Robert senior's father and two younger half-brothers.
Robert senior's art collection: Richard S. Kennedy, *The Dramatic Imagination of Robert Browning: A Literary Life* (Columbia, Missouri: University of Missouri Press, 2007), p. 9.

p. 164 His half-brother Reuben says his library 'comprised [...] the critical points of ancient and modern history, the lore of the Middle Ages, all political combinations of parties, their description and consequences; and especially the lives of the poets and painters.' Kelley et al., Biographical note citing G & M, p. 8, and *Reconstruction*, J42. (The feast of Charles the Martyr is to remain in the Anglican calendar till 1859.)
'Dear Mr Kenyon...' EBB to RB 31 January 1846, #2195. Migraines: RB to EBB 12 May 1845, #1912; RB to EBB 13 May 1845, #1914.

p. 165   No *'femmelette...'*: 'He has too much genius for it. Men of high imagination never subject themselves to the conventions of society [...] He lives in the world, but loathes it.' EBB to Mitford 14 April 1845, #1885. 'Indian Empire...' EBB to George Goodin MB 1 April 1846, #2285. 'Imperialist' is first used in the early years of the nineteenth century of Napoleon I's expansionism. D. A. Lake: 'Imperialism: political aspects' in Elsevier, *International Encyclopedia of the Social & Behavioral Sciences* 2001, pp. 7232–4.
     The Condition and Treatment of Children employed in the Mines and Collieries of the United Kingdom Carefully compiled from the appendix to the first report of the Commissioners With copious extracts from the evidence, and illustrative engravings (London: William Strange, 1842). *Blackwood's Edinburgh Magazine* vol. LIV, no. CCCXXXIV (August 1843), pp. 260–62.

p. 166   'As a woman... Lift my voice...' EBB to Clementia Taylor 2 April 1845, #1878.

p. 167   'Blood of a slave...' EBB to RB 20 December 1845, #2144.

p. 168   The Revd John Tittle arrived on St Kitts in 1730, 'Appointed by the SPG [...] as attorney for Ponds and Lucas Estate [...] Privateers kept seizing his ships, which were then diverted to New York, where his brother lived! The SPG eventually dismissed him [...] However, sustained by local support, and secure in his two cures of St. Peter's and St. George's, he refused to accept dismissal. He married between 1731 and 1733 Margaret Strachan, daughter of the surgeon Dr. George Strachan of St. Kitts. Their daughter, Margaret Tittle, married in 1778 the first Robert Browning; and their son Robert, born in 1781, was sent to St. Kitts to work on his mother's plantation [the] prosperous Anderson Estate, which the Revd Tittle had managed for William Coleman, the London merchant, and himself.' Kathleen D. Manchester, *Historic Heritage of St. Kitts, Nevis, Anguilla* (Trinidad: the Author, 1971) pp. 16–17.
     'I never showed them...' EBB to Arabella MB 12 January 1851, #2899. 'Swindling' Kenyon: 'I feel trodden down by either his too great penetration or too great unconsciousness.' EBB to RB 31 January 1846, #2195. 'Secrets indeed...' EBB to RB 12 August 1846, #2535.

p. 169   Surtees is made captain after exchanging to 83rd Foot Regiment; he won't be promoted to major for fifteen years.
     Aunt Hedley: 'At dinner my aunt said to Papa .. "I have not seen Ba all day—and when I went to her room, to my astonishment a gentleman was sitting there". "Who was *that*" said Papa's eyes to Arabel—"Mr Browning called here today," she answered—"And Ba bowed her head", continued my aunt, "as if she meant to signify to me that I was not to come in"— "Oh," cried Henrietta, "*that* must have been a mistake of yours. Perhaps she meant just the contrary."' EBB to RB 15 July 1846, #2484; EBB to RB 13 July 1846, #2482.
     'Why should not...' RB to EBB 12 June 1846, #2411.

p. 170   'Therefore decide…' EBB to RB 9 September 1846, #2593. 'Married directly…' RB to EBB 10 September 1846, #2594. Uncle Sam's shares: 'Stormie told me the other day that I had eight thousand pounds in the funds,—of which the interest comes to me quarterly […] from forty to forty five pounds Papa gives me every three months, the income tax being first deducted. […] Then there is the ship money .. a little under two hundred a year on an average […] the annual amount of which […] has been added to the Fund-money until this year, when I was directed to sign a paper which invested […] the annual return in the Eastern Railroad [to] increase by doubling almost […] Then there are the ten shares in Drury Lane Theatre—out of which, comes nothing.' EBB to RB 5 August 1846, #2526.

'Stormie told me this morning…' EBB to RBB 6 August 1846, #2528.

p. 171   'Sixteen pounds a year…' EBB to RBB 22 July 1846, #2499. Thanking Wilson for standing witness because Robert's closest friend, Captain Pritchard, is away: RB to EBB 12 September 1845, #2597; RB to EBB 13 September 1846, #2600.

p. 172   'It *does* make us laugh…' EBB to Arabella MB 13 September 1847, #2701. 'Emotion & confusion…' EBB to RB 13 September 1846, #2599. 'You shall have the ring…' EBB to RB 10 September 1846 #2596.

p. 173   On journalists: EBB to RB 12 September 1846, #2598. On Mr Boyd: EBB to RB 30 June 1846, #2446. 'Grave faces…' #2598. EBB continues: 'I kept saying, "What nonsense, .. what fancies you do have to be sure", .. trembling in my heart with every look they cast at me—.' 'I will be docile…' EBB to RB 16 September 1846, #2608.

p. 174   Timetable muddles: EBB to RB 18 September 1846, #2613. Le Havre is still Havre-de-Grace. *The Railway Times* vol. IX, no. 38 (19 September 1846), p. 1368. https://books.google.co.uk/books?id=w2I3AQAAMAAJ& pg=PA1368&lpg=PA1368&dq=london+weather+12+september+1846&sour ce=bl&ots=Ac9wp3yUFY&sig=ACfU3UohYWNaMIMqvuaf6akTMW T6Dw8x3g&hl=en&sa=X&ved=2ahUKEwjU9NSVx_fhAhVaShUIHVp tCNEQ6AEwFHoECAgQAQ#v=onepage&q=london%20weather%20 12%20september%201846&f=false [retrieved 30 April 2019].

At EBB's request, the newspaper text substitutes plain 'Saturday' for a date, leaving room for the belief that it takes place on the day they leave the country. EBB to RB 14 September 1846, #2604.

p. 175   EBB puts off friends, and cancels Miss Mitford.

'My dearest George… I knew…' EBB to George Goodin MB 17–18 September 1846, #2616.

45 New Cavendish Street was then 9 Great Marylebone Street. The family firm of Hodgson's also had a stationers and bookshop at 6 Great Marylebone Street, on the actual corner of the terrace where the Barretts lived. https://www.ucl.ac.uk/bartlett/architecture/sites/bartlett/files/ chapter15_devonshire, pp. 4, 25 [retrieved 1 May 2019].

'After the Havre… Now five horses…' EBB to Arabella MB 26 September 1846, #2620. They arrive in Le Havre six months before the new boat train service direct to Paris. https://en.wikipedia.org/wiki/Paris–Le_Havre_railway [retrieved 2 May 2019].

p. 176   'I prevailed… We were deposited… She came…' #2620.

p. 177   'Just a pretty…' EBB to Henrietta MB 23 November 1847, #2711. In Robert, on the other hand, Anna Jameson sees 'inexhaustible wit, & learning & good humour'. EBB to Mitford 2 October 1846, #2622; EBB to Arabella MB 16–19 October 1846, #2624. 'Death warrant… Very hard letters…' EBB to Arabella MB 2 October 1846, #2621. 'He will wish…' EBB to RB 14 September 1846, #2604. '"Imprudence" into "Prudence" …' #2621.

p. 178   'We hear… I want…' EBB to Julia Martin 22 October 1846, #2625. Fontaine de Vaucluse: #2624. 'Nearly as much attention…' #2622. 'Glittering… A thousand mountains…' #2624.

p. 179   'Beautiful Genoa… And now this is… You would certainly smile…' #2624. Their companions stay in Pisa a month, then go on to Rome where Jameson researches her masterpiece, *Sacred and Legendary Art*. https://www.wantedinrome.com/news/tracing-the-footsteps-of-romes-foreign-writers-and-artists.html [retrieved 26 November 2019]. 'We have our dinners from the Trattoria…' EBB to Julia Martin 5–9 November 1846, #2627.

p. 180   'Infinitely more… We are going to be busy…' #2624. 'The ordering of the dinner…' EBB to Mitford 5–8 November 1846, #2626.

p. 181   'Lizards…' #2627. 'Won't call me *improved*…' #2626. 'Towards evening…In the first moment…' EBB and RB to Arabel and Henrietta MB 26 March 1847, #2663. 'So dreadfully affected…' EBB to Henrietta MB 31 March 1847, #2664.

p. 182   'Wilson…' #2663.

SEVENTH FRAME

p. 183   Gillian Rose, Preface in *Judaism and Modernity: Philosophical Essays* (Oxford: Blackwell, 1993), p. v.

BOOK EIGHT

Epigraph   *AL* Bk 5, Ll. 227–29.

p. 185   'I persuaded…' EBB to Henrietta MB *c.*24–30 April 1847, #2670.

p. 186   '& saucers &c &c…' EBB to Arabella MB, 29–30 May 1847, #2680. 'A bottle… A bad artist…' EBB to Henrietta MB 23–24 November 1847, #2711. In 1849 Geddie marries her 'bad artist', becoming working partner to Rome-based Scottish painter and art-photographer Robert Macpherson (1814–72), and herself a photographer and engraver and eventually her aunt's biographer. '*Matrimonio*…' EBB to Henrietta MB [?24]–30 April 1847, #2670. Greetings: EBB to Arabella MB 6 May 1847, #2672.

Thomas Carlyle to RB, 23 June 1847, #2682; quoted in EBB to Henrietta MB 9 July 1847, #2684.

Curtis will write up his visit in *Harper's New Monthly Magazine*, September 1861, as an obituary. EBB to Henrietta MB 16 May 1847, #2678. 'Half past ten...' #2680.

p. 187   'I dream...' EBB to Arabella MB 12 April 1847, #2668. Brotherly contact: EBB to Henrietta MB 21–24 February 1848, #2719. Criticism: 'That [Henry] shd be hindered in the legitimate & honorable desire of taking a step out into life for himself.' EBB to Arabella MB 6 May 1847, #2672. 'Disposed to scold...' Henrietta MB to Samuel MB 14–15 July 1839, SD1018.

p. 188   Daisy's bride, a Barrett cousin, is thought to have mental health problems. Stormie's estate is Bryngwyn, in Montgomeryshire. R. A. Barrett, *The Barretts of Jamaica*. For Uncle Sam's daughter see p. 184; for Stormie's daughters see pp. 138–39, 181; for Sette's daughter see p. 139.

EBB's enjoyment: Frances Hanford to Frances Parthenope Nightingale 21 May 1847, SD1320.

p. 189   'On their arrival...' #2681. 'We could not lead...' EBB to RB 2 July 1846, #2455. The Ugolino connection is made later: EBB to Arabella MB 10–11 May 1848, #2731. 'The eight windows...' EBB to Arabella MB 26 July 1847, #2686.

p. 190   'At about eight... The green plaid...' EBB to Arabella MB 6 May 1847, #2672.

'We have taken Anunziata [sic] with us in our <place> of residence': #2686.

'Little front-caps...' EBB to Henrietta MB 9 July 1847, #2684. Robert 'hates ribbon, & prefers everything as simple & quiet as possible.'

'Thin...' EBB to Arabella MB 22–25 June 1847, #2681. 'For above three hours... EBB to Arabella MB 13 September 1847, #2701.

p. 191   'The windows...' #2701. 'Milky way...' EBB to Henrietta MB 21–24 February 1848, #2719.

The 'little baby-house' is almost certainly number 8 Piazza de' Pitti. EBB to Henrietta MB 23–24 November 1847, #2711. 'Such tiny rooms! [...] But the situation, .. nothing cd be perfecter than the situation [...] a bad staircase, steep & narrow .. & on the second floor the people agreeing to take us for twenty scudi a month, that is four pounds, nine shillings—': EBB to Henrietta MB 20 October 1847, #2707.

'In came...' #2719.

p. 192   'My usual health...' EBB to Mitford 22 February 1848, #2720. Morning sickness: #2719. EBB miscarries on 16 March. EBB to Henrietta MB 15 March to 1 April 1848, #2724. Possibly a sedentary life and low BMI mean light periods, hard to differentiate from problematic spotting. Though EBB thinks 'there must be a great mistake in the *time*... Of course it is natural...' #2720.

Casa Guidi Windows Part 1 Ll. 478–81, 516–22.

p. 193   *Blackwood's* turns down the poem in October 1848. EBB supplies a limited number of notes for the first, book publication. Cooperative ideas realised as *Ateliers Nationaux*. 'Really we are not communists…' EBB to Kenyon 1 May 1848, #2730.

p. 194   'As if the hope of the world…' #2730.
          The Globe and Traveller (10 June 1851), p. 2.

p. 195   'Next summer we shall let…' EBB to Arabella MB 10–11 May 1848, #2731. She continues: 'Florence is the cheapest place in Italy, which brings it to being the cheapest place in the world. Also this is the cheapest moment for Florence, through the panic.'
          'The carpet… We wanted… The bedrooms…' EBB to Henrietta MB 18–20 November 1848, #2751.

p. 196   Again, perhaps at first EBB doesn't realise she's pregnant.

p. 197   Domett is Colonial Secretary 1862–63. 'I cannot well…' RB to Domett 22 May 1842, #964. Meeting Elizabeth: 'I have some important objects in view with respect to my future life—' RB to Alfred Domett 13 July 1846, #2483.
          RB and EBB visit Dante's tomb in the pre-dawn because they're leaving for Florence and prefer travelling in the night cool. And because, not having registered the required paperwork, they aren't actually allowed in. In 1810 Dante's actual bones were hidden from the occupying French in a pillar in the adjoining cloister.
          'He looked east…' EBB to Mitford 24 August 1848, #2744.

p. 198   Wilson also wants to call Dr Harding for RB. 'Most active members… Wineglass…' EBB to Arabella MB 7–11 October 1848, #2748. EBB suspects quinsy too: EBB & RB to Mary Louisa Boyle 3 December 1848, #2754.
          Mahony has nursing experience, from nursing in Cork Cholera Hospital during the 1832–33 epidemic. Thomas Francis Woodlock, *Catholic Encyclopedia* vol. 12 (1913 edition). https://en.wikisource.org/wiki/Catholic_Encyclopedia_(1913)/Father_Prout [retrieved 11 June 2019].
          'He plants himself…' #2748.

p. 199   'Disagreeableness… Little dear…' #2748. The couple have just one night off from Mahony in two months.
          Vanity Fair completes a nineteen-part serialisation in *Punch* in July 1848. EBB reads it in volume form. EBB to Mitford 30 April 1849, #2787. *The Fraserians*, an 1835 group-portrait line drawing by Daniel Maclise, also includes Samuel Taylor Coleridge and Robert Southey, although they weren't regular contributors. As for sententiousness, Virginia Woolf will be right to say that 'the long years of seclusion had done [EBB] irreparable damage as an artist'. 'I want to be…' RB to EBB 3 August 1846 #2521. 'Oh to be with you…' RB to EBB 7 August 1846, #2529. 'Society *by flashes*…' #2792.

p. 200 'Laughed a little...' EBB to Henrietta MB 16 May 1847, #2678.
'Robert came in from his walk the other evening with an "Ah, ha! I have
been kissed by somebody since I saw you last." I suppose he meant to
make me dreadfully jealous; instead [...] it came into my head that you
and Arabel were in Florence [...] Robert seeing me quite gasp for breath,
hastened to explain that it was only his haunting friend, Father Prout,—
who spending an hour or two in Florence on his road to Rome, of course
met Robert, & *kissed him* in the street, mouth to mouth, a good deal to his
surprise.' EBB to Henrietta MB 23–24 November, 1847, #2711.
'Mrs Jameson says...' #2678. 'A strange sort of person...' Mitford to
Charles Boner, 22 February 1847, SD1310.
'At a young ladies' school in Chelsea, Mary received an education strongly
rooted in literature and French': 'Mary Russell Mitford (1787–1855)' in *The
Brownings' Correspondence*, vol. 3, pp. 319–321.
'Femmelette' is used in Julien Chevalier's *L'inversion de l'instinct sexuel
au point de vue médico-légal* of 1885. Cited in Jeffrey Merrick, Bryant T.
Ragan, Bryant T. Ragan, Jr, *Homosexuality in Modern France* (Oxford:
Oxford University Press, 1996), pp. 159–60. G. R. Emile Batault's 1885
categorisation of male hysterics in the Salpêtrière Hospital contrasts a
'perfumed and pomaded *femmelette*' with a 'robust working man' of healthy
masculinity: G. R. Emile Batault, *Contribution à l'étude de l'hystérie chez
l'homme* (Paris: republished Hachette, 2017). In the twenty-first century
femmelette will be campily reappropriated by the French gay community,
like the English 'queer'.

p. 201 Alfred Domett also goes on to a scandalously passionate heterosexual
relationship, apparently conducting an affair with his future wife, Mary
George, a married Wellington school teacher for years. 'Alfred Domett'
in *Te Ara: The Encyclopedia of New Zealand* https://teara.govt.nz/en/
biographies/1d15/domett-alfred [retrieved 14 June 2019]. https://www.
wikitree.com/wiki/Nelson-14202 'The Church of England in the Early
Days of Ahuriri', *Daily Telegraph*, issue 5511, 27 April 1889 [retrieved 14
June 2019].

p. 202 'I wd have sent...' #2748. In the same letter EBB admits her tumble and
describes Mahony: 'Not over refined in the way of him, though so highly
cultivated in intellectual respects. Then it is a grace in these fathers of the
church, to be "fraternal" they think.'
'The *second life*...' EBB to Henrietta MB 18–20 November 1848, #2751.

p. 203 Righi 'may get from forty to seventy pounds a year perhaps, which in
Florence is a high point of prosperity.' #2751. RB to Arabella MB and
Henrietta MB 18 March 1849, #2779.
'The nurse says...' RB to Arabella MB and Henrietta MB 9 March 1849,
#2776. '& I comforted myself...The first cry...' EBB to Anna Jameson 30
April 1849, #2785. Birth announcement: #2776. 'Her perfect goodness...'
#2779. 'Little fellow...' RB to Arabella MB and Henrietta MB 13 March

1849, #2778. Doesn't breast-feed: 'Tho' Ba is inconvenienced a little [...] seeing that she does not nourish the infant herself'. #2779.

p. 204   Looking for *balie*: #2778. 'Mighty woman...' #2779. 'Nobody was ever...' EBB to Mitford 10 October 1848, #2749. 'Just because...' EBB to Julia Martin 14 May 1849, #2791. RB's mother was already unconscious when the news of the birth arrived.

Chapman and Hall has taken on both poets from the dilatory Moxon. 'One heap...' Mitford to Charles Boner, 22 February 1847, SD1310. 'Lord Tennyson manfully tackled it, but [...] "There were only two lines in it that I understood, and they were both lies; they were the opening and closing lines, *'Who will may hear Sordello's story told,'* and *'Who would has heard Sordello's story told!'* " [...] "My wife," [Carlyle] writes, "has read through 'Sordello' without being able to make out whether 'Sordello' was a man, or a city, or a book."' William Sharp, *Life of Robert Browning* (London: Walter Scott Ltd, 1897) chapter 5, pp. 93–113.
The Eclectic Review (August 1849), pp. 203–14; *The Atlas* (13 January 1849), pp. 33–34; *The English Review* (June 1849), pp. 354–86; *Graham's American Monthly Magazine of Literature and Art* (December 1849), pp. 378–79; *The Mornng Post* (9 February 1849), p. 6.

p. 205   'So longingly...' EBB to Henrietta MB 23–25 May 1849, #2793. 'If your...' EBB to Sarianna Browning 2 May 1849, #2789.

Christening: 'Ba told me I should greatly oblige *her* by not only giving our child that name, but by always calling him by it.' He has a Nonconformist's christening 'at the French Evangelical Protestant Church, being the chapel of the Prussian Legation at Florence', RB to Sarianna Browning 2 July 1849, #2800. Moïse Droin, the Genevan-born progressive educationalist and pastor of the Lutheran Evangelical Church 1835–50, has published liturgical verse. That it's actually the *German* Lutheran Evangelical Church we know from Claire Keller, *Une passion italienne: Le général Ostermann-Tolstoï et Maria Pagliari* (Geneva: Éditions Slatkine, 2016) page number not given: https://books.google.co.uk/books?i d=gyIiCwAAQBAJ&pg=PT145&lpg=PT145&dq=Moïse+Droin&source= bl&ots=MwGYKIIhgm&sig=ACfU3U2DdPPX46kKg13BJ7zt4gb7fKkpeg &hl=en&sa=X&ved=2ahUKEwias_iTgYXjAhXoQUEAHUXJBiw4ChD oATAFegQICRAB#v=onepage&q=Moïse%20Droin&f=false [retrieved 25 June 2019].

'Nerves were unstrung...' EBB to Arabella MB *c.*23–25 June 1849, #2797.

p. 206   'Prices... Some suggestion of it...' #2797. 'Flush, Baby...' EBB to Arabella MB 4 July 1849, #2801.

p. 207   '...Bosnian': Edmund Gosse, *Critical Kit-kats* (London: William Heinemann, 1896). 'The truth is that though they were written several years ago, I never showed them to Robert till last [year] .. I felt shy about them altogether .. even to him. I had heard him express himself strongly against "personal" poetry & I shrank back.—[...] But when Robert saw them, he was much touched & pleased—&, thinking highly of the poetry, he did not like, .. could not consent, he said, that they should be lost to my volumes: so we agreed to slip them in under some sort of veil, & after much consideration chose the "Portuguese." Observe—the poem which precedes them, is "Catarina to Camoens". In a loving fancy, he had always associated me with Catarina, and the poem had affected him to tears, he said, again & again.' EBB to Arabella MB 12 January 1851, #2899.

Robert 'is much better': EBB to Arabella MB 31 August 1849, #2812.

p. 208   *The Christian Register* (28 September 1850), p. 154. *The English Review* (December 1850), pp. 320–32. *The Morning Post* (13 December 1850), p. 2. *The Athenaeum* (30 November 1850), pp. 1242–44. *Harper's New Monthly Magazine* (October 1850), p. 714.

Despite fainting, at Christmas EBB was still 'hoping that the poor little resolute creature may not be weakened by the peril she has run—.' EBB to Henrietta MB 22 December 1849, #2826.

'Generally obtuse…' EBB to Henrietta (MB) Cook 15 April 1850, #2842.

p. 209   'I grieve…' #2826. Arabella MB to Henrietta (MB) Cook 8 April 1850, SD1420. 'What emotion…' #2842.

Advocacy of EBB for laureateship: *The Athenaeum* vol. 1 (1850), p. 585 https://babel.hathitrust.org/cgi/pt?id=chi.25738790&view=1up&seq=591 [retrieved 26 June 2019]. Thought to be by either literary editor Henry Chorley (Martin Garrett, *A Browning Chronology* (Basingstoke, Hants: Palgrave, 2000), p. 83) or T. K. Hervey (Kelley et al., online *Chronology*).

'It's curious…' EBB to Arabella MB 14–16 June 1850, #2861. EBB goes on: 'To say nothing of my own husband's rights! At the same time it is just possible, that the choosers may escape from the difficulty of choice by choosing a woman, & in that case, may choose me. (They *wont* though.)' Louise Bogan becomes the first female annual US Laureate ninety-five years from now.

p. 210   'Appeals…' EBB to Mary Louisa Boyle 5 December 1850, #2891; EBB to Miss Mitford 13 December 1850, #2895.

'A hundred ounces…' as estimated by Dr Harding. RB to Kenyon 29 July 1850, #2869. They now don't really need the extra room that their landlord has let them rent since spring. 'Perfectly white & black…' EBB to Eliza Anne Ogilvy 28 August 1850, #2875. 'Except the blackberries…' EBB to Sarianna Browning *c.*7 September 1850, #2877.

p. 211   Poems (1850): *The Athenaeum* notes 'Diffuseness, ruggedness, *concetti*, and at times colloquialisms'.

On 13 August 1850 the Brownings had lost one of their few intellectual and genuine Florentine friendships when the American feminist Margaret Fuller d'Ossoli, her husband, an Italian count, and their infant son, around Pen's age, drowned off the American coast.

p. 212   Venice: 'Robert & I were sitting outside the caffè in the piazza of St Mark last night at nearly ten, taking our coffee & listening to music, & watching the soundless crowd drift backwards & forwards through that grand square'; EBB to Arabella MB 16 May 1851, #2917. They're travelling with the Ogilvies, Casa Guidi neighbours. 'Robert & I... An old man...' EBB to Arabella MB 5 June 1851, #2920.

p. 213   The quick route is via Basle and Strasbourg. Tennyson's offer: his letter delights the Brownings because it's autographed. EBB to Arabella MB 21 July 1851, #2930. 'The idea... It is a position... Thank God...' EBB to Eliza Ogilvy 25 July–1 August 1851, #2931. 'Henry has...' EBB to Julia Martin 23 August 1851, #2941. 'Dear George...' EBB to Henrietta Cook 6 October 1851, #2962. 'Very violent...' EBB to Julia Martin 17 September 1851, #2945.

p. 214   'Mr Arnauld [sic]... There's kindness... The quality... Paris...' EBB to Julia Martin 6 August 1851, #2936.

p. 215   'Miseries...' They move into No. 138 on 10 October 1851. Carlyle to RB 10 October 1851, #2964; EBB to Sarianna Browning c.7 October 1851, #2963; EBB to Arabella MB 12–14 October 1851, #2965. 'A drawing room...' EBB to Anna Jameson 21 October 1851, #2969. 'Has taken to...' #2965. '*Peninni*...' EBB to Eliza Ogilvy 17 October 1851, #2967. By Christmas, Elizabeth borrows the coinage: 'He's really a darling more & more, the sweetest little Peninni of a child that ever was seen.' EBB to Arabella MB 25 December 1851, #2988. In her sketch of his new hat he looks like Flush! EBB to Arabella and Henrietta MB, 19 October 1849, #2819. This is also where we read of Righi's disappearance. Pen's costume: EBB to Henrietta Cook 2 November 1851, #2974. 'Do you know...' EBB to Henrietta Cook 1 December 1852, #3149.

p. 216   Desirée: EBB to Arabella MB 31 October–23 November 1851, #2973. £800: equivalent to about £110,757.73 in 2020: http://www.in2013dollars.com/uk/inflation/1852?amount=800 [retrieved 29 June 2019]. 'To the heart...' EBB to Anna Jameson 7 July 1852, #3060. 'Neither Robert nor I had apprehended the real character of the letters.' She goes on to repeat the untruth that Mrs von Müller was a bigamist, and 'an intriguing woman': there's no evidence of this, as the judge pointed out in summing up. The case is reported in *The Times* (2 July 1852), p. 7; *The Morning Chronicle* (2 July 1852), pp. 7–8; and in *Galignani's Messenger* (5 July 1852).

p. 217   RB and Milsand finally meet in mid-December. Letter of introduction: #2972. 'She seemed...' EBB to Kenyon 15–16 February 1852, #3005.

p. 218   Robert senior had moved to Bayswater, perhaps to elude Mrs von Müller, earlier that year. Wilson stays: 'I have learnt the use of Wilson.' EBB to Henrietta Cook 21 August 1851, #2938. 'Only bone...' EBB to Jameson 4 January 1853, #3156. 'To my deep joy... We have no fires...' EBB to Arabella MB 13–15 November 1852, #3146.

p. 219   'Neither I nor Baby...' #2792. EBB continues, 'We are like the church bells of San Felice opposite, which, with a sublime impartiality rang when the Grand Duke ran away & when he was invited back again, when the general assembly met & when it would'nt meet any more, when the republic was declared and when it was denied.'. 'Kissing Pen...' EBB to Arabella MB 13–15 November 1852, #3146. 'A very happy winter...' EBB to Jameson 17 March 1853, #3179.

BOOK NINE

Epigraph   *AL* Bk. 9, L. 939.

p. 222   'Well—here's...' EBB to Arabella MB 11–12 September 1853, #3266. 'Likely indeed... Cheerful little blue room...' EBB and RB to George Goodin MB 16–18 July 1853, #3227. 'Our little Penini...' EBB to Hiram Powers 1 August 1853, #3242.
'An artist must...' EBB to Henry Fothergill Chorley, influential literary critic of *The Athenaeum*, 10 August 1853, #3246. She continues, 'We, neither of us, show our work to one another till it is finished.'

p. 223   'There was...' #3227. 'She & I...' #3246.
Although EBB is said to have called herself 'a Swedenborgian' in an unlocated 1857 letter to Henrietta, just two months later she writes that 'I object much to seeing Christ's name in the category with Shakespeare's or even Swedenborg's.' EBB to Henrietta Cook 8–9 October 1857, #4070; EBB to James Jackson Jarvis 5 December 1857, #4103. Swedenborgian friends include Euphrasia Fanny Haworth, family friend Charles Augustus Tulk, and a Wimpole Street neighbour, homeopath James John Garth Wilkinson.

p. 224   Bulwer-Lytton is a British diplomatic attaché in Florence. 'The subject deepens...' EBB to Miss Mitford *c.*26 October 1853, #3278.

p. 225   'To see Rome...' EBB to George Goodin MB 7–8 October 1853, #3274.
'Remember unless...' EBB to Emelyn Story 18 November 1853, #3290.
'Which is considered...' EBB to Arabella MB 28–29 November 1853, #3292.

p. 226   The Storys: #3290. 'Robert & I... She may not live...' #3292.

p. 227   'We had no night-room... This dust...' #3292.
Thackeray's wife has been locked up since their third daughter's birth in 1840.
'The greatest woman...' These journal entries record slightly later London meetings with EBB in September 1855, by which time Anne is eighteen. Hester Thackeray Ritchie, ed, *The Letters and Journals of Anne Thackeray Ritchie with Many letters of William Makepeace Thackeray* (New York and London: Harper and brothers, 1924), pp. 77–78.
The Secretary is August Emil Braun. Anne Thomson, his literary wife, commissioned EBB for *Classical Album* (April 1845).

p. 228   'The talk was...' EBB to Miss Mitford 10 May 1854, #3413.

p. 229   'Delicate, pale... I have'nt taken...' #3413. 'He died...' EBB to Arabella MB 17–20 June 1854, #3434. 'Our own child...' RB to William Wetmore Story 11 June 1854, #3430.

p. 230   'Lameness...' EBB to Arabella MB 12 September 1854, #3468. 'At home...'

'Florence, June 30, 1854' in *The Critic* (1 August 1854) pp. 422–23. Cited in Kelley et al, fn. 5 to #3468.

The David Lyon dividend may be £175. #3468.

'The cough…' EBB to Eliza Ogilvy 6 March 1855, #3530. 'Constantly supposes…' EBB to Sarianna Browning late January 1855, #3512.

p. 231   Arabella's availability: EBB to Arabella MB 10 January 1855, #3508. "Not […] the best use… Since the siege…' EBB to Anna Jameson 24 February 1855, #3524.

Arabella does raise Emma, child of her second cousin Samuel Goodin Barrett; bizarrely, Elizabeth feels that Henrietta should give up one of her children to Arabella to raise.

'Robert & I…' #3508.

p. 232   '*In blots…*' #3530.

p. 233   *AL* Bk. 5, LL. 41, 43, 45–49, 57–64, 66, 69, 72–73.

p. 234   'Stocks… People have been so kind…' EBB to Anna Jameson 2 February 1857, #3963.

p. 235   Emily Dickinson, #312. *AL* Bk. 4, Ll. 1212–18.

p. 236   'Punch…' #3508. 'A single lady…' EBB to Arabella MB 12 March 1850, #2836. She continues, 'I liked her little dog extremely—& by no means disliked her.'

'Lives here alone…' #3413. 'He feels…' #3508. EBB continues, 'Upon Wilson's thanking him very much for the compliment to herself, he condescended to make another exception in her favour.'

p. 237   'But with an Italian .. a Tuscan […] there is no legal marriage, except by the act ecclesiastical'; EBB to Arabella MB 10 July 1855, #3575; EBB to Alfred MB 9 July 1855, #3574.

'Half America…' EBB to Henrietta Cook 13 July 1855, #3578.

Sarianna and Arabella are also present for that September reading.

Papa and the 'mesmerizer': EBB to Henrietta Cook 27 August 1855, #3604.

p. 238   The Barretts leave home on 30 August, ostensibly so that Wimpole Street can be redecorated, and return by the 27 September reading. 'Tears enough…' #3575. 'Little warm, sunny, shabby…' Ritchie, ed, *The Letters and Journals of Anne Thackeray Ritchie*, p. 82.

p. 239   'Old charm…' #3574. *AL* Bk. 6, Ll. 79–84. EBB fair-copies the first two books in January, the next three in February, and the sixth by 13 March.

RB's *Men and Women* reviewed: In November (UK) and December (America). Anon. in *The Literary Gazette* (1 December 1855), pp. 758–59; Margaret Oliphant in *Blackwood's Edinburgh Magazine* (February 1856), p. 137; Henry Fothergill Chorley in *The Athenaeum* (17 November 1855), pp. 1327–28.

RB's *Shelley 'Letters'* reviewed: *The Literary Gazette* (21 February 1852), pp. 173–75; John Forster in *The Examiner* (21 February 1852), pp. 117–18; Henry Fothergill Chorley in *The Athenaeum* (21 February 1852), p. 214. Anon. in *The Leader* (28 February 1852), pp. 205–206; Anon. in the

Manchester Guardian (3 March 1852), p. 147; George Henry Lewes in *The Westminster Review*, April 1852, pp. 502–11.

EBB's *Poems (1856)* adds *Casa Guidi Windows* and three uncollected poems to *Poems (1850)*.

p. 240   'Always a weight…' #3578.

Kenyon's bequest won't be available for a year. His will dates from the week before his death. SD1993. Bryan Waller Procter to EBB *c.*4 December 1856, #3931.

p. 241   'Shed tears…' EBB to Anna Jameson 2 February 1857, #3963. 'I think…' John Ruskin to RB 27 November 1856, #3927. Further correspondence admiring *AL*: Leigh Hunt to EBB and RB 31 December 1856, #3949. #3927. John Ruskin to RB 28 December 1856, #3947.

p. 242   Mostly enthusiastic: though a year after *AL*'s publication John Nichols in the *Westminster Review* 'has leisure to be censorious' about form and versification in particular. *AL* reviewed: Anon. in *The Globe and Traveller* (20 November 1856), p. 1. Charles Hamilton Aidé in *Edinburgh Weekly Review* (28 February 1857), pp. 7–9. Henry Fothergill Chorley in *The Athenaeum* (22 November 1856), pp. 1425–27. Anon. in *The Albion* (6 December 1856), p. 585. Anon. in *New-York Daily Tribune* (20 December 1856), pp. 5–6. Anon. in *New-York Daily Times* (9 December 1856), p. 2. George Eliot in *The Westminster Review* (January 1857), pp. 306–310. Perceptively, Coventry Patmore admires the *Sonnets from the Portuguese*: at least one ranks 'with the very best of Milton and Wordsworth. […] Nothing is more untrue than the common notion that deep and subtle thought is foreign to passion.' In *Aurora Leigh*, she 'seldom goes out of her way for an image'. *The North British Review* (February 1857), pp. 443–62.

p. 243   'There has been…' #3963. 'I shall try…' #3578. 'Yet when it came…' EBB to Henrietta Cook 13 May 1857, #3999. 'Without a word…' EBB to Arabella MB *c.*29 April 1857, #3991.

p. 244   In less than a fortnight RB is able to report that EBB 'will get over the blow' of Papa's death. RB to Arabella MB [?29] April 1857 #3992.

They're staying at Casa Betti. Annunziata's details: source is 'Simonetta Berbeglia, of Arezzo', cited in Kelley et al, note to EBB to Sarianna Browning c.9 September 1857, #4043. 'When I wanted…' EBB to Arabella MB 12 April 1858, #4164.

p. 245   RB on mediums: John Casey, *After Lives: A Guide to Heaven, Hell and Purgatory* (Oxford: Oxford University Press, 2009), p. 373.

'A bad winter…' #4164.

p. 246   Tuberculosis in Le Havre: Adolphe Lecadre, 'Etude statistique, hygiénique et médicale relative au mouvement de la population du Havre en 1868' in *Recueil des publications de la Société Impériale Havraise d'Etudes Diverses* (1868): pp. 45–114, 91. Cited in David S. Barnes, *The Making of a Social Disease: Tuberculosis in Nineteenth-Century France* (Berkeley: University of California Press, 1995), Chapter 6: https://publishing.cdlib.org/

ucpressebooks/view?docId=ft8t1nb5rp&chunk.id=ch6&toc.depth=1&toc.
id=ch6&brand=ucpress [retrieved December 2019]. We can't be certain
EBB was free of tuberculosis by her death. 'Plenty of distraction...' EBB
to Isa Blagden 7 January 1859, #4315.

p. 247   'Beautiful dream...' EBB to Eliza Ogilvy 17 October 1859, #4508, Eton.
EBB will publish 'Napoleon III in Italy' in *Poems Before Congress* next year.
In Marciano, as EBB recovered, 'The Brownings almost invariably came
over in the afternoon to tea on the grass terrace'. Marchesa Edith Marion
Peruzzi de' Medici (née Story) in *The Living Age* vol. 285 (1915), p. 554.

p. 248   'Ill-directed flight...' Julia Ward Howe, *Words for the Hour* (Boston:
Ticknor and Fields, 1857), pp. 145–47.

p. 249   RB appreciated: EBB to Sarianna Browning 7 April 1860, #4644, Lilly.

p. 250   RB's new persona poems will appear in 1864's *Dramatis Personae*.
'Approaching antagonism...' William Michael Rossetti, *Some
Reminiscences* vol. 1 (Cambridge: Cambridge University Press, Cambridge
Library Collection, 1906 reissued 2013) p. 239.
Via Felice is now Via Sistina.

p. 251   'Lord Walter's Wife' portrays the double standard by which unfaithful
women are condemned but men are not.
EBB's heart is 'heavy': EBB to Sarianna Browning 19 January 1861,
#61047-00 [*c.*28 March 1861], MS at Lilly.

p. 254   Philip Larkin, 'An Arundel Tomb' in Archie Burnett, ed, *The Complete
Poems* (London: Faber, 2012), pp. 71–72.
'Slender, fragile...': At nine, Pen appeared 'At once less childlike and less
manly than would befit that age'; Nathaniel Hawthorne, *Notes of Travel*
(Boston: Houghton, Mifflin, 1870), pp. 69–70.

p. 255   A memorial tablet for EBB: Simone Luigi Peruzzi to RB 21 June 1859,
#4433.
Though the Casa Guidi images don't take, Rome is at the cutting edge of
contemporary photographic practices. Beth Saunders, 'The Rise of Paper
Photography in Italy, 1839–55' in *Heilbrunn Timeline of Art History* (New
York: The Metropolitan Museum of Art, 2000), http://www.metmuseum.
org/toah/hd/rppi/hd_rppi.htm (April 2017) [retrieved 14 December 2019].

Index

EBB = Elizabeth Barrett Browning; RB = Robert Browning.
All works are by EBB unless otherwise stated.
Colour plates are indicated by 'Pl.'
References to information in the Notes are indicated by '*n*'; e.g. 280*n*87 indicates the note(s) on page 280 referring to page 87 in the main text.

Abbeville (France) 28
Abinger, James Scarlett, 1st Baron 18
abolitionism 8, 17, 29, 80–83, 162–3, 165, 167, 249, 279*n*82
Ackland, Joss 5
Aeschylus 141; *Prometheus Bound/Unbound* (EBB trans.) 87, 94, 100, 101, 104, 207, 280*n*87
age of consent 48, 272*n*48
Aix-en-Provence 178
Akhmatova, Anna 134
Albert, Prince consort 288*n*134
Albert Edward, Prince of Wales (*later* King Edward VII) 247
Albion, The (magazine) 242
Allnatt, Richard Hopkins ('Dr Allnutt') 192
Altham, Roger 265*n*16
American Civil War 224
Amiens (France) 28
Ancona (Italy) 196–7
Andersen, Hans Christian 252
Anglo-Sikh War, First (1845–46) 165
anti-Catholicism 68, 136
Anti-Corn Law League 166
anti-imperialism 165, 292*n*165

Armenian Renaissance 212
'Arnauld, Mr' *see* Arnould, Joseph
Arno, River 151, 252
Arnould, Joseph ('Mr Arnauld') 214
Arquà Petrarca (Italy) 212
Artaud, William 22, 24, 267*n*22, Pl.
Arthurian legend 105
Assisi 225
asthma 100
Athena (goddess) 27
Athenaeum, The (magazine) 178, 209; EBB's works published in 67, 128, 129, 130, 135, 285*n*116, 287*n*128; reviews of EBB's works 87, 92, 107, 108, 127, 211, 242, 249, 280*n*87, 299*n*211; reviews of RB's works 239
Atlas, The (magazine) 107, 140, 141, 204, 249, 284*n*107
'August Voice, An' 248
Aukerian, Haroutiun 212
Aurora Leigh: characterisation 4, 9–10, 11, 12, 36, 183, 232, 233–4; dedication 240; editions and reprints 235, 243, 246, 250; frontispiece 1–3, 37, 263*n*1–3; influence and significance 9, 235; influences on 59;

later criticism 5; planning and writing 135, 219, 222–3, 231–5, 239, 240–41, 302n239; publication and reception 2, 9, 234–5, 241–3, 303n242; structure, plot and themes 2, 9–10, 36, 37, 183, 232–5, 241; quoted v, 1, 4, 9, 10, 11, 12, 13, 17, 20, 38, 48, 49, 59–60, 74, 99, 126, 151, 185, 194, 232–3, 235, 239

Austen, Jane 5, 108

Authors' Club of New York 3

Avignon 178

Babbacombe (Devon) 118

Bagni di Lucca (Italy) 205–6, 222–3, 244

Baker, William 266n17

Bancroft, George 131

Baptist War (Jamaica; 1831–32) 80, 81–2

Baptists 81, 276n68

Barclay, Constance, photograph of RB and Pen Pl.

Barker, Edmund Henry 65

Barlow, Thomas Oldham 2, 3, 263n2, Pl.

Baron, John 38–9, 42

Barrett, Edward (EBB's great-grandfather) 15, 29, 84

Barrett, Elizabeth (EBB's grandmother) see Moulton, Elizabeth

Barrett, George Goodin (EBB's great-uncle) 30, 268n30

Barrett, Hercie (EBB's four times great-grandfather) 29

Barrett, Richard (EBB's cousin) 81, 84, 114

Barrett, Samuel (EBB's cousin; 'Handsome Sam') 84

Barrett, Samuel (EBB's great-uncle) 85

Barrett, Samuel Goodin (EBB's cousin) 139, 302n231

Barrett, Susanna Maria (EBB's cousin) 139

Barretts of Wimpole Street, The (Besier) 4–5, 6; film and TV adaptations 5

Barry, Dr (Torquay physician) 112–13, 114, 285n114

Barthes, Roland, 'The Death of the Author' 263n4

Basingstoke (Hampshire) 120

Bate, Gerardine (later Macpherson) 176–7, 179, 186, 294n179, 294n186

Bath (Somerset) 75, 77, 270n38

Battle of Marathon, The 10–11, 27, 65, 104, 256

Beaumont, Sir George 60

Belle Sauvage, La (boat) 117

Bellow, Saul 5

Bell's Weekly Messenger (newspaper) 249

Benkhausen, George de 290n147

Berlin 195

'Bertha in the Lane' 134

Besier, Rudolf, The Barretts of Wimpole Street 4–5, 6

Biondi, Madame (midwife) 203, 219

bisexuality see homosexuality and bisexuality

Bishop, William 137, 288n137

Blackwood's Magazine 107, 141–2, 165, 189, 192–3, 239, 249, 296n193

Blagden, Isa 236, 253, 254, 255

Blake, William, 'Jerusalem' 166

Blanc, Louis 193

Bloom, Harold 5

Boccaccio, Giovanni: The Decameron 36; Divine Comedy 284n107

Bogan, Louise 299n209

Bologna 212

Bonaparte, Charles-Louis-Napoléon see Napoleon III, Emperor

Boner, Charles 200

'Book of the Poets, The' 36, 128–9, 287n128

Bookseller, The (magazine) 249

Bordman, Nelly 65, 177

Boston Miscellany, The (magazine) 131

Boswell, James, Life of Samuel Johnson 12

Boulogne 28, 54

Bourges (France) 178

Boyd, Anne Lowry 60–61, 64, 68, 275n64, 276n68

Boyd, Annie (later Hayes) 61, 64, 68, 276n68, 280n88

Boyd, Hugh Stuart 60–69, 77, 78, 87, 90, 101, 128, 159, 161, 168, 173, 202–3, 274n61, 275n63–4, 276n68, 277n77, 280n87

Brady, Mathew 3, 263n3

Braun, August Emil 227, 301n227

Brighton 74–5; Pavilion 270n34

Brontë sisters 5, 8, 56, 108, 233; Charlotte Brontë 8, 12, 108, 264n12; Emily Brontë 5, 36

Brown, Ford Madox 237

Brown, Lancelot 'Capability' 58

Browne, Sir Thomas 164

Browning, Elizabeth Barrett: family background 8, 16–18, 28–33; birth and christening 8, 15, 33; childhood and adolescence 6, 8, 10–11, 13–16, 19–34, 38–45, 48–54, 56, 151–2, Pl.; life at Hope End, Herefordshire 13–15, 20–22, 28, 49–50, 87; family holidays 15, 21, 24–5,

28, 33, 54, 78, 267n25; first writings 8,
10–11, 22–5, 27–8, 268n27; developing
political awareness 26–7; first printed book
10, 27; confinement in Gloucester during
illness 38–45, 48, 52, 271n42–3, 272n44,
Pl.; sixteenth birthday 48; returns home as
invalid 44, 48–50, 56–7; further youthful
writings 51–4; first published poems 53–4,
104, 273n53–4; nineteenth birthday 53;
stays with grandmother in Hastings 54;
twentieth birthday 54; publication of *An
Essay on Mind* 54–8, 61, 104, 273n54–5;
friendship and correspondence with Sir
Uvedale Price 58–66, 62, 63, 274n62;
beginning of friendship with John Kenyon
57–8, 109; relationship with Hugh Stuart
Boyd 60–69, 77, 78, 87, 90, 101, 159, 161,
168, 173, 202–3, 275n63–4, 277n77; death
of mother 65, 69–71, 227; father's financial
problems 67, 69, 76, 84, 275n67; father
forced to sell Hope End 74–6, 84; family
moves to Sidmouth 74–6; life in Sidmouth
74, 76–9, 84, 86–8, 277n78–9, 278n79;
publication of Aeschylus translations 87,
101, 104, 280n87; friendship with Revd
George Hunter 86, 279–80n86, 284n108;
publication of 'Stanzas Addressed to Miss
Landon' 87–8, 92; family leaves Sidmouth
and moves to London 88–9, 280n88;
family life at Gloucester Place 89–90,
95–6, 99–102; introduction to London
literary scene 90–96; regular publication of
poems in literary magazines 92; beginning
of friendship with Mary Russell Mitford
58, 93–6, 100–101; publication of *The
Seraphim* 96, 101, 107–8, 128, 284n107;
death of Uncle Sam 102, 227; family moves
to Wimpole Street 101–3; family life at
Wimpole Street 104–5, 138–40; continued
development as writer 104–10; three-year
convalescent confinement in Torquay 110–
22, 132; death of brother Sam 114–15, 227,
285n115; death of brother Edward 116–18,
126, 131, 216, 227, 251; resumes writing
119–20, 122; acquires pet spaniel Flush 58,
120–22; returns to London 122–3, 126–7,
286n122; resumption of literary activities
in London 123, 127–36; Flush kidnapped
136–8, 173, 288n138; publication of *Poems
(1844)* 32, 129–30, 134–5, 140–42; first
correspondence with RB 142–6, 162,
289n145; first meeting with RB 146–8;

their courtship and romance 148, 152,
154–63, 199; plans to over-winter in Italy
152–5, 158, 160; strengthening health and
resumption of social activities in London
160–61; planning of elopement with RB
8, 162, 168–71; writing of *Sonnets from
the Portuguese* 168; marriage ceremony
170–73, 174, 186, 293n171; couple travels
via France to Italy 173–9, 200; arrival in
Livorno and journey on to Pisa 151, 179,
199, 200; in Pisa 151, 177–8, 179–82,
294n179; first pregnancy and miscarriage
181–2, 185, 203; couple moves to Florence
185; in Florence 185–212; first wedding
anniversary 190–91; second pregnancy and
miscarriage 192, 295n192; third pregnancy
196, 198, 202–3, 296n196; three-week tour
of coast and Apennines 196–8; RB visited
by Francis Sylvester Mahony 197, 198–202,
297n200; death of Hugh Stuart Boyd 202–
3; birth of son Pen 203; death of mother-
in-law 204, 205; Pen's infanthood and early
childhood 203–4, 205, 212, 215–16, 219,
222–3, 226–7, 229–30, 236, 244, 298n203,
298n205, 300n215; family trip to Bagni di
Lucca 205–6, 207; fourth pregnancy and
miscarriage 206, 208, 299n208; publication
of *Poems (1850)* 207–8, 209, 210–11,
233; final pregnancy and miscarriage 208,
210; sister Henrietta's marriage 208–9;
suggested as potential Poet Laureate
209–10, 299n209; summer in Siena 210;
writing and publication of *Casa Guidi
Windows* 194, 210–11, 229, 233; eighteen
months' travelling 211–18; in northern
Italy 212–13; in Paris 213, 215–17, 218; in
London 213–14, 217–18; family returns
to Florence 218–19; writing of *Aurora
Leigh* 219, 222–3, 225, 231–5, 239, 240–41,
302n239; seventh wedding anniversary in
Bagni di Lucca 222–3; day trip to Prato
Fiorito 224–5; six months in Rome 225–9;
family returns to Florence 229, 236; death
of Flush 229; father injured in accident
230; death of Mary Russell Mitford 230;
family travels again to France and England
236–43; in Paris 237, 238–9; in London
237–8, 239–40, 244–5; visits Isle of Wight
and Somerset 240–41; last meeting with
John Kenyon 240–41; family returns to
Florence 243; publication of *Aurora Leigh*
9, 234–5, 241–3, 303n242; death of father

243–4, 303n244; summer at Bagni di
Lucca 244; back in Florence 245; family
spends summer in Paris and Normandy 3,
245–6; photographic session with Macaire
brothers at Le Havre 1–2, 3, 245–6, Pl.;
winter in Rome 246–7, 304n247; family
returns to Florence at outbreak of Franco-
Austrian hostilities 247; summers at Siena
and winters in Rome 247–52; publication
of *Poems Before Congress* 249–50, 304n247;
death of sister Henrietta 251, 252; last
poem 8–9, 252; final return to Florence
252; last weeks 220–21, 252–3; death 4,
253–4; funeral 10, 254–5; posthumous
works 251
Character & characteristics: abolitionism 8,
19–20, 29, 82, 83–84, 167, 249; anti-
imperialism 165; appearance 1, 2–3, 4,
22, 32, 93, 140, 220–21, 227, 252, 263n2,
272n44; art appreciation 161; biographies
and studies 261, 263n6; charm 93, 227;
confidence 8, 61, 101; determination 49,
53, 105, 187, 248; dislike of paying social
visits 61–2, 146; dress 190; early literary
ambitions 8, 11, 22–4, 52–3; ethnicity and
racial heritage 8, 29–31, 167–8; female
friendships 77–8, 93, 109, 161, 236;
finances 102, 104, 156, 162, 170, 186–7,
212, 229, 230, 240, 293n170; as 'ghost
in the machine' 7, 224; gift for love 193;
good traveller 111, 178; hairstyle 140, 171,
272n44, 289n140; high-spiritedness 40,
94; intellectual snobbery 76; international
reputation 130–31, 140–41, 211, 241–2,
243; late-riser 99, 112; linguistic abilities
22, 24, 25, 28, 94; literary significance
and influence 4, 235; love of the sea 78,
89; male friendships 57, 63, 77, 86, 109,
120, 158–9; names and nicknames ix, 15,
32, 207; obedience 53; opium/morphine-
taking 43, 44, 132, 161, 181, 202, 203,
248, 253, 254; pets 6, 22, 58, 89, 100,
120–22, 136–38, 229, 267n22; political
awareness 26–7, 165–67, 193–4, 249–50;
portraits and likenesses 1–4, 9, 22, 46, 93,
220–21, 245, 246, 252, 261n1–3, 267n22,
289n140, Pl.; possible humped back 263n2,
272n44; pragmatism 209; pregnancies
and miscarriages 108, 181, 192, 193, 196,
198, 202–3, 206, 208, 210, 238, 295n192;
racial views 8, 29–31, 82, 83–4, 166–7;
relationship with father 22, 28, 56, 61, 66,

86–7, 153–5, 177; relationship with mother
19; religion and spirituality 7, 54–5, 68–9,
86, 104–5, 108, 132, 133, 158, 202, 223–4,
244–5, 248, 276n69, 279n86, 301n223;
reputation 4–7, 11, 43, 92, 108, 130–31,
145, 206, 209, 256–7; self-discipline 53;
sexuality 105, 109, 156, 157, 159; shyness
61–2, 91, 92, 94–5, 144, 220; solitariness
49, 61, 131, 223; supernatural interests 132,
133, 223–4, 244–5, 248; tomboy 21, 25,
106; views on America 131
Health: first illness and confinement
in Gloucester 38–45, 56; supposed
hypochondria 43–4; subsequent invalid
status 48–50, 56–7; develops chronic cough
on moving to London 90, 99; persistent
susceptibility to chest infections 92,
99–100, 110; development of chronic lung
disease 110, 114, 263n2, 284n110; three-
year convalescent confinement in Torquay
110–22, 132; advised to over-winter in
Italy 152–3; illness and sexuality 156, 157;
strengthening health during courtship with
RB 160–61; suffers fall during pregnancy
202; blood loss following final miscarriage
210; develops pulmonary disease during
travels to Paris and London 211–12,
214, 216, 217, 218; recovery on return to
Florence 218, 219; severe chest infection
during Italian winter 230, 236; gastric fever
during summer at Bagni di Lucca 244;
further chest infections and deteriorating
health 245, 246, 247, 249, 303n246; final
illness 252–3
Writings see 'An August Voice'; *Aurora
Leigh*; *The Battle of Marathon*; 'Bertha in
the Lane'; 'The Book of the Poets'; *Casa
Guidi Windows*; 'Catarina to Camoens';
'The Cry of the Children'; 'A Curse for a
Nation'; 'De Profundis'; 'The Dead Pan';
'The Development of Genius'; 'A Drama
of Exile'; *An Essay on Mind*; 'Essay on
Woman'; 'Glimpses into My Own Life and
Literary Character'; 'Hiram Powers' "Greek
Slave"'; 'The House of Clouds'; 'Isobel's
Child'; 'King Victor Emmanuel Entering
Florence'; *Last Poems*; 'The Lay of the
Brown Rosary'; 'A Lay of the Early Rose';
'Lessons from the Gorse'; 'Little Mattie';
'Lord Walter's Wife'; 'A Meditation in
Tuscany'; 'A Musical Instrument'; 'My
Character and Bro's Compared'; 'Napoleon

III in Italy'; 'Nature's Remorses'; 'Night
and the Merry Man'; 'The North and the
South'; 'On a Portrait of Wordsworth
by B. R. Haydon'; 'On the Cruelty of
Forcement to Man'; *Poems (1844)*; *Poems
(1850)*; *Poems (1853)*; *Poems (1856)*;
Poems Before Congress; *Prometheus Bound/
Unbound* (trans.); *Psyche Apocalypté*;
'Rhapsody of Life's Progress'; 'Riga's Song';
'Romance of the Ganges'; 'The Romaunt
of Margret'; 'The Romaunt of the Page';
'The Runaway Slave at Pilgrim's Point'; 'A
Sea-Side Meditation'; *The Seraphim*; 'The
Sleep'; *Sonnets from the Portuguese*; 'Stanzas
Addressed to Miss Landon'; 'Stanzas
on the Death of Lord Byron'; 'A Tale of
Villafranca'; 'A Thought on Thoughts';
'Thoughts versus Words'; *Two Poems by
Elizabeth Barrett and Robert Browning*; 'The
Virgin Mary to Child Jesus'; 'A Vision of
Poets'; 'Where's Agnes?'; 'Wine of Cyprus'
Browning, Margaret (*née* Tittle; RB's
grandmother) 168, 292n168
Browning, Margaret (RB's aunt) 163
Browning, Reuben (RB's father's half-brother)
291n164
Browning, Robert 'Rob' (RB's grandfather)
163, 292n168
Browning, Robert (RB's father) 162–4,
281n91, 291n163–4, 292n168; scandal and
European exile 215, 216, 218, 237, 245,
255, 300n218
Browning, Robert: family background 147,
162–4, 168, 292n168; birth 164; childhood
and education 147, 164; as young man
in London 91–2, 94, 130, 142, 147, 200,
281n91; publication of *Paracelsus* 91, 92,
281n91; early travels 142, 147, 290n147;
first correspondence with EBB 142–6, 162,
289n145; first meeting with EBB 146–8;
their courtship and romance 148, 152,
154–63, 199; planning of elopement 8, 162,
168–71; marriage ceremony 170–73, 174,
186, 293n171; couple travels via France to
Italy 173–9, 200; arrival in Livorno and
journey on to Pisa 151, 179, 199, 200; in
Pisa 151, 177–8, 179–82, 249n79; and
EBB's first pregnancy and miscarriage
181–2; couple moves to Florence 185;
in Florence 185–212; first wedding
anniversary 190–91; and EBB's second
miscarriage 192; three-week tour of coast

and Apennines 196–8; visited by Francis
Sylvester Mahony 197, 198–202, 297n200;
publication of *Poems 1849* 189, 204–5; birth
of son Pen 203–4; death of mother 204,
205; Pen's infanthood and early childhood
205, 212, 229–30, 298n205; family trip to
Bagni di Lucca 205–6, 207; and publication
of EBB's *Sonnets from the Portuguese* 206–7,
298–9n207; publication of *Christmas-
Eve and Easter-Day* 207; and EBB's final
miscarriage 210; summer in Siena 210;
eighteen months' travelling with EBB and
Pen 211–18; in northern Italy 212–13; in
Paris 213, 215–17, 218; in London 213–14,
217–18; and father's scandal and European
exile 216, 218, 300n216; family returns
to Florence 218–19; writing of *Men and
Women* 216–17, 219, 222, 228–29, 231;
seventh wedding anniversary in Bagni di
Lucca 222–3; day trip to Prato Fiorito
224–5; six months in Rome 225–9; family
returns to Florence 229, 236; and EBB's
serious chest infection during Italian winter
230, 236; family travels again to France and
England 236–43; in Paris 237, 238–9; in
London 237–8, 239–40, 244–5; publication
of *Men and Women* 231, 239; visits Isle of
Wight with EBB 240; family returns to
Florence 243; death of father-in-law 244,
303n244; summer at Bagni di Lucca 244;
winter in Florence 245; family spends
summer in Paris and Normandy 3, 245–6;
and EBB's photographic portrait sitting at
Le Havre 3–4, 245, 263n3; winter in Rome
246–7, 304n247; family returns to Florence
at outbreak of Franco-Austrian hostilities
247; last family summers at Siena and
winters in Rome 247–52; EBB's final
return to Florence 252; and EBB's final
illness and death 252–4; at EBB's funeral
255; widower 251, 255–6, Pl.; death 256
Character & characteristics: abolitionism
8; amateur artist 3, 246, 251–2; anti-
authoritarianism 159; appearance 146, 147,
200, 227, Pl.; EBB's views on works 122,
128–9, 145; feminine qualities 159, 164–5,
200–201; finances 156, 159, 186, 192;
health 146, 164, 191, 197, 198, 202, 205,
207, 245, 290n159, 299n207; portraits and
likenesses 146–7, 246, Pl.; religion 69, 147,
223, 224; reputation 91, 92, 145, 204–5,
207, 216–17, 236, 256; sexuality 200–202;

views on EBB's works 142, 143–4, 168;
views on spiritualism 245, 250
Writings: *Christmas-Eve and Easter-Day* 207;
Dramatic Lyrics 228; *Dramatis Personae* 245,
251, 304*n*250; 'By the Fireside' 224–5; 'The
Guardian Angel: A picture at Fano' 196–7;
'House' 201; *Letters of Percy Bysshe Shelley*
(ed.) 215, 239; *Men and Women* 216–17,
219, 228–9, 239, 302*n*239; 'Mr Sludge,
"The Medium"' 245; 'My Last Duchess' 47,
228; *Paracelsus* 91, 92, 122, 281*n*91; 'Pippa
Passes' 122, 204, 289*n*145; *Poems 1849* 189,
204–5; *The Ring and the Book* 259; *Sordello*
129, 145, 204, 298*n*204; *Strafford* 92, 204;
'Two in the Campagna' 228; *Two Poems by
Elizabeth Barrett and Robert Browning* 229
Browning, Robert Wiedeman Barrett (EBB's
son; 'Pen'): birth 203; infanthood and early
childhood 203–4, 205–6, 210, 229–30, 236,
298*n*203, Pl.; christening 205, 298*n*205;
nickname 205, 215, 300*n*215; childhood
illnesses 210, 226–7, 229, 244; travelling
with parents 205–6, 212, 215–16, 218, 219,
222–3, 226–7, 237–8, 245; later childhood
250, 252, 254, 255–6; mother's death and
funeral 254–5; later life 44, 256, Pl.; death
256
Browning, Sarah Anna (*née* Wiedemann; RB's
mother) 162, 164; death 204, 205, 298*n*204
Browning, Sarianna (RB's sister) 162, 177,
205, 215, 216, 218, 237, 245, 255, 256,
302*n*237
Bryant, William Cullen 245
Bryngwyn (Montgomeryshire) 188, 295*n*188
Buchanan, Anne 44
Bulwer-Lytton, Robert (*later* 1st Earl of
Lytton) 224, 227, 236, 244, 301*n*224
Byron, Allegra 188
Byron, George Byron, 6th Baron 6, 52–3,
106, 141, 201, 284*n*108; European exile
151–2, 188, 201, 212, 225, 290*n*152; *Childe
Harold's Pilgrimage* 53, 101, 134, 152; *Don
Juan* 52, 134, 135, 258; 'The Giaour: A
Turkish Tale' 290*n*152

C. S. Francis & Co (publishers) 3, 241, 263*n*1
Caistor (Lincolnshire) 285*n*111
Calais 28
Calvino, Italo 35
Cameron, Julia Margaret 1
Camões, Luís de 134, 207
Campbell, Thomas 211

Carboneria (revolutionary group) 190
Carden, John 42–3, 45, 69
Carlyle, Jane 217
Carlyle, Thomas 146, 186, 214, 215, 217, 237,
239, 298*n*204; *Sartor Resartus* 107
Carter, Matilda 286*n*119
Cartesianism 7, 55, 224
Cartier-Bresson, Henri, photographs of
Gandhi 72
Cary, Henry Francis 95
Casa Guidi Windows 194, 210–11, 229, 233,
303*n*239, Pl.
Cash, Johnny 28–29
'Catarina to Camoens' 134, 207, 299*n*207
Catholicism 138; anti-Catholicism 68, 138;
Oxford Movement 85
Cava de' Tirreni (Italy) 162
Cavour, Camillo Benso, Count of 239, 252,
253, 255
Chambers, William Frederick 99, 110, 111,
113, 152, 152–3
Chapman and Hall (publishers) 204, 207,
229, 249, 298*n*204
Charles Albert, King of Piedmont-Sardinia
195–6
Charles I, King 164
Charles II, King 29
Charterhouse (school) 31, 273*n*51
Chatterton, Thomas 6
Chaucer, Geoffrey 128; *The Canterbury Tales*
36, 134
Cheltenham (Gloucestershire) 28, 38, 53,
69–70, 227, 270*n*38
Chepstow (Monmouthshire) 59
Cheshunt (Hertfordshire) 164
Chopin, Frédéric 157
Chorley, Henry Fothergill 178, 242, 249,
281*n*91, 299*n*209, 301*n*223
Christian Register, The (newspaper) 208
Christian's Monthly Magazine, The 186
chromatology 149–50
Cinnamon Hill (Jamaica) 18, 28–9, 34,
80–81, 85, Pl.
Clare, John 6
Clarke, Adam 283*n*103
Clarke, Carlyle 117, 118
Clarke, Thomas 266*n*17
Clarkson, Thomas 83, 279*n*82
Clifton (Bristol) 119
Cocks, Lady Margaret 77–8, 79, 80
Coddington, Fannie (*later* Browning) 256
Colburn, Henry 169, 283*n*101

Coleridge, Samuel Taylor 90, 93, 141, 281*n*90, 296*n*199; 'The Rime of the Ancient Mariner' 288*n*134
Colwall (Herefordshire) 13, 76, 77
Commeline, James 77, 277*n*77
Commeline, Maria 77
communism 165, 193–4
Congregationalism 86, 276*n*68, 279*n*86
consumption *see* tuberculosis
Cook, Altham 215
Cook, Henrietta *see* Moulton-Barrett, Henrietta
Cook, William Surtees 168–9, 187, 188, 208–9, 217, 251, 292*n*169
Cooke, Tommy (Gloucester nurse/medic) 42, 53, 271*n*42, 273*n*53
Corn Laws 166, 167
Cornhill Magazine 250, 252
'Cornwall, Barry' *see* Procter, Bryan Waller
Corsica 237
Cother, William 39–41, 42, 43, 271*n*39
Cottrell, Henry, Count 191, 219, 223
Cottrell, Sophia, Countess 191, 219
Cousin, Victor 237
Cowes (Isle of Wight) 240
Cowley, Abraham 60
Coxhoe Hall (Co. Durham) 33, 65
Crawford, Louisa 248
cricket 75
Critic, The (magazine) 249; feature article on EBB and RB's life in Florence 230, 233
Cronos (Greek god) 154
Crow, Elizabeth (*later* Treherne) 111–12, 122, 136–7, 138–9, 140, 238, 285*n*111, 288–9*n*139
'Cry of the Children, The' 165–6
'Curse for a Nation, A' 249
Curtis, George William 186, 295*n*186
Cushman, Charlotte 246

Dacre, Barbarina Brand, Lady (*earlier* Wilmot) 94, 95, 96, 109, 282*n*95
Daily News (London newspaper) 198, 209, 242, 249, 288*n*135
D'Alessandri, Antonio 220, 252, Pl.
Dall'Ongaro, Francesco 251
Dante Alighieri: tomb 197, 296*n*197; *Divine Comedy* 189
David Lyon (ship) 102, 170, 212, 229, 230
Dawlish (Devon) 117
'De Profundis' 251
dead, communication with 223–4, 245

'Dead Pan, The' 142
Denham, Sir John 60
Descartes, René 7, 55; *see also* Cartesianism
'Development of Genius, The' 61
Diana, Princess of Wales (*earlier* Lady Diana Spencer) 220
Dickens, Charles 135, 224, 239, 288*n*135
Dickinson, Emily 9, 134, 235
Dieppe 215
Dilke, Charles Wentworth 128
Dispensationalism 54–5
Disraeli, Benjamin (*later* 1st Earl of Beaconsfield) 165
Domett, Alfred 197, 201–2, 296*n*197, 297*n*201
Dominicans 85
Dowglass, Fanny 162, 286*n*122
Downton Castle (Herefordshire) 274*n*59
'Drama of Exile, A' 140
Droin, Moïse 298*n*205
Dublin 85
Duncan, James 54
Dundee 164
Dyer, George, Bacon portraits 150
dystonia 45

Eastbourne (Sussex) 74–5, 238
Eastnor Castle (Herefordshire) 26
Eckley, Sophie 244–5, 246, 248
Eclectic Review, The (magazine) 204, 211
Edgeworth, Maria 8
Edinburgh Weekly Review (magazine) 242
Eikon Basilike (Charles I attrib.) 164
Elgin, Elizabeth Bruce, Countess of 245
Eliot, George 5, 9, 108, 233, 264*n*8; on *Aurora Leigh* 242–3
Elliott and Fry (photographers) 3, Pl.
encephalomyelitis 44, 272*n*44
Engels, Friedrich, *The Communist Manifesto* 165, 194
English Review, The (journal) 204, 208, 211
Epsom (Surrey) 32, 269*n*32
Essay on Mind, An 54–8, 61, 95, 104, 152, 251
'Essay on Woman' 26
Evening Mirror (New York newspaper) 140–41
Examiner, The (journal) 107, 186, 204, 249, 284*n*107

Factory Act (1844) 166
Fano (Italy) 196–7
Fanon, Frantz, *The Wretched of the Earth* 165

farming 20, 266–7n20
Fenton Hall (Northumberland) 265–6n16
Ferdinand II, King of the Two Sicilies 196
Ferrier, James 141–2
'Field, Michael' (Katharine Bradley and Edith Cooper) 9, 235, 264n9
Fielding, Henry, *Tom Jones* 64
Findens' Tableaux (annual) 94, 119, 127, 282n94
First Sikh War (1845–46) 165
Florence 185–6, 188–90, 218–19, 247, 250, 252, 254–5, 296n195, Pl.; Palazzo/Casa Guidi 189–90, 191, 194–5, 203, 255, 259, Pl.; Piazza de' Pitti 191–2, 295n191; Via delle Belle Donne 185; Via Maggio 191; Villa Brichieri 254, 255
Flush (spaniel) 6, 58, 120–22, 123, Pl.; kidnapped 136–8, 173, 288n138; travels to Italy with EBB 175, 177, 178; in Italy 190, 191, 197–8, 205, 206; death 229; *Flush: A Biography* (Woolf) 6
Fontaine de Vaucluse (France) 178
Forster, John 186, 204, 214, 303n239
Forster, Margaret, *Elizabeth Barrett Browning* 261, 263n6, 284n110
Fourier, Charles 193
Fox, Charles James 60
Fox, Eliza Bridell 246
Foxley (Herefordshire) 58
framing structures, literary 35–7
Francis & Co (publishers) 3, 241, 263n1
Franco-Austrian War (1859) 247
Fraser's Magazine 199, 211, 296n199
Freiburg, University of 46–7
Frocester (Gloucestershire) 111
Fuller, Margaret 299n211

Galignani's Messenger (newspaper) 209, 300n216
Galileo Galilei 188
Gandhi, Mahatma, Cartier-Bresson photographs 72
Garibaldi, Giuseppe 211, 250
Genoa 178–9, 218, 243, 246
George, Mary (*later* Domett) 297n201
Gibbon, Edward, on Homer 55
Gielgud, Sir John 5
Gilgamesh (Sumerian epic poem) 35–6
Gilpin, William 59, 274n59
Giovine Italia, La (Young Italy movement) 131, 190
Glasgow University 79, 278n79

'Glimpses into My Own Life and Literary Character' 23
Glisson, Francis 41
Globe and Traveller, The (newspaper) 53, 194, 209, 242
Gloucester 38–9, 41–2; County Lunatic Asylum 39; General Infirmary 38; Pump Room 38, 270n38; Spa Hotel 38, 42, 48, 270n38
Godey's Lady's Book (magazine) 140
Godwin, William, *Memoirs of the Author of a Vindication of the Rights of Woman* 12, 264n12
Goethe, Johann Wolfgang von 90, 211; *The Sorrows of Young Werther* 26
Gordigiani, Michele, portrait of EBB Pl.
Gordin, Madame (tutor) 24
Gordon, Anne Elizabeth (*later* Moulton-Barrett) 278n81
Gosforth (Northumberland): Kenton Lodge 16; St Nicholas's Church 33
Gothic Revivalism 136
Graham-Clarke, Arabella (EBB's aunt; 'Bummy') 15, 41, 64, 69–70, 111, 187–8, 209, 231, 276n69
Graham-Clarke, Arabella (*née* Altham; EBB's grandmother) 16, 23, 69, 265–6n16
Graham-Clarke, John (EBB's grandfather) 16–19, 30, 33, 204, 265n16, 266n16–17, 266n19, 276n69
Graham-Clarke, Mary (EBB's mother) *see* Moulton-Barrett, Mary
Graham's American Monthly Magazine 131, 204
Grammar Schools Act (1840) 288n135
Grand Tour 59, 152, 228
Gray, Thomas 60
Great Western Railway 161
Greenwood, John 81
Greer, Germaine, *Slip-Shod Sibyls* 159, 263n6
Grenzboten, Die (journal) 211
Grey, Charles Grey, 2nd Earl 82
Grisanowsky, E. G. T. 247
Guercino (Giovanni Barbieri) 196
Gurney, Arthur Thompson 208

Hanford, Compton John 186
Hanford, Frances ('Fanny') 186, 188
Harding, Dr (physician in Florence) 202, 203, 296n198, 299n210
Hare, Augustus William 90

Hare, Julius Charles 90
Harness, William 95, 96
Harper's New Monthly Magazine 208, 295*n*186
Harrow School 31–2
Hastings (Sussex) 54
Hastings, Lady Flora 288*n*134
Havannah (poodle) 22, 267*n*22, Pl.
Haworth, Euphrasia Fanny 245, 301*n*223
Hawthorne, Nathaniel 131, 245, 246, 254, 304*n*254
Hawthorne, Sophia 245
Haydon, Benjamin Robert 130, 133, 160, 282*n*93, 287*n*130
Hayes, Henry William 276*n*68
Hayter, Charles 267*n*22
Hedley, Arabella 169
Hedley, Jane 111, 169, 284*n*111
Hedley, Robert 111, 284*n*111
Heidegger, Martin 47
Helena, Grand Duchess of Russia 74
Hemans, Felicia 88, 208, 280*n*88
Henry VIII, King, Holbein portrait 72
Heraud, John Abraham 186
Herder, Johann Gottfried 90
Hervey, Thomas Kibble 299*n*209
Hewitt, C. A. 34, 270*n*34
Heywood, Thomas 270*n*34
'Hiram Powers' "Greek Slave"' 186
Hogarth, William 163
Hogg, James 93
Hogg, Thomas Jefferson 199
Hoggart, Richard 135
Holbein, Hans, the Younger, portrait of Henry VIII 72
Holland, Henry 270*n*34
Holland-Martin, Lady Anne 5
Home, Daniel Dunglas 245
Homer 52, 55, 106, 146, 167; *Odyssey* 134
homosexuality and bisexuality 109, 200–201, 206, 297*n*201
Hope End (Herefordshire) 13–15, 20–22, 28, 34, 49–50, 60, 70, 75–6, 128, 206, 265*n*14, 265*n*16, 270*n*34, Pl.
Hoppner, Richard and Isabella 188–9
Horne, Richard Hengist 105, 119–20, 290*n*152; *A New Spirit of the Age* 105, 147
Hosmer, Harriet 236; bronze cast of EBB and RB's hands Pl.
'House of Clouds, The' 287*n*128
Howe, Julia Ward 90; 'One Word More with E.B.B.' 248

Howick, Henry Grey, Viscount (*later* 3rd Earl Grey) 80, 278*n*80
Hughes, Ted 251
Hume, David 26
Hunt, Leigh 209, 241
Hunt, William Holman 237
Hunter, George 86, 279–80*n*86, 284*n*108
Hunter, Mary 86, 111, 284*n*107, 284*n*108
Huntingdon, Selina Hastings, Countess of 31
Husserl, Edmund 47
hypnotherapy *see* mesmerism
hypochondria 43–4

imperialism 165, 292*n*165
imprisoned woman, as cultural figure 105, 108
Independent, The (American magazine) 250, 251
industrialisation 20, 166, 241
Irigaray, Luce 98
Irving, Edward 55, 273*n*55
Isaacson, Mary (*later* Altham) 265*n*16
Isle of Wight 74–5, 240
'Isobel's Child' 96
Italian unification *see* Risorgimento

Jago, Mr (physician) 177
Jamaica 18, 28–30, 79–84, 188, 268*n*30, 278*n*80–81; religion 68, 81, 278*n*81; slavery 17, 29, 80–83, 278*n*80; sugar production 17, 29, 80, 266*n*17 *see also* Cinnamon Hill
Jameson, Anna 161, 162, 176–7, 179, 186, 200, 218, 231, 236, 245, 250; *Legends of the Madonna* 214; *Sacred and Legendary Art* 294*n*179
Jelf, Sir James 270*n*38
Jenner, Edward 39
Jewish Expositor and Friend of Israel, The (journal) 54
Joan of Arc 28, 133
Johnson, Samuel, *Lives of the Most Eminent English Poets* 12
Jones, Jennifer 5
Jonson, Ben 164
Judaism 54
Julius Caesar 52
Jung, Johann Heinrich *see* Stilling, Heinrich

Kavaler-Adler, Susan, *The Compulsion to Create* 159
Keats, John 88, 141; death 6, 52, 152, 252
Keble, John 85
Kelley, Philip 5, 261
Kemble, Fanny 214, 228

Kenyon, John: background and early life 57–8, 90, 164; appearance and character 58, 91; friendship with EBB 57–8, 63, 109, 122; literary life in London 90–91, 100, 281n90; makes introductions for EBB 58, 90–93, 94, 96; and publication of EBB's works 101, 130; buys house in Torquay 132–3, 286n122; and EBB's introduction to RB 58, 142–3, 146; EBB's social outings with 161; and EBB's secret romance and marriage to RB 168, 177, 186, 187; during EBB and RB's visits to England 214, 218, 237, 240–41; financial support for EBB and RB 58, 218, 229, 240; later life and death 229, 240–41, 303n240; EBB's correspondence with 106, 193; writings 100

'King Victor Emmanuel Entering Florence' 250

Kingsley, Charles 217

Kinney, Elizabeth 223, 236

Kinney, William 223

Kipling, Rudyard 9

Knibb, William 81

Knickerbocker, The (magazine) 140

Knight, Charles 273n54

Knight, Richard Payne 274n59

La Spezia (Italy) 206

Ladies of Llangollen (Eleanor Butler and Sarah Ponsonby) 95

Lamartine, Alphonse de 193

Lamb, Charles 90, 93

Lamb, Joseph 265n16

Lamb, Mary 90

Lancasterian System (education method) 288n135

Landon, Laetitia Elizabeth 87, 88

Landor, Walter Savage 90, 91, 93, 106, 244, 250, 281n91

Langland, William 128

Langley, Henry G. 140, 141

Lapotaire, Jane 5

Larkin, Philip, 'An Arundel Tomb' 254

Last Poems 251

Laughton, Charles 5

Lawrence, Sir Thomas, *Sarah Barrett Moulton: Pinkie* 265n15

'Lay of the Brown Rosary, The' 136

'Lay of the Early Rose, A' 133–4

Le Havre 1, 3, 174, 175, 245–6, 293n174

Ledbury (Herefordshire) 75, 76; Parish Church 267n21

Leghorn *see* Livorno

Lehmann, Rudolf 246

Leighton, Sir Frederic 227, 237, 246

Lena, Annunziata 244, 253, 255, 303n244

Lenin, Vladimir, *Imperialism* 165

Leonardo da Vinci, *The Last Supper* 212

Leopold II, Grand Duke of Tuscany 191, 247, 300n219

'Lessons from the Gorse' 287n128

Levi, Primo 6

Levinas, Emmanuel 46–7, 220

Ley, James and Louisa 191

Liberator, The (magazine) 211

Liberty Bell, The (abolitionist anthology; 1848) 167

Lincoln, Abraham 224

Lincoln, Mary Todd 224

literacy 135, 264n11, 288n135

Literary Gazette, The 107, 211, 239

Little Bookham (Surrey) 170

'Little Mattie' 251

Livorno (Leghorn) 151, 152, 179, 199, 200, 206, 237, 243, 246

Locke, John 26; *An Essay Concerning Human Understanding* 23

Lockhart, John Gibson 228; *Life of Robert Burns* 12

London: Bayswater 300n218; Camden 90, 138; Covent Garden 91, 92; Crawford Street 103, 283n103; Ealing 245; Grays Inn Road 135; Hampstead Heath 173; Hodgson's British and Foreign Subscription Library 175, 293n175; London Zoo 93; Marylebone 51, 85, 89–90, 103, 136, 171–2, 213, 293n175; Paddington Chapel 171; Regent Square Chapel 95; Regent's Park 93, 160; Shoreditch 173; St John's Wood 173; St Marylebone parish church 171–2; Vauxhall 174; Warwick Crescent 255; York Street Chapel 164 *see also* New Cross (Surrey)

London (Barrett family homes): Gloucester Place 89–90, 95, 103; Wimpole Street 101–4, 136, 170, 213, 238

London Ragged School Union 135, 229, 288n135

'Lord Walter's Wife' 251

Losh, James 266n17

Loudon, John Claudius 34

Lowell, James Russell 131, 141, 167

Lowry, Malcolm 6

Lowry, Wilson 275n64

Lucas, John, portraits of Mary Russell
   Mitford 282*n*93
Lucerne 212
Lushington, Vernon 250
Lyon 178, 218

Macaire, Louis Cyrus 3, 245, 246, Pl.
Macaire-Warnod, Jean Victor 3, 246
Mackenzie, Mary 246
Maclise, Daniel, *The Fraserians* 296*n*199
MacNeice, Louis 184
Macpherson, Gerardine *see* Bate, Gerardine
Macpherson, Robert 186, 294*n*186
Macready, William Charles 91, 92, 204, 239
Madeira 8, 32, 269*n*32
Magenta, Battle of (1859) 247
Mahony, Francis Sylvester ('Father Prout')
   197, 198–202, 245, 296*n*198, 297*n*200
Malvern (Worcestershire) 13–14, 61, 62, 128;
   Festival Theatre 5
Manchester Guardian (newspaper) 211, 249
Mantua 196, 212
Marciano (Italy) 247, 250
Marseille 178, 190, 237, 243
Martin, James 77, 277*n*76
Martin, Julia (*née* Vignoles) 76–8, 178, 180–
   81, 214, 244, 277*n*76
Martineau, Harriet 131–2, 146
Martinique 85
Marx, Karl, *The Communist Manifesto* 165,
   194
Mason, Cyrus 163
Mathews, Cornelius 131; *Poems on Man*
   287*n*131
Mazzini, Giuseppe 211, 217
McSwiney, Daniel 57, 267*n*24, 274*n*57
measles 43, 44
'Meditation in Tuscany, A' 192–3, 194, 210,
   296*n*193
Medwin, Thomas 199
Melville, Herman 131
Mérimée, Prosper 237
Merleau-Ponty, Maurice 184
mesmerism 132, 237
Methodism 68–9, 81, 276*n*68–9
Metropolitan Magazine, The 107, 284*n*107
Mew, Charlotte 9, 235
Michelangelo 161, 206; tomb 188
Mignaty, George 255
Mignet, François-Auguste 237
Milan 212
Millais, Sir John Everett, *Mariana* 105

Milnes, J. N., 'The Illnesses of Elizabeth
   Barrett Browning' 272*n*44
Milnes, Richard Monckton (*later* 1st Baron
   Houghton) 178
Miłosz, Czesław 46
Milsand, Joseph 217, 245
Milton, John 60, 141, 303*n*242; *Paradise Lost*
   22, 154, 161, 284*n*107; *Paradise Regain'd*
   164; *Poems on Several Occasions* 164; 'When
   I consider how my light is spent' 258
mirrors, two-way 124–5, 259
Missolonghi (Italy) 152
Mitford, George 94
Mitford, Mary Russell: appearance and
   character 93–4; early life and education
   297*n*200; life in Berkshire 93, 94, 126,
   282*n*93, 287*n*126; literary life and
   reputation 93–4, 108–9, 282*n*94; beginning
   of friendship with EBB 58, 93–9, 100–101;
   support for EBB and publication of her
   works 94, 101, 109, 122, 127, 130, 285*n*116;
   affection for EBB 109, 120; gives EBB
   spaniel Flush 58, 120–22; visits EBB at
   Wimpole Street 139; views on RB 147,
   164–5, 200–201, 204; and EBB's secret
   marriage and flight to Italy 177, 178; and
   EBB's life in Italy 192; during EBB and
   RB's visits to England 214; publication
   of memoirs 216; death 230; EBB's
   correspondence with 101, 103, 109, 118,
   123, 129, 132–3, 138, 143, 146, 148, 154,
   181, 192, 204, 224, 284*n*109, 288*n*139,
   292*n*165; *Belford Regis* 282*n*93; *Our Village*
   93, 112, 282*n*93; *Recollections of a Literary
   Life* 216; *Sketches of English Character and
   Scenery* 93
Modena (Italy) 212
Montego Bay (Jamaica) 28, 278*n*81
Monthly Christian Spectator, The 211
Monthly Chronicle, The 107
Monthly Review, The 107
Moore, John Collingham 58
Moore, Thomas 12
Moorhouse, Paul 149–50
Moravian Church 81, 82
More, Sir Thomas, *Utopia* 164
Morning Chronicle, The (London newspaper)
   211
Morning Post, The (London newspaper)
   204–5, 208
morphine *see* opium and morphine
Morris, Jane 2

Motherwell, William 141

Moulton, Charles (EBB's grandfather) 18, 32, 269*n*32

Moulton, Edward Barrett (EBB's father) *see* Moulton-Barrett, Edward Barrett

Moulton, Elizabeth (*née* Barrett; EBB's grandmother; 'Grandmama'): family background 18; leaves Jamaica for England 18, 265*n*15; EBB named after 15; and EBB's childhood and upbringing 21, 28, 51, 53, 78; life in London 51, 89; EBB stays with at Hastings 54; death 75–6; legacies 85, 102

Moulton, George Goodin (EBB's uncle) 265*n*15

Moulton, Robert (EBB's great-uncle) 32, 269*n*32

Moulton, Sarah (EBB's aunt; 'Pinkie') 15, 18, 265*n*15

Moulton-Barrett, Alfred (EBB's brother; 'Daisy') 15, 50, 115, 137, 188, 213, 237, 244, 288*n*138, 289*n*140, 295*n*188, Pl.

Moulton-Barrett, Amelia (EBB's sister-in-law) 245

Moulton-Barrett, Arabella (EBB's sister): childhood and adolescence 22–3, 42–3, 49, 50, 267*n*25; ill-health 42–3, 49; and EBB's relationship with Hugh Stuart Boyd 62; family moves to Sidmouth 76; life in Sidmouth 77, 78, 79, 277*n*78, 278*n*79; family moves to London 88–9; life in London 111, 156, 160; with EBB during convalescence in Torquay 111, 114, 116, 118, 121; death of brother Edward 117; and kidnapping of EBB's spaniel Flush 288*n*138; and EBB's plans to travel to Italy 153, 160; and EBB's secret romance and marriage to RB 156, 171, 172, 173, 175, 187; religious life 171; work with Ragged Schools Union 135, 229; and sister Henrietta's marriage 209; during EBB and RB's visits to England 213, 240; visits EBB at Le Havre 245; later life 230–31, 302*n*231, 302*n*237; EBB's correspondence with 106, 112, 168, 186–7, 194–5, 209, 226, 227, 238, 243, 245, 298–9*n*207, 299–300*n*212, 300*n*215

Moulton-Barrett, Charles (EBB's brother; 'Stormie'): appearance and character 79, 278*n*79; birth 15; nickname 15; childhood and adolescence 42, 50, 79, 278*n*79; family moves to London 88–9; sent on business

to family estates in Jamaica 79, 126, 187, 285*n*114; visits Egypt with brother Henry 152; and EBB's marriage to RB 187; marriage and children 188, 298*n*188; death of father 244; later life 79, 188, 295*n*188

Moulton-Barrett, Edward Barrett (EBB's father; 'Papa'): family background and wealth 14, 18, 28–30; appearance and character 31, 34, 49, 64, 75–6, 153; birth 14, 28; childhood and early life 18, 28–9, 30, 31–2, 75, 84, 269*n*32; marriage to Mary Graham-Clarke 18, 33; early married life 16, 18–19, 33–4, 269*n*33; moves family to Hope End estate in Herefordshire 14–16, 19, 34, 75, 153; family life and children's upbringing 21, 26, 28, 56–7; encouragement of EBB's literary ambitions 8, 22, 26, 27, 53–54, 104; political and religious views 27, 68–9, 75, 76, 81, 104–5, 153, 166; and EBB's first illness and confinement in Gloucester 40, 42; and EBB's early works 53–4, 61, 87, 101, 104; and EBB's relationship with Hugh Stuart Boyd 62; death of wife 70, 75; financial problems 67, 69, 76, 84, 275*n*67; forced to sell Hope End 74–6, 84, 153; moves family to Sidmouth 74–6; life in Sidmouth 79, 87–8, 278*n*79; sends sons on business to family estates in Jamaica 79–80, 84, 102, 153, 285*n*114; business trips to London 84–5, 279*n*84; falls ill in London 84–5; family leaves Sidmouth and moves to London 88–9; family life at Gloucester Place 89–90, 95–6, 101; death of brother Sam 102, 283*n*102; family moves to Wimpole Street 101–4, 153; family life at Wimpole Street 104–5, 115–16; and EBB's chronic lung disease and three-year convalescence in Torquay 110, 113, 115, 118, 119, 122, 285*n*115; death of son Sam 115–16, 153, 285*n*115; death of son Edward 117–18, 283*n*104; contemplates buying estate in Wales 119; permits EBB to return to London 122–3; and kidnapping of EBB's spaniel Flush 137–8, 288*n*138; and EBB's secret romance with RB 152, 156, 174–5, 292*n*169; and EBB's plans to travel to Italy 152, 153–5, 160; temporarily relocates family to Little Bookham, Surrey 170, 171, 173; reaction to EBB's secret wedding and flight to Italy 177, 187, 213–14; and other children's

relationships and marriages 188, 209,
243–4; during EBB and RB's visits to
England 213–14, 237–8, 240; injured in
accident 230; declining health 237; death
188, 243–4
Moulton-Barrett, Edward (EBB's brother;
'Bro'): appearance and character 53, 116,
Pl.; birth 33; childhood and adolescence
15, 24, 25, 31, 33, 42, 50, 51, 53, 77, 89,
265n15, 273n51, Pl.; EBB's closeness to
25, 42, 51, 53, 77, 118, 158; and EBB's
ill-health 42, 51, 271n42; and EBB's
relationship with Hugh Stuart Boyd
62; death of mother 70; family moves
to Sidmouth 76; life in Sidmouth 77,
277n79; sent on business to family
estates in Jamaica 79–80, 82–4, 152, 153,
279n82; returns to England 84; family
moves to London 88–9; with EBB during
convalescence in Torquay 111, 113, 116,
152, 285n113; death in drowning accident
116–18, 126, 131, 216, 227, 251, 283n104
Moulton-Barrett, George (EBB's brother):
appearance and character 79; childhood
and adolescence 50, 79, 278n79; family
moves to London 88–9; legal career
79, 88, 126, 281n91; with EBB during
convalescence in Torquay 111, 112; and
publication of EBB's works 129; and EBB's
plans to travel to Italy 153, 160; and EBB's
secret marriage and flight to Italy 175,
177, 187; during EBB and RB's visits to
London 213, 237, 240; and father's injury
in accident 230; visits EBB at Le Havre
245; later life 91, 266n19, 277n77; EBB's
correspondence with 225
Moulton-Barrett, Henrietta (later Cook;
EBB's sister; 'Addles'): appearance and
character 50–51, 61–2, 102; childhood
and adolescence 15, 22, 39, 48, 49, 50–51,
61–2; closeness to brother Sam 102; ill-
health 39, 42–3, 44; on EBB's sixteenth
birthday 48; stays with grandmother in
Hastings 54; and EBB's relationship with
Hugh Stuart Boyd 62; death of mother
69–70; family moves to Sidmouth 76;
life in Sidmouth 77, 79, 277n79, 278n79;
family moves to London 88–9; and EBB's
friendship with John Kenyon 109; with
EBB during convalescence in Torquay
111, 116, 118–19, 187, 284n111; death of
brothers Sam and Edward 117, 118–19;

family life at Wimpole Street 139, 153,
156; courtship with Surtees Cook 155,
164, 168–9, 187, 188; and EBB's secret
romance and marriage to RB 156, 173, 187;
and EBB's life in Italy 190, 192, 295n191;
marriage and children 188, 203, 208–9,
215, 302n231; family life in Taunton 213,
215, 241; during EBB and RB's visits
to England 213, 214, 217, 241; death
of father 243–4; death 251, 252; EBB's
correspondence with 38, 61–2, 187, 192,
240, 243, 295n191, 297n200, 301n223
Moulton-Barrett, Henry (EBB's brother):
appearance and character 115–16;
childhood and adolescence 50, 278n79;
travelling as young man 115–16, 126, 152;
and kidnapping of EBB's spaniel Flush
137–8; relationship with father 153, 187,
295n187; and EBB's marriage to RB 187;
marriage 245; visits EBB at Le Havre 245
Moulton-Barrett, Mary (née Graham-
Clarke; EBB's mother; 'Mamma'): family
background 16–18; appearance and
character 19; birth and childhood 16, 19;
marriage to Edward Moulton-Barrett
18, 33; early married life 16, 33, 265n16,
269n33; family moves to Hope End estate
in Herefordshire 16, 19, 75, 265n16; family
life and children's upbringing 26, 28, 50, 62,
268n28; encouragement of EBB's literary
ambitions 22, 26, 53–4; poetry-writing
and drawing 23, Pl.; and EBB's first illness
and confinement in Gloucester 41, 43;
and EBB's first publishing successes 53–4;
death of mother 69, 276n69; declining
health 62, 69–70; death 65, 69–71, 227
Moulton-Barrett, Mary (EBB's sister), death
aged four 21, 23, 70, 267n21
Moulton-Barrett, Mary Clementina (EBB's
aunt) 80–81
Moulton-Barrett, Octavius (EBB's brother;
'Occy') 69, 115, 126, 213
Moulton-Barrett, Samuel Barrett (EBB's
uncle): childhood and early life 18, 32,
269n32; EBB's childhood visits and trips
with 21, 28; on EBB's character 193;
political career 27, 32, 80, 89, 278n80; and
EBB's ill-health 41–2; and publication
of EBB's works 54, 273n54; as potential
mentor to EBB 57; returns to Jamaica
80; life in Jamaica and management of
family estates 80–82, 83, 84, 102, 110, 188,

278n81, 283n102; illegitimate daughter
188, 295n188; death 102, 227, 283n102;
bequest to EBB 102, 170, 283n102; EBB's
correspondence with 24, 57
Moulton-Barrett, Samuel (EBB's brother):
appearance and character 102–3, Pl.;
childhood and adolescence 50, 51, 77, 89,
273n51, Pl.; closeness to sister Henrietta
102, 118; family moves to Sidmouth 76;
life in Sidmouth 77; sent on business to
family estates in Jamaica 84, 88, 102, 114,
115, 152, 153, 285n114; returns to England
102–3; life in London 103; death 114–15,
118, 153, 227, 285n115
Moulton-Barrett, Septimus (EBB's brother;
'Sette'): appearance and character 116; birth
48, 273n48; childhood and adolescence
50, 76, 115–16; family moves to Sidmouth
76; family moves to London 88–9; family
life in London 115–16; legal training 126;
and kidnapping of EBB's spaniel Flush
137; joins brother Stormie in Jamaica 188;
illegitimate daughter 188, 295n188; during
EBB and RB's visits to London 213
Mountcashell, Margaret King, Lady 282n95
Moxon, Edward 129–30, 134–5, 140, 215,
239, 287n130, 287n131, 298n204
Müller, Minny von 216, 300n216
Mushet, Harriet 66
'Musical Instrument, A' 97
'My Character and Bro's Compared' 23–4

Naples 250
Napoleon I, Emperor 133, 287n130, 292n165
Napoleon III, Emperor 216, 218, 219, 247,
249, 250
'Napoleon III in Italy' 247
Napoleonic Wars 54, 59
Nash, John 270n34
National Schools 288n135
'Nature's Remorses' 251
Nether Stowey (Somerset) 90
New Cross (Surrey) 142, 163, 213
New Monthly Magazine, The 87, 92, 280n87,
289n140
New York 103, 131; Authors' Club 3
New-York Daily Times 242
New-York Daily Tribune 130, 263n3, 303n242
New-York Weekly Tribune 130
New Zealand 197
Newcastle upon Tyne 16, 17–18, 21, 30,
165–6, 166 see also Gosforth

Newman, John Henry 85
Nichols, John 303n242
'Night and the Merry Man' 96
Nightingale, Florence 42, 231
Nonconformism 68–9, 79, 81, 85–6, 135, 147,
153, 164, 223, 276n68, 278n81, 288n135 see
also Methodism
'North and the South, The' 8–9, 252
North British Review (journal) 242, 303n242
nursing 42, 231
Nuttall, George Ricketts 39, 40, 42, 270–
71n39, 271n40
Nuttall, Thomas 270–71n39

Ogilvy, David and Eliza 300n212
'On a Portrait of Wordsworth by B. R.
Haydon' 130
'On the Cruelty of Forcement to Man' 8, 27,
268n27
One Thousand and One Nights (Islamic Golden
Age folktales) 36
opium and morphine 43, 44, 132, 161, 181,
202, 203, 248, 253, 254
orientalism 34, 165, 270n34, 290n152
Orléans (France) 175, 177
Orme, Mrs (governess) 119
Ossoli, Giovanni d' 299n211
Ossoli, Margaret Fuller d' 299n211
Overbury Court (Worcestershire) 277n76
Ovid 52
Owen, Robert 224
Oxford Anthology of English Literature
(Kermode et al. eds) 5
Oxford Movement 85

Padua 212
Page, William 226, 246
Paine (Farnham family) 217
Paine, Thomas 26
Palgrave, Francis Turner 218
Pan (god) 97
Paris (landmarks and places): Champs-
Élysées 215, 237, 239; Hôtel aux Armes
de la Ville de Paris 176, 213, 215; Hôtel
de la Ville l'Évêque 218; Hôtel de Rivoli
28; Jardin des Plantes 28; Louvre 28, 239;
Messagerie Hotel 176; Opéra Comique 28;
Théâtre Français 28; Tuileries 28
Paris, EBB visits: in childhood 28; on route
to Italy following marriage 176–7; with RB
and Pen (1851–52) 213, 215–17, 218; with
RB and Pen (1855–56) 237, 238–9; with

RB and Pen (1858) 245, 246
Parma 212
Patmore, Coventry 141, 217, 242, 303*n*242; *The Angel in the House* 57
Perugia 225
Peruzzi, Simone Luigi 255
pet kidnapping 136–8, 173, 288*n*138
Peters, Elissa 30, 268*n*30
Petrarch 178, 212
photography 1–4, 72, 97–8, 220–21, 245–6, 252, 255, 304*n*255, Pl.
Picturesque (aesthetic) 34, 49, 58–9, 60, 141, 274*n*59
Pisa 151, 152, 177–8, 179–82, 189
Pius IX, Pope 196
Plath, Sylvia 134, 251
Plato 24, 67
Plymouth 110
Plymouth Brethren 85
Poe, Edgar Allan 140–41
Poems (1844) 32, 129–30, 134–5, 140–42, 207, 289*n*140
Poems (1850) 186, 189, 207–8, 209, 233, 287*n*131, 299*n*211, 303*n*239
Poems (1853) 219
Poems (1856) 239, 303*n*239
Poems Before Congress 249–50, 304*n*247
Poet Laureate, appointment of 209–10, 299*n*209
poliomyelitis 44
Pope, Alexander 10, 52, 60; *The Dunciad* 52; 'Essay on Man' 26; *Iliad* (trans.) 22; *The Rape of the Lock* 52
portraiture 72–3, 150, 161, 220, 258–9; portraits and likenesses of EBB 1–4, 9, 22, 46, 93, 220–21, 245, 246, 252, 261*n*1–3, 267*n*22, 289*n*140, Pl. *see also* photography
Portsmouth 174
Powers, Hiram 186
Prato Fiorito (Italy) 203, 224–5
pregnancy 108, 138–9, 238, 244; EBB's pregnancies 181, 192, 193, 196, 198, 202–3, 206, 208, 210, 238, 295*n*192
Pre-Raphaelite Brotherhood 2, 237
Press, The (newspaper) 249
press-ganging 27, 268*n*27
Price, Sir Uvedale 58–60, 62, 63, 274*n*62; *An Essay on the Modern Pronunciation of the Greek and Latin Languages* 62, 275*n*63; *An Essay on the Picturesque* 58–9
Prince, Mary 82–3, 279*n*82

Pringle, Thomas 82–3
Prinsep, Valentine Cameron, drawing of EBB Pl.
Pritchard, James 293*n*171
Procter, Bryan Waller ('Barry Cornwall') 90, 178, 214, 281*n*91
Prometheus Bound/Unbound (Aeschylus; EBB trans.) 87, 94, 95, 100, 101, 207, 280*n*87
Prospective Review, The (journal) 211
Proudhon, Pierre-Joseph 193
'Prout, Father' *see* Mahony, Francis Sylvester
Psyche Apocalypté 119–20, 127
Pugin, Augustus 136
Punch (magazine) 199, 296*n*199

Quadrilatero (fortresses) 196
Quarterly Review, The 107

race and racism 8, 29–31, 85 *see also* slavery and slave trade
Radetzky, Joseph, Count 196
Ragged Schools 135, 229, 288*n*135
railways 161, 174, 175, 178, 294*n*175
Ramsgate (Kent) 14, 25, 267*n*25
Raphael 161
Ravenna 197, 296*n*197
Read, Thomas Buchanan 214, Pl.
Reade, John 217
Reading (Berkshire) 93, 120
Rembrandt van Rijn, self-portraits 73, 161
Report of the Children's Employment Commission (1842) 165, 292*n*165
Revista Britannica (journal) 211
Revolutions of 1848 193–4, 195–6
Revue des deux mondes, La (journal) 217
Rham, William Lewis 33
'Rhapsody of Life's Progress' 133, 287*n*131
Ricasoli, Bettino, 2nd Baron 253
Richmond (Yorkshire), parliamentary constituency 32, 80, 278*n*80
'Riga's Song' 251
Righi, Signor (member of ducal guard in Florence) 203, 210, 297*n*203, 300*n*215
Riley, Bridget 149–50
Rimini 197
Risorgimento 190–91, 193, 195–6, 247, 249–50
Ristori, Adelaide 237, 246
Robinson, Henry Crabb 90, 91, 281*n*90
Rogers, Samuel 161, 214
Romagnoli, Ferdinando 236–7, 238, 244, 256, 302*n*237
Romagnoli, Orestes Wilson 238, 244

Roman Catholicism *see* Catholicism
'Romance of the Ganges' 96, 282n94
'Romaunt of Margret, The' 92, 101
'Romaunt of the Page, The' 136
Rome 152, 200, 225–9, 246–7, 247–52, Pl.
Rose, Gillian, *Judaism and Modernity* 183
Ross on Wye (Herefordshire) 59
Rossetti, Dante Gabriel 180, 214, 237, 239;
  portrait of EBB 2–3, 4, 9, 46, 245, 263n2,
  Pl.
Rossetti, William Michael 250, 263n2
Roth, Philip 5
Rouen 28, 175–76
Rousseau, Jean-Jacques 26; *Confessions* 11–12
Rubens, Sir Peter Paul 161
'Runaway Slave at Pilgrim's Point, The' 166–7,
  168, 241
Ruskin, Effie (*née* Gray) 218
Ruskin, John 78, 218, 237; on *Aurora Leigh* 5,
  9, 241; *Modern Painters* 239
Russell, Odo (*later* 1st Baron Ampthill)
  247
Rutter, Elizabeth 16, 266n16
Ryle, Gilbert 7

Said, Edward, *Orientalism* 165
Sand, George 108, 157, 217, 236, 300n217
Sartoris, Adelaide (*née* Kemble) 228, 237
Sartoris, Edward John 228
Saturday Review, The (magazine) 249
Saunders and Otley (publishers) 96
Scarlett, James (*later* 1st Baron Abinger) 18
Scarlett, Philip 269n32
Scheherazade (*One Thousand and One Nights*
  character) 36
Schiller, Friedrich 90
Scotsman, The (newspaper) 211
Scully, Dr (Torquay physician) 114, 122
séances 223–4, 245
'Sea-Side Meditation, A' 54
self-portraiture 73, 161, 258–9
Seraphim, The 96, 101, 107–8, 127, 128, 207,
  280n87, 284n107
Seurat, Georges 149
Severn, Joseph 252
Seward, Anna 95
sexuality 57, 105, 109, 156, 235, 272n48;
  homosexuality and bisexuality 109, 200–
  201, 206, 297n201
Shaftesbury, Anthony Ashley-Cooper, 7th
  Earl of 135
Shakespeare, William 128, 186, 209, 241,

301n223; sexuality 201, 206; *Measure for
  Measure* 105; *Othello* 22; *The Tempest* 22
Sharp, William, *Life of Robert Browning*
  298n204
Sharpe, Samuel 81, 278n81
Shearer, Norma 5
Shelley, Clara 189
Shelley, Mary 5, 8, 108, 129, 189, 205–6,
  282n95; *Frankenstein* 6, 36, 56, 233
Shelley, Percy Bysshe 52, 53, 107, 135, 141,
  188, 282n95, 284n108; in Italy 152, 188–9,
  205–6, 225; death 152, 246; *Adonais* 52,
  88; *Letters of Percy Bysshe Shelley* (forgery)
  215, 239; *Poetical Works* (1839) 129; 'Rarely,
  rarely comest thou' 143
Shepherd, Lady Mary 109
Siddal, Lizzie 2
Sidmouth (Devon) 74–5, 86–8, 103, 277n78–
  9; Belle Vue (*later* Cedar Shade) 79, 88,
  277n79; Marsh Congregational Chapel
  86, 108; Rafarel House 74, 75, 78–9, 88,
  277n78
Siena 210, 247, 250
Sikh War, First (1845–46) 165
Silverthorne, James 171
Sitwell, Dame Edith 5
Slavery Abolition Act (1833) 82, 83
slavery and slave trade 17, 19–20, 29, 31, 76,
  80–84, 153, 166–7, 249, 269n32, 278n80 *see
  also* abolitionism
'Sleep, The' 255
Smiles, Samuel, *The Life of George Stephenson*
  264n12
Smith, Ann 283n103
Smith, Charlotte Turner 207
Smith, Stevie 5
Sobraon, Battle of (1846) 165
Society for the Propagation of the Gospel
  (SPG) 168, 292n168
Solferino, Battle of (1859) 247
Somers, John Cocks, 1st Earl 26–7, 78; *A
  Defence of the Constitution of Great Britain*
  27
Sonnets from the Portuguese 5, 32, 168, 173,
  206–7, 298–9n207, 303n242
Southampton 174
Southey, Robert 90, 123, 281n90, 296n199;
  Life of Nelson 12
Spectator, The (magazine) 141, 249
Spencer, Bernard 184
Spencer, Lady Diana (*later* Princess of Wales)
  220

Spender, Sir Stephen, 'One More New
  Botched Beginning' 183–4
Spenser, Edmund 53, 60, 128; *The Faerie
  Queene* 128, 134
spinal disease and treatment 40–45
spiritualism 7, 223–4, 244–5, 248
St Gotthard Pass (Switzerland) 212
St Kitts 162, 163, 168, 292*n*168
'Stanzas Addressed to Miss Landon' 87–8,
  92
'Stanzas on the Death of Lord Byron' 53–4,
  88, 273*n*53
Stendhal syndrome 161
Sterne, Laurence, *Tristram Shandy* 36
Stilling, Heinrich (Johann Heinrich Jung),
  Theory of Pneumatology 133
Stoddard, Richard Henry 3
Story, Edith (*later* Marchesa Peruzzi de'
  Medici) 226–7, 229, 304*n*247
Story, Emelyn 223, 225, 226–7, 246
Story, Joe 226, 227
Story, William Wetmore 223, 225, 226–7,
  229, 246, 252
Stowe, Harriet Beecher 243
Strachan, George 168, 292*n*168
Strachan, Margaret (*later* Tittle) 168,
  292*n*168
Stratford de Redcliffe, Stratford Canning, 1st
  Viscount 247
Stratten, James 171
Sublime and Beautiful (aesthetic) 58–9, 60
suffrage, women's 8, 48
sugar production and trade 17, 29, 80,
  265*n*16, 266*n*17
Sunbeam, The (magazine) 107
Sunday schools 86, 288*n*135
Surtees, Aubone 266*n*16
Surtees, Mary (*née* Altham) 266*n*16
Swallowfield (Berkshire) 282*n*93
Swedenborgianism 223, 301*n*223
Swinburne, Algernon 9

table-rapping 223–4, 245
'Tale of Villafranca, A' 248
Talfourd, Field 246
Talfourd, Sir Thomas Noon 91, 281*n*91; *Ion*
  91, 93, 94, 200
tardive dystonia 45
Tasso, Torquato 144
Taunton (Somerset) 213, 215, 241
Taylor, Sir Henry 217
TB *see* tuberculosis

Teignmouth (Devon) 117
Teniers, David, the Younger 163–4
Tennyson, Alfred Tennyson, 1st Baron
  128–9, 130, 141, 146, 209–10, 298*n*204,
  300*n*213; EBB meets 213, 223, 237; 'The
  Lady of Shalott' 105, 136; 'Mariana' 105;
  In Memoriam 210; *Poems* (1842) 129; 'The
  Princess' 225
Tennyson, Emily Tennyson, Lady 213
Tennyson, Frederick 236
Tennyson, Hallam (*later* 2nd Baron
  Tennyson) 218
Terni (Italy) 225
Thackeray, Isabella 227, 301*n*227
Thackeray, William Makepeace 227, 251, 252;
  Vanity Fair 199, 296*n*199
Thackeray Ritchie, Anne 227, 236, 238,
  301*n*227
Thames Ditton (Surrey) 214
third dimension, in art 149–50
Thomson, Anne 301*n*227
'Thought on Thoughts, A' 87
'Thoughts versus Words' 66–7
Three Mile Cross (Berkshire) 93, 282*n*93
Thurlbear (Somerset), Stoke Court 251
Tighe, George 282*n*95
Tighe, Mary 95, 280*n*88, 282*n*95
Times, The (newspaper) 203; publication of
  EBB's poems 87, 280*n*87
Tintern Abbey (Monmouthshire) 59
Tintoretto 161
Tiresias (mythological figure) 146
Titian 161
Tittle, John 163, 168, 291*n*163, 292*n*168
Tittle, Margaret (*later* Browning) 168,
  292*n*168
Tittle, Margaret (*née* Strachan) 292*n*168
Toleration Act (1688) 81
Torquay (Devon) 110–22, 132–3, 277*n*79,
  284*n*111; Beacon Terrace 111, 113–14; The
  Braddens 111, 284*n*111
Tree, Ellen (*later* Kean) 91
Treherne, Elizabeth *see* Crow, Elizabeth
Treherne, William 138
Trepsack, Mary ('Treppy'): family background
  and ethnicity 18, 85, 279*n*85; early life in
  Jamaica 85; friendship with Barrett family
  18, 85; and Barrett children's upbringing
  28, 53, 273*n*51, 279*n*85; and publication
  of EBB's works 54; life in London 85, 89;
  EBB meets in London 161, 168; and EBB's
  secret romance and marriage to RB 168,

187; and EBB's sister Henrietta's marriage 209; later life and death 230, 243
Trepsack, William 85
Trilling, Lionel 5
Trinity Hall (Cambridge) 32
tuberculosis (TB) 38–9, 102, 110, 152, 246, 284n110, 303n246
Tulk, Charles Augustus 191, 301n223
Turin 218
Turner, J. M. W. 218; *The Angel Standing in the Sun* 108
Twickenham (Middlesex) 213
Two Poems by Elizabeth Barrett and Robert Browning 229

Ugolino family 189, 295n189
United States Magazine and Democratic Review 131, 140
Updike, John 5

Valpy, Abraham John 87, 91, 101
Vanneck, Charles 117
Vasari, Giorgio 179
Venice 188, 196, 212, 299n212; Ca' Rezzonico 256
Ventnor (Isle of Wight) 240
Verona 196
Victor Emmanuel II, King of Italy 249, 250
Victoria, Queen 134, 288n134; accession 134, 288n134; marriage and children 116, 285–6n116, 288n134
Vienna 195
Vienna, Congress of (1815) 190
Vignoles, John 277n76
Villafranca, Treaty of (1859) 247
Virgil 52
'Virgin Mary to Child Jesus' 96
'Vision of Poets, A' 136
Voltaire 26

Waddell, Hope 115
Wallis, Henry, 'The Death of Chatterton' 6
Waterhouse, John William 105
Weir, J. G., 'The Illnesses of Elizabeth Barrett Browning' 272n44
Weiss, Ellen Buchanan 44
Wellington, Arthur Wellesley, 1st Duke of 130
Westminster Review (journal) 242, 303n242
Wheatley, Phillis 31, 269n31
'Where's Agnes?' 248
Whiggism 27, 60, 83, 131, 147, 162

Whipple, Edwin Percy 204
Wilberforce, William 83, 279n82
Wilde, Oscar 9; *The Ballad of Reading Gaol* 154
Wilkinson, James John Garth 301n223
Wilson, Dr (physician in Florence) 252
Wilson, Effingham 281n91
Wilson, Elizabeth (*later* Romagnoli): appearance and character 139–40, 180; background and early life 139; maid to EBB 139–40; and EBB's romance with RB 156, 171; witness at EBB's wedding 171–2, 173; travels to Italy with EBB 171, 173–4, 175; in Italy 179, 180, 181–2, 185, 190, 191, 195, 203; engagement to Signor Righi 203, 210, 237, 297n203, 300n215; and birth of EBB's son Pen 203; and Pen's upbringing 205, 218, 223; travelling with Brownings to Paris and London 212, 215–16, 218, 237, 238; marriage to Ferdinando Romagnoli 236–7, 238, 256, 302n237; pregnancies and children 238, 244; leaves service as EBB's maid 244; later life 244, 256
'Wine of Cyprus' 133–4
Wolfe, Charles, *Poetical Remains* 12
Wollstonecraft, Mary 282n95; *A Vindication of the Rights of Woman* 26, 287n127
Wood, Marshall 263n3
Woolf, Virginia 5; on EBB 6, 263n6, 296n199; *A Room of One's Own* 11, 104; *Flush: A Biography* 6
Wordsworth, William 59, 90, 128–9, 141, 146, 209, 281n91; EBB meets 93; Haydon portrait 130, 287n130; death 209; 'By the Side of Rydal Mere' 128; 'Lines Written a Few Miles above Tintern Abbey' 59; *Poems, Chiefly of Early and Late Years* 129; 'On a Portrait of the Duke of Wellington by Haydon' 130, 287n130; *The Prelude* 128; 'Scorn not the Sonnet' 201
Worthing (Sussex) 267n25
Wreford, Henry 247
Wroth, Lady Mary 207
Wye, River 20, 58, 59; Wye Tour 59

Yazor (Herefordshire) 58, 62
Yellow Fever 115
Young, D. A. B., 'The Illnesses of Elizabeth Barrett Browning' 44, 263n2, 272n44
Young America movement 131
Young Italy movement *see Giovine Italia, La*